AF600582

MODERN REALISM IN ENGLISH-CANADIAN FICTION

COLIN HILL

Modern Realism in English-Canadian Fiction

UNIVERSITY OF TORONTO PRESS
Toronto Buffalo London

Toronto Buffalo London
www.utppublishing.com

ISBN 978-1-4426-4056-6

Library and Archives Canada Cataloguing in Publication

Hill, Colin, 1970–
Modern realism in English-Canadian fiction / Colin Hill.

Includes bibliographical references and index.
ISBN 978-1-4426-4056-6

1. Canadian fiction (English) – 20th century – History and criticism.
2. Realism in literature. 3. Modernism (Literature) – Canada. I. Title.

PS8191.R37H54 2012 C813'.520912 C2011-907911-9

A section of chapter 2 was previously published in *Canadian Literature* 195. Sections of chapter 4 have been published in different forms in *Journal of Canadian Studies* 44.3 (2010) and in *The Canadian Modernists Meet: Essays on Modernism, Antimodernism and Modernity*, ed. Dean Irvine (2005).

University of Toronto Press acknowledges the financial assistance to its publishing program of the Canada Council for the Arts and the Ontario Arts Council.

Canada Council for the Arts
Conseil des Arts du Canada

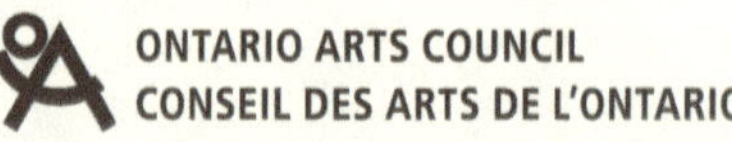

This book has been published with the help of a grant from the Canadian Federation for the Humanities and Social Sciences, through the Aid to Scholarly Publications Program, using funds provided by the Social Sciences and Humanities Research Council of Canada.

University of Toronto Press acknowledges the financial support of the Government of Canada through the Canada Book Fund for its publishing activities.

For Olivier

Contents

Acknowledgments

I am indebted to many people for their assistance, advice, and support as I was writing this book. I would like to express my thanks to editors, colleagues, teachers, friends, students, archivists, and librarians: D.M.R. Bentley, Gregory Betts, Marie-Thérèse Blanc, Donna Bennett, Jared Bland, Nick Bradley, Russell Brown, Marlys Chevrefils, George Elliott Clarke, Brian Corman, Melba Cuddy-Keane, Malcolm Davidson, Jeannine DeLombard, Gaby Divay, Andrew DuBois, Michel Ducharme, Dennis Duffy, Kevin Flynn, Carole Gerson, Alex Gillespie, Marlene Goldman, Allan Hepburn, Miranda Hickman, Patrick Howlett, Linda Hutcheon, Dean Irvine, Daniela Janes, Stephen Johnson, Maggie Kilgour, James Leahy, Robert Lecker, Andrew Lesk, Mark Levine, Jody Mason, Brandon McFarlane, David McKnight, Alex MacLeod, Randy McLeod, Nick Mount, Siobhan McMenemy, Frances Mundy, Heather Murray, John O'Connor, Medrie Purdham, Maggie Redekop, Mari Ruti, Patricia Simoes, Sam Solecki, Carl Spadoni, David Staines, Olivier St-Hilaire, Leslie Thomson, Brian Trehearne, Alan Twigg, Ryan Van Huijstee, Dan White, Malcolm Woodland, Kailin Wright, Herb Wyile, and Tim Yu.

My research would not have been possible without financial support from the Connaught Fund at University of Toronto, the Social Sciences and Humanities Research Council of Canada, and McGill University in the form of two awards (the Max Bell Fellowship in Canadian and Northern Studies and the Hugh MacLennan for the Study of English Fellowship).

MODERN REALISM IN ENGLISH-CANADIAN FICTION

1
The Modern-Realist Movement: Contexts, Aesthetics, Origins

Interest in Canadian literature reached unprecedented levels in the years immediately preceding and following the national centennial celebrations of 1967. Hugh MacLennan, then Canada's pre-eminent writer, was at the height of his fame and entering the final period of an illustrious career that produced a record five Governor General's Awards. His name had become almost synonymous with Canadian literature and critics were beginning to take stock of his achievements. Remarkably, in the years bracketed by Expo '67 and the 1976 Summer Olympics (both hosted by MacLennan's adopted hometown), no fewer than six book-length studies of MacLennan and his work were published. While these books were varied in their appraisals and critical dispositions, they were unanimous that MacLennan was an important Canadian originator whose legacy included the awakening of national – perhaps even international – interest in Canadian literature. Many of MacLennan's readers past and present consider the publication of *Barometer Rising* in 1941 a watershed moment in national literary development.[1] No earlier novel so captured the national imagination by speaking of Canadian experience in a manner at once tied to the native soil and evocative of a cultural mythology. But if *Barometer Rising* marks the beginning of contemporary Canadian fiction then Canadian fiction has a problematic beginning indeed. For one thing, MacLennan's first published novel appeared just as four decades of high-modernist experiment in Europe and America were reaching scattered points of exhaustion. But the style and technique of *Barometer Rising* are remarkably conservative and bear much more likeness to well-known Victorian novels than to works by modernist innovators such as Virginia Woolf, James Joyce, Djuna Barnes, or William Faulkner. If *Barometer Rising* is an originary novel at the fountainhead of contemporary Canadian fiction then Robert Kroetsch was right when he rhetorically obliterated Canadian modernist fiction with a now infamous quip: 'Canadian literature evolved directly from Victorian into Postmodern.'[2]

Literary tastes have obviously changed since MacLennan was at the height of his fame, and *Barometer Rising* perhaps no longer reads like the archetypal Canadian novel it may never have been. MacLennan's reputation – like those of his most famous and canonical Canadian contemporaries, Morley Callaghan and Frederick Philip Grove – has fallen into steep decline. As contemporary Canadian fiction becomes increasingly inventive, international, and reflective of cultural diversity, early twentieth-century Canadian fiction to some readers appears increasingly conservative, outmoded, culturally monolithic, insular, even irrelevant: as Glenn Willmott summarizes, 'often seen as a lingering afterlife of Victorian literature or as an ambivalent precursor of postmodern literature, this period has always seemed a "transitional phase," as John Moss once put it.'[3] Current international debates that are broadening and decentring established conceptions of modernist writing have so far done relatively little to reinvigorate and reassess modern Canadian fiction. It may be surprising, then, that the work of MacLennan and his contemporaries and forerunners can still reveal much about the nature of modern Canadian writing and the origins of contemporary Canadian fiction. Although it is one of Canadian literature's best-kept secrets, in the decade before *Barometer Rising* was published MacLennan was a very different kind of writer than his well-known novels suggest. While travelling widely in Europe and America during the politically charged 1930s, and spending time in the Soviet Union and Nazi Germany, MacLennan produced two still-unpublished modernist novels: *So All Their Praises,* finished in 1933, and *Man Should Rejoice,* finished in 1937. Both of these novels are set outside the Canadian milieu that nearly all of MacLennan's published writing treats. They are written in highly experimental modernist styles and are deliberately evocative of novels by illustrious and canonical modernists, most notably Joyce and Hemingway. It is remarkable, given the common characterization of MacLennan as a conservative realist dedicated to the literary representation of Canada, that he participated in the international modernist revolution so uncompromisingly. So why have many critics and readers so resoundingly endorsed his conservative prose and neglected his cosmopolitan experimental writing? Why did MacLennan abandon his early modernist experiments for a conservative realism? How many of

MacLennan's contemporaries and forerunners have been similarly misunderstood and misrepresented? Why is some of Canada's best modernist fiction still almost unknown, and how might its consideration help us reimagine entrenched ideas about modern writing in Canada?

While work by a few recent critics has made it increasingly difficult to claim that Canada lacks a modernist fiction, there is nothing approaching a consensus about its aesthetic qualities, temporal and generic boundaries, or relation to contemporaneous European and American modernisms. Judging by most international standards, modernist fiction seems scarce in Canada, and individual works that fit established definitions of modernism tend to appear sporadically, at wide intervals, with little apparent connection to larger literary patterns, movements, or national and international sensibilities. The best-known Canadian fiction of the early twentieth century – works by MacLennan, Ostenso, Callaghan, Grove, and Ross for example – seems unlike the canonical modernist literatures of Europe and the United States and remains difficult to account for using established international, generic, temporal, and aesthetic concepts, markers, and models. Accordingly, theories of modernist Canadian fiction usually require elaborate qualifications and a multi-generic redefinition of the term for use in a Canadian context. Some contemporary scholars, and most notably Willmott, have offered original and sophisticated arguments that help to negotiate the labyrinth of 'isms' – realism, romanticism, naturalism, modernism – that is early twentieth-century Canadian writing.[4] Willmott's work has demonstrated the existence of links between Canadian and foreign aesthetics, and shown that the standard definitions of these loaded terms do not easily apply in the Canadian context. Other critics, including Brian Trehearne, Candida Rifkind, Carole Gerson, Sandra Djwa, Tracy Ware, D.M.R. Bentley, Nick Mount, and Dean Irvine, have done much to reconstruct and understand the genealogies of early twentieth-century Canadian literary cultures and the aesthetics and influences of individual modern writers. But despite this recent attention (most of it concerned primarily with poetry) the study of modernist Canadian prose is still in its early stages. A comprehensive modernist literary history is yet to be written, modernist archives and special collections remain tantalizingly unplundered, and modernist Canadian fiction has not yet been examined in a sustained way through the lenses of modernist and international critical theories.

This book appears at a moment when a remarkable renaissance of interest in modernist Canadian writing is occurring. It tells the story of Canada's forgotten modern-realist movement, or, more specifically, of a group of writers who deliberately and against much resistance modernized Canadian fiction in the early twentieth century. The modern transformation of Canadian fiction began with the emergence of their dynamic, experimental, and polemical modern-realist movement in the 1920s. Authors, critics, readers, and publishers of the period greeted their movement with boisterous enthusiasm and heralded it as the indisputable and long-sought revolutionary break with outmoded aesthetics, including both romanticism, still the dominant mode of Canadian fiction at the end of the First World War, and the European nineteenth-century realism that had been exerting inconstant influence in Canada since about 1850. Canada's modern-realist movement was driven by three dozen writers who produced, between 1919 and 1950, about one hundred novels and scattered works of short fiction. Some of these writers are the best known of the period: Morley Callaghan, Hugh Garner, Frederick Philip Grove, Raymond Knister, Hugh MacLennan, Martha Ostenso, Sinclair Ross, and Robert J.C. Stead. Other modern realists who played important roles have been forgotten almost entirely, if they were ever known at all: Irene Baird, Bertram Brooker, Ethel Chapman, Philip Child, Douglas Durkin, Wilfrid Eggleston, Hubert Evans, Gwethalyn Graham, Vera Lysenko, Joyce Marshall, Edward McCourt, Thomas Murtha, Len Peterson, Jessie Georgina Sime, A.M. Stephen, Arthur Stringer, and Christine Van Der Mark, among others.

The emergence of modern realism is the most significant event in the development of Canadian fiction before the contemporary period. It has been of central and lasting importance to the development of Canada's national literature. Its legacy continues to exert fresh influences on even the most recent generation of Canadian authors. This book explores modern-realist fiction and the ideas, aesthetic principles, ideological formations, historical development, and legacy of the movement out of which it grew. Such an exploration necessarily challenges some critical assumptions about modern Canadian writing and established schools of Canadian literary theory and helps to make sense of the problematic styles and aesthetics of some of Canada's most important modern writers. Canada's modern-realist movement provides a critical paradigm for many of the best known and widely read works of the early twentieth century and invites a reconsideration of the significance of many works that remain obscure or unpublished to the present day.

Only a handful of Canadian writers of the early twentieth century produced indisputably modernist works of fiction that are obviously akin to international examples – Sheila Watson, A.M. Klein, and Elizabeth Smart are perhaps most remarkable in this regard. The bulk of the 'serious' fiction written in Canada in the same period is 'modern-realist' and not conveniently accounted for with established definitions, generic boundaries, aesthetic concepts, genealogies, and temporal boundaries commonly associated with Anglo-American modernisms. Aesthetically, the modern realists sought a direct, immediate, contemporary, idiomatically correct language, and a narrative objectivism and impersonality. They demonstrated a sustained and experimental interest in psychological writing and the epistemological representation of human consciousness. They directed the technical innovations they undertook in these respects toward a mimetic representation of a contemporary world, usually Canadian, and, much as European and American modernists did, explored the cultural conditions and great 'themes' of 'modernity': moral relativism, modern technology, the forces of urbanization and industrialization, modern social and political ideals, moral and religious change and decline, human sexuality, evolving gender roles, and modern historical events, including the Great Depression and two world wars. But the modern realists were neither belatedly imitating an antiquated nineteenth-century realism in their work, nor clumsily duplicating comparatively sophisticated modernist techniques. The modern realists were aware of foreign modernisms and realisms, to be sure, but they arrived at their own modern-realist aesthetic through persistent, thoughtful, self-reflexive, and often idiosyncratic experiment. While the modern realists shared many assumptions about writing with their boldest modernist counterparts – a belief in art for art's sake, a desire to extricate the author from the text, a fundamental conviction that the great 'truths' about humankind (or the truth that there are none) could be found through a probing and literary representation of human consciousness – they ultimately stopped short of endorsing some of the boldest technical experiments of the high modernists: extreme fragmentation, dissonant multivocality, highly subjectivist renderings of human consciousness, overt and sustained impressionism, surrealism, and expressionism. This book explores the often experimental aesthetic of the modern realists and highlights points of convergence and divergence, both among writers of the various modern-realist sub-genres and among the modern realists and their foreign modernist contemporaries.

Any theoretical framework for early twentieth-century Canadian fiction will find the concepts 'modernism' and 'realism' unavoidable and enormously problematic. Both concepts within and beyond Canada are vigorously contested. Either grouping of movements and aesthetics can be argued to incorporate many if not most elements of the other. Willmott highlights the atypical nature of modernism in Canadian prose when he asks, 'What kind of modernism is this? Answers have succeeded to the extent that modernism has been recognized to be a monster with many heads.'[5] In literary histories, modernism and its competing and constitutive forms are usually posited as reactions to the outmoded antithetical realisms that precede, inform, and antagonize them. There is nothing approaching a consensus about how Canadian modernisms and realisms ought to be situated relative to other foreign and indigenous literary modes. To complicate matters, the term 'realism' in Canada has a long history of critical usage and few if any literary terms have been applied with less precision. The term immediately evokes the nineteenth-century realism that preceded modernist forms of innovation in the European context, and many documents discussed in this study show Canada's modern realists drawing important distinctions between themselves and writers such as Tolstoy, Balzac, Dickens, Hardy, and George Eliot. To the modern realists and early twentieth-century Canadian critics, however, the term 'realism' was absolutely *not* synonymous with nineteenth-century fiction: much as the term 'modernism' does today, 'realism' then signified numerous, and often competing or contradictory, concepts, formations, groupings, techniques, and aesthetics. Most often, when the term 'realism' appeared in the formative literary magazines of the 1920s, especially *Canadian Bookman* and *The Canadian Forum*, discussed later, it was aligned, explicitly or otherwise, with the 'modern': as Adrian MacDonald wrote in the *Bookman* in 1922, 'the unique claim of realism as a school of fiction is its appeal to the scientific spirit. That impulse which sent the modern world into the laboratory, is the one upon which the realist strives to found his popularity.'[6] In these same magazines, 'realism' is often positioned opposite another prevalent mode of Canadian fiction of the period: as Sandra Djwa observes in '*The Canadian Forum*: Literary Catalyst,' critics of the period 'wished to counter an old romanticism with a new realism.'[7]

For many of the same writers and critics, 'realism' was an antidote to the romantic 'idealism' that stifled critical thought in Canada. Fiction that embodied the worst kinds of this idealism was opposed by the *Canadian Bookman* in its manifestos, including its opening prospectus, which positioned the new magazine opposite 'the merely sentimental, narcotic, idea-less books, miscalled books of the imagination, which have formed the literary food of too many of us who did not wish to be bothered with ideas.'[8] Other early critics saw realism to be precisely what was needed to further the causes of idealism in Canada's most nationalistic decade. This attitude is especially prevalent in the 1920s rhetoric of the Canadian Authors Association, whose leaders, as Mary Vipond points out, believed that 'the real roots of the English-Canadian identity lay in its rural and small town past,' and encouraged tales of local colour that offered 'real' portraits of regional settings cast in an idyllic light.[9] Realism of the period has also been linked both to a documentary, journalistic style of writing – as in Pacey's assertion that 'realism' reflects the 'actual conditions of Canadian life'[10] – and to a more imaginative literary possibility, loosely defined in Lionel Stevenson's 1924 'Manifesto for a National Literature,' as 'acknowledging the so-called "realities" of life's pantheistic.'[11] And, while 'realism' was often associated, as I have suggested, with older and more conservative forms of foreign fiction, it was an indisputably contemporary form, both to the modern realists, and to conservative segments of the literary world who used 'realism' as a euphemism for 'sexually explicit': in a 1924 article by Hilda Glynn-Ward, 'A Plea for Purity,' readers were warned that 'there has come over the literature of the day the foetid breath of decadence. They call it realism,' when it is in fact, Glynn-Ward warns, 'the dopish ravings of the modern sex-writers.'[12]

Criticism since the 1920s has used the term 'realism' less frequently and often with less precision. While there have been scattered discussions of the realist aspects of works by a few individual writers, and of some of the 'types' of realism found in Canadian writing, there have been very few sustained critical discussions of Canadian realism, and even fewer that consider realism a modern literary form. The most substantial literary-historical reading of Canada's realism appears not surprisingly in *Literary History of Canada* (1965–90). Here, Desmond Pacey writes a chapter that briefly surveys realist fiction of the period, with special attention to Grove and Callaghan, yet he asserts that 'realism, and especially urban realism, was a very unusual commodity in Canadian fiction between the wars. Such realism as there was developed almost exclusively on the prairies, where there was a distinctive pattern of life.'[13] While Pacey's treatment of Canadian realism remains the most comprehensive on record, it nevertheless emphasizes the supposedly regional concerns of Canada's realists, their rural subject matter, intellectual and creative isolation, lack of innovation, and stylistic shortcomings.

Most recent studies consider Canadian realism only peripherally if at all. The most recent edition of *The Oxford Companion to Canadian Literature* (1997), in 'Novels in English, 1920–1940,' identifies 'a period in Canadian fiction when the realistic novel emerges' before it surveys various types of fiction of the same period while avoiding realism almost entirely.[14] In *Canadian Literature in English* (1985), W.J. Keith discusses the contributions of some major writers who could be considered realists, but his informative discussions make almost no mention of their realism beyond his opening assertion that 'the popularity of most of these writers can be explained by their shrewd but often crude blend of romance and realism.'[15] Elizabeth Waterston's *Survey: A Short History of Canadian Literature* (1973) discusses Canadian fiction of the period with no discussion of realism at all. In their anthology of historically significant critical articles, *Canadian Novelists and the Novel* (1981), Douglas Daymond and Leslie Monkman offer a promising section entitled 'The Rise of Realism,' but most of their judicious selections discuss realism only indirectly, and the modern-realist manifestos of the *Canadian Bookman* are not represented. Other literary histories have represented Canadian realism with greater attention to its modernist affinities. *George Woodcock's Introduction to Canadian Fiction* (1993) identifies 'a tradition founded in realism but ready to learn from modernist and post-modernist innovatory techniques.'[16] E.L. Bobak's 'Seeking "Direct, Honest Realism": The Canadian Novel of the 1920s' (1981) captures the sense in which realism emerged during the period as a coherent and rebellious movement by suggesting that it met with considerable resistance from a conservative literary culture: 'opposition to realism was often extreme.'[17] Bobak however suggests that Canadian realism is fundamentally derivative, and proposes that it was transplanted belatedly from abroad: 'Realism, an ideal medium for the objective reporting of social phenomena, had still not made its way into Canadian fiction in the early decades of the twentieth century ... Even today in Canada, the nineteenth-century realists are exerting fresh influences.'[18]

Canadian realism, then, has not often been considered in a sustained manner and alongside contemporaneous modernisms. Accordingly, some fallacies about realism and its writers appear across the full spectrum of Canadian criticism. Lack of acknowledgment that Canada's experimental modern realism was brought into being deliberately and consciously has typecast its writers, by default, in passive and imitative roles. Sometimes this passivity is described in terms of literary influence, and Canadian realists become derivative imitators of the outmoded aesthetics of other countries. T.D. MacLulich's *Between Europe and America: The Canadian Tradition in Fiction* (1988) has rightly observed a tendency in Canadian criticism to represent the realists in this way: 'not until well into the present century do the best Canadian novelists begin, as Hugo McPherson puts it, "to create Canada in the way that Hawthorne, a century earlier, helped to create New England."'[19] Elsewhere, and more frequently, realism is seen as the product of deterministic regional and geographical influences. Alison Calder has drawn much-needed attention to this problem in discussions of prairie realism: 'Criticism of prairie realism is predicated on a belief in the primacy of the land. Geographic determinism is evident even in the critical label: *prairie* realism.'[20] That readers sometimes accept *both* of these contradictory theses – how can a Canadian realism be both an imitation of foreign modes and the product of geographical determinism? – is made evident in Pacey's formative *Creative Writing in Canada*, where he offers them almost side by side: 'at every stage of its progress [Canadian culture] has been strongly influenced by English, American, and ... European models ... Canadian literature thus far has been almost wholly an inevitable response to a geographical and climactic situation, and this it should and must remain.'[21]

Coming to terms with modern realism requires a movement beyond some of the established critical definitions and dichotomies imposed on Canadian fiction by other traditions, and the now rich and substantial body of criticism on Canadian poetry, which follows a different literary development. Some help can be gleaned from recent international scholarship that has broadened definitions of the term 'modernism' well beyond the boundaries of the canonical high modernism of Joyce, Woolf, Eliot, Pound, and others. In *Bad Modernisms* (2006), Douglas Mao and Rebecca L. Walkowitz conclude that the term 'modernist' is increasingly used to connote disparate authors and texts: 'new modernist studies has extended the designation "modernist" beyond such familiar figures ... and embraced ... other cultural producers hitherto seen as neglecting or resisting modernist innovation.'[22] Yet such a wholesale reimagining of modernism is not necessary to bring the modern realists, who were clearly modernist innovators if not exactly 'familiar figures' on the international stage, under its rubric. More exactingly, several recent critics have questioned the antagonistic relationship that supposedly exists between literary modernisms and realisms. Chris Baldick's *The Oxford English Literary History: The Modern Movement* (2004), for example, sees strong continuities between late Victorian and modernist writing. He points out that virtuosic and radically experimental modernism, while representing a very small portion of the modern writing in the British tradition, has erroneously come to appear antithetical to works by more traditional modern writers such as Dorothy Richardson, D.H. Lawrence, and E.M. Forster. He accordingly presents a convincing argument for the inclusion of British modern realism within a larger modernist tradition: 'The modern movement, then, as understood by writers who had grown up with it, was a broad church that embraced a variety of forms, techniques, styles, and attitudes, all of which were in some way innovative and in some way representative of new twentieth-century modes of awareness.'[23]

By the same token, Canadian modern realism only appears conservative in retrospect and alongside canonical forms of high-modernist innovation. If Canadian modern realism in this respect suffers from the same critical problem as its British counterpart, a host of other forces and critical assumptions has further disconnected it from its modernist affinities. Nationalist readings of Canadian fiction have notoriously ignored international influences in their quests to identify national theses, thematic patterns, and regional portraits. The historical record shows, however, that Canada's modern realists and their critics at home and abroad considered their work innovative and part of the general revolution in twentieth-century fiction retrospectively termed 'modernism.' Although it may be inconvenient, Canada's modern realism cannot be fully understood without attention to the larger international modernist revolution it participates in.

It is necessary to adjust some critical terms and paradigms to account for the peculiar and multi-generic aesthetic of modern realism (this includes a rethinking of the stark oppositional relationship between modernism and realism mentioned earlier), but such critical distinctions cannot be abandoned altogether. Much Canadian criticism has denied the modern realists a precise and coherent aesthetic and inferred that their work is merely a hodgepodge of accidental and often incompatible influences. In his introduction to *Modern Times: A Critical Anthology* (1982), John Moss conflates realism, modernism, and a host of other aesthetics in the Canadian novel of the period:

> Modernism in the novel has become virtually synonymous with realism. But realism, ironically, has come to mean romance ... In Canadian fiction, romantic-realism begins with the novels of Frederick Philip Grove and remains the dominant mode to the present day. There have been a few

> outstanding exceptions, but not until the super-realism of Munro ... did the modernist conventions in Canada begin to crumble.
>
> Certainly the conventions of modernism are devoutly upheld by the fictions of Callaghan, MacLennan, and Wilson ... Grove's *Settlers of the Marsh* and Ostenso's *Wild Geese* ... both blend romance with realism as early examples of Canadian modernist fiction.[24]

If this application of terminology is not amply representative of the problematic coexistence of twentieth-century 'isms' in Canadian fiction, Moss goes on to argue that Elizabeth Smart's *By Grand Central Station I Sat Down and Wept*, one of the few indisputably modernist novels produced in Canada, is an *exception* to his definition of modernism: it 'def[ies] such conventions,' but is nevertheless 'thoroughly modern, philosophically (and possibly postmodern as well).'[25] Moss is stating what so many others have sensed all along: the usual dichotomy between realism and modernism does not work in the Canadian context, and these terms are frequently applied idiosyncratically by authors and critics alike. At the same time, Moss's attention to problems of terminology suggests that modern Canadian fiction needs an exacting and exhaustive re-evaluation. It is not enough to move beyond old patterns and dichotomies simply by denying that they exist or inviting different evaluative methods and critical practices: think of Northrop Frye's notorious gesture in 'Conclusion to a *Literary History of Canada.*' Modern realism contains elements of various other recognizable forms and aesthetics. But its borrowing and reinventing was neither wholesale nor accidental. Modern realism came into being as a result of tireless experiment with both new and established literary models and forms from both Canada and abroad.

The most overarching rereading of modern Canadian fiction is Glenn Willmott's *Unreal Country: Modernity in the Canadian Novel in English* (2002). Willmott, like some of the most innovative contemporary scholars of international modernism, broadens definitions and perspectives: 'modernism need not be limited for Canadian literary-critical purposes to models provided by an Anglo-American canon or by its formalist critical orthodoxy.'[26] Willmott proposes a kind of multi-generic 'modernity at large' which is for the most part unbounded by established generic and temporal markers.[27] Borrowing the phrase 'modernity at large' from Arjun Appadurai, Willmott suggests that 'the old antinomy that had loomed above the work of fiction for modern Canadian writers – the titanic contest of realism and romance – is not an antinomy at all.'[28] In place of this generic dichotomy, he proposes a new, modern, Canadian super-genre that, while more developed than that intimated by Moss, is not markedly dissimilar. He argues that his application of the concept of 'modernity at large,' derived as it is from postmodern criticism, 'provides a coherent frame of reference for modern Canadian fiction in English':[29]

> The new romance will register the primacy of the (contingent) event over the (cosmogenetic) world, rather than the other way around. By the same proposition, realism too is turned inside out. The conventional function of realism, to register the interrelations and values of a given, secular world, or 'what is,' is eroded by the uneven and unstable, slash-and-burn transvaluations of a material life subject to the unpredictable synapses of global economy, media, and mobility. A self-ironicizing realism is now required to register these unevenly signifying events, which mark the shifting social limits and vectors of global flows themselves; it is required, however ephemerally and paradoxically self-consciously, as a provisional ground for the imagination 'at large.' The third formal term, which ... lies behind these inverted shells of romance and realism alike, belongs to modernism.[30]

Willmott's argument for the presence of these contingent, ironized, and degraded forms of modernism, romanticism, and realism in some well-known Canadian texts is convincing, and offers some of the best evidence that the restrictive oppositions critics have found useful in the past are in need of re-evaluation.

Aesthetic and generic boundaries are not the only ones that are difficult to draw in modern Canadian writing: workable temporal or genealogical models have proven equally elusive. In 'Losing the Line: The Field of Our Modernism' (1989), Dennis Duffy writes that 'something is obviously missing from our culture, something that ought to have reposed between barbarism and decadence, between late romanticism and postmodernism. What is missing?'[31] This 'missing' part of our literary development is, in Duffy's view, a Canadian modernism, but one that is impossible to pin down temporally: 'literary modernism ... was not a pure, univocal phenomenon ... Linear, processional models of our national literary development are as problematic as they are seductive.'[32] The assertion that a Canadian modernism will not look like those of other countries is refreshing, and Duffy's acknowledgment that it will happen on its own timeline is liberating. But it is possible to open the door to such a Canadian modernism too widely, and deny the presence of a 'processional model of our national literary development' altogether. Duffy's model makes sense if we are talking about Canada's indisputably high-modernist texts. Such works are indeed few and far between in Canadian fiction, and do seem to appear sporadically and independently, with little connection to a larger national or international movement: Smart's *By Grand Central Station I Sat Down and Wept* (1945), Sheila Watson's *Deep Hollow Creek* (ca 1933), MacLennan's *So All Their Praises* (1933) and *Man Should Rejoice* (1937), A.M. Klein's *The Second Scroll* (1951), to name just some of those written before Watson's *The Double Hook* (1959), which Frank Davey considers 'the first truly modern Canadian novel.'[33] But however unclear the genealogy of Canadian modernism may be, the modern-realist movement *does* have a clear emergence, evolution, and exhaustion.

Canada's modern realism has never been considered the product of a coherent national movement. This may be because of the regionalist lens through which Canadian fiction is often read. It may also be because both realism and modernism are often posited as foreign aesthetics conceived and shaped by international movements long before they travel in degenerated forms to Canada. This argument, advanced most prominently in T.D. MacLulich's *Between Europe and America: The Canadian Tradition in Fiction* (1988), emphasizes the realists' reluctance to take up experimental forms and places these writers in a passive mode by casting them as failed modernists: 'it may be useful to remind ourselves just how gingerly our authors took up the innovative techniques used by the leading European and American writers of modernist prose.'[34] MacLulich draws an important link between 'the movement towards realism' and 'the arrival of modernism in Canadian fiction,' but positions these forces in adversarial roles and suggests that Canadian 'realism' impeded the arrival of foreign 'modernism' to Canada: 'Our first generation of modernist writers did not venture very far into the more experimental regions of modernist technique. Instead, the task was to define the principal features of the Canadian social world and to articulate the typical ways in which Canadians were responding to that world ... modernism came into Canadian fiction in such a tentative and unspectacular fashion.'[35] The assertion that modernism 'came into' Canadian writing from outside denies the experimental and innovative literary impulse that the modern realists considered the core of their aesthetic, and suggests that the more 'documentary' impulse of realism was irreconcilably at odds with the aims of modernist fiction. But, as we shall see, the unique techniques of the modern realists grow out of their largely successful experiments to balance the objectivist stance of the traditional realist with the subjective perspectivism of the high-modernist form.

As a scholar of Canadian literature with a strong interest in Anglo-American modernism, I have spent much of the past ten years building on the work of these critics and determining why there is little modernist fiction in Canada that resembles foreign examples. To these ends, I began at the foundational level with a large bibliographical project and tracked down close to four hundred Canadian novels of the period, many of which have been all but lost to Canadian literature. While this reading did not immediately explain the lack of an indigenous modernist fiction, it did produce a surprising proliferation of writing that might be loosely called 'realist.' This realism comes from all parts of the country, deals almost as often with urban as rural environments, and looks very little like the nineteenth-century realisms of other countries with which its few famous works have sometimes been compared. More strikingly, much of this realism is indisputably modern in both subject matter and technique. I broadened my research to include the literary periodicals and criticism that surround these works, and I pursued some of the most significant and prolific realist authors into archival collections across the country.

This book offers an overview of the modern-realist movement as a whole and traces its development and proliferation over three decades. Modern-realist fiction can be divided into several overlapping subgenres – most prominently prairie realism, urban realism, and social realism – although such subdivisions are largely arbitrary, and key aesthetic aims and ideals were shared by all of the modern realists, regardless of their geographical origins, ideological dispositions, or subject matter. Generic and temporal boundaries are difficult to establish in any literary tradition, and well-known discussions of Canada's cultural and geographical heterogeneity suggest that such tasks may be especially difficult in the Canadian context. Furthermore, in a literary tradition that tends to emphasize, even celebrate, the 'isolation' of its writers and a corresponding lack of coherent schools, I refer to a modern-realist 'movement' cautiously, but deliberately. I do not mean to suggest that the modern realists were a close-knit group of writers colluding on a common endeavour. Yet neither am I suggesting that they merely shared in some vague way a few loosely defined beliefs about writing. The sheer number of documents in which the various modern realists articulate similar convictions about 'realism' and 'modernity' in Canadian fiction, often referring to their compatriots and modernist contemporaries from other countries, indicates an unmistakable and coherent pattern of thought. Even more convincing evidence is found in the fiction itself: several dozen seemingly disparate writers executed remarkably similar strategies in their modern realism.

Perhaps the most immediate evidence of a coherent modern-realist movement comparable to other modernist movements is found in the manifestos and polemical articles published in Canada's little magazines of the 1920s. Chapter 2 reads these statements and demonstrates that the modern realists participated in the same 'international revolutionary climate,' replete with 'self-conscious formations, declarations and manifestos ... and self-conscious, militant and collective positioning' that gave rise to the other modernist "isms."'[36] The emphasis of this narrative is not, however, rigidly literary-historical, and its structure is designed to reflect the range of forms and aesthetics that make up modern realism, not to present a fixed, chronological timeline. My most important aim is a coherent reading of the modern-realist aesthetic, and an articulation of its modern techniques, concerns, subject matter, and writerly assumptions. To this end, I provide two broad chapters that reconsider and reconstitute the most significant forms of modern-realist fiction. Chapter 4 offers a re-evaluation of prairie realism through an emphasis on its under-acknowledged modern concerns and experimental techniques, and a refutation of critical myths about its regional relevance and geographical determinism. Chapter 6 explores Canada's largely ignored urban and social realism, foregrounding their modern subjects, innovative forms of reportage, and opposition to the socialist realism for which they are sometimes mistaken. Subdividing modern realism along these lines perpetuates the myth that these various forms of realism are in conflict, and, to be sure, I draw some distinctions between the various modern-realist sub-genres. My intention, however, is to bridge, to a great extent, the rural/urban divide in concepts of Canadian realism. Many of the works I discuss appear in both chapters: Douglas Durkin's *The Magpie*, for example, is a social-realist novel set in Winnipeg in the 1920s that crosses the boundaries that supposedly divide various types of realistic writing in Canada. To a degree, also, my divided discussion of the main types of realism has been predetermined by accepted critical definitions that I wish to challenge: for example, only by questioning the atypicality and regional relevance of prairie realism in a focused chapter am I able to argue that such characterizations are misleading.

These two broad chapters are grounded by three others that provide readings of the oeuvres of three of the most important modern realists. Chapter 3 explores Raymond Knister's pioneering modern realism and shows how his career, which emerged almost contingently with the movement as a whole, defined realism unmistakably in experimental terms. Chapter 5 investigates the most eclectic of the modern realists, Frederick Philip Grove, and reveals that his realism reflects a struggle to balance a competing modernity and traditionalism, something that is true of much modern realism. Chapter 7 approaches the realism of Morley Callaghan, the period's most cosmopolitan and internationally recognized Canadian writer of fiction, and articulates the distinction between modern realism and high modernism through a consideration of his techniques and writerly assumptions. Approaching the modern-realist movement from this range of perspectives allows both an overview of its boundaries, concerns, and preoccupations, and a focused reading of its precise and specific applications in the work of some of its most significant proponents. The final chapter offers some speculations about the significance of this reconstruction of the modern-realist movement for Canadian fiction and criticism more generally.

As I began reading through works of modern realism, I discovered that they were far more numerous than I had imagined and literary histories have indicated, and that some of the most remarkable works of Canadian fiction of the period have been forgotten, or neglected right from the start. Alongside some of the most canonical works of modern realism – Grove's *Settlers of the Marsh*, Ostenso's *Wild Geese*, MacLennan's *Barometer Rising*, Callaghan's *Such Is My Beloved* – I consider a sampling of lesser-known works. Some of these are by writers whose reputations are not yet firmly established – Irene Baird, Edward McCourt, Arthur Stringer, J.G. Sime, Christine Van Der Mark, Bertram Brooker, Douglas Durkin, Wilfrid Eggleston, Philip Child, A.M. Stephen, Len Peterson, and Gwethalyn Graham, to name just some. Works by these writers are in many cases of equal or superior 'quality' to the better-known works of canonical authors and resist some canonical stereotypes. Even the least remarkable of these forgotten works are worth reconsidering, if for no other reason than to reveal the surprising diversity of modern realism, and the fact that Canada's canonical authors were writing, not in literary isolation, but in the context of a movement that, like almost any literary movement, has both its central and its peripheral figures.

Such breadth of scope inevitably means that some things have been left out. I might have included, for example, individual author chapters on several other modern realists with a significant body of work: Irene Baird, Robert J.C. Stead, Sinclair Ross, Hugh Garner, J.G. Sime, Edward McCourt. While all of these writers are treated in my broad chapters on the proliferation of modern realism – and my treatment of Baird's pioneering modern realism can be found in the introduction to a recent critical edition of *Waste Heritage*[37] – I have limited my in-depth readings to a group of three writers who represent a fair cross-section of the aesthetic approaches to modern realism taken by writers of the period. Conveniently, these writers also produced a large body of fiction between 1919 and 1950, were articulate literary critics, left behind substantial archival materials, and have been the subject of significant critical attention. While I am able to treat many other modern realists less exactingly, I admit a certain frustration at not having the space to offer closer readings of many of the works I explore. In some cases, this does not prove problematic: novels such as *As For Me and My House*, *Fruits of the Earth*, and *More Joy in Heaven* have been widely read, and will not suffer from my relatively quick treatment here. In other cases, brief discussions of lesser-known but highly significant works of the period – Sime's *Sister Woman*, McCourt's *Music at the Close*, A.M. Stephen's *The Gleaming Archway* – may be vaguely unsatisfying. This is an inevitable result of my determination to keep the modern-realist movement as a whole near the centre of my discussion. While I have dispensed with much of the close reading I might otherwise have provided, I have still endeavoured to provide a general sense of the lesser-known works I explore. And if this project has some value, perhaps others will bring more attention to bear upon some of the little-known works of modern realism that are treated here only briefly.

Much as the modernist movements that blossomed in Europe in the early twentieth century have their origins in dynamic social and intellectual changes that occurred in the previous century, the realist impulse in Canadian fiction that crystallized into a movement in the 1920s can be traced back to the years preceding Confederation. Robert Lecker writes that 'ever since the nineteenth century, canonical activity in Canada has been driven by different applications of the national-referential ideal, and by the assumption that a country without a national literature is no country at all.'[38] It is hardly necessary here to offer a detailed re-examination of the nineteenth-century 'national-referential ideal' already amply explored by Lecker and others. But it is important to distinguish from the outset the largely romantic 'national-referential ideal' of Canada's nineteenth-century writers from the far more contemporary, realistic, and mimetic 'ideal' that is part of the modern-realist aesthetic. Three years before Confederation, the first major Canadian literary anthology, E.H. Dewart's *Selections from Canadian Poets* (1864), complained about the lack of recognition accorded Canadian writing that sought to present a 'faithful' representation of Canada:

> Let any Canadian bard presume to think that the wild-flowers which formed the garlands of his sunny childhood, the sweet song-birds that sang him to sleep in infancy, or the magnificent lakes, forests, and rivers of his native land, are as worthy of being enshrined in lyric numbers, and capable of awakening memories of days as bright, associations as tender, and scenery as beautiful, as ever was sung by hoary harper of the olden time, and he is more likely to secure contempt than sympathy or admiration.[39]

This attitude is reflected by William Douw Lighthall in the preface to *Songs from the Great Dominion* (1889):

> The poets whose songs fill this book are voices cheerful with the consciousness of youth, might, public wealth, and heroism. Through them, taken all together, you may catch something of the great Niagara falling, of brown rivers rushing with foam, of the crack of the rifle in the haunts of the moose and the caribou, the lament of vanishing races singing their death-song as they are swept on to the cataract of oblivion ... Now, who are those who are drinking these inspirations and breathing them into song? In communing with them, we shall try to transport you to the Canadian clime itself.[40]

Of course, these writers are talking about poetry, not fiction, but their evocations of a 'national-referential ideal' are unmistakable. While the modern realists would also place much emphasis on representing Canada in their work, it is easy to distinguish between the idealistic and romantic aims of these early anthologists and the attention to the 'actual conditions of Canadian life' that Pacey identifies as one of the key defining features of early twentieth-century realism.[41] Indeed, part of the reason for the persistence of the 'national-referential ideal' in Canadian fiction has been its propensity to become manifest in numerous genres and modes. Lecker's identification of this ideal in early, pre-realist Canadian writing is crucial because it suggests that, contrary to what some have asserted, realism is not merely a predetermined form that develops by default when the nation becomes the subject of literary attention. The modern realists, of course, had a referential ideal in mind – the mimetic representation of a modern, contemporary Canada. But this was far from being their sole interest, and their modern realism developed as a complex and experimental form, growing out of a particular application of the 'national-referential ideal,' and a range of other concerns having little or nothing to do with nationalism or geography: psychology, large socio-political forces, and the general cultural conditions of the twentieth-century.

Generally speaking, the idealistic, romantic-realist tone of Dewart and Lighthall persisted almost unchallenged in Canadian writing until about 1920. Only a few Canadian writers of the first two decades of the century carried out literary projects that can be more than loosely defined as 'realist.' Even in these few cases, Canadian writers generally approached realism as a vague technique to communicate larger idealistic values, and no overarching realist aesthetic appears to have guided their efforts. As Cal Smiley argues,

> the idealism of these authors was inextricably linked to the conventions of the literary romance. Larger-than-life characters, exaggerated emotions, episodic plots, a central love story, and the neat resolution of all story elements were the basic ingredients of most novels. Still, the inspiration for many works changed as writers shifted towards characters and incidents based on their own observations ... Writers increasingly insisted on the 'reality' of their stories. They did so, however, while staying within the limitations of the romantic conventions that supported their idealism and generated sales.[42]

Duncan Campbell Scott's *In the Village of Viger* (1896) and Sara Jeannette Duncan's *The Imperialist* (1904), both reminiscent of the work of earlier English writers, offer what might be the most accomplished and clear-cut examples of traditional realism in Canada fiction. Also noteworthy in this regard are the early novels of Nellie McClung, including *Sowing Seeds in Danny* (1908) and *The Second Chance* (1910), the latter being an early social-realist work that broadly examines the situation of women in the period. Lucy Maud Montgomery's well-known *Anne of Green Gables* (1908) was among the best of the many realistic local-colour works produced at the time, and its vivid portrait of Prince Edward Island endures to the present day. Ralph Connor [Rev. Charles William Gordon], the high-profile and best-selling Canadian author of the period, produced numerous moralistic works – including his best-known work *Glengarry School Days* (1902) – that were uncommonly attentive to the specific details of their settings and are still considered to be among the pioneering realist fictions in Canada. But whatever the significance of these early examples of realistic writing, they have much more in common with European and American nineteenth-century realism than with Canadian modern realism. And unlike both the modern and nineteenth-century realists, these early Canadian realists neither wrote as part of a larger realist movement nor undertook a serious and sustained writerly contemplation of the modern realist form.

The general realist *impulse* in Canadian writing required a modern and energetic literary movement for it to complete its transformation into a full-fledged realist *aesthetic*. For this movement to begin required two mutually dependent factors: a group of writers and critics, however loosely bound together, had to propose a set of formal aims and principles that would define their modern realism, and a public forum had to be made available wherein these writers could debate and exchange their ideas. The realist impulse present in the minds of Canada's writers and critics before 1920 crystallized into the modern-realist movement with the appearance of the *Canadian Bookman* and *The Canadian Forum* in 1919 and 1920. These magazines, with their interests in contemporary subjects, combative dispositions, nationalistic fervour, and notions of self-importance, provided an ideal space for a heated debate about the new writing in Canada. Over the next decade and a half, these magazines, and especially the *Bookman*, would print most of the manifestos of the modern-realist movement, and would give a voice, in one form or another, to most of the important writers of the period. Like many of the other literary movements that communally define 'modernism,' the Canadian modern-realist movement had a heightened sense of its significance, and positioned itself somewhat contradictorily as both a revolutionary departure from literary tradition, and the natural culmination of a literary past. To understand the precise nature of modern realism, and exactly how it came into being in the 1920s, we must now turn our attention specifically to the little magazines and their manifestos.

2

Manifestos for a Modern Realism: *Canadian Bookman* and *The Canadian Forum* in the 1920s

The same cataclysmic event that ended and inaugurated modernist movements in other countries – Futurism, Dada, Surrealism – was an impetus for a modern fiction in Canada. The Canadian experience of the Great War fuelled nationalism to an unprecedented degree and led writers, artists, and critics to believe that the national culture was coming of age. A new-found sense of importance led to boisterous and sustained demands from readers and writers for new, modern forms of Canadian art and literature. As Mary Vipond writes of the 1920s, 'What is most important about the decade … is not the informal communication patterns binding Canadian artists and intellectuals, but the extent to which these links became formalized, institutionalized, and made nation-wide.'[1] In January 1919, a little more than a year before the first Group of Seven exhibition was held at the Art Museum of Toronto in May 1920, an unsigned editorial published in the first issue of *Canadian Bookman* insisted, 'it is impossible to converse for five minutes with any of the leading booksellers of Canada without perceiving how greatly enhanced a sense of the importance and public serviceability of the book business has been developed as a result of conditions during the world war.'[2] In keeping with this new national spirit, Canadians established two major literary magazines dedicated to the proliferation of modern writing in the two years following the Great War: *Canadian Bookman* in 1919 and *The Canadian Forum* in 1920. In their inaugural issues, both magazines forcefully and polemically declared that their aims were nationalistic and self-confidently positioned themselves at the vanguard of a new and defining era in Canadian cultural life. Despite these similarities, critical examinations of these two magazines have held them in unequal regard, and literary histories have tended to cast them as arch-rivals: while *The Canadian Forum* is usually praised for its intellectual and cosmopolitan contributions to Canadian literature, *Canadian Bookman* is almost always dismissed as uncritical and backward-looking. The forgotten debates about modern writing that occurred in the pages of Canada's two most important literary magazines of the 1920s reveal that Canada's new literary realism was neither derived from foreign models nor geographically predetermined: it was brought to life through the deliberate and painstaking efforts of writers and critics who were responding to the general cultural conditions of the twentieth-century world in their groundbreaking stories, manifestos, book reviews, letters, critical articles, and public statements. These same individuals were utterly convinced that twentieth-century Canada required a new, serious literary form that was up to the task of exploring both the contemporary world and the modern human condition in its broadest sense.

Conventional appraisals of *The Canadian Forum* and *Canadian Bookman* are partly responsible for obscuring the originary and transformative modern realism that both journals advocated. Canada's literary histories have tended to overemphasize the rather superficial quarrel between contributors to these two magazines in the 1920s: the *Bookman*, in its early years, was forced to defend itself against frequent, scathing, and unprovoked attacks from the *Forum*, which expressed outrage at its supposedly low critical standards. While it is true that these two magazines often perceived themselves to be adversaries on the national stage because of this debate about literary standards, the conflict between them was not the result of a fundamental philosophical or aesthetic disagreement about Canadian fiction. Throughout the 1920s and beyond, articles, reviews, literary manifestos, and mission statements in both magazines would, whatever their competing aims in other areas, argue unmistakably for a new, modern-realist aesthetic. While their conceptions of what this modern realism ought to look like were often vague and sometimes in conflict, both the *Bookman* and *Forum* offered passionate and coherent statements in support of the new form. More significantly, both magazines characterized Canada's emerging realism in palpably modern terms, and equated many of the subjects and techniques of the modern realists with those of the best-known European and American modernists.

Canadian Bookman published its first issue in January 1919 under the general editorship of B.K. Sandwell, a journalist, McGill University lecturer, and co-founder of the Canadian Authors Association (CAA).

The magazine appeared regularly until 1939 – with the exception of a few issues that did not appear in 1937 – when it merged with the official organ of the CAA, *The Canadian Author*, to become *The Canadian Author and Bookman*. Many critics have rightly noted that the articles published in the *Bookman* are nationalistic and self-celebratory in tone, and frequently exhibit an irritating and self-congratulatory boosterism.[3] One reason why Canadian realism has scarcely been recognized as a modern form of writing arising out of a distinct literary movement in the 1920s is this: critics have so persistently celebrated the *Forum* and denigrated the *Bookman* that it now appears almost ludicrous to suggest that there are significant similarities between the two. Tellingly, there has been no sustained critical study of major ideas common to both journals. But if we acknowledge from the outset that the *Forum* triumphed in the debate about literary standards then we can begin to explore these journals' surprising mutual advocacy of the modern movement in Canadian fiction.

The persistent reprobation of the *Bookman* seems to derive primarily from the fact that it was, for a very brief period from 1921 to 1922, an official publication of the much-maligned Canadian Authors Association. This role, as Wynne Francis argues, 'meant that the policy of the magazine was adapted to the needs of that essentially conservative and professional oriented organization, resorting in the twenties to a noisy boosterism that favoured quantity over quality and patriotism over literary worth. Deservedly or not, the reputation of both the Association and its house organs has suffered from this stigma ever since.'[4] Vipond lists a number of reasons why the CAA has been 'open to a certain amount of ridicule,' including the rapid expansion in membership that welcomed '"practically anyone who professed an interest in literature," as Madge Macbeth puts it, "and whose cheques would be honoured by a bank."'[5] While the *Bookman* included some of the most important critical articles and literary contributions of the period – including those of Frederick Philip Grove, Raymond Knister, Robert J.C. Stead, Lorne Pierce, Lawren Harris, Georges Bugnet, Beaumont S. Cornell, Marcus Adeney, and Lionel Stevenson, to name a few – the majority of its pages were filled with book reviews and articles by amateur writers, and it is the worst of these pieces that give the magazine the bad reputation that has overshadowed its important contribution.

One revealing example, 'Standards of Criticism,' an early unsigned manifesto published in the second issue of the *Bookman* in 1919, inadvertently opened the floodgates to bad fiction and criticism. This article was written largely in defence of the realist aesthetic that was emerging in Canadian writing and the value of the regional fiction favoured by the CAA: 'When a Canadian writer endeavours to express something of what he has honestly seen and diligently studied in the social or psychological or natural phenomenon of Canada, we propose to extend to him all of the encouragement that we can.'[6] But in its quest to find new Canadian writing that met its criteria, this article was overzealous, and spelled out the loose, or at least different, standards by which Canadian work ought to be evaluated: 'We are indeed going to have various standards of criticism, and ... we can imagine no utility or vitality or reasonableness in criticism which has only one standard and seeks to apply it indiscriminately to all artistic works.'[7] This manifesto validated the 'boosterish' impulse evident in most Canadian criticism of the period and set the tone for many articles that would be published in the *Bookman* during its early years. These articles are, as one would expect, celebratory, nationalistic, and uninterested in the question of artistic merit: as W. Garland Foster wrote in the December 1924 issue, Canadian writers should 'reflect the life of the country at its best and reflecting, beautify it.'[8] A similarly uncritical attitude is expressed in a book review signed 'A.E.S.S.,' which appeared in the May 1924 number: 'The publication of local literature is to be commended and encouraged, whatever the quality.'[9] These pedestrian articles and opinions provided easy fodder for critics of Canadian boosterism, no matter how much backtracking Sandwell did in response to the snickers and denunciations that came from many sides, and especially from the young modernists among the more cosmopolitan of *The Canadian Forum* contributors, including Douglas Bush and A.J.M. Smith. As Smith wrote in a letter to Raymond Knister in 1927, 'it seems to me that before Canada can have a modern and individual literature our critical standards must be thoroughly overhauled and some counter irritant provided to offset the traditional gentility of journals like *The Canadian Bookman* [*sic*]... which [is] vitiating public taste and distorting literary values.'[10] It is remarkable that Smith, at the forefront of the movement for a modern poetry in Canada, was so caught up in the debates about literary value that he neglected to acknowledge the loud calls for a modern fiction that were made by some of his most loyal sympathizers, including Raymond Knister, also a leading Canadian modernist poet, in the very same issues of the *Bookman* that printed the boosterish pieces.

What the opponents of the *Bookman* found most distasteful, however, was the commercial aspect of the magazine and its complicity in the constant efforts of Canadian publishers to sell more books. Even before its formal affiliation with the CAA, the magazine unambiguously allied itself with the material promotion of Canadian writing. As it stated in 'Bookishness in Canada,' an unsigned article that appeared in the inaugural issue in January 1919, 'the Book is a singularly composite product. To place the completed article in the hands of the consumer requires the services of the author, for the making of it; the publisher, for the physical production of it; the bookseller and the library for the distribution of it ... It is these common interests, the interests of the Book itself, which the *Canadian Bookman* is designed and pledged to serve.'[11] This attitude is reflected in numerous other articles in the magazine, including the revealingly titled 'Canadian Book Trade's Golden Era: "Just Around the Corner, if Booksellers do their Part,"' published in April 1922. Such fervently naive pieces, and the *Bookman*'s almost unequivocal support for Canadian Book Week, an annual CAA-supported event geared toward the marketing of Canadian books, provoked negative responses ranging from the cautiously critical to the vitriolic. In May 1921, an editorial written by Barker Fairley was published in the *Forum* pointing out a key contradiction in the position of the CAA, and by extension the *Bookman*: 'Its first object is "To act for the mutual benefit and protection of the interests of Canadian Authors and for the maintenance of high ideals and practice in the literary profession." But there are two objects here, not one, and they very often conflict with one another.'[12] Less generously, Douglas Bush remarked in the *Forum* in December 1926 that

> as each Canadian Book Week or gathering of the Authors' Association recedes into the past and the echoes of mutual adulation roll comfortably from soul to soul, there rises insistently in one's bosom the impolite query: 'Do Canadian authors ever read anything?' It would seem incredible that intelligent persons who were abreast of the contemporary movement could hold the opinions which most of our *literati* exuberantly express about their own works and their friends' ... The salvation of Canadian literature would be a nation-wide attack of writer's cramp, lasting at least a decade.[13]

The Canadian Authors Association, of course, did not develop as an organization devoted to high critical standards, but rather as 'a trades guild for Canadian writers, to protect them *vis-à-vis* the other interests involved in the publishing business ... Beginning as a professional pressure group, it became more and more an association for a wide variety of individuals interested in vaguely cultural activities.'[14] Its metamorphosis from this sort of trade organization into chief advocate of Canadian Book Week is neither difficult to imagine nor particularly surprising. But the dual role of the CAA meant that critics who took aim at the uncritical tendency in Canadian writing were also targeting those who wished to sell Canadian books. *Canadian Bookman*, a loud, prolific, and visible supporter of Canadian publishers, became synonymous with the CAA and was an easy mark for critics and writers with all sorts of complaints: low critical standards, nationalism, social conservatism, the commercialization of Canadian literature, the proliferation of regionalism, sentimentalism, and the ignorance of foreign writing. But, while the *Bookman* is 'guilty' of all of these 'affronts' to some degree, as Mulvihill suggests, 'both Smith and Bush had as their immediate target the Canadian Authors Association and to some extent the *Bookman* was simply caught in the crossfire.'[15]

I have spent some time looking at these criticisms of the *Bookman* because Canada's literary histories have so persistently placed *The Canadian Forum* at the centre of Canadian literary culture of the 1920s that its importance is difficult to challenge. Yet the *Forum* of the 1920s said very little about Canadian fiction and published only a very limited range of short stories by a select group of individuals, most of whom were somehow connected with the editors of the journal, who were themselves generally far more interested in public affairs and politics than in literature. I do not mean to suggest that the *Bookman*'s contribution to the development of Canadian modern realism has been deliberately overlooked. Rather, critics have been understandably captivated by numerous other important literary debates of the period, all of which see the *Bookman* taking naive, conservative, and nationalistic positions: the magazine often implies that a Canadian subject is more important than literary skill, that regionalism is more important than cosmopolitanism, that literature ought to have an engaged social role by upholding high moral standards. Not surprisingly, most have assumed that a magazine striking such postures could have little to contribute to our understanding of serious writing in Canada.

Canadian Bookman's most serious and thoughtful contributors directed the nationalistic impulse in a more profitable direction and changed the course of Canadian literary development profoundly. These men and women advanced a new modern-realist fiction that was unlike, in just about every way imaginable, the romantic, conservative, and uncritical forms of fiction that the magazine is ironically infamous for endorsing. Modern realism is fully engaged in the contemporary moment, socially conscious and often progressive, frequently anti-nationalistic and critical of accepted cultural 'values,' technically radical by Canadian standards of the period, profoundly concerned with human psychology, and as thematically modern as any but the most radical modern works of early twentieth-century literature. A series of manifestos and articles published in the *Bookman* in the 1920s established a sense of urgency about Canada's need for modern writing and offered initial definitions of the new modern realism and its characteristics. This effort was reflected in many of the book reviews that the *Bookman* printed from the early 1920s through to its amalgamation with *The Canadian Author* in 1939. Although the essential creative works of modern realism would not be published in the *Bookman* (which published very little creative work), the magazine's series of manifestos for a modern realism would have a wide-ranging and formative impact on Canadian literature for decades to come.

Canadian Bookman's unsigned prospectus, which appeared at the beginning of the inaugural January 1919 issue, revealed that the magazine considered itself a revolutionary catalyst and sought to oppose status-quo literary values with a new, modern form of realism. Like other innovative modes of expression, including most of the competing movements that collectively make up literary modernism, Canada's modern realism began with a manifesto, or a 'testimony of a historical present tense spoken in the impassioned voice of its participants. The manifesto declares a position; the manifesto refuses dialogue or discussion; the manifesto fosters antagonism and scorns conciliation. It is univocal, unilateral, single-minded.'[16] The *Bookman*'s first manifesto, 'The New Era,' firmly establishes the magazine in the 'historical present' and declares boisterously that 'the first issue of the new *Canadian Bookman* appears at a moment which happens also to mark the beginning of a new era in the history of mankind, and, very particularly, in the history of Canada.'[17] It demonstrates the 'antagonism' of the modernist manifesto, clearly refusing any 'conciliation' between an obsolete past and the new era it is initiating: 'We stand today, along with the other great nations of a purified world, at the beginning of a new era which will certainly be vastly different from both the era of force and the era of materialism which preceded it.'[18]

The prospectus heralds a new national era dawning in the wake of the Great War and defines this era specifically in cultural and literary terms. It places the *Bookman* by implication at the centre of a Canadian literary coming-of-age that will contrast favourably with a materialistic era that culminated in war: 'It will be in one respect an era of ideas, an era of profound and general thought ... if this era is to be an era of ideas, it follows that it is also to be an era of books, since books are the one great medium through which ideas of [*sic*] communicated and perpetuated ... The *Canadian Bookman* itself is one of the phenomena of the new era.'[19] This sense of the arrival of a 'new era' is found everywhere in the pages of the magazine: it is the only magazine of the 1920s regularly to publish reviews of new works of Canadian fiction, it speaks out on most of the pressing cultural issues of the day, and it shows a strong interest in the social and political development of Canada.

The *Bookman*'s prospectus also 'declares a position' in support of a new form of modern writing worthy of this 'new era' and, in enumerating its literary standards, ironically foreshadows the rhetoric that critics of the magazine would use against it in years to come: the new books will not be 'the merely sentimental, narcotic, idea-less books, miscalled books of the imagination, which have formed the literary food of too many of us who did not wish to be bothered with ideas.'[20] While this first manifesto would not define the new writing specifically in terms of the modern realism it would shortly advocate, it hinted at the mimetic nature of this new fiction and called for 'real books, containing real ideas about the important things of life ... It was this conviction, of the coming of an era of ideas and of books, which was strong in the minds of the founders of the new *Canadian Bookman* and which led them to select the present as an appropriate time.'[21] The leap from a call for 'real books' and 'real ideas about the important things of life' to demanding a realism up to the task of exploring the modern world was subsequently made in short order, and over the next few months and years numerous authors and critics weighed in on the subject, defining and refining the modern-realist aesthetic.

The *Canadian Bookman* of the 1920s and '30s might be read as a series of small articles that, following the lead of the 1919 prospectus, evoke the language and tone of the manifesto and cumulatively offer a passionate and persistent call for a Canadian modern realism, enumerate its characteristics, and offer critical commentary on the first exemplary creative works as they emerged across Canada in the 1920s. The enthusiastic and urgent spirit of the prospectus would carry on unabated in virtually every aspect of the *Bookman* until the arrival of the 1930s and the scaling back, both of nationalistic pride in Canada in general, and of the size and format of the magazine itself. While this enthusiasm would often translate into the boosterish attitudes and expressions mentioned earlier, it would also lead a number of contributors to turn their attention seriously to the task of determining exactly what was wrong with Canadian literature and what writers and critics needed to do to bring it into the modern era. Their solution, in short, was for writers to engage the contemporary world with their fiction and for critics to advocate a new realist aesthetic against what would prove to be considerable resistance. After the first manifestos appeared in the *Bookman*, it would be more than a decade before the small-minded criticisms of this new form's supposed vulgarity, explicitness, and lack of moral conscience subsided and enduring works of modern realism were numerous enough to constitute a major literary movement and Canadian genre.

The first significant *Bookman* article to follow the prospectus and call for a modern realism was J.M. Gibbon's 'The Coming Canadian Novel,' published in July 1919. Douglas Daymond and Leslie Monkman credit Gibbon with being one of the regular *Bookman* contributors who sought 'to bridge traditional values and radical literary innovation.'[22] For his part, Gibbon, after praising both English and American literature for veracious 'observation of contemporary or recent life,' laments the lack of a similar quality in Canadian fiction, revealing that, from the start, there were important *Bookman* critics interested in looking judiciously at the national literature and directing it toward realism: 'The novel should realistically reflect contemporary life ... There has been no memorable picture in fiction of either Montreal or Toronto, for instance, although Montreal has a population almost as large as Boston, and Toronto is no mean city.'[23] The premise of Gibbon's article is relatively straightforward, and he states concretely what many of the anticipators of Canadian modern realism had been saying in approximate terms all along. But the shifting of focus to the 'contemporary' setting distinguishes this new attitude from that of many earlier writers who believed that while Canadian writing ought to be about Canada, this writing could as easily be romantic as realist. Gibbon also suggests that the new realism will render the contemporary Canadian subject matter in a style of writing that is both creative and documentary: 'Wherever in the modern world there is activity, there is the creative and imaginative reporter.'[24] Gibbon even anticipates the proliferation of Canadian social realism in the 1930s when he argues that the new realism ought to reflect a contemporary environment because of its social importance: 'The host of English realists from Dickens to the present day are such creative reporters, voicing the problems and the spirit of a century of social turmoil and upheaval.'[25]

Importantly, Gibbon is not acting as a 'booster' of the Canadian fiction that already exists but is among the first to advocate for a new, modern fiction. His discussion laments the absence of a flourishing modern realism in Canadian literature: 'The Englishman who looked for a representative picture of Canadian life in the Canadian novel would be disappointed.'[26] Gibbon echoes the revolutionary tone of the *Bookman*'s prospectus and frames his own article as a manifesto by closing with a prophetic summons for modern realists to appear on the Canadian literary scene and describe the contemporary Canadian 'spirit' as Gorki and Balzac did for Russia and France in their own periods: 'Canada is still waiting – but will not have to wait long – for her prophet – or more likely her group of prophets who shall interpret her many-sided, but always vigorous, life to her own people and to the Nations who have accepted her as Come of Age.'[27] Although Gibbon's article is still thickly cloaked in the rhetoric of romantic nationalism and celebration of the Canadian spirit, it takes the important step of redirecting the boosterish impulse away from an uncritical celebration of Canadian literature as it is toward a confident and enthusiastic advocacy of what it might be, should the modern-realist moment come to pass. Gibbon also makes a point about the promotion of Canadian books that refutes many of the *Forum*'s criticisms of the *Bookman* that would follow in the early 1920s. He argues that 'there are good reasons for this dearth of Canadian life in Canadian fiction, which like most good reasons are economic … the realistic novel had no place – what was wanted was the goody-goody love story with a happy ending.'[28] Rather than suggesting either that Canadian books ought to be celebrated, whatever their quality, or that Canadian books had already achieved a level of quality that ought to be celebrated, Gibbon argues that the promotion of Canadian books, and the economic benefit for Canadian publishers, will lead to a higher quality of 'realistic' literature.

While Gibbon defines Canadian modern realism imprecisely in terms of its documentary properties, other 1920s contributions to the *Bookman* would be more complex and exacting. One of the first Canadian critics to insist that the new writing in Canada ought to do more than simply and accurately reflect a Canadian environment or society was Beaumont S. Cornell, writing in 'The Essential Training of the Novelist,' which appeared in the *Bookman* in June 1921. Cornell, himself the author of two novels of the period – *Renaissance* (1922) and a realist novel set in Ontario, *Lantern Marsh* (1923) – vigorously argues that the new writing in Canada must supplement its documentary impulse with philosophical and psychological interpretation. Cornell argues that literature ought 'to be an exponent of life's meaning' and that this requires a movement beyond 'the boring, even distressing, facts of actual existence.'[29] Cornell concedes that the novel is essentially a realistic form of expression – 'the novel is tied up inseparably with actuality. It is the next thing to reality because it is always an estimate of human life' – but adds that higher forms of literature require a 'subjective' interpretation of the world to supplement an 'objective' rendering of reality: 'The noblest intention of fiction, then, is to interpret life; and since this requires much more than a skilful pen, the essential training of the novelist begins when he commences to observe life reflectively ... He must appraise, compare, judge, select, emphasize – in short interpret ... for he is dealing with the great objective reality ... It is not sufficient that he should be a reporter, standing aloof, coldly observing the pageant of existence.'[30]

While Cornell's argument that literature ought to strive to be 'subjective' appears unnecessary by contemporary critical standards, his suggestion that 'objective' writing is already, in 1921, becoming the default style for modern Canadian writing – the *Bookman* had already praised the realism of novels by Robert J. C. Stead, Douglas Durkin, and Arthur Stringer – gives a clear indication of the quick pace of change in Canadian literary circles. More importantly, Cornell is beginning to define the 'modern' component of Canadian realism. Contrary to a popular interpretation, Canadian writers of the 1920s were not engaged in the unproblematic transplantation of a nineteenth-century realist aesthetic into a Canadian milieu. While more precise definitions of the modern and interpretive component of realism would be articulated by later critics, Cornell is highlighting a problem with nineteenth-century realism that led to some of the more experimental high-modernist techniques. While neither Cornell's article nor his own novels explicitly advocate or exhibit the boldest subjectivist devices of modernist innovation, his argument hints at the complexities of Canadian realism and demands that it do more than document and reflect. The discomfort that Cornell expresses with writing that is 'engaged simply in "holding up the mirror to nature"' is loudly echoed in the writings of the important modern realists who would follow and explore this problem much more rigorously and exhaustively.

A more precise definition of the new modern realism and its characteristics would begin to take shape with the publication of Adrian Mac-

Donald's article, 'English Realism to a Canadian,' in September 1922. MacDonald draws some important contrasts between Canadian realism and the form and spirit of realism in the European, or essentially English, traditions. While the tone of his article is somewhat pedestrian – 'To a somewhat romantic Canadian ... the contemporary English novel is at first somewhat disconcerting' – MacDonald's musings on the English novel, perhaps unwittingly, touch upon a number of concepts of relevance to the development of modern realism in Canada.[31] The most crucial of these observations is that, on some level at least, the new modern realism is incompatible with an idealistic nationalism. In reviewing his selection of European high-realist fictions, MacDonald remarks that these novels 'recount not the vain successes of men, but their failures,' and that 'all this dismal sense of failure is quite foreign to the optimistic spirit of our dominion. We Canadians are born with the conviction that ... there are no limits to what we may accomplish.'[32] Building upon Gibbon's assertion that the new modern realism ought primarily to explore the contemporary world, MacDonald suggests that to do just this will mean extending the scope of the Canadian novel beyond those areas of life, contemporary or otherwise, that can be easily idealized, idyllized, and celebrated. This would be the realization behind an essential shift in the mind-set of Canadian writers as modern realism began to proliferate in the later 1920s and 1930s. One need only compare romantic prairie novels such as Stead's *The Homesteaders* (1916) and Ethel Chapman's *God's Green Country* (1922) to their bleaker, more famous, 'prairie-realist' counterparts, published in the years that would follow, to find evidence of a shift in writerly disposition.

MacDonald's 1922 article also enumerated some of the characteristics of modern realism, or, as he called it, 'the method of the new school.'[33] Not surprisingly, a prominent feature of this 'method' would be the high-realist's assertion that a writer ought 'to be exact in detail.'[34] MacDonald also identifies the fictional representation of a 'deep sense of the ineffectiveness of man,' again emphasizing the need for fiction to cast off its romantic and idealistic sensibilities in a manner reminiscent of European and American Naturalists – Zola, Ibsen, Strindberg, Hardy, Wharton, Dreiser, Norris, and Crane.[35] On the subject of style, MacDonald advocates a 'simple, idiomatic, carefully wrought English,' which is the one feature that perhaps most immediately distinguishes Canadian modern-realist fiction both from its European high-realist counterparts and from most of the few pre-1920s fictions written in Canada that gesture toward a realist aesthetic, most notably Duncan Campbell Scott's

In the Village of Viger (1896), Ralph Connor's *The Man From Glengarry* (1901), Sara Jeannette Duncan's *The Imperialist* (1904), and Frederick Niven's pre-1920s novels, including *A Wilderness of Monkeys* (1911).[36]

A related aspect of style advocated by MacDonald that would become an almost ubiquitous feature of modern-realist fiction is a form of implied narrative objectivity, at least insofar as this concept is synonymous with an author's attempt to 'avoid the appearance of over-conscious artistry' and to support an 'appeal to the scientific spirit.'[37] MacDonald also defines the new modern realism as having an instructive purpose: 'The novel is no longer to be looked upon as the mere amusement of an idle hour, but its covers are to be opened with minds alert for revelations of new truths,' and it ought to be actively involved in 'criticizing our existing institutions.'[38] Such an impulse underlies the didacticism that is evident in many Canadian social-realist novels of the period. The most enigmatic characteristic identified by MacDonald is 'psychological realism,' though this feature would also rise to prominence in the modern-realist novel and would be one of the chief characteristics distinguishing early modern-realist fictions from the more romantic works that preceded them.[39] Finally, MacDonald leaves no doubt that he believes this new realism ought to be pursued by Canadian writers, readers, and critics, and he recalls the earlier manifestos published in the *Bookman* with his assertion that 'any Canadian with a taste for letters will soon find himself reacting favourably to the art of these stories ... his staple food in the way of fiction will henceforth be novels flavoured with the spirit of realism.'[40]

Lorne Pierce championed the emerging realism from a conservative angle in 'Canadian Literature and the National Ideal,' which appeared in the *Bookman* in September 1925. Pierce's celebratory tone in praise of the new trend in Canadian literature is easily detectable, and he reveals that in a few short years modern realism had moved beyond its initial phase: 'We have happily left behind the times when Canadian literature was supposed to ape the themes and methods of England, and also those hectic days when the proper attitude towards our new school of native letters was one of sheer rhapsody, as noisy as it was uncritical.'[41] Among the features of the new writing that elicit Pierce's approval, and in his view follow naturally from our 'National Ideal,' is 'Realism,' which among other things is defined as follows: 'everything crystal clear, and "facts-is-facts."'[42] Pierce's conservative credentials in both the social and literary realm are evident: he was a Methodist and later United Church minister, and his landmark anthology, *Our*

Canadian Literature: Representative Prose and Verse (1922), co-edited with Albert Durrant Watson, had only recently revealed in its preface an 'insistence upon the physical and ethical quality of men and women,' and offered a view of literature in which 'the actual poet is he who presents reality in the beautiful garments of revealing art.'[43] In his *Bookman* article, Pierce praises Canadian realism for the fact that, despite its proliferation as a literary form, 'we have escaped sex, psycho-analysis, and morbid ventures into the dim unknown.'[44] Like many of the other critics who openly advocated a new realism in the pages of the *Bookman*, Pierce phrased his call for this new literature in the language of the manifesto: 'We are at the very beginning of things – not the end. For the rest we need ... utter fidelity to the truth ... a determination to be ourselves.'[45] Of course, Pierce's most conservative comments reveal that he was not advocating the same kind of realism as were most other critics of the day. But they are testimony that the new realism was being noticed by all segments of the Canadian literary world by the mid-1920s.

Certainly, modern realism owes some of its success and proliferation as a form to the fact that it appealed both to the more radical, innovative segments of the Canadian literary community, including leftists of various stripes, who saw it as a modern form that reflected and commented upon a contemporary society in transition, and the conservative segment of the literary world that included Lorne Pierce and much of the membership of the Canadian Authors Association, which, except in the very few cases in which 'realist' and 'sexually explicit' could be conceived as synonymous, felt that realism was an unthreatening form. The conservatives also were attracted to the new realism because it had the potential to offer morally inoffensive sketches of small, local environments. With its purported fidelity to facts, truth, and scientific principles, realism could be made to seem an antidote to the amoral, relativistic, experimental high-modernist fiction that was making its presence felt through reviews of foreign works in both the *Bookman* and *The Canadian Forum* in the 1920s.

A more moderate critic, Francis Dickie, applauded the frankness of the new realism in his October 1925 *Bookman* article 'Realism in Canadian Fiction.' Rather than expressing pride in the fact that Canadian writers tended to avoid more sordid matters in their fiction, Dickie remarks, speaking of the European novelists, that 'all take account and deal frankly with life as a whole as no Canadian writer has yet done in the novel.'[46] In the Canadian situation, Dickie can only offer a limited form of praise, identifying a 'second type' of 'kindlier realism; novels in which sex, for one fundamental, appears clad more conventionally ... In Canada there has been something of an approach toward realism of this second type, at least.'[47] A number of insights into the phenomenon of Canadian modern realism emerge from Dickie's discussion. On the simplest level, Dickie demonstrates that realism is a modern literary form acceptable to at least some of those writers and critics who seek to move beyond the more traditional and conservative types of Canadian writing. Dickie's advocacy of a modern realism, however, does not derive solely from his approval of its potential subject matter. Rather, Dickie argues that the incorporation of all aspects of life into Canadian fiction, including a discussion of sexuality – 'accurateness and vividness' requires that 'sex ... tak[e] its proper place' in the novel – will ameliorate the style of Canadian writers: 'Canadian fiction as yet has not enough artistic balance without which no great literature is possible. That artistic balance will come with the advent of realism.'[48] Dickie indicates that the emerging realism interested critics not merely because it might serve a nationalistic project and celebrate Canada through mimetic depictions, or because it might be a vehicle for social change, or because it was a new and unexamined literary form. Like many of his contemporaries, Dickie was most intrigued by the unmistakeably modern style of the new realism, and how a new 'artistic balance,' or a developing interest in modern aesthetics, might transform Canadian writing.

Most of these initial *Bookman* articles discuss modern realism in passionate but relatively general terms. They communicate why a new Canadian fiction is needed and offer an overview of the immediate characteristics of the new realism they advocate. While these articles obviously consider the new realism to be 'modern,' not all of them discuss it in a manner that immediately or obviously suggests that it has affinities with other forms of modernist literature, or deserves inclusion among the established, various, competing, and contradictory modernist aesthetics and movements. Exact boundaries between realisms and modernisms, whether temporal, regional, national, generic, aesthetic, or ideological, are notoriously difficult to draw in any literary tradition, and the Canadian situation provides no exception. 'What makes Canadian realism "modern"?' is a question that most critics of the early twentieth century rarely asked and almost never answered directly. Probably, the new modern realism was so unlike the Canadian fiction that preceded it that critics and writers felt no need to question its essential modernity. From a contemporary perspective, however, it appears problematic that Canadians were writing modern realism while dissimilar forms of modernist writing were appearing in other countries. Were Canadians ignorant of foreign and experimental modernisms? Did they see their modern realism as a national branch or regional application of an international modernism? Were such issues of any interest to writers of the period? Certainly, modern realism in Canada is a hybrid genre that incorporates techniques commonly associated with European and American realisms and naturalisms, and various modernist movements, while remaining distinct from all of these forms.

The literary-historical timeline further complicates distinctions. Modern realism's rise to pre-eminence in Canadian prose fiction in the 1920s occurs at a time when the European and American realist traditions had been all but exhausted and eclipsed by a new generation of heterogeneous and innovative modernist authors. A majority of Canadian critics and writers appears not to have perceived that a shift towards modernism, in radical terms, was taking place in any literary tradition, Canadian or foreign. A reading of the letters and book reviews published in Canadian journals of the 1920s makes it clear that the average reader, and even the average critic, had very little awareness, much less understanding, of the movements and range of aesthetics critics have retrospectively termed 'modernism.' These individuals tended instead to view contemporary works by leading modernists such as Joyce and Woolf as experiments which differed from accepted works of realism only in the degree to which they were willing to experiment with literary technique to express an essential 'realism' or 'reality.' A review of Virginia Woolf's *To the Lighthouse*, published in the *Bookman* in September 1927, calls Woolf 'the chief exponent of the modern novel,' yet offers no more sophisticated technical analysis of the book than to remark that it is an 'ably-drawn ... character study ... containing touches of beautiful prose.'[49] Such banal reviews were not the sole property of the *Bookman*. In 1926, *The Canadian Forum* summarized Joyce's short story 'The Dead' as 'simply a representation of the fine and complex sensations of a man during a single evening.'[50]

While neither reviewer's analysis is essentially incorrect, their understatements of the technical achievements of these two modernist classics are as blatant as they are typical of conceptions of modern fiction in 1920s journals. An especially conspicuous example of Canadian critical ignorance of modernist innovation and experiment is a review of T.S.

Eliot's *The Waste Land* (1922), by John Hurley, which appeared in the *Bookman* in May 1923. Not only is the title of the poem misspelled in the review, but it is mistakenly attributed to T.G. Elliott, the author and editors perhaps half-confusing the American poet with T.R. Elliott, a writer of dismal Canadian historical-romance novels, including *Hugh Layal: A Romance of the Up-Country* (1927). Nevertheless, the poem is judged unremarkable: 'One reads his poem with ... a deep sense of disappointment at his [Eliot's] deliberately wrought incoherence ... "The Waste Land" is really a very small plateau, confined within the limits of Mr. Elliott's ... cool brain.'[51]

But the best articles printed in the 1920s magazines indicated more precisely what made the new realism 'modern' and how it was related to the literatures of other nations. An especially articulate, incisive, and prolific critic of the new modern realism was Lionel Stevenson, and his work does much to clarify the interplay of realist and modernist aesthetics in Canadian prose. Best known for his critical work *Appraisals of Canadian Literature* (1926), Stevenson was a frequent contributor to the *Bookman* in the mid-1920s, and his articles enumerate many of the key characteristics of modern realism. In 'The Fatal Gift,' published in the *Bookman* in 1923, Stevenson echoes many of his contemporaries with a call for a more refined and direct use of language in literature: 'The man who undertakes to write to-day has too many words at his command. Impressive words and whole glib phrases are stored profusely in his memory and transfer themselves thence on to paper with scarcely an effort of the intellect ... If our language is to be vitalized, it must first be condensed.'[52] Here, Stevenson draws an important contrast between the modern-realist novel and both the European novel of the nineteenth century and the early twentieth-century Canadian novel. The form of writing that Stevenson favours contrasts with the verbose, philosophical, expansive novels of George Eliot, Dickens, Thackeray, or Duncan and Connor in the Canadian context. Stevenson argues for a language that exhibits 'extreme simplicity. Every word is brief and entirely familiar; not a phrase is distorted or far-fetched.'[53] The sort of unencumbered, direct writing that Stevenson advocates here is not unlike the less-experimental strain of modernist prose – perhaps best exemplified by writers such as Ernest Hemingway, Jean Rhys, and Sherwood Anderson – that would have an important impact on so many Canadian writers, including Knister, Callaghan, Baird, and to a lesser extent MacLennan.

Stevenson believed this new style, and the realism that it both reflected and facilitated, to be unarguably modern. In 'The Outlook for Canadian Fiction,' which was published in the *Bookman* in July 1924, Stevenson concedes 'the most beautiful prose written in Canada' to the romantic novelists writing around the turn of the century.[54] The modern writing, or 'new impulse,' he celebrates involves a rejection of 'beautiful' words in favour of a 'harshness that is loosely termed realism.'[55] The new, and even revolutionary, direct style Stevenson endorses entails more than a refinement of language; it involves an exacting and realistic treatment of its subject matter: 'The tradition is no longer satisfactory. Almost without exception, the note-worthy new novels show a determined effort toward more serious treatment of life.'[56] The realist aesthetic, then, is both new and experimental, but Stevenson is hardly celebrating experiment for its own sake. To him, and to so many Canadian writers and critics of the period who expressed similar views less articulately, realism was both new and very familiar, and as such it embodied a complex but workable contradiction. Modern realism represented an unmistakable break from the literary style that preceded it, yet it did so by offering a representation, not of the new and uncharted high-modernist terrain of the unconscious, or of the obscure and outré, or of the spiritual and symbolic, but rather of something that was very well known if under-represented to Canadian writers: the familiar, actual conditions of Canadian life.

In his enigmatic 1927 *Bookman* article, 'Is Canadian Poetry Modern?' Stevenson takes his call for a national literature to a new level, and in the process offers a view of what makes Canadian realism modern that is broadly in line with the working definitions of other critics and writers. Stevenson begins by showing contempt for the most experimental high modernism: speaking of Gertrude Stein's work, he remarks, 'In such cases "modernity" consists in a startling extreme of a current fashion, sweeping into temporary notoriety by ostentatious novelty, making an almost physical assault on the sensibilities of the reader.'[57] Modernity, to Stevenson, is not located in the experimental or technical features of a literary work, yet it is an essential and desirable feature of literature: 'modernity is the essential characteristic which distinguishes true and permanent literature from mere word-spinning.'[58] Where, then, can the essence of a text's modernity be located if not in its technical aspects? Stevenson offers his answer in terms that provide the central tenet of a definition of Canadian modern realism: he insists upon drawing a distinction between 'genuine modernity and revolutionary innovation.'[59] He argues that modern writers are involved with

> fully interpreting the actual vital spirit of their times, free of outworn conventions and yet avoiding all self-conscious affectation of revolt; their eyes turned neither toward the past nor toward the future, but ... absorbed in the entertaining spectacle of life around them, and their transference of that life into art was immortal because the spark of actual life was in it ... there is nothing apologetic or experimental or defiant in the attitude of the true modernists ... the satisfying effect of utter reality ... results from the author's complete identification with the immediate subject matter.[60]

Realism, in Stevenson's view, is modern when it is engaged in capturing its contemporary spirit to the fullest degree possible, and this is a revolutionary act: 'direct identification with the spirit of any age means necessarily a severance from moribund traditions, even though they are still observed by the majority.'[61] Yet literary experiment and technical innovation are neither characteristic nor atypical of the modern; a modern literature is involved in a representation of its contemporary environment by whatever technical means necessary. This view, although rarely articulated by the earliest critics of modern realism, would appear to have been very widely held in Stevenson's day, judging by the number of modern-realist authors who do exactly as Stevenson advocates, and the number of later critics and writers who say more or less the same thing. This begins to explain why Canadian realists believed they were creating a modern literature in the 1920s at the same time that high-modernist experiments in the literary magazines seemed, from a contemporary perspective, to be contradicting them. It also begins to explain why so many of the experimental techniques that Canadian writers attempt – Grove's temporal shifts in *The Master of the Mill*, Knister's handling of multiple points of view in his unpublished novel *Group Portrait*, Baird's 'reportage,' Callaghan's psychological realism, and MacLennan's 'kaleidoscopic' technique from his unpublished first novel – do not closely resemble related techniques in high-modernist fictions. The Canadian modern realists are not being self-consciously experimental; they are being modern in the sense that they are attempting to represent their contemporary environment, and for the most ambitious of these writers, this activity leads them to employ new forms that might best be viewed as complementing this realism, rather than dimly reflecting high-modernist methods. The legacy of the *Canadian Bookman* of the 1920s comprises mainly these and other articles that boisterously advocate and define the new modern realism. The *Bookman*'s role in Canadian literary history is crucial: it provided a vital forum where writers and critics could articulate the purposes and techniques of their new aesthetic. Without such a forum, it is difficult to imagine how so many literary figures of the day might have reached (or discovered) a near consensus about new writing in Canada, and there might not have been a coherent modern-realist movement at all.

By the mid-1920s, discussions of modern realism were nearly ubiquitous in the *Bookman*, and evidence that it was on the minds of a broad reading public can be found in many of the minor and otherwise unremarkable items published in the magazine: advertisements, announcements, gossip columns. But the best proof that the movement was gaining ground is the appearance of increasing amounts of modern-realist fiction itself. Such works began to surface with regularity as the early manifestos were being published in the *Bookman*. Stead's essentially romantic novels of the late teens were beginning to exhibit unmitigated characteristics of modern realism by the publication of *Dennison Grant* in 1920. Knister's modern-realist short stories appeared in print as early as 1922. By 1925, Grove and Ostenso had published the first famous modern-realist novels, *Settlers of the Marsh* and *Wild Geese*. The sheer number of book reviews published during the period that noticed and praised realist tendencies in new Canadian works confirms this. An unsigned review of Stead's new novel, *The Cow Puncher*, appeared in the *Bookman* in January 1919 and directed one of Canada's early realists toward the aesthetic he would develop in his next few novels: 'It will certainly be of value when Mr. Stead takes to the portrayal of more normal and more accurately observed Canadian life [including] ... a life-like and sincere picture of the normal, every-day, routine events which make up most of the life even of a Westerner at this advanced date in "Canada's Century."'[62] Similarly, the unnamed reviewer of Luke Allan's sensationalistic adventure novel, *Blue Pete: Half-Breed* (1921), remarked that 'Canadians with a real knowledge of their West will note in it some signs of an ability to do something more than describe gunfights, suggesting that Mr. Allan may eventually turn to a much more artistic and serious portrayal of Western life.'[63] In 1923, a notice of Ethel Chapman's *God's Green Country* (1922) described the novel in a single line, choosing to emphasize its documentary and didactic qualities: 'An all-Canadian novel showing how conditions in rural life may be improved by the application of modern methods.'[64] A review of Grove's *Settlers of the Marsh* by Georges Bugnet, himself the author of a realistic novel written in French about the life of a part-Native woman, entitled

Nipsya (1924), appeared in December 1925 and equated Grove's abilities as a writer with his realist aesthetic: 'Grove has certainly the marks of a gifted writer who knows how to curb his imagination to let facts, real facts, predominate.'[65] By October 1926, as evidence that realism was being accepted as the new modern form by critics, if not yet by the majority of Canadian authors, T.D. Rimmer remarked, in a short article entitled 'Recent Canadian Novels,' that 'it is rather peculiar that the majority of Canadian authors still evince a warm partiality towards adventure and story-telling instead of devoting their talent to the interpretation of contemporary life and the processes that govern individual reactions.'[66]

Such positive reviews of modern-realist works are found not only in the *Bookman*. Despite its comparative critical neglect of prose, *The Canadian Forum* published occasional reviews of Canadian books in the 1920s. These reviews reveal that the *Forum* endorsed the modern-realist writing of the *Bookman*, irrespective of the debates that divided these magazines on other issues. An unsigned 1923 review of Grove's first book of sketches, *Over Prairie Trails* (1922), offered praise for its accurate, unsensational depiction of life on the Manitoba prairie: 'There is incident, but, thank Heaven, no plot. I do not know of a more vivid or authentic description of inland Canadian weather. There is combined the naturalist's scientific accuracy and attention to detail with the poet's interpretive affection.'[67] A review of Pierce and Watson's *A Book of Canadian Prose and Verse* (1922), also appearing unsigned in the *Forum* in 1923, was critical of the verse, but claimed: 'It is a different matter with the prose ... even when, occasionally, the style is inferior, the material is vivid and authentic and deals with the actual life of the people.'[68] Even Frederick Niven, a writer of historical romances and some of the dullest realist novels of the period, was praised for his technique in a review in May 1927: 'Niven, in his descriptions, has an uncanny knack of selecting the essential details, and illuminating them with his own emotional colouring.'[69] The *Forum*'s praise of these works proves that the modern-realist movement was not contained in the pages of a single magazine with a supposedly regionalist, uncritical, and commercial agenda. The *Forum*'s endorsement of the *Bookman*'s new realism is in fact rather remarkable when one considers how irreconcilably opposed these two magazines are in most literary histories. But why would Canada's most sophisticated, cosmopolitan, and modernist magazine of the period offer support for the realist aesthetic of its rival? The answers to this question reveal fallacies in critical conceptions of 1920s literary culture, and offer more evidence that modern realism has important affinities with the kinds of modernist writing usually associated with the *Forum*.

The Canadian Forum began publishing in October 1920 under the watchful eyes of four members of the faculty of the University of Toronto: Barker Fairley, S.H. Hooke, Gilbert Jackson, and C.B. Sissons. It was a direct descendant of *The Rebel* (1917–20), a noisy University College magazine that was abandoned when its founders turned their attention to the creation of their new and more ambitious journal. The *Forum* has long been considered to mark a crucial turning point in Canadian literary history and has been credited with playing a decisive role in the introduction of literary modernism to Canada.[70] It has certainly received far more credit for its impact on Canadian literature than has the *Canadian Bookman*. Even in its most recent edition, *The Oxford Companion to Canadian Literature* does not provide an entry for the *Bookman*, but its entry on the *Forum* remarks that 'it has always been faithful to its title by allowing discussions of issues from all sides.'[71] Few would dispute the *Forum*'s key function in the development, dissemination, and critical discussion of Canadian poetry: nearly all of Canada's important modern poets published in the *Forum* in the 1920s, and the magazine published numerous landmark critical pieces on the subject. But the critical discussion of prose made up a far larger proportion of the *Bookman*'s literary pages than the *Forum*'s, and the latter was not entirely, or even predominantly, devoted to the discussion of literature, allotting far fewer pages to literary topics than the *Bookman* in an average issue.

The *Forum* did, however, publish dozens of short stories by Canadian writers alongside many of the most significant modernist poems of the 1920s. This makes the *Forum*'s support of the *Bookman* aesthetic especially surprising and revealing: it offered acclaim for modern-realist fiction at the same time as it was regularly publishing – and critically ignoring – its own brand of modern short stories. While the *Forum* obviously took its role of purveyor of Canadian poetry very seriously, it was not nearly so discriminating in its choice of stories, and almost none of the fiction it published in the 1920s and '30s is known today. In keeping with its general aesthetic tastes, the stories the *Forum* printed often bear a superficial resemblance to the experimental modernist short story, often sharing with it an economy of style, unity of effect, structural irony, impersonal narrative, and interest in representing subjective states. At the same time, the majority of these stories share much more with the popular magazine fiction of the day, and they appear flashy, insincere, short-sighted, and ultimately disposable. Many of the pieces of *Forum* short fiction are little more than snide, humorous anecdotes, satirical pieces on current events, sensationalistic action or adventure stories, or moralistic and didactic sketches. The editors appear to have made little effort to seek out new Canadian writing, and many if not most of the stories that appeared in the *Forum* in the 1920s were written by the people who held editorial positions for the magazine – including J.D. Robins (by far the most frequent contributor of fiction), Richard de Brisay, and Gilbert Norwood. The result of this cliquish, narrow editorial approach is a body of monotonous fiction, characterized by in-jokes, self-importance, snobbishness, and closed-mindedness. While the stories are nevertheless almost universally competent and remarkably concise, they are also largely academic and artless, and their concision appears to be less a deliberate aesthetic choice than a mere by-product of the space constraints of the magazine.

The fiction of the *Canadian Forum*, however, should not be dismissed outright. A few enduring pieces did appear in the 1920s and early 1930s, and some of the *Forum* stories exhibit stylistic techniques that are characteristic of the most innovative high-modernist writing. Perhaps the best-known piece to appear in the 1920s was Raymond Knister's groundbreaking modern-realist short story 'The Strawstack,' published in October 1923. While the *Forum* did not publish fiction by as significant a Canadian writer again until the early 1930s, more prominent names began to appear with some frequency around the time of the journal's tenth anniversary: Leo Kennedy's 'Portion of Your Breath' appeared in January 1930, and his 'We All Got to Die' followed in December of the same year, as part of an issue that also included Leon Edel's 'The Eternal Footman Snickers,' with its obvious allusions to T.S. Eliot's 'The Love Song of J. Alfred Prufrock.' A story by Dorothy Livesay entitled 'Beach Sunday' appeared in January 1931, and L.A. MacKay's 'Three Men' appeared in April 1931. But the most remarkable of the *Forum* short stories were by lesser-known individuals. Robert Beattie's 'Island Night' (November 1920) pushed an objective, impersonal form of narration to an experimental extreme, and this technique, with variations, also appeared in Olaf Olafsen's 'The Victim' (July 1924) and John T. Jones's 'Wagon Wheels' (October 1926). J.D. Robins's 'The Walls of Jericho' (July 1921) used a pattern of allusion to structure the narrative, and a similar preoccupation with allusion, perhaps encouraged by the frequent use of this device by the *Forum* poets of the period, can be found in Margaret Ray's 'St. George and the Dragon' (December 1927) and in another Robins story, 'David, Son of Thalia,' which appeared in December 1928. A direct and ironic approach to dialogue and setting appears in Mary Q. Innis's 'The Quarrel' (August 1922) and in Paul A.W. Wallace's 'The Romance of the West' (March 1923). Perhaps most strikingly, some of the techniques associated with the representation of human consciousness also appear: J. Ansel Anderson employs a Jamesian centre-of-consciousness technique in 'The Coward' (August 1925), J.H. Simpson creates an impressionistic narrative voice in 'Orchard Way' (August 1931), and Eleanor McNaught's 'September Sonata' (March 1932) offers a fragmented, stream-of-consciousness narrative.

At first, it is tempting to argue that these few *Forum* stories represent an important Canadian contribution to international modernist writing, or at very least a significant offshoot of foreign high modernism. Yet such an argument is difficult to sustain. For one thing, remarkable stories are a very small minority of those that appeared in the *Forum* in the 1920s and '30s. More significantly, the journal that printed these stories, the same journal that is so often praised for its modernist innovation, completely disregarded these stories critically; a glance through the *Forum* of the 1920s reveals that short fiction appears with regularity, yet the magazine appears almost unaware of its existence, interested instead – when it considers literature at all – in both Canadian poetry, and prose from Europe and the United States. And the major prose writers of the period, even those who contended that they were at the centre of the new movement in writing, were, at their most supportive, silent on the subject of the fiction of the *Forum*. Raymond Knister, Canada's first major modern realist and an author of short fiction published in the magazine, was dismissive of the *Forum*'s over-all literary relevance in an essay entitled 'Canadian Letter,' which he wrote for *This Quarter*, a Parisian journal devoted to experimental writing that also published some of his poems and modern-realist stories: 'The *Canadian Forum*, perhaps the most important and intelligent magazine we have, calls itself "A Journal of Literature and Politics," cogently except that the literature is rather consistently omitted.'[72] Knister also specifically dismissed the Canadian short fiction of the period in another essay written around the same time, 'The Canadian Short Story,' first published in the *Bookman* in 1923: 'Most people have ... left [the Canadian short story] unregarded in the magazines ... the short story is preeminently a commercial article ... reduced to a formula so regular that ... anyone can turn out a story to conform ... I have never yet seen a good story by a Canadian author in a Canadian magazine.'[73]

That Knister's views on the Canadian short story were widely held by his contemporaries is suggested by their almost utter silence on the issue: Knister is one of the very few critics of the period to consider the subject of the Canadian short story worth any commentary at all. But despite his negative valuation, Knister was optimistic, both in his own short fiction with its tireless experimentation and evolution and in his article: 'What, approximately is wrong with the Canadian short story? The question is not in itself encouraging, though a search for answers to it may reveal potentialities as well as pitfalls.'[74] Knister's question brings another one to mind that is more difficult to answer: why did the *Forum* and the literary public of the 1920s ignore this magazine's high-modernist fiction just as literary nationalism was running high, and Canadian critics, especially those clustered around the *Bookman* and *Forum*, were seemingly desperate to find Canadian literature of value?

A few indirect answers to this question arise out of a closer examination of the critical attitudes to fiction held by Canadian modernist *poets* of the period, and of practical problems associated with publishing magazine fiction in the 1920s. These answers are especially important as they help to define further the relation of modern realism to foreign modernisms. The practical reasons for the neglect of these short stories are not complicated. The best-known creative writers who published in the *Forum* were singularly or primarily poets – E.J. Pratt, A.J.M. Smith, Robert Finch, Dorothy Livesay, F.R. Scott, Leo Kennedy, and A.M. Klein – so the magazine's relative disregard of prose is perhaps to be expected, especially as most of these poets were also among the literary critics of the time. Also, Canadian poetry was, in general, much more highly regarded than was Canadian fiction in the 1920s; it at least had an established tradition, represented by the Confederation poets, even if the young modernists who published in the *Forum* wrote largely against this tradition. So the stature gap between poetry and prose may partly explain the *Forum*'s disregard of its own short fiction. There are also material and physical aspects of the magazine to consider: the brevity of the poem better suited the *Forum*'s concise art-deco format than did the short story, and poetry certainly did appear with much greater frequency. Probably for similar reasons, most of the pieces of short fiction published in the *Forum* were so pared down, very often to a single page in length, that they are difficult to equate with longer, more 'serious' prose forms such as the novel. The *Forum* published reviews of novels (almost all of them foreign) during the period, and it treated the novel as *the* serious, socially relevant prose genre. So the *Forum* seems to have had no pretensions about the significance of the fiction it published. It was treated without the seriousness reserved for poetry, regarded as entertainment, and included as a regular, predictable feature of the journal that amounted to little more than, as Knister puts it, 'a pleasant, more or less innocuous way of passing a quarter of an hour.'[75]

Experimental modernist techniques were highly valued in the Canadian poetry of the 1920s, especially by the writers and critics grouped around the *Forum*, even if a very small proportion of Canadian poetry of the period is experimental. Yet similar innovation, when it occurred in a contemporaneous body of fiction in the same journal, went totally disregarded. This is a contradiction, however, only when experimental modernism is seen as an innovative mode in sharp contrast to a traditional and conservative realism. In fact, the *Forum*'s modernist poets expressed ideas similar to those expressed in the modern-realist manifestos of the *Bookman*. In other words, the modernist poets of the *Forum* had more in common with modern-realist than high-modernist prose writers. As Sandra Djwa points out, 'the younger poets, led by Smith, believed they were totally rejecting the old romantic tradition: they decried the sentimental, nationalist verse of their immediate contemporaries and predecessors; they wished to counter an old romanticism with a new realism, rhetoric with imagism, conventional metrics with the subtlety of half-rhyme; above all, they wished to broaden the subject matter of poetry.'[76] Crucially, Djwa's argument recalls Stevenson's characterization of the relationship between high modernism and realism, published in the *Bookman* in 1927, that I paraphrased earlier: literary experiment and technical innovation are neither characteristic nor atypical of the modern; a modern literature is involved in the representation of its contemporary environment, by whatever technical means necessary.

Even one of the most sophisticated of Canada's modernist poets, A.J.M. Smith, echoed this reading of realism as experimental, modern, and new. In his 'Introduction' to *The Book of Canadian Poetry* (1943), Smith recalls that

> the modern revival began in the twenties with a simplification of technique ... Canadian poets turned against rhetoric, sought a sharper more objective imagery, and limited themselves as far as possible to the language of everyday and the rhythms of speech. These reforms were largely the work of younger poets whose outlook was native rather than cosmopolitan and whose aims were those of realism. These poets sought to render with a

new faithfulness much that had been passed over as 'unpoetic' by previous generations.[77]

Smith posits modernist innovation, not as the polar opposite, but as the logical, experimental extension of the realistic impulse in poetry. Of course Djwa, Stevenson, and Smith are all talking about poetry – an indication of the marginal role prose played in Canadian literary circles in the 1920s – and the techniques of prose and poetry have important dissimilarities. In prose, to a greater extent than in poetry, the most experimental modernist literary techniques – extreme fragmentation, stream of consciousness, juxtaposition – are associated with the representation of individual consciousness. It is also difficult for a poem to be 'realist' in the same sense as a work of fiction, and it is no accident that all of the major schools of realism – prairie realism, social realism, urban realism, socialist realism – are almost exclusively concerned with fiction. Canadian modern realism, with its quest for objectivity, its ubiquitous third-person narrators, and its fidelity to the mimetic representation of Canada, rarely requires such radical literary techniques for the communication of its modern version of reality. Modern fiction, for Canadian prose writers of the 1920s, involved reflecting the contemporary world accurately and directly, and this is not what the *Forum* short-story writers generally achieve. The self-consciously experimental *Forum* stories, then, are at best seen as isolated experiments, conducted by individual writers (almost none of whom built lasting literary reputations) interested in experimenting, in a largely virtuosic and self-referential manner, with the techniques they had become aware of through their reading of foreign writers.

That these stories went unregarded by the 'cosmopolitan' literary world of the 1920s is significant because it reveals that while the *Forum* was confident about the poetry it published and considered itself at the forefront of the new movement in Canadian poetry, it enjoyed no such self-assurance when it came to fiction. Its poetry was the best in Canada, its poets were the leading poets of the age, and its aesthetic principles for poetry were well-defined, if often disputed, debated, and challenged. On the other hand, it did not even consider the fiction it published worthy of serious critical comment: few important Canadian fiction writers of the period published in the *Forum* (and not one did regularly), and it had no clearly defined aesthetic principles about fiction. If the *Forum*'s silence on the issue of its own fiction, or the anxiety that it apparently felt about the quality of the work it published, is not enough to suggest that the legitimate claim to modernity in Canadian prose belongs to the modern realists, then consider this: the few articles published in the *Forum* in the 1920s that *do* discuss fiction endorse, almost without exception, neither foreign high modernism nor the fiction published in its own pages, but the works of Canada's modern realists. The main contribution of the *Forum* to Canadian prose, then, was not the introduction of a modernist aesthetic comparable to that which it helped bring to Canadian poetry. While explicit statements on Canadian fiction are relatively few in the *Forum*, the accumulation of its commentary in the area amounts to its advocacy, not of the majority of its own stories, with their slight, popular approach, or of the small experimental strain of prose it published, but rather of the modern-realist movement championed in the *Bookman*.

The *Forum*'s initial prospectus of October 1920, entitled 'Three Years Have Passed,' would see the magazine mark its territory every bit as polemically as the *Bookman*'s had nearly two years before, though it did so with only an implicit endorsement of literary realism. The magazine did, however, come out strongly in favour of new forms in literature, and the editors cast themselves as important figures in the ongoing struggle to forge a new literature in Canada that, in their minds, had begun with the *Forum*'s forerunner, *The Rebel*. Using a third-person past tense to grant themselves mythical status, the *Forum*'s founders wrote: 'Their [the founders'] rebellion – still in progress – was against the conventions, not against society. Their excursions into politics were neither numerous nor protracted. It was in the field of arts and letters, that they flaunted their banners as a rule.'[78] While some might assume that the new forms of literature advocated by the *Forum* were the experimental modernisms of Europe and America, the opening editorial expresses its nationalistic sentiments, along lines similar to those of the *Bookman*, by demanding a distinctly Canadian literature:

> Too often our convictions are borrowed from London, Paris, or New York. Real independence is … a spiritual thing. No country has reached its full stature, which makes its goods at home, but not its faith and its philosophy. Such a magazine as the 'Canadian Nation,' whatever has been said of its activities, is in itself a recognition of this truth. It is just as much a part of the 'Made In Canada' movement, as the Canadian Manufacturers Association. So too would 'The Canadian Forum' be considered.[79]

If the editors of the *Forum* are not subscribing to the belief held by so many *Bookman* critics of the period – namely that Canada ought to represent itself in its literature along the lines proposed by the modern realists and their forerunners – they have nevertheless failed to offer an alternative. But regardless of whether writers and critics associated with the *Forum* arrived at their support of modern realism accidentally, or as a result of influence from the *Bookman*, or simply because – when they considered literature at all – they were too busy discussing poetry to hold strong modernist opinions on prose, supportive references to the emerging realism are relatively common in its pages.

Many of the positive reactions to the emerging realism expressed in the *Forum* may have their origin in Huntley K. Gordon's 'Canadian Poetry,' published in March 1921, the first article in the *Forum* to discuss realism in any protracted manner. Gordon's sentiments sound as though they might have been extracted from the *Bookman*, and he comes out in favour of a body of national verse that strives toward the realistic depiction of Canada. In Gordon's words, 'English Canada fails to produce a distinctive verse of literary value ... and if we are to produce a poetry of any value, we must shun derivative expression and sentiment ... We have our own expressions ... [and] we must learn to use and purify them, and develop a native tradition, or die to literature.'[80] Criticizing Archibald Lampman, whom he claims is too derivative of European poets, and allying himself with the modern movement in Canadian poetry, Gordon argues that 'only by the reality of its impression can poetry succeed, and seldom does Canadian poetry achieve reality.'[81]

Statements such as Gordon's, emphasizing Canadian nationalism and the realist forms it usually privileges, are surprisingly common in the magazine. An article by Barker Fairley entitled 'Artists and Authors,' for instance, appeared in the *Forum* in December 1921 and also reflected the sentiments of the *Bookman*'s modern-realist advocates, lashing out against 'the narcotic of cheap writing' and lamenting the lack of a representative aesthetic in Canadian prose: 'We cannot yet say of any Canadian book that it expresses the strength and character of the Canadian people ... We have hardly a book that remotely expresses us ... We have nothing in Canada which we can put in the hands of a visitor from Mars and say, "Read that if you want to know what we are like."'[82] In the very act of advocating a form of literary realism, this article vocally criticizes the CAA and their 'orgy of mutual congratulation.'[83] The fact that this article, and others published in the *Forum*, position themselves simultaneously in favour of the realism advocated by the *Bookman* and against the CAA – which Desmond Pacey and Wynne Francis have suggested is almost synonymous with that magazine – suggests that something is amiss in critical conceptions of the period, and that even in the 1920s critics were overlooking the *Bookman*'s most significant contributions to Canadian literature.

The most vocal of the *Forum* critics were opposed to what they perceived to be the boosterism of the CAA and its house organs, but this opposition should not be equated with a sweeping rejection of the *Bookman* and its support of realism in Canadian writing. Not a single significant article critical of modern realism appeared in the *Forum* in the 1920s. There was, however, a peripheral concern among many of the *Forum* critics that more conventional notions of realism were somehow too limiting, and they, like many of their *Bookman* counterparts, pressed Canadian writers to move beyond the merely referential in their fiction. In a letter published in the *Forum* as an article entitled 'The Canadian Novel' in June 1922, J. Addison Reid wrote in response to a friend's request for a representative Canadian novel: 'You wish to send someone ... a Canadian novel which will be really representative of Canada ... The greatest novelists, I would say, are those who are masters in the interpretation of human emotions, which are not national but universal.'[84]

Reid cautions against the type of fiction that merely recreates a particular locale, setting, or nation in literature, demanding that a larger purpose be part of the new writing in Canada. Alfred Gordon makes this point more directly in a letter to the editor printed as an article entitled 'Canadian Culture?' in March 1922. Implying his opposition to the boosterism and nationalism of the CAA and the *Bookman*, Gordon concedes, nevertheless, that an essential realism should form the basis of modern writing: 'The artist of course deals with reality ... but never as reality; and art thus not being of the practical world, it cannot be served by a practical conception, such as that of nationalism ... to presume there is such a thing as "the national art" which the Canadian writer can achieve by "trying," or by using Canadian "settings," is to betray ignorance of the real nature of art.'[85] The key contribution of the *Forum* to the creation of Canadian modern realism is its few articles such as Gordon's. The *Forum* gave its tacit approval to the movement advocated by the *Bookman* but insisted that realism be more than a technique or a naive philosophy. In other words, the complementary role the *Forum* played was to direct Canadian writing toward a more serious aesthetic contemplation of realism.

These calls for a Canadian prose concerned with more than a simple reflection of life are not, however, calls for a consciously experimental Canadian prose. As I have suggested, the *Forum* did not advocate an experimental high-modernist fiction in its critical articles, but rather tended to support Stevenson's claim that realism is a modern form of writing. John H. Creighton's 'The Fiction of James Joyce,' which appeared in the *Forum* in July 1926, was one of several critical articles in the magazine that offered an analysis of what would later become the high-modernist classics. These articles, without exception in the 1920s, do *not* praise innovative literary techniques or advocate experimentalism in Canadian prose. Rather, they ignore the modernist techniques in the works they consider, or they consider them un-Canadian, or they awkwardly dismiss them as incomprehensible and irritating. Creighton's article is not significant for an outright rejection of modernist experiment, but for a characterization of modernism as simply an inventive and highly successful form of realism. In his discussion of *A Portrait of the Artist as a Young Man* (1914), Creighton writes:

> *A Portrait* is realism of the spirit, springing from a conviction that life is not to be caught and held in the solid, material mould of the old realism of Bennett, Galsworthy, Dreiser, and Wells; it is a realism that places emphasis on the heterogeneous impressions, emotions, feelings, and thoughts of life rather than on its facts, whether people, houses, streets, clothes, food, furniture, or hotels. Despite its lack of balance it brings us close to life – as close as we have ever been in fiction.[86]

The *Forum*, then, lends its important endorsement to the notion of modern realism put forth by the best of the *Bookman* critics; literary modernism is an extreme or heightened form of realism; by the same token, realism is a subdued form of modernism approaching the same subject matter as its more innovative counterpart with less experimental virtuosity. Even the most experimental Canadian journal of the period affirmed that modern fiction was realist at heart, and no one could deny that, by 1930, modern realism was far and away the dominant aesthetic in serious Canadian prose.

The originators and early advocates of modern realism in the 1920s were a diverse group of writers and critics, from all parts of Canada, both formal conservatives and literary innovators, both celebrators of all things Canadian and imitators of foreign modes and models. The aims and techniques associated with Canadian modern realism are almost as many and diverse as their advocates, who, writing in their prospectuses, editorials, articles, and manifestos, offered the first incisive critical comments on Canada's modern fiction. Unfortunately, a critical tradition that polarizes the *Bookman* and *Forum* in its discussions of poetry and politics has obscured the dynamic emergence of modern realism in the 1920s and the complexity and richness of the debate that supported it. Still, however revealing and significant the critical discussions of modern realism in the *Bookman* and *Forum* may be, neither venue published a significant amount of this new fiction. The boldest and most important contribution to the modern-realist movement was made by the writers of this fiction themselves, not by the critics who evaluated it.

3
Raymond Knister: Revolutionary Modern Realist

No writer who experimented with realism in the 1920s did so as imaginatively as Canada's first major modern realist, Raymond Knister. His critical opinions on modern realism, expressed in articles, correspondence, and creative work, offer ambitious and probing definitions of the genre as a whole. The fact that Knister's critics tend to consider him, contradictorily but accurately, the pre-eminent Canadian prose realist and experimentalist of the 1920s, highlights his literary significance and draws attention to the interdependence of the realist and experimental impulses in writing of the period. Although his reputation as a prose writer rests almost singularly upon his first published novel, *White Narcissus* (1929), he produced much significant work in his short career. His first short story appeared in January 1922, and he created prolifically until his untimely death by drowning in 1932. In one decade, Knister produced about one hundred poems, half as many short stories and sketches, four novels (two remain unpublished), and dozens of critical works, including essays, reviews, editorials, and a landmark anthology of Canadian short fiction. This impressive oeuvre constitutes the first sustained creative expressions of the modern-realist aesthetic in Canada. Knister wrote deliberately as a modern realist from the very start of his career, when works of realism, modern or otherwise, were almost non-existent in Canada and *Canadian Bookman* was only issuing its initial manifestos on the subject. He was an incisive critic and an indefatigable letter writer, and this largely unpublished portion of his work, together with his published writing, reveals that his thoughts on the emerging modern realism were frequent, probing, influential, revolutionary, and articulately expressed.

Knister's own literary production accounts for only part of his significance to the early development of Canadian modern realism. His dual role as pre-eminent realist *and* experimentalist of the 1920s means that he and his work embody a number of tensions and contradictions that reflect and magnify those inherent in the larger modern-realist movement. He was the earliest Canadian writer to couple Lecker's 'national-referential ideal'[1] with a wholly realistic aesthetic, and to be noticed in the modernist literary circles of Europe and America: in this sense, he reflects the multiple origins and influences of the larger movement of which he is a part and personifies the term 'modern realist.' He advocated an international standard in Canadian writing and championed Canadian subjects and issues in fiction, thus arguing from both points of view in one of the key literary debates of his day. He was at once devoted to experiment and innovation, yet critical of the avant-garde movements of the period; in this sense, he exemplified the relation of Canadian modern realism to other modernisms. Knister's short career was a largely successful literary struggle to negotiate conflicting and competing impulses, ideas, and positions. This same struggle, which was the catalyst for much of his most ambitious work, is also typical of many of those encountered by later Canadian modern realists, writing in other regions and contexts.

Knister is also important as he was an intensely individualistic yet well-connected writer, and his circle of influence and influences was wide. He was almost unique among his contemporaries (Callaghan is the only other prose writer who can make this claim) in that he was associated with significant writers and critics in Canada, the United States, and Europe. In his own country, he corresponded with the most significant literary figures of the period, including Frederick Philip Grove, Morley Callaghan, Dorothy Livesay, Leo Kennedy, A.J.M. Smith, Mazo De la Roche, Duncan Campbell Scott, Lawrence Burpee, Sir John Willison, W.A. Deacon, Hugh Eayrs, Merrill Denison, Pelham Edgar, and Lorne Pierce, among many others. He published some of his first works in *The Midland,* an experimental American journal devoted to the publication of modern writing, and from 1923 to 1924 lived in Iowa as its associate editor. Knister published poetry and prose in *This Quarter,* a Parisian journal that favoured experimental writing and included works by such illustrious modernists as James Joyce, Ezra Pound, Ernest Hemingway, Carl Sandburg, Djuna Barnes, and e.e. cummings. Yet despite his many connections to foreign writers and awareness of their literary techniques, Knister remained committed to the modern realism that he maintained was synonymous with the new writing in Canada. In pursuit of his own ambitious literary projects, Knister would undertake numerous experiments with the realist form, and his views on the subject would evolve and expand, broadening, clarifying, and defining the genre of modern realism, both to himself, and for the movement as a whole.

Knister's pioneering, even revolutionary, role in Canadian literary history has occasionally been acknowledged by his critics.[2] Much of Knister's own abundant criticism confirms, supports, and attempts to direct the dramatic changes taking place in Canadian writing in the 1920s. In an essay probably written in 1923, 'Canadian Letter,' Knister identifies the new realist movement and explicitly supports the *Bookman*'s formative role: 'It was not until our adoption of *Maria Chapdelaine* on its appearance in English, *circa* 1921, that these guesses, warnings, hopes, deprecations, and plaints [for a new literature] began to be heard generally, and now the *Canadian Bookman* lends an impartial ear to tens of these voices – which is a good augury.'[3] In this same essay, drawing attention to the sense of promise in the emerging Canadian literary scene, Knister remarks, reflecting his own dual attachment to literary models and individual experiment, 'we have room for all schools, space to be free of all schools.'[4] In 'Canadian Literature: A General Impression,' probably written between 1920 and 1923, Knister was already remarking upon 'the presses' that 'continue to pour forth an increasing number of volumes by Canadian authors until, not unnaturally we have begun to experience a desire to know our position,' thereby highlighting both the material profusion of Canadian writing in the 1920s, and the fast-growing critical awareness of the same.[5] In 'Canadian Literati,' also written in the 1920s, Knister reflects and affirms the optimistic and energetic literary spirit of the times in his discussion of 'our noble determination to make an all-Canadian literature where none was.'[6] In this piece, Knister draws attention to the significance of his own role in the new literary movement, presenting himself, with some modesty, as exemplary of Canada's new writers: 'I may be pardoned for offering myself as *corpus vila*.'[7] By 1928, Knister was taking it upon himself to define the new canon of Canadian prose in his ground-breaking anthology *Canadian Short Stories*. Although much of the material Knister included was not written in the 1920s – he includes stories by Leacock, Roberts, and Scott, for example – he nevertheless declares the anthology to be indicative of the revolution underway in Canadian, and even foreign, writing: 'Literature as a whole is changing, new fields are being broken … and the changes in other countries show counterparts in our development … There has been a sudden growth of consciousness.'[8] Knister embraced his role as a harbinger of literary change, and wrote manifestos that judiciously avoid the excessive boosterism of the worst of the *Bookman* critics but are unmistakably optimistic and celebratory of the new realism.

For all of his advocacy of the new writing, and in spite of positioning himself at the vanguard of a new era, Knister was one neither to abandon his influences nor to discount the values and standards of a literary tradition, indigenous or foreign. He was also reluctant to join with the most nationalistic *Bookman* voices and champion Canadian subjects and issues as the only suitable topics for Canadian fiction. Although the vast majority of his work is about Canada, and he has certainly been praised for his vivid depiction of Ontario farm life, throughout his career he remained deeply ambivalent about nationalistic literature. While steadfastly convinced that Canada ought to have a modern literature particular to its own circumstances, he disputed a popular claim of the period that a literature that did not reflect Canada was somehow 'un-Canadian.' Grove's reply to a letter from Knister shows that they were in fundamental agreement on this issue: 'What you say with regard to "really indigenous work" is quite right. I don't care one particle about any indigenous setting. So long as the work turned out by any Canadian writer is worth its salt, it will be Canadian, no matter whether it deals with Canada or China.'[9] Knister's argument against restricting the subject matter of the Canadian novel, reflected in Grove's letter, also implies opposition to Sandwell's advocacy of 'various standards of criticism,' discussed earlier. The Canadian writer who works with foreign modes, models, and subjects will inevitably be judged in relation to those who have trodden this ground before, and Knister welcomes the comparison. While Knister enthusiastically endorses modern writing in Canada, he insists that a literary work, Canadian or otherwise, ought to be judged on its 'literary' merits, not on the basis of its subject matter or nationalistic assertions. Knister, then, comes out on the sides of both the *Bookman* and the *Forum*, the so-called 'boosters' and the so-called 'knockers' of nationalist literature, demonstrating that this polarizing debate was of more interest to critics and editors than to writers. Yet whether this double stance is the result of a deliberate aesthetic choice, or simply the inevitable conclusion of writing and reading widely, is not entirely clear: as he writes in 'Canadian Literature: A General Impression,' 'many critics have made outcry at the imitative and exotic nature of Canadian genius, without stopping to consider that even were the disregard of models desirable, it is not possible.'[10]

By all estimations, Knister was remarkably well read, and he tried to familiarize himself with as many different types of writing as he reasonably could. Among the most revealing of Knister's papers in the McMaster collection is a long 'List of Books Read By J. Raymond Knister From September 1914 to Mid 1924,' in which he records the hundreds of works he read in his formative years.[11] His readings range from the most traditional of the realists – Austen, Dickens, Turgenev, Thackeray, Howells, Balzac, George Eliot – to the leading modernist writers of his period – Conrad, James, Anderson, Lawrence, Dos Passos, T.S. Eliot. His reading of Canadian authors was less extensive but included many of the best-known writers of the time, including Grove, Stringer, Leacock, De la Roche, Pickthall, and Durkin. Knister had a deep sense of literary tradition – this is apparent in so many of his letters that compare and discuss other authors – and he believed that literary influence was both desirable and unavoidable. The idea that a modern writing in Canada could appear suddenly and independently of other literary traditions was apparently unthinkable. As he wrote in a letter to Lorne Pierce in 1925, 'I have no objection to the idea of any Canadian using the forms which traditionally belong to other literatures ... Nor is it well that the writer should be ignorant of other literatures. But it is not likely that we will reach indigenous Canadian forms at the first try, so that experiment has always seemed perilous.'[12]

Knister's disbelief in a literature that is entirely homegrown is a rejection of the nationalistic impulse in Canadian writing, and by implication a denial that the essential preoccupation of Canadian realists ought to be the 'national-referential ideal.' This stance frees Knister, and potentially his contemporaries and literary descendants, to develop the modern-realist aesthetic along lines that are not pre-eminently documentary. Knister is proposing a realist form of writing that has an individualistic artistic vision at its core. As Stevens argues, Knister 'was ... trying to assess his own ideas in light of those past writings, examining recent developments in Canada and other literatures, testing personal ideas against those he was constantly encountering in his own wide reading.'[13] The logic of Knister's implicit argument is perhaps surprising, but sound: he counters the emerging, deterministic 1920s notion that a respect for traditional and foreign literary modes will lead to a literature that is derivative and imitative with a suggestion that an isolationist literature grounded solely in a Canadian context will, also deterministically, produce writing that is narrow and unimaginative. Both of these sets of circumstances, if unchallenged, limit individual expression and are therefore in Knister's view to be avoided. The alternative he proposed was to acknowledge all influences and to subscribe wholly to none. The 'new era' of modern Canadian writing represented not so much a break with the past, but the awakening of a critically creative spirit and the unique interpretation of both ancestral forms and contemporary, indigenous subjects by a new generation of experimental, individualistic writers. As early as 1932, Leo Kennedy, Knister's first serious critic, identified this individualistic characteristic of his writing: 'He does not, consciously or unconsciously, emulate any school of writing ... His experiments with form and matter are not in any predefined direction; he is drawing on himself rather than his reading, and modelling his subject in a way native to himself.'[14]

Despite his acknowledgment of various influences and aesthetics, both realist and modernist, both foreign and Canadian, Knister's critics often characterize him as an unproblematically realistic writer whose chief contribution to Canadian letters was the creation of its first truly representative stories.[15] Such critical statements are accurate evaluations of many of Knister's sketches and to a degree of some of Knister's earliest fiction, which is experimental only insofar as it provides the first stylistically rigorous examples of the new modern realism outlined in the journals of the 1920s. Were these early efforts Knister's sole contribution to Canadian prose, he would still more than merit discussion in the context of the emergence of modern realism in Canada: while even his first published work is predated by other works approaching the modern-realist form, including works by Robert J.C. Stead and Jessie Georgina Sime, Knister's early stories achieve an unprecedentedly concise, impersonal rendering of their subject matter, at least by Canadian standards. Knister is not unlike Richard Milne, the central character of *White Narcissus*, who muses upon an important step in the development of his writing as it moves from the old romanticism to the new realism: 'He foresaw ... a further development in his own art. An increasing surface hardness seemed to be an inevitable accompaniment to the progress of the significant novelists of his and an earlier day.'[16] Yet the 'failures' of Knister's early stories are as significant in understanding his development of a modern realism as are their successes. Knister's growing preoccupation with representing something beyond surface realism – human psychology – led him to acknowledge and transcend the limitations of the traditional realist form.

On the most obvious level, however, all of Knister's stories offer a purportedly accurate, recognizable, faithful reflection of 'ordinary' life. With their Canadian settings – most of Knister's stories are set on farms in southwestern Ontario – they also reflect a predominant attitude expressed in the literary journals of the day: fiction ought to present a portrait of the distinctly Canadian locale. Mimetic, idiomatically correct dialogue is one of the simplest modern-realist techniques used by Knister to create an illusion of reality. His stories do not describe rural speech patterns: they recreate them. Many of Knister's stories are, in fact, structured almost entirely around conversations – 'Horace the Haymow' being perhaps the best example – with very few interjections by an overarching narrative voice. This technique, although not particularly innovative or experimental, contributes to an objectivist tone that prevails in most of the stories. Much as Hemingway does more famously in his short stories of the same period – including 'Hills Like White Elephants,' 'A Clean Well-Lighted Place,' and 'The Killers' (1927) – Knister all but eliminates the subjective, evaluating narrator and permits the reader to read (or hear) a dialogue directly, as it is spoken. The modern-realist aesthetic is highly impersonal, and Knister's narrators are almost always reporters, not the interpreters, judges, and evaluators who often narrate more traditional realist fiction.

The near elimination of a subjective, contextualizing narrative voice contributes to a larger, more immediately apparent aspect of the modern realism that informs Knister's stories: a remarkable precision of language and concision of expression. Usually, Knister's fiction strives to present the 'thing itself' and reads almost as a prose equivalent of the imagist poem. Knister's writing is compact, and his sentences are generally short and to the point. While his vocabulary is large, his diction is direct and unambiguous, as this short passage from 'The One Thing' reveals: 'It was January. The night was already quite dark. A thaw had broken up the road, which was now a mass of hummocked and holey clay, with a pair of deep narrow channels jaggedly traversing it longitudinally.'[17] Knister does not reject longer, unusual words but he only employs diction that is incisive and descriptive, almost always avoiding words that are in any way vague or allusive. As he wrote in a letter to W.A. Deacon, 'I am for a Spartan plainness of diction in whatever kind.'[18] This economy of style also applies to the emplotment of his stories. His paragraphs are unusually short, focused, and typically limited to the expression of small, closely related ideas that move the narrative forward directly. As he writes in 'The Loading' (1924), 'Jesse and his son entered the stable in silence. The boy was making for the box containing the curry-combs and brushes, when he saw that his father took down a collar from the peg. He also lifted down a collar and began to unbuckle its top. Jesse went over to a stall.'[19] Knister's stories aim to create a believable and realistic setting by offering specific, recognizable details, in this case those pertaining to everyday Ontario farm life. Yet the descriptions characteristic of Knister's modern realism differ from those found in more traditional realist fiction. His settings, and the objects that help to evoke them, are presented 'as is.' They are rarely symbolic, and rarely serve to connect the action or concerns of a given story to a larger social context. While Knister's emphasis in his stories is upon the routine lives of his characters, they are not presented as typical, or as somehow representative of general experiences.

Direct, purportedly objective, unmediated, impersonal expression, then, is the most fundamental tenet of Knister's modern realism. In contrast to the ever-present, congenial, admittedly subjective narrators of much traditional realist fiction, Knister's narrators are all but transparent, and scarcely distinguishable from the abstracted author himself. His own aesthetic aims and writerly intentions are far more visible and detectable in most of these stories than any narrative persona. While no 'personality' tells most of these stories, the presentation of directly observable facts apparently unmediated by a consciousness highlights the author's aesthetic achievement of a refinement of expression and unity of effect. Knister's stories are almost journalistic in style – more so, even, than many of his sketches – and their subjects are presented as though the reader is observing directly, as this passage from 'Indian Summer,' probably written in 1921, reveals: 'As she replaced the switch and turned again to her visitor there was a little flush about the rather thin brown face, with its slight hollow back of and below the mouth. Momentarily silence came.'[20] The matter-of-fact description is obviously impersonal, as is the dehumanized objectification of the subject's face, which is treated as a simple object under observation. Whatever emotion or significance is attributed to the face must be projected onto it from a reader's standpoint. This is the case in so many of Knister's stories in which the objective renderings of subject matter provide little indication of what a typical or appropriate psychological response to the subject matter might be. In one respect, Knister is undertaking a relatively straightforward realist project and attempting to present a clearly identifiable locale with objectivity, disinterestedness, and an emphasis upon surface appearances. At the same time, and to a remarkable extent, Knister's impersonal stories are autotelic, or aesthetically self-contained, much as some imagist poems are, and they make little or no attempt to refer to an extratextual world. Knister's realism contrasts sharply, in this latter respect, with most nineteenth-century realist fiction that is deliberately and referentially situated in a larger sociocultural milieu. The impersonality and near autotelism of Knister's stories, even when they are set in a rural environment that Canadian critics so often associate with a referential realism, demonstrate an important modern-realist affinity with the high modernists.

The exploration of human psychology and consciousness is equally if not more characteristic of Knister's fiction. Even the stories I have mentioned so far, with their cold rendering of facts, are largely structured around psychological states or developments in the minds of their central characters. Knister's most straightforward stories, including 'The One Thing,' offer descriptions and observations that cumulatively evoke a reflective psychological impression. His more complex works are less static, and emplotted over a psychological process, such as the form of spiritual transformation that takes place in 'The Strawstack' (1923). Denham remarks that, for Knister, 'realism is a notoriously tricky term, implying both a concern for accurate representation of the surface textures of ordinary life and the necessity of getting below the surface to an interpretation of the underlying social and psychological forces that are not easily accessible to ordinary observation.'[21] To this end, many of Knister's stories – including 'Mist Green Oats' (1922), 'The Loading' (1924), and 'The Strawstack' – build toward a grand revelation, or psychological realization, following an almost Joycean progression from ignorance or naivety to epiphany. One effect of this emphasis upon psychological development is that the action of many of the stories initially occurs internally, rather than in the external, physical world. In 'Mist Green Oats,' for example, changes in consciousness direct the action of the story, even when such actions are banal. As we follow the growth of the central figure, an adolescent boy, events follow his shifting states of mind, including, in this case, the sudden emergence of a memory: 'The victuals were cold, but his dinner was awaiting him on the table in the kitchen. When a few minutes later he began to take the dishes away he left off abruptly, remembering that he should have time for such tasks in the evening, when the work outside was done.'[22]

Knister's stories, with their various approaches to exploring psychology, are most remarkable when they strive to reconcile an apparent incompatibility between an inner, subjective, psychological subject matter, and the cold, objective modern-realist style. As I have argued, his aesthetic is largely referential, even if he is ambivalent about the importance of a Canadian subject matter and frequently willing to create works that approach autotelism. When Knister attempts to represent human consciousness in his stories, he finds that a simple realist aesthetic, with its emphasis upon external, observable facts, is technically inadequate. In his best stories, the points at which a straightforward realist aesthetic fails to offer a convincing representation of human consciousness mark the points of departure for his boldest technical experiments. His less successful works embody unresolved struggles to achieve the same effect, but in failure are usually highly revealing of his literary aims and intentions. In 'The Loading,' for example, Knister creates an entirely omniscient third-person narrator who attempts to offer insight into the subjective thoughts and emotions of various characters from an impersonal perspective. The result of this approach is psychological description that is often banal, melodramatic, heavy-handed, and at times even unintentionally almost humorous: 'Unaccountable pity for everyone and everything enwrapped him.'[23] In 'Indian Summer,' these psychological descriptions are perhaps more skilfully handled, yet they remain rendered entirely from an outside perspective, and the genuineness of the thoughts and emotions is lost amid the excessively precise diction: 'She followed the old course of invidiously admiring content unthinkingly, as if uncertain how to bring out what was on her mind.'[24] In 'Mist Green Oats,' similar passages are still narrated from a third-person perspective, yet Knister makes a primitive attempt to generate a mimetic impression of consciousness through the employment of a tone and rhythm that sympathetically mimics the characters' thoughts. In this passage, written in the past tense, he strives to give it an immediacy through the use of vigorous, active diction and the awkward insertion of the word 'now': 'As he moved about he was not oppressed now by a sense of haste, by a fear, almost, of something unknown threatening their determination which yet chivied and lured the men of farms through those ontreading days of late spring.'[25] In the final analysis, most of these attempts to present a realistic rendering of psychological states are somewhat clumsy and unconvincing. Many of Knister's experiments with the same aim in mind, however, prove more successful, largely because his persistence leads him eventually to define realism more broadly than many of his earliest stories would suggest was possible.

A dissatisfaction with traditional realism was brewing in Knister's mind from early on in his career, and his early experiments with impersonality reflect this anxiety in an early form. As he wrote in 'Canadian Literature: A General Impression' (ca 1923), 'Realism is not ... to be accepted as an end in itself, nor, at its best as an unmixed good, but as bringing up a depth of knowledge and conviction and authenticity of feeling together with a more revealing portrayal of our inner life.'[26] Knister would identify this problem with realism again in a revealing letter to his friend Elizabeth Frankfurth, written on *Midland* letterhead in 1924: 'How to impart a hint of the wonder and mystery behind the circumstances, yet remain true to these latter?'[27] Suggesting that this problem was becoming a career-long preoccupation for him, and for writers of modern-realist fiction in general, he acknowledged the importance of resolving it in his 'Introduction' to his anthology, *Canadian Short Stories*, in 1928: 'What is known as realism is only a means to an end, the end being a personal projection of the world. In passing beyond realism, even while they employ it, the significant writers of our time are achieving a portion of evolution.'[28] Towards the end of his career, in a 1930 manifesto defending realism published in *Saturday Night* entitled 'Dissecting the "T.B.M.,"' Knister argues that realism does more than document and reflect; it names and emphasizes the significant, hidden aspects of life: 'Realism has a function as criticism ... of life ... [its purpose is to] heighten life ... we must be true to life – writers and readers both. Because if we don't come to grips with it we shall miss the real thing underneath.'[29] Knister's dissatisfaction with traditional realism periodically led him to experiment with the realist form in ways that approximate the most experimental techniques of high modernism, including stream of consciousness, extreme fragmentation, multivocality, interior monologue, and impressionistic writing. Curiously, Knister's struggle to stretch the boundaries of realism to include representations of consciousness does not progress uniformly or undistractedly from failure to achievement, or from conservative realism to innovative modernism. Written around the same time as many of his early 'failures' are some of Knister's most experimental fictions – the surrealist 'Eric Mirth or the Larger I,' for example, was written before 'The Loading,' and many of his last works, including the novella 'Innocent Man' and the short story 'Hackman's Night,' are technically very similar to Knister's most conservative realist fictions. As Philip Child – himself a significant modern realist – writes, 'Knister continued the struggle courageously, never compromising the integrity of his vision for a commercial success, learning and experimenting as he went, making mistakes sometimes to be sure.'[30]

An immediately obvious narrative strategy for the writer who wishes to explore human psychology in fiction is the employment of a first-person narrative voice. A few of Knister's stories do deviate from the standard third-person, omniscient narrative model, and his work provides a number of experiments with subjective narration. In one respect, the use of a first-person narrative voice hardly seems experimental or innovative. While it is true that first-person narratives had occasionally appeared before in Canada – Frances Brooke's *The History of Emily Montague* (1796), Susanna Moodie's *Roughing It in the Bush* (1852), and Stringer's prairie trilogy (1915–22) come to mind – all but a tiny handful of the hundreds of Canadian novels written before 1920 are narrated in the third person, and Knister was certainly breaking with a firmly established norm in his first-person stories. In addition, the modern-realist ideal, with its emphasis upon real events, real people, and real settings, almost seems to demand the purportedly objective, omniscient perspective. Knister's most straightforward first-person narrative appears in 'Grapes,' an initially unpublished short story probably written in 1922. Strangely, in this story, as in the similarly narrated story entitled 'The First Day of Spring' (1924–5), Knister does not fully realize the creative possibilities of the first-person form, and his narrator functions almost as his third-person counterparts do. While these two first-person narratives are, of course, rendered from a particular character's perspective, they offer very little insight into the minds of the characters discussed, or even into the minds of the narrators themselves. For example, while recounting a series of memories, the narrator of 'Grapes' remarks: 'Those were busy days though I do not seem to have been impressed by the fact,' revealing, by describing his thoughts as an outsider would, that he is even less omniscient and knowing about his own consciousness than a third-person narrator would be.[31] In these straightforward first-person stories, Knister's narrators do not speak their own thoughts aloud or provide substantial insight into their own mental states, deliberately or otherwise. In fact, they are, if anything, more coldly analytical than their third-person counterparts, standing aloof and analysing their own emotions and actions: 'Possibly the grown-ups influenced my half-conscious reflections, or my uneasiness required romantic invention.'[32]

A more complex and innovative employment of first-person narration can be found in another unpublished short story entitled 'Banking

Hours' (ca 1923). Knister probes the psychology of his narrator both directly, by having the main character analyse his own psychological processes as the narrators of 'Grapes' and 'Spring' do, and indirectly, creating an unreliable narrative and structural irony in which the speaker undermines his own interpretation of events unwittingly. Unlike the first-person narrators of the stories mentioned previously, this narrator, although unnamed, is highly personal, characterized, and emotionally involved. As the young man relates the story of having his honesty secretly tested by the manager of the bank at which he works through the use of a clever ploy, his voice is highly revealing of his personality and thought processes: 'I wanted the job all right, let me tell you, because I always have liked the idea of it ... I thought that any day when I could call myself a banker would be – well, anyone knows what I mean if they've wanted something terribly bad, without thinking it could be possible.'[33] On the simplest level, Knister avoids describing the detailed psychology of his character directly in this story, instead allowing thoughts and emotions to be either readily apparent in the narrator's words, or easily inferred by the reader. While 'Banking Hours' does not offer the almost scientific study of life evident in so many of Knister's fictions, it is, on one level perhaps, more objective, in that the character's thought processes are presented 'as is,' often without any comment or analysis. In fact, the fullest psychological portrait of the narrator in this story emerges when the reader pieces together the story that is unintentionally revealed: the unreliable narrator depicts himself as the wronged party, unjustly tested, unerring and in control, yet his own statements suggest otherwise: 'I couldn't just fly off the handle like I wanted'; 'I would have been the maddest I've been in my life'; 'If I could do anything that would make those kind of people pay, I would do it'; 'I know I'll never trust myself to be civil to that old hick if he comes in again'; 'I was nearly boiling all the way to her door.'[34] In 'Banking Hours,' then, Knister's narrator highlights subjectivity and foregrounds unreliability to present both a story firmly grounded in recognizable details – the story abounds with factual descriptions of banking business – and a highly convincing psychological portrait. Yet Knister does not carry this experiment to its boldest conclusion, instead stopping far short of the bald, epistemological representation of consciousness, and he even apparently feels the need to justify the first-person perspective by framing the story as a possible letter: 'As it is I think I may just send some of this to old George to let him see what's on my mind. Or perhaps I'll be satisfied just getting it off my chest, and burn the whole business.'[35] Knister's decision to account for the story in this manner suggests that he is aware of the unconventionality of his work, and perhaps wary of the possibility that highly subjective narration will compromise the objective aesthetic that he persistently and forcefully advocates.

In another first-person narrative written around the same time Knister comes far closer to the mimetic representation of consciousness. In what may be his most ambitious and enigmatic story, 'Eric Mirth or the Larger I' (ca 1920–3), the narrator attempts, through surreal imagery, to communicate an epiphanic spiritual awakening that he characterizes as a 'perception of the infinitude of the Allness,'[36] not unlike the state of being (or non-being) that Virginia Woolf would later explore from numerous perspectives in *The Waves* (1931). Knister invents his own diction ('periodicy' 'unrageneracy') suggesting that the state he represents is not easily described in conventional terms. In attempting to express the boundlessness of this experience, the narrative voice speaks predominantly in the present tense, yet shifts in and out of the past tense. At the same time, the over-all flow of the narrative is essentially epistemological: 'As I sit here and the waves of memory flood my soul, they float back to me first recollections, initial surgings of the valid I ... [*Knister's ellipsis*] My mother, for I was but three years old, was spanking me, expurgating the unragenerацy of the under-soul. Suddenly it seemed, I was seized by an awareness of the veracity of periodicy. This was but a dawning. As I sat – stood, afterwards, unfolded to me by way of specific experimental documentation, realization of the philosophy of punishment, the oneness of obliquity and castigation.'[37] While Knister generally allows the narrative to follow the speaker's shifting thought processes, analytical, contextualizing passages are offered to ground the narrative within a stable temporal framework: 'Intertwined, inextricably with this come my first memories of my grandfather.'[38] And Knister's unconventional style in this story means that it is not always clear whether many of the passages are to be read as interior monologues, or merely poetic musings of a narrator being consciously rhetorical: 'I was to turn to real-estate. I should always turn to real-estate, manifesting itself in and manifesting one thing or another ... Power, of change, Change, Overturn and turnover. The world needed the vibration of it – the golden real of it ... [*Knister's ellipses*].'[39] These techniques are representative of Knister's desire to explore human thought processes in fiction, and of his willingness to experiment boldly with the realist form, rather than simply abandoning it, towards the achievement of this end.

In 'The Strawstack,' a story published in the *The Canadian Forum* in 1923, Knister offers another experiment aimed at heightening the psychological realism of his fiction, this time employing a third-person narrative. While Knister would later question the success of this particular story, his comments in this regard also reveal that he was well aware that his work was treading on new territory: 'I had a story in the Oct. Can. Forum which was written about two and one half years ago which strikes me at once as so immaturely melodramatic and yet in some ways worthwhile that I don't know what to think of it.'[40] In this story, the narrative voice, which is highly impersonal and omniscient, makes little attempt to mimic the flow of consciousness of the central character, although some attempt is made to offer commentary on the unnamed character's thoughts: 'It occurred to him that it was wrong, that he should be ashamed and repentant.'[41] Yet this story differs from Knister's other early 'objectivist' fictions in that the third-person narrative voice – its language, tone, pacing, and style – is cleverly manipulated to reflect the nature of the central character's psychological states: 'The place was the same, with the sorrowful sameness he found in the chances of life, in its monotonous recurrence, unescapable; the horrible rise and sinking of the sun, moons.'[42] Knister occasionally circumvents the impersonal and objective tone of the narrator, adding a crucial subjective element to the story, by providing symbolic descriptive passages that mirror the inner contents of the central character's mind: 'The trees were shrunken, grizzled, and unkempt, stood vagabonds, in an air of desperately-attempted sturdy carelessness.'[43] The evocation of a mood through the highly stylized, even symbolic, use of language, first attempted by Knister in 'The Strawstack,' would prove to be one of the most successful and recurring methods he found to convey the subjective contents of consciousness within the larger objective framework of the typical modern-realist story.

'The Fate of Mrs. Lucier,' published in Paris in *This Quarter* in 1925, offers another of Knister's most successful and enduring narrative techniques employed to achieve psychological realism. For the most part, 'Mrs. Lucier' differs minimally from most of Knister's straightforward third-person narratives and employs a narrative voice that is, again, highly impersonal, omniscient, and purportedly objective. Nevertheless, 'Mrs. Lucier' represents a refinement, or perhaps a perfection, of the style and techniques that Knister developed in earlier stories, including 'The Loading,' 'The One Thing,' and 'Mist Green Oats.' The most remarkable difference between 'Mrs. Lucier' and these earlier works derives from Knister's employment of a centre-of-consciousness technique:[44]

> How long before the street car would come? She had forgotten whether it was due at seventeen minutes after seven or seventeen minutes to eight. At least the wait was always endless, each time she had to remind herself that it would really come to an end. What if the car should be late reaching the city – a night like this? Lyniol would be worried ... [*Knister's ellipsis*] Perhaps he would go away and leave her to get home alone. The streets were so misleading at night, and where could she inquire the way?[45]

Through the use of a transparent, uncharacterized third-person voice that speaks from the point of view of Mrs. Lucier – a technique used to great effect by Joyce in several stories in *Dubliners* (1914) including 'The Dead' – the story retains its pretence to objectivity and conveys the thought processes of a character from an internal point of view. In passages such as the one cited above, Knister achieves a kind of aesthetic reconciliation between the objective thrust of his realist project and his desire to depict subjective psychological states. While 'Mrs. Lucier' still does not jettison psychological analysis from an external perspective – 'Her heart leaped. With trepidation and quivering foretaste of triumph Mrs. Lucier marched to her suitcase' – the centre-of-consciousness technique allows Knister to keep both an internal and external perspective simultaneously and interactively at the forefront of his narrative.[46]

White Narcissus (written 1925–7; published 1929) is Knister's best-known work, and most of the sparse criticism on Knister's prose focuses upon this novel. Part of the reason Knister's significance as an experimentalist has sometimes been understated is that *White Narcissus* is generally characterized as a relatively straightforward work of realism, significant for paving the way for many of the more successful realist works that other writers would create after it.[47] The realist properties of this novel are undeniable – the techniques of his early modern-realist works, including concision, direct expression, and mimetic dialogue, are obvious throughout. Also, the length of the novel relative to the short stories means that Knister's portrait of a recognizable locale and depiction of the daily lives of characters are especially developed and vivid. But *White Narcissus* also exhibits some of the experimental techniques geared toward the creation of a heightened sense of psychological realism. This novel's reputation as the representative work of Knister's oeuvre is probably appropriate inasmuch as it represents the refinement of many of the techniques he had experimented with beforehand. But *White Narcissus*, in and of itself, gives a skewed impression of Knister's oeuvre: it is more melodramatic and implausible than most of his other works, and it avoids his most adventurous and perhaps significant technical experiments with first-person and unreliable narration.

White Narcissus nevertheless marks the crystallization of many of Knister's innovative techniques. His narrator, although omniscient and detached, offers sustained symbolic and personified descriptions in the manner of 'The Strawstack,' and these same passages frequently reflect the psychological states of characters in their tone and style: 'The road made fitful efforts at directness, and would ignore the swing of the high river banks, only a little farther on to skirt a depression, a sunken, rich flat, bearing rank, blue-green oats surrounded by drooping willows, elms through which only a glimpse of the brown ripples of water could be seen.'[48] This novel also builds upon the kind of direct, psychological analysis present in earlier stories by offering descriptions of mental states that are less cold, stolid, and artless than many previous examples: 'Yet it was complete content that embraced his mind as he lay in his room that night, and the thought which came to him, whether then or through the hours of sleep, was that nothing mattered.'[49] Knister supplements these external observations with passages that speak partly from within the consciousness of the novel's main character, Richard Milne, and while the narrator is omniscient, his voice is frequently filtered through Milne's own point of view. The most convincing passages in the novel combine centre-of-consciousness narrative with concise, descriptive observations that are neither excessively scientific nor inappropriately verbose, and result in a seamless alternation between two complementary perspectives: 'Was Ada thinking this? She had been looking at him with starry eyes in the pearl dusk. Did she think his decision mere complacent briskness? Now, wearily she rose from the bench, and he with her, and before she could turn into the house, he led her half by force down the veranda and they walked in silence.'[50] The psychological impact of *White Narcissus* is cumulative. There are no sustained passages that step outside of the main narrative and follow Milne's thoughts in an unmediated fashion. Still, the impression generated by the third-person narration is predominantly subjective. The story is both grounded in realistic observation and plainly coloured by an individual perspective. Kennedy makes this point precisely: 'This book is distinctly an experiment in a *genre*. In it, Knister relaxes the strict objectivity of the early stories in favour of a "style" ... While farm life and manners are identifiable and immediate, they are viewed through the coloured spectacles of a temperament and a prevailing mood.'[51] *White Narcissus*, then, is not among the most radically experimental of Knister's fictions, yet it provides perhaps his most balanced example of psychological realism.

Knister's most ambitious experimental writing is found in his unpublished novel, *Group Portrait*, probably written in 1923. Although written before *White Narcissus*, it is more self-consciously innovative, thereby reinforcing the idea that Knister's career is not accurately viewed as a linear progression from a traditional realism to experimental modernism. His attempts to render human consciousness mimetically are more pronounced and varied in *Group Portrait* than in any other single work, and it is his only work of fiction to explore the thoughts of more than a single character (unless his objective third-person narrators are considered characters in the stories they narrate). Knister's techniques in this novel anticipate those that would be developed by William Faulkner in his landmark novels *The Sound and the Fury* (1929) and *As I Lay Dying* (1930): multivocality, fragmentation, and interior monologue. Knister's correspondence makes it clear that he was aware that his efforts in this novel were highly experimental and that he intended the narrative to be structured primarily upon a subjective principle. As he wrote to Frankfurth, 'In fact ... since you enquire about my novel ... each chapter will be recorded as it is seen by one of the characters, and colored by his or her vision. There will be about a dozen points of view, so that superficially the piece will lack unity ... My aim is a picture of a farm family, neither typical nor atypical, and instead of a dramatic conflict of interest there will be a failure of the wills of these individuals to impinge on each other.'[52]

These comments suggest that the novel will rather simply manipulate point of view, perhaps along the same lines of the then unwritten *White Narcissus*, but this novel also uses a variety of techniques to mimic thought processes and to imitate the ebb and flow of human consciousness. While a third-person narrative framework is provided to help connect the various fragments of centre of consciousness that come from at least ten different points of view, analytical comments on the characters' thoughts from an external perspective are minimal. Interestingly, the third-person narrator, from the first paragraph of the book, is neither purportedly objective nor impersonal, and he addresses the reader directly, in the manner of many nineteenth-century narrators: 'Over the tangle of hay in which he reclined guiding the team, he watched the shadowed lake swing from sight. The farms lay smoothly along the banks of the lake shore. They were of gravel, coarse and smaller, and yellow sand in places. This was their surface, and the surface of farms, down to a few feet, counts; a farmer would not need to tell you.'[53] This third-person narrator with a discernible personality is perhaps created to provide a level of comfort that might potentially offset the disorienting shifts in perspective that rapidly follow his introduction and subsequently appear unrelentingly in a loosely connected series of juxtaposed fragments.

The first unconventional manipulation of point of view along these lines emerges in the second paragraph of the novel. Almost as soon as the third-person narrator has established a presence, the narrative voice shifts unexpectedly into the second-person: 'To come early was to find great washes and streaks of light color, unsuspected as you strolled, unless accompanied, along away from the sunset to the bank.'[54] As the novel unfolds, it becomes apparent that second-person narration is sometimes used as an intermediary technique to make the transitions from a third-person objective perspective to subjective centre-of-consciousness passages less abrupt. Many of these centre-of-consciousness sections are similar to those discussed in relation to Knister's other stories: 'Robina couldn't help her mother with the threshing meals – how could she when she was finishing the dress she was to wear in the evening. She was to sing at the social. She'd been asked ... [*Knister's ellipsis*].'[55] Relatively lengthy sections of the novel use this technique to forward the action of the story and simultaneously permit the action to be witnessed from an internal perspective, effectively eliminating the need for the third-person narrator to offer excessive commentary from above. Other centre-of-consciousness passages more closely resemble internal monologues, and many of these portray characters speaking their internal thoughts in the second person, again possibly doing so to help acclimatize the reader to what Knister perceives to be a radical form of realism: 'When you thought of it, though it did seem ridiculous, it made a difference, she being all dressed up, and they, in dusty shirts and red- or blue-handkerchiefed necks ... [*Knister's ellipsis*] Though they came to the social with other girls; or went away from it perhaps with them. Glad enough they'd be if she –'[56] These second-person passages, at once addressing the reader directly and mimicking thought processes in the minds of the figures who make up the group portrait, elicit reader involvement in the story and add an additional subjective layer to the narrative. At the same time, in this above passage and in many others, Knister uses ellipses and dashes to end sections of the text abruptly, emphasizing the inconstant flow of the mind and creating an effect of fragmented multivocality. Whether or not the various fragments of the novel eventually merge into a cohesive impression, or 'group portrait,' is a subject for debate, yet Knister's experiments in this important work mark the closest point that he came to duplicating the innovative techniques characteristic of much high-modernist fiction. This novel also offers some of the clearest indications that the techniques of modernism and modern realism are, in their more conservative and radical forms respectively, one and the same. Yet, as is the case with some of the most revealing works of Canadian modern realism, this novel has never been published. A future determination of Knister's significance in the development of early-twentieth century Canadian writing will be largely predicated upon his efforts in *Group Portrait* and in several of his other lesser-known works.

As Leo Kennedy wrote in 1932, 'To those who revel in American experimentalists, and adumbrate the poppycock that outside of Callaghan's pages there is no experimental work to be found, I submit the novels, stories, and trivia of Raymond Knister again ... The keynote of Knister's literary career up to the present is experiment. This sufficiently explains why it is that his place has been that of a minor and little-known artist in the departments of *belles lettres*.'[57] While Knister did not live to see these first significant critical affirmations of his pioneering spirit published in the *Forum* in September 1932 – he drowned while swimming alone in Lake St Clair on 29 August of the same year – it is clear that he was keenly aware of his role as an experimentalist and that he embraced it as enthusiastically as he did the modern-realist aesthetic. In fact, he considered modern realism and experimentalism to be contingent terms. While Knister probably did not communicate substantially with foreign writers of modernist prose, he considered himself and his modern realism to belong to a larger, experimental movement prevalent in the literary circles of his time. His correspondence with Ernest Walsh, editor of *This Quarter*, is revealing in this regard. Writing in response to Knister's submission of work to his modernist journal, Walsh offered a series of comments that strongly encourage the experimental impulse in Knister's writing: 'Your stuff is real. The story we took. Keep at it. Lets [*sic*] see more of your things. Poems not so good. Dig all you can out of your surroundings. Don't play safe. Try anything. You may manage something really big if you risk failure in trying. Study our men. Note Hemingway and McAlmon.'[58] Interestingly, Walsh's letter is both offering the American modernists as a model for Knister's prose and emphasizing the importance of a realism in writing – 'Dig all you can out of your surroundings' – reinforcing what Knister knew all along: the new realism is modern. Knister's responses to Walsh were enthusiastic, and he was very eager to accept the role of experimentalist proffered to him from Paris, then the centre of a vibrant expatriate scene. Just as significant were Knister's assertions that his writing was already experimental: 'I have written a novel (twice) [*Group Portrait*] which I think shows a real technical innovation. The usual structural functions are reversed.'[59] Perhaps even more tellingly, Knister considered his work to be comparable to that of the writers endorsed by Walsh: 'Hemingway's prose is real and earnest! I doubt if there is a word wrong in "Big Two-Hearted River." I see fully achieved in it the effect I have occasionally tried for. (One story of mine you might have liked is "Mist Green Oats") ... The others are all interesting, and I must, particularly, see more of Robert McAlmon's work ... But of course my major satisfaction is in being one of these fine fellows myself.'[60] The form of modern realism that Knister advocates, and effectively defines in his own creative writing, is not in his mind, or Walsh's for that matter, significantly different from the less-experimental strain of modernist prose that I have already attributed to the writers that Walsh mentions, and to others including Rhys, Anderson, Fitzgerald, and Lawrence.

Yet Knister drew a clear distinction between his form of experiment and the writing of the more extreme modernists of the period. To him, experimentalism was a necessity, but not an end in itself. In accordance with his wide reading and reluctance to abandon literary tradition, Knister did not perceive his era to mark a bold break with the past. As he wrote to Merrill Denison of the *Bookman* in 1923, anticipating the seminal argument that Stevenson would make in that journal four years later, 'the matter of modern movements in literature and the drama is interesting to me ... I think that while there must be experiment, the main line of tradition will be continued, and change will be represented by a curve rather than a corner. Much of the stuff in a magazine such as "Broom" for instance I think is bunk ... though any of these experiments may prove of value to one who can apply them to a vision of his own and to a knowledge of the tradition.'[61] Even after his publication in *This Quarter* and his correspondence with Walsh, Knister's essential views on experimentalism in writing remained largely unchanged. Writing to

Frankfurth several months after his exchange of letters with Walsh, he would again, this time indirectly, express a relatively conservative view on the issue: 'Gertrude Stein? I'm not learned enough to say whether her writings have any value to psychology; they seem to me exercises in the association of ideas. But I can't see their relation to literature.'[62] Again, we return to the view of modern writing expressed by Stevenson in 'Is Canadian Poetry Modern?' Experiment, for both Stevenson and Knister, is not in and of itself particularly desirable or even characteristic of the modern impulse in literature. Knister's assertion that 'change will be represented by a curve rather than a corner' reaffirms his own modern-realist aesthetic, with its links to tradition, and its innovative strategies that follow from its psychological emphasis. Yet Knister is not opposed to the experimental trend in fiction: he would even suggest, in the midst of writing his most traditional major work in 1931 – the fictional biography of Keats that would be published posthumously under the title *My Star Predominant* (1934) – to a probably baffled Grove that 'I may use the present book as material for a new one altogether. It would be an interesting attempt ... to translate the ... profound mind of Keats into the modern manner of interior monologue. Possibly also a book say after the pattern of Joyce's "Portrait of the Artist as a Young Man."'[63] Knister's experiments are neither eclectic attempts to create a profoundly new form of writing that departs from tradition nor half-successful emulations of high-modernist techniques. They are focused, deliberate, and individualistic efforts to achieve a more penetrating realism than Canada had previously known, a realism that could simultaneously document a surface world of appearances and the hidden processes of human consciousness: a modern realism.

The last major project of Knister's career, *My Star Predominant*, is not easily placed alongside Knister's earlier work and suggests that in his final years he may have been moving away from the modern realism he helped to shape and define. While to a degree this novel is realist in a traditional sense, and well-written and well-researched, it offers none of the experimental writing that characterizes Knister's most significant fiction. Was Knister in the process of abandoning his earlier views on writing? A curious and very rough novel plan that Knister wrote three weeks before his death, entitled 'Via Faust,' offers the last and perhaps the most ambiguous of Knister's statements on realism. While Waddington has cautioned against an autobiographical interpretation of 'Via Faust,'[64] there are clearly some parallels to be drawn between Knister's career and that of the unnamed writer-protagonist of the unwritten novel. In his early career, the writer struggles with the expression of a traditional realism in his work: 'He decides a la Keats that the truth about life is its beauty, etc, and grimly struggles to put this into his novels, realistic.'[65] Certainly, this character's efforts parallel Knister's attempts to 'impart a hint of the wonder and mystery behind the circumstances, yet remain true to these latter.'[66] A later stage outlined in the life of the writer, a Faust figure, is less clear and leaves Knister's final views on realism open to speculation: 'Decides that one must pass beyond the Keats-Shakespeare stage to the Goethean and beyond that, if possible. But these preoccupations and ideas, he notes, take the greatest writers away from realism. Tolstoi to an ethical world, Goethe to creation but cerebral more than instinctive, Anatole France to brilliant generalization and satire, no effort at realism.'[67] Certainly, Knister is again adumbrating his career-long conviction that a traditional realist form is inadequate to the task of representing the lofty 'preoccupations and ideas' that he associates with a number of writers in this passage. And, as I have argued, these same concerns are the catalyst behind Knister's boldest experiments with the realist form. Yet whether he is suggesting that great literature is not realistic (great writers do not bother with a limited form such as realism) and negating his own life's work, or suggesting that truly great writing attains a plateau at which it becomes effortlessly realistic, is unclear.

Knister's own hard-won modern realism can, on one level, be seen as the result of a persistent effort to create fiction that appeared effortless, and this may partly explain his own distaste for literature that foregrounds its own experiment, or ambition, or conscious effort. If nothing else, 'Via Faust' suggests that, however diverted from his modern-realist project Knister may have become with his work on *My Star Predominant*, he was, until his death, still exploring the creative possibilities of modern realism. Of course, it is not possible to know where Knister's fiction might have led Canadian writing in the 1930s and beyond. This truism aside, Knister was the first writer of prose in Canada to think seriously about modern fiction, to consciously direct the changes that were taking place in Canadian literary circles, and to arrive at a practicable modern-realist aesthetic in his work. With Knister's premature death, Canadian modern realism undoubtedly lost its most experimental and perhaps most committed advocate.

4
The Proliferation of Modern Realism in Canada, Part 1: Prairie Realism Re-evaluated

At the time of Raymond Knister's death in 1932, modern realism was already established as the dominant form for serious fiction in Canada, and it was evolving in a variety of individual oeuvres and several broader regional, ideological, and aesthetic contexts. Of the various realist 'schools' that proliferated in the decades after the First World War, none has been as influential, widely discussed, and critically problematic as prairie realism. In the broadest sense, this chapter re-evaluates prairie realism in the context of the larger modern-realist movement of which it is a part. To do this, it is necessary to engage prominent critical conceptions of prairie writing that have contributed to its characterization as conservative, monolithic, derivative, and isolated from larger movements and trends in early twentieth-century Canadian culture. Some of the most influential critics of prairie realism have focused on the ubiquitous presence of a deterministic landscape and have implied that the genre as a whole is homogeneous, anomalous, predictable, and limited in subject matter and technique. Edward McCourt's much-cited *The Canadian West in Fiction* (1949) built a foundation for geographical criticism when it emphasized the regional relevance and mimetic aesthetic of prairie writing: 'It is the purpose of this book to examine some of the prose fiction written about the Canadian West by native Westerners and others, and to attempt an estimate of the extent to which it is an artistic re-creation of the prairie way of life.'[1]

More exclusively thematic in its approach, though no less inclined toward the geographical thesis, Laurence Ricou's *Vertical Man / Horizontal World: Man and Landscape in Canadian Prairie Fiction* (1973) unified all of prairie writing with a single vivid image that stresses the isolating effect of prairie geography on writers and their fictional characters: 'The basic image of a single human figure amidst the vast flatness of the landscape serves to unify and describe all prairie fiction.'[2] In 1977, Dick Harrison's *Unnamed Country: The Struggle for a Canadian Prairie Fiction* argued that 'prairie fiction is about a basically European society spreading itself across a very un-European landscape. It is rooted in that first settlement process.'[3] Even Deborah Keahey's relatively recent book-length study, *Making It Home: Place in Canadian Prairie Literature* (1998), while challenging the traditional geographical reading of 'prairie literature' in which 'place has overwhelmingly been defined in narrow, deterministic terms,' still asserts that geography provides an overarching, universalizing interpretation, if appropriately reimagined: 'What is needed for the Canadian Prairies ... is a more flexible concept of the *relationship between* home and place ... Rather than discard the notion of place entirely and replace it with a notion of culture, then, place must instead be reimagined as a creation of the social, psychological, and cultural relationships that people have to particular landscapes or physical spaces.'[4] And this is just the beginning: numerous other critics use these same geographical concepts and metaphors as starting points for their analyses.[5]

The quantity of this criticism, its pedagogical utility, and its often convincing analyses mean it has become almost monolithic and difficult to contest: as Susan Jackel observes in the most recent edition of *The Oxford Companion to Canadian Literature*, 'critical approaches to prairie writing continue for the most part to hew to the environmentalism of Edward McCourt.'[6] However valuable a geographical approach to prairie writing may be, it has nevertheless had the unfortunate and unintended consequence of obscuring the achievements and failures of individual writers and through repetition has established a critical view of prairie writing now so firmly entrenched that it is difficult to challenge. At the same time, the term 'prairie realism' is highly misleading, and the fiction it denotes is more diverse, contradictory, complicated, and informed by national and international ideas and aesthetics than the geographical thesis suggests. Not only is prairie realism not rigidly bounded or defined by a geographical place called the prairie: like the modern realism that includes it, prairie realism can only be partly accounted for under the rubric of 'realism.' Some scholars have highlighted the need to reconsider established notions of prairie realism by exploring, in individual texts, the modern aesthetics, concepts, and issues that are inadequately accounted for by more traditional readings.[7] More broadly, Alison Calder's 'Reassessing Prairie Realism' (1997) convincingly argues for a re-examination of the significance and boundaries of the genre as a whole, and she asks us to consider 'what happens to the writers of the last fifty years whose works do not fit into a "realistic" and therefore tragic view of prairie existence.'[8] Donna Bennett's 'Conflicted Vision: A Consideration of Canon and Genre in English-Canadian Literature' (1991) suggests that prairie realism is a form of literary modernism that has been unfairly treated by Canadian critics: 'It is important to grasp the effect upon Canadian canon-making of one segment of Canadian modernist writing [prairie realism] remaining virtually unrecognized as aesthetically significant.'[9] These and other challenges to monolithic conceptions of prairie realism suggest that it is far more complex than is sometimes imagined and might be re-evaluated in a manner that accounts for its 'modernity' in inclusive terms.[10]

I contend that prairie realism is not a conservative, mimetic, and regional genre at the periphery of Canadian literary development. It is a major, even central, component of the modern-realist movement that was unfolding across Canada in the early twentieth century. Prairie realism was among the most modern forms of writing to appear in Canada before 1950, and its writers carried out some of the boldest literary experiments of their period. Accordingly, I propose a configuration of 'prairie realism' that is paradoxically both broader and narrower, more specific and more inclusive than most. The genre can usefully be expanded to include any realistic novel written in residence on or about the prairie, regardless of whether or not it treats the traditional homesteading subject, the prairie 'region,' rural life, or some variation of any or all of these. Numerous critics have counted the detailed depiction of traditional farm life among the chief defining characteristics of the prairie-realist novel. A more inclusive view of the genre acknowledges that its authors were not nearly so preoccupied with geography or uniformly rural and regional, but were writing about the same modern and cosmopolitan themes and issues as modern realists and modernists in other countries. Prairie realism includes the novels of Bertram Brooker, Douglas Durkin, and Nellie McClung, for example, despite their predominantly urban prairie settings that make them difficult to situate within the traditional boundaries of the genre. In keeping with my assertion that the geographical boundaries of prairie fiction are arbitrary and that prairie realism and modern realism are all but synonymous, I consider a handful of novels written by so-called 'prairie' writers that are not even set on the prairie, including, for example, Grove's *Master of the Mill* (1944), set in north-western Ontario. Nevertheless, the term 'prairie realism' – signifying regionalism on the one hand and derivation from nineteenth-century realism on the other – has been firmly established, and to replace it with a new term such as 'modern prairie realism' or 'prairie modern realism' would be cumbersome and misleading in other respects.

From the start, critics have emphasized the real struggles faced by prairie writers who wished to create without a supportive literary culture and in the shadow of an overwhelming geographical presence. W.J. Keith, for example, suggests that the efforts of the prairie realists ought to be considered 'isolated attempts to come to grips with the country and its people in imaginative terms.'[11] The origins of the myth of the isolated prairie writer are not difficult to uncover. One need only recall the most memorable characters of the best-known prairie-realist novels of the period to find fictional characters who fit the stereotype: Niels Lindstedt of Grove's *Settlers of the Marsh* (1925), Caleb Gare of Ostenso's *Wild Geese* (1925), Gander Stake of Stead's *Grain* (1926), Mrs Bentley of Ross's *As For Me and My House* (1941). These fictional characters have become the archetypal figures of prairie realism, and their lives are better known to readers than are those of even the most canonical prairie writers. Consequently, the prairie realists themselves are easily presumed to be writing autobiography. This perilous assumption was made as early as January 1927, when a *Canadian Bookman* review signed H.M.R. insisted that *New Furrows* (1926), a little-known novel by Flos Jewell Williams, was an 'authentic' rendering of 'the first-hand experience of the author, who for many years has lived in the west.'[12] Similarly, an early essay on Grove – who has suffered and benefited more than others from the misanthropic stereotype of the prairie artist – appeared in *The Canadian Forum* in 1932 and set the tone for much of the early, reductive, biographical reading of Grove's fiction that would follow. In this piece, Robert Ayre creates a derogatory portrait of Grove, the archetypal prairie writer – 'Frederick Philip Grove is a solitary giant, treading his own lonely trail, heedless of his contemporaries, unhurried, undistracted ... Grove shrinks from ... modern life ... and gives himself to the slow rhythms of the grudging prairie' – before using this biographical caricature to account for Grove's fictional characters: 'The inner meaning of Len's union in death with Lydia is that a sensitive man cannot live without ideals ... this, too, [as with Grove] is a denial of life.'[13] In a more contemporary study, Ricou conflates the circumstances of real-life prairie authors with those of their fictional characters: 'When a character in a prairie fiction is either an artist, or of artistic temperament, the writer's creative responses to the environment are objectified. The absence of feature in the bleak and empty landscape, like the absence of feature in the social and cultural life of the prairie, leaves the aspiring artist without stimulus, without encouragement, and without the varieties of human intercourse which are his traditional subject.'[14] In other words, the fictional image of the isolated prairie dweller has become a compelling lens through which critics often evaluate the conditions surrounding the production of prairie writing itself. As Calder says, 'the prairie that the prairie realists construct becomes real for these critics, and that constructed prairie is then used as a standard of evaluation to measure other books.'[15]

As compelling as this myth may be, and as easy as it is to find it thematically reflected in much prairie-realist fiction, it is responsible for at least one misreading of the phenomenon of prairie realism as a whole: prairie writers of the early twentieth century are, in Canada's literary histories, erroneously located far from the centre of Canada's literary culture, and their works are often viewed as regional efforts of dubious significance to the development of a national fiction. In such a paradigm, the amateurish, anomalous, imitative, and insignificant prairie author is rarely considered part of the experimental, 'modern' writing of eastern Canada. This attitude toward prairie realism can be traced back to *The Canadian Forum* of the 1920s and '30s, which considered the genre antithetical to the modern writing it favoured and deliberately denigrated, satirized, and dismissed it. As I have already discussed, the *Forum*'s view of Canadian literature in the 1920s won the claim to legitimacy, and its version of the events of the period is now enshrined in most literary histories. While the *Bookman* of the 1920s regularly considered even some of the most obscure works by prairie writers, only a tiny handful were reviewed in the *Forum* during the same period, and almost nothing in these reviews was positive. None of Grove's novels of the 1920s, for example, was considered worthy of comment in the *Forum*, although his two books of nature sketches were reviewed. In May 1923, an unsigned piece examined *Over Prairie Trails* (1922). It offered some tepid praise of Grove's realist technique but was written in the typically dismissive and patronizing tone that the *Forum* critics often employed in their discussion of western writers: 'Over prairie trails in a buggy or cutter seems to an Easterner to promise a minimum of interest.'[16] While the reviewer does reluctantly concede that Grove occasionally offers a 'fascinating narrative,' he or she indulges in the kind of personal attacks on the prairie realist that are characteristic of other

Forum articles, and emphasizes the stereotype of the isolated prairie writer: 'a moody man's moods ... Mr. Grove of the book is a queer man, and a stubborn, whose opinion of us is not very high.'[17] A review of Grove's other work of prairie non-fiction, *The Turn of the Year* (1923), also unsigned, appeared in the February 1924 issue of the *Forum*. While the reviewer of this book of nature sketches found less fault with the Grove persona – 'the moody bitterness ... which expected no understanding appreciation from us ... is noticeably absent' – he or she nevertheless found relatively little value in the book's descriptive power: 'there is ... a fatiguing minuteness of sustained description which calls for dilution with incident.'[18] The only 1920s prairie novel reviewed in the *Forum*, Stead's *Grain* (1926), was similarly derided in an unsigned review in the January 1927 issue. While the writer acknowledged 'vivid accounts of farming operations in the West,' he or she nevertheless found the book mundane, commenting on Stead's 'kindly realism' and remarking that 'the book strives for no cosmic proportions.'[19] The reviewer was also unable to distinguish this ground-breaking prairie-realist work – also one of the most serious and slow-moving novels of the period – from the most sensationalistic forms of action and adventure fiction set on the western frontier: 'it looks like a prostitution to a story-craving public.'[20]

More blatantly indicative of the *Forum*'s dismissive attitude to prairie realism are the short stories it published that satirize prairie novelists and novels. One such example, 'The Romance of the West' by Paul A. W. Wallace, appeared in the March 1923 issue, mocking the nationalistic ambitions of prairie writers, holding up their realist aesthetic for ridicule, and diminishing their efforts with derogatory references to their regional concerns: 'Jedidiah Jennings had an itch of the pen, and an appetite for journalistic fame. Seeking lands to scoop, he became fired with the notion to write up Canadian prairie life, or, as his own phrase ran, to interpret in literature the land where history is being made ... But Jennings was too careful an artist to rest content with getting his romance second hand. He took an excursion ticket west for genuine local colour.'[21] If this story leaves some doubt as to whether the *Forum* was critical of all prairie fiction, or merely the most sensationalist forms of western romance, Robert Ayre's 'The Pollyanna Farmer,' which appeared in the November 1930 issue, suggested that even the most serious realistic fiction by prairie writers was not up to the *Forum*'s cosmopolitan literary standards. Ayre's story – comprising thirty-two chapters of approximately one paragraph in length – is a parody of the prairie-realist novel, invoking almost every cliché of the genre imaginable. He begins the story with an English emigrant named Bellow travelling west, and satirizes the prairie writer's trademark descriptions of the physical world: 'Wire fences, and stubble, and dejected stooks from last year's harvest humbled by the winter, rusted machinery, black earth and snow ... Prairie and more prairie, and still more.'[22] He spoofs the awkward sentimentality of the worst prairie novels: '"I feel like the Swiss Family Robinson," said Bellow. He was of a romantic temperament.'[23] Critiquing the slow pace of the prairie-realist novel and the destructive forces of nature described by many prairie novelists, he reduces the action of entire chapters to a single line: '*Chapter Fourteen* / The first crop of the Bellows fell before the assault of the rust, cutworm, and sawfly after it had been thinned out by drifting and flooding.'[24] The commonplace protagonist of the prairie novel, and the prairie author's penchant for mimetic dialogue, are similarly held up for ridicule: '"I don't know about these 'ere turnips," said Alf, wiping the sweat off his brow. "Blimee if I don't think I've gone and planted them upside down."'[25] Implausible plot twists are parodied by the deus ex machina ending of Ayre's story in which 'Oil was discovered on the farm. Incredible quantities of oil, and fortunes were being made over-night.'[26] And any doubt that Ayre intends the story to discredit both the place of prairie novels in Canadian literature as a whole, and the nationalistic aims of the movement celebrated in the rival *Canadian Bookman*, is obliterated by his ironic one-line opening 'Preface': 'Here, at last, is the Great Canadian Novel.'[27]

Certainly, many of the characteristics of prairie fiction derided in the reviews, articles, and satires of the *Forum* are not difficult to find even in some of the most accomplished works of the period. There are few if any prairie-realist novels written in the 1920s and '30s that are wholly satisfying aesthetically or free of romantic and nationalistic sensibilities that remain nearly ubiquitous in Canadian fiction long after the emergence of modern realism. In spite of this, the *Forum*'s attitude to prairie writing is excessively cursory and dismissive and obviously motivated by the well-documented desire of central Canadian writers and critics of the period to establish a modern literature in Canada that was, they believed, in just about every way imaginable, unlike even the most serious and ambitious works of the prairie realists. As the *Forum*'s views of Canadian literature in the 1920s have eclipsed those of the *Bookman*, not only is modern realism absent from literary histories, but the individual writerly struggles of prairie realists to change the direction of Canadian fiction have often been overlooked.

At first, some general facts about Canadian literary culture of the period appear to justify the *Forum*'s neglect. There can be little doubt that the institutionalized literary cultures in western Canada in the early twentieth century paled in contrast with those of Montreal and Toronto; while Winnipeg remained Canada's third-largest city until well into the twentieth century, there were almost no publishing houses of note in western Canada before 1950, the most modern and significant literary magazines of the period were published in the east, and the largest markets for Canadian fiction were in the United States, England, and the most populous eastern provinces. Yet individual prairie writers themselves, whatever the general indifference to literary enterprise in the west, were often far more connected to their modern-realist counterparts than most literary histories suggest, and a survey of literary periodicals of the day – most importantly *Canadian Bookman* – reveals that prairie writers played leading roles in the national movement for a new Canadian fiction.

Prairie writers themselves have done almost nothing to dispel the notion of their literary isolation. In several notable cases, and for dubious reasons, they have deliberately perpetuated it. In an article which appeared in *The Canadian Forum* in August 1931, 'Apologia Pro Vita et Opere Suo,' Grove responded to criticism of his writing published in the magazine by suggesting that he was not connected to the literary world it endorsed and ought not to be judged by its literary standards: 'Metaphorically speaking, I live in the wilderness and cannot afford to take part in the activities of my fellows ... we artists need solitude above all.'[28] In Grove's infamous Governor General's Award–winning autobiography, *In Search of Myself* (1946), tellingly called 'My Life as a Writer in Canada,' he blames cultural isolation and Canada's indifference to literature for his failure to achieve greater recognition as a writer, something he is apparently convinced he warrants: 'Half a century ago, that Frenchman [André Gide] had considered *me* as the most lavishly endowed among the young men then living within his orbit ... What, so I asked myself, had been the reason of my thus grievously disappointing my friend? ... the chief reason ... was that I never had an audience.'[29] A more direct and specific statement on the cultural isolation of the prairie writer appears in *Literary Friends* (1980), the memoirs of Wilfrid Eggleston, author of a little-known prairie-realist novel, *The High Plains* (1938). Like Grove, Eggleston suggests that the lack of an audience leads to economic hardship and greatly hinders prairie writers in their quest for literary achievement. Somewhat paradoxically, however, Eggleston, like some critics, equates the absence of literary culture on the prairie with the presence of traditional literary influence, and he emphasizes the imitative impulse in prairie writing: 'The market for sophisticated works on the agricultural frontier was virtually non-existent ... The struggling craftsmen imitated the best models within their reach ... The isolated writer is almost doomed to be a generation or so behind the times, mastering, it may be, a literary fashion just about the time it has run its course and become passé and unremarkable in the livelier centres of sophisticated culture.'[30] Such assertions by both Grove and Eggleston become suspect when we recognize that they are emphasizing their own cultural isolation as a way of justifying their own perceived failures as writers. Grove's autobiography, revealed by D.O. Spettigue to be largely fictional, takes the form of an apologia for his literary underachievement relative to Gide, whom he claims to have known as a young man. And Eggleston insists that economic hardship, not lack of talent, led him away from his 'lofty ambitions' and his literary pursuits: 'If I could not make Canadian writing my vocation, no one could deny me a series of hobbies.'[31]

In spite of these writers' grim descriptions of early twentieth-century prairie culture, numerous other sources suggest that literary life on the prairies was not quite so bleak. McCourt, for example, offers a surprisingly vibrant characterization of early prairie literary life in *The Canadian West In Fiction* (1949): 'In the Canadian West the first community institution seems to have been either a church or a police barracks; the second, one is tempted to feel, a Literary Society ... Other indications of the emphasis placed by the early settlers interested in literature or ... culture are to be found in the literary controversies which from time to time enlivened the correspondence columns of the prairie newspapers.'[32] In support of his claims, McCourt notes the remarkably precocious founding of the Fort MacLeod Literary and Historical Society in 1884, and the creation of the Regina Literary and Music society in 1885. Other sources reveal that McCourt's observations on late nineteenth-century prairie culture are equally true of the 1920s, when the works of prairie realism began to appear with some frequency. On the first list of 'Members Admitted to the Canadian Authors' Association,' which was printed in the September 1921 issue of the *Canadian Bookman*, 95 of the 247 'regular' members of the new association are from the four western provinces, making western Canadians substantially over-represented on a per-capita basis relative to their eastern counterparts.[33] David Arnason's *The Development of Prairie Realism* also does much to challenge the myth of the isolated prairie writer, proposing instead that they share a common intellectual heritage. Arnason identifies a number of general European intellectual trends and concepts common to the major prairie realists, including a 'belie[f] in human progress,' an acceptance of so-called 'new psychologies,' and a general attitude of 'liberal humanism.'[34]

However limited prairie literary culture of the early twentieth century might have been, and however much economic pressures undeniably presented hardships for prairie writers (as they have for all but a handful of Canadian authors up to the present day), the prairie realists did not live entirely, or even primarily, within a closed sphere of prairie literary culture. Even the most basic facts of the prairie realists' biographies suggest important connections to a larger Canadian literary scene. All three of the prairie-realist autobiographers – Grove, Eggleston, McClung – regardless of their other statements, had substantial literary connections. Grove took three nationwide reading tours in 1928–9, sponsored by the Canadian Club, that were well attended and well covered by the Canadian literary periodicals and newspapers of the day. He served in 1930–1 as 'President and Editor of the Ariston Publishers,' an endeavour that helped him establish numerous literary friendships, including one with Raymond Knister.[35] He was a frequent contributor to and subject of the Canadian literary periodicals of the day, including the *Bookman* and to a lesser extent the *Forum*, and his letters reveal his connections to dozens of significant literary figures of the period, including Marcus Adeney, W.J. Alexander, Richard Crouch, Pelham Edgar, Barker Fairley, Watson Kirkconnell, Hugh MacLennan, Desmond Pacey, Lorne Pierce, E.J. Pratt, and Carleton Stanley. Eggleston, despite his lower profile, was just as connected to the national scene: his memoirs discuss his numerous literary friends and acquaintances, including Grove, Knister, Pratt, Edgar, Bliss Carman, Sir Charles G.D. Roberts, and many others. McClung's literary and political activities made her national and international connections. She travelled extensively in Canada, was a prominent member of the CAA, served on the CBC's board of governors, and was a Canadian delegate at the League of Nations conference in Geneva.[36]

All of the other prominent prairie realists also deviate from the stereotype of the isolated writer to varying and significant degrees. Stead spent most of his early years in Manitoba, where he was the editor of several journals and newspapers, including *The Southern Manitoba Review*. He moved to Ottawa in 1919, where he wrote his prairie-realist novels, and served as the president of the Canadian Authors Association in 1923–4. Ostenso and Durkin both wrote their best-known prairie-realist novels – *Wild Geese* (1925) and *The Magpie* (1923) respectively – after settling in New York City, where they lived relatively cosmopolitan lives: 'Durkin's sister had already made her name as an opera singer in New York, and she drew Durkin and Ostenso into the glittering world of New York society.'[37] McCourt was born in Ireland, emigrated to Alberta, and attended Oxford University as a Rhodes scholar before accepting lecturing posts in Ontario and New Brunswick; his novels, beginning with *Music at the Close* (1947), were written after his relocation to Saskatoon in 1944. Stringer was Ontario-born and lived in both Montreal and Toronto before moving in 1914 to Alberta, where he wrote his prairie trilogy – *The Prairie Wife* (1915), *The Prairie Mother* (1920), and *The Prairie Child* (1921). In the same year that the last instalment of his trilogy was published, he moved to New Jersey, where he spent the rest of his life and effectively became an American writer. Born in England, Brooker established a creative reputation as an avant-garde abstract painter; he left the prairie for Toronto fifteen years before the appearance of the only novel he published in his lifetime, *Think of the Earth* (1936). Ross's best novel, *As For Me and My House* (1941), was written long after he had left small-town Saskatchewan for Winnipeg in 1933, but before his departure for England as a soldier in 1942 and his eventual settlement in Montreal in 1946. And even W.O. Mitchell, who spent a larger portion of his adult life on the prairie than most of the others, published his work in numerous widely circulating magazines of the period, including *The Atlantic Monthly*.

Admittedly, these biographical facts provide only circumstantial evidence of significant literary connections, but they certainly indicate that prairie literary culture of the period was far from insular. More concrete evidence of the role played by prairie realists in the larger modern-realist movement is found in the literary periodicals of the period. In fact, an examination of the *Canadian Bookman* of the 1920s reveals that the birth of modern realism and the emergence of prairie realism occurred simultaneously and contingently: prairie realism did *not* develop independently or after the fact as a particular regional application of the larger, national literary sensibility. Emerging works of prairie fiction were considered in the *Bookman* alongside the manifestos for a Canadian modern realism and, as they appeared throughout the 1920s, were billed as groundbreaking works of fiction with national relevance, at the vanguard of literary experiment and change, and were considered the exemplary works of modern realism in Canada. The *Bookman* of the 1920s reviewed most of the new prairie novels as they appeared. The majority of the novels reviewed by the *Bookman* in the 1920s were prairie novels. Almost without exception the magazine's reviewers discussed new prairie fiction in relation to the new modern writing in Canada.

Although typically celebratory in their attitudes to new Canadian writing, many of the *Bookman* reviewers of the period are surprisingly reserved in their praise of the least realistic new works by prairie authors. In fact, most of these reviews appear to be directing Canada's prairie writers toward the emerging modern-realist aesthetic, and writers appear in kind to be responding, becoming more realist in their approach to literary endeavour as the decade wears on. At the same time, the reviewers consider new works of prairie-realist fiction to be exemplary of the new writing in Canada, and the *Bookman* manifestos shape much of their discussion of modern realism with new prairie fiction in mind. In the first issue of the *Bookman* in January 1919, the first prairie realist, Robert J.C. Stead, is encouraged by the unnamed reviewer of his romantically emplotted third novel, *The Cow Puncher* (1918), to make a move toward more realistic writing. Remarking that Stead's novel 'falls between the two stools' of the 'romantic' and the modern 'life-like and sincere picture of the normal,' the reviewer prophesies that 'it will certainly be of value when Mr. Stead takes to the portrayal of more normal and more accurately observed Canadian life.'[38] In the October 1919 issue of the *Bookman*, an unsigned reviewer had similar advice for Douglas Durkin, objecting to the sensationalism of *The Heart of Cherry McBain* (1919): 'Mr. Durkin can write excellent narrative and description, and his literary abilities seem worthy of much better material than this outworn theme of the youthful fighting man ... We are convinced that there are deeper and finer themes than this in the Canadian West and that Mr. Durkin knows them or will find them.'[39] Despite its improbable premise, unrealistic dialogue, and generally romantic tone, B.K. Sandwell, in the December 1920 *Bookman*, praised Arthur Stringer's *The Prairie Mother* (1920) as a novel about 'human life as lived by ordinary human beings,' and he held it up as an example for other writers of the period to follow: 'It is when we read books like this that we begin to feel something of the appalling waste of time and intellectual abilities, and even costly paper and binding, that is involved when men who could write truthfully and nobly about Canadian life spend their talents upon commercial novels of intrigue, of crime, of adventure.'[40] And a prominent *Bookman* reviewer, Austin Bothwell, directed another important writer of the period toward realism in a review of *Purple Springs* (1921) that appeared in the December 1921 issue. Accusing Nellie McClung of having 'falsified the record' in her fictional account of the 'decline and fall of the notorious Roblin government,' Bothwell muses that 'if she had stuck resolutely, if not to the facts, to the spirit of facts, she might have enriched our literature permanently.'[41]

As prairie-realist novels began to appear with more regularity later in the decade, the *Bookman* critics turned from their pleas for realist fiction to appear to a celebration of the new novels as they arrive, and they openly equated a realistic aesthetic with artistic accomplishment. When Stead's fifth novel, *Neighbours* (1922), was published, an unnamed reviewer in the November 1922 *Bookman* announced that it marked 'entirely new ground, and much richer and more productive ground ... the whole picture is drawn with ... much faithful observation ... 'The Cow Puncher' made him a best-seller; 'Neighbours' makes him an artist.'[42] In February 1924, an unsigned review acclaimed Durkin's social-realist prairie novel set in Winnipeg, *The Magpie* (1923): 'It is a very fair story of Canada in general and Winnipeg in particular at more or less the present moment ... as a resumé of the situation in all its nebulous, overgrown, loose-endedness, it is distinctly striking.'[43] An omnibus review by Georges Bugnet in the December 1925 *Bookman* drew attention to the realist properties of Grove's *Settlers of the Marsh* (1925) and Ostenso's *Wild Geese* (1925), lauding the former's 'accurate and penetrating analysis' and the latter's realistic achievement and literary promise: 'If Miss Ostenso ... can write such a strong and realistic novel for a *début*, we may expect from her a real masterpiece, perhaps Canadian, in a few years.'[44] In January 1927, the *Bookman* featured a review of Stead's *Grain* (1926) by T.D. Rimmer that remarked upon the 'convincing' depiction of 'intimate detail of prairie life.'[45] A March 1929 review by A.S.M. of another almost unknown prairie-realist novel, Chas. W. Peterson's *Fruits of the Earth* (1928), not to be confused with Grove's novel of the same name published five years later, suggested that 'particular attention should be paid to [Peterson's] prologue, in which the author has summed up his subject in a brilliant and realistic manner.'[46] Reflecting the growing emphasis on realism in Canadian literary circles of the day, Peterson's 'Preface' to the novel states his realistic aims in no uncertain terms: 'There seems a persistent demand for a plain, unvarnished story of the prairie farm, truthfully portraying ... pioneer life, without introducing the artificial glamour of the conventional roaring cowpuncher.'[47] And these are by no means the only examples of such reviews of prairie fiction; in issue after issue, the *Bookman* critics sought out the new modern realism in the works they reviewed, and they found it more often in the works of prairie writers than anywhere else.

Numerous *Bookman* articles exploring the social aspects of Canada's literary circles in the 1920s indicate that the major prairie writers, including McClung, Grove, and Stead, were regarded as cultural celebrities and stimulated both gossip and adulation.[48] Prairie novels in the 1920s and '30s received more 'official' recognition than new works from eastern Canada: Ostenso's *Wild Geese* (1925) won the famous $13,500 *Pictorial Review* prize for best novel, Grove was awarded the Lorne Pierce medal in 1934, and the first two Governor General's Awards for fiction, presented in 1937 and 1938, went to prairie novels – Brooker's *Think of the Earth* (1936) and Laura Goodman Salverson's *The Dark Weaver* (1937). Prairie books were also among the best-sellers in Canadian fiction from the very beginning: two of Ralph Connor's first three books – *Black Rock: A Tale of the Selkirks* (1898), *The Sky Pilot: A Tale of the Foothills* (1899), and *The Man From Glengarry* (1901) – which together sold more than five million copies, were set in western Canada.[49] McClung's *Sowing Seeds in Danny* (1908) was for a time the best-selling novel in Canadian history. Many of Stead's novels made the best-seller lists in Canada, England, and Australia,[50] *The Cow Puncher* (1918) alone selling 70,000 copies.[51] And Grove's first two Canadian books of prairie sketches, *Over Prairie Trails* (1922) and *The Turn of the Year* (1923), were widely reviewed and among his best-selling works upon their publication. But the best indication of the 'modernity' and extra-regional relevance of prairie realism is in the fiction itself, which undertakes a surprising range of technical experiments with the realist form, and explores some of the most modern subjects of the twentieth-century world.

The dominant approach to prairie realism for most of the past century has been thematic, and critics have written prolifically about the uncomfortable relation of humans to their natural environment, the homesteading subject, and the rural way of life. Such themes are natural extensions of the geographical thesis, and it is neither surprising nor inappropriate that they have been widely discussed. But the dangers of geographical readings become apparent when critics use them to offer definitive and encompassing interpretations of the genre as a whole. Ricou, for example, uses a highly creative interpretation of the prairie landscape to make his geographical thesis unequivocal: 'The basic image of a single human figure amidst the vast flatness of the landscape serves to unify and describe all prairie fiction.'[52] To support this, he creates an imaginary, personified prairie landscape that takes on a series of archetypal personae: 'Benign,' 'Implacable,' 'Invisible,' 'Obsessive,' 'Internalized,' 'Eternal,' and 'Bewildering.'[53] Although Ricou and other thematic critics with similar concerns – including Angus, Dahlie, Elder, Harrison, Kreisel, McCourt, and Thacker – deserve much credit for defining a major literary genre and enumerating its thematic patterns, their studies ironically marginalize the very prairie fiction they have consolidated by downplaying both its important affinities with the rest of early twentieth-century literature and individual texts that resist larger schematizations.

Brooker's *Think of the Earth* (1936), a novel that was all but forgotten for decades until reissued in a critical edition by Glenn Willmott in 2000, demonstrates this phenomenon. Despite being set in an archetypal prairie town in 1907, its claim to cultural relevance as the winner of the first Governor General's Award for fiction, and the link it embodies between prairie writing and the experimental artistic circles that Brooker moved in, *Think of the Earth* is not treated substantially in any of the first three, foundational, book-length studies of prairie writing; McCourt and Ricou do not mention Brooker's novel, and Harrison excludes it from his larger analysis on the basis that it does not fit the geographical thesis: '*Think of the Earth* is its title but not its tendency; the action could have been set on the fringe of anywhere.'[54] Yet *Think of the Earth* is among the most remarkable novels written in Canada before 1950. Its exploration of religious decline and urbanization and its emphasis upon human psychology and spirituality make it one example of prairie realism that cannot be accounted for without acknowledging the genre's modernist affinities. And Brooker's novel is hardly alone in this regard. The interest that prairie-realist fiction shows in modern technology, the forces of urbanization and industrialization, modern social and political ideals, moral and religious change and decline, human sexuality, evolving gender roles, and central historical events of the modernist age – including the two world wars and Great Depression – place it among the most thematically modern writing produced in Canada in the early twentieth century.

Like the Canadian urban and social realists discussed later, and numerous international modernist writers, prairie realists express ambivalence about technological change and reveal it to be a liberating and threatening force, associated at once with twentieth-century notions of progress and dehumanization. While the prairie realists do not always discuss technology in the sweeping fashion of the urban realists, or in the ideological terms of many of the social realists, they do often provide detailed descriptions of new machinery and its effects on the lives of prairie inhabitants. Frequently, these are agricultural machines, possibly explaining why this concern was overlooked by the cosmopolitan *Forum* critics of the 1920s and '30s who perhaps considered this type of technological innovation part of a regional preoccupation with prairie life and detailed description of landscape. One of the earliest prairie-realist representations of the machine appears in Stead's *Grain* (1926). New agricultural equipment, in this case the 'threshing machine,' represents both the promise of the future and a threat to traditional life and the financial security of homesteaders: 'Bill Powers was the chief thresherman of the community. He had graduated from the old horse-power days in the steam-engine class in the early nineties, and was now wearing out his third machine, which, with the assistance of his homestead quarter, carried the accumulated mortgages passed on by its predecessors.'[55]

In other cases, the prairie realists juxtapose vivid descriptions of the machine with images of rural life to highlight the hurried pace of cultural change. Realistic description of landscape is an unmistakable feature of Eggleston's *The High Plains* (1938), yet his technical descriptions of machines shatter the placid surface of his pastoralism and emphasize, almost mimetically, the speed of technological development in early twentieth-century Canada and its effects upon the lives of prairie dwellers: 'The pant of the loader became more laboured, the separator emitted a low moan, rapidly rising in pitch to a thin whine as a hundred wheels and pulleys, rocking arms and steel elbows, sieves and fans, endless chains of buckets, whirled and vibrated in a perfect frenzy of concerted motion ... David, looking on, felt that it was the satisfying culmination of their homestead venture.'[56] The machine is also frequently used to symbolic ends by the prairie realists, allowing them to comment indirectly on the larger social, political, and cultural forces that inform their works. Grove's *The Master of the Mill* (1944) plays upon the popular prairie-realist convention of investing symbolic significance in the landscape by superimposing a grand-scale technological image over the natural setting and imbuing it with allusive meaning. His mill is at once a powerful representation of progress and technological achievement, and an embodiment of the dehumanizing forces of global capitalism: 'Its image lay on the mirror-smooth water like a fairy palace inverted ... that mill stood as a symbol and monument of the world-order ... of a ruthless capitalism which had once been an exploiter of human labour but had gradually learned ... to dispense with that labour, making itself independent, ruling the country by its sheer power and producing wealth.'[57] These descriptions of machines suggest that the prairie world these authors represent is far more connected to outside forces and modern influences than some characterizations suggest. Importantly, the modern forces in motion on the early twentieth-century prairie, transforming lifestyles and challenging belief systems, are the same ones critiqued and celebrated in the urban and social-realist novels of Canada and much of the rest of the world.

The prairie realists commonly accompany images of the machine with descriptions of a rural prairie being urbanized and industrialized. Much as prairie writers view the machine with ambivalence, these larger modern forces are rarely depicted as either wholly malevolent or benign. The threatening encroachment of the modern world and its values is a key concern even in some of the first prairie-realist novels. Stead's *Homesteaders* (1916), which spans the period between 1882 and about 1910, is set against the backdrop of a prairie landscape that is quickly changing, and the cacophonous language that Stead uses to describe this process draws attention to many of the negative aspects of modernization: 'Railways had supplanted ox-cart ... as the freighters of the plains ... The vast sweep of the horizon, once undefiled by any work of man, was pierced and broken with elevators, villages, and farm buildings, and the whiff of coal smoke.'[58] Reflecting the competing attitudes that prairie realists of the period have about modernization, Eggleston's *The High Plains* (1938) conversely sees it as a largely positive and civilizing force: 'The coming of the railroad transformed the life of the ... community almost overnight. In the swift superficial metamorphosis of the frontier, the village of Thora sprang up and supplanted the agricultural outpost, just as the outpost had replaced the wild desolation of the range.'[59] The archetypal prairie town of Poplar Plains in Brooker's *Think of the Earth* (1936) presents a predominantly urban setting for modern change on the prairie and opens with a reference to the quick pace of urban development and its inherent constructive and destructive forces: 'He had been there thirty years and the place had changed beyond belief ... a second railroad was coming through ... Jim Conover's farm had been torn up with steam shovels and turned into a huge gravel pit.'[60] And, perhaps owing to its later date of composition and its author's leftist convictions, Vera Lysenko's *Yellow Boots*

(1954), an almost unknown work of prairie realism, expresses a wholly negative view of the industrial world that has reached the prairies and likens the situation to the transformation of Europe during the Industrial Revolution: 'The factory ... was a modern one, well-lighted, with big panes of glass and modern machines ... Some of the older workers recalled songs they had sung ... regarding exploitation within the European factories – the terrible speed-up, the whip of the foreman, the child labour.'[61] Such images of an urban world at odds with the rural landscape and a traditional way of life, however they are characterized, are a constant if peripheral concern for the prairie realists. It is worth noting that the geographical thesis, with its emphasis upon human struggle solely in relation to a threatening *natural* environment, denies the prairie-realist concern with a number of the most fundamental and modern subjects of the twentieth-century novel.

The prairie realists also frequently raise the dominant and contemporary social issues of their day and explore early twentieth-century society and politics from a variety of ideological perspectives. In his last novel, *Dry Water* (1935), Stead offers a detailed exploration of the effects of modern economics on the lives of prairie farmers. Donald Strand, an honest, hard-working, traditional homesteader, is manipulated by bankers into believing that his values are compatible with the new economy of modern Canada. His banker, Mr Sutherland, lures him with flattery and platitudes into collaboration with the very forces that threaten his livelihood: '"The source of all wealth is still in the land ... wealth is accumulating at an unprecedented and ever-accelerating pace. We are entering a new era, Mr. Strand. But we will do well to still give honor to the homely virtues of industry and enterprise."'[62] In the end, the downfall of the Strands is representative of the impending decline of traditional ways of life and of the subjugation of rural Canada to urban interests and values. In his earlier novel, *The Smoking Flax* (1924), Stead explores changing social demographics and the contrast of traditional ways of life with modern sensibilities. Cal, a university graduate with a degree in sociology, comes to work on the Stake family farm and attempts to apply his sociological theories to farm life: 'Of what use was his higher education if he could not grapple with a situation of this kind; if he must leave this farm as crude and ugly as he had found it?'[63] The romantic conclusion of the novel brings Cal's modern sensibilities together with a traditional way of living, suggesting a possible reconciliation between the forces that so often compete in prairie-realist novels: Cal marries Minnie, the attractive daughter of farmer Jackson Stake, and the closing scene emphasizes pastoral beauty and harmony – 'The world is at peace, and, it might be asleep, save for the slow shuttling of the ploughs back and forth across the summer fallows' – as Cal and Minnie make plans to go to the 'Electric theatre.'[64]

Durkin's *The Magpie* (1923), another novel exploring modern politics and social concerns, is perhaps more representative of the period by virtue of its pessimism. Here, no such reconciliation is possible between traditional and modern views of the world. The protagonist, Craig Forrester, is a trader on the Winnipeg grain exchange and finds himself torn between his progressive social conscience and his hypocritical involvement in a capitalist society that exploits farmers and industrial workers. Images of the prairie landscape and references to large socio-political events, often juxtaposed with one another, constantly flow through Craig's mind, representing the two worlds, the modern and the traditional, between which he feels caught: 'Before a week has gone the water is lying in pools in the lowlands ... Bolshevism had risen like a black cloud in the east and was threatening to overcome Polish resistance ... It was thus he argued with himself as he walked westward along the avenue thronging with late afternoon shoppers.'[65] At the end of the novel, disillusioned by the moral decay of the modern world and the social disruption caused by events that include the Winnipeg general strike in 1919, Forrester returns to his childhood home and takes up a traditional way of life, reinforcing a common prairie-realist critique of modern society that runs throughout *The Magpie*.

Similarly, the prairie realists' exploration of moral change and the decline of traditional religious beliefs and systems is at odds with conservative characterizations of the genre. In Grove's *Our Daily Bread* (1928), generational conflict within a single family is representative of larger conflicts between generations and competing notions of family and community found in Canadian society. In Grove's novel, a homesteading patriarch named John Elliott struggles to impose his time-honoured values upon his children, who have more modern sensibilities, and his failure in this endeavour is paralleled by his physical decline and emotional disintegration. Elliott's story begins with an account of his worldly success and a description of his rural empire built over the years through 'introspection, dreams, ideas,' and old-fashioned hard work.[66] By the end of the novel, Elliott is a broken man; in declining health and feeling abandoned by his children, who leave the homestead to pursue their own more modern pursuits, he 'passes from hand to hand' before dying and symbolically taking a way of life with him: 'Henceforth, [the Elliott children's] eyes would be focused on their own, individual futures.'[67]

In Brooker's *Think of the Earth* (1936), changing moral and social values are explored in an overtly religious context when Tavistock, a mad eccentric who believes himself to be a modern Christ figure, arrives in a prairie town and, in what he conceives to be part of his messianic role, begins prophesying a murder and preaching an almost Nietzschean moral relativism: 'Do you think it is possible for us – you or me – to experience ... suffering, without *ourselves* committing a murder?'[68] The Canon, a traditional Anglican minister who has long theological discussions with Tavistock, becomes increasingly frustrated as his traditional religious knowledge fails to rebut the modern Christ figure's perspective on human existence: '"Don't ask me," said the Canon ... "I'm just an old-fashioned parson who believes in original sin."'[69] The ending of the novel is enigmatic and closes with Tavistock's partial acceptance by the prairie community and his final assertion that the traditional moral and religious concepts of good and evil do not adequately define the modern condition: 'As soon as I saw – what I saw – the perfection of everything – the harmony of good and evil – I knew there was no need ... for Christ – or any new Christs.'[70]

While the particular theological issues raised by Brooker's novel are hardly typical of prairie realism in general, a modernist notion that religion is losing (or has lost) its relevance in the modern world is found in numerous other works, including, most famously, Ross's *As For Me and My House* (1941). Mrs Bentley, a preacher's wife whose diary provides the novel's first-person narrative, comments on the superficiality and hypocrisy that characterize the religious beliefs of her community: 'In return for their thousand dollars a year they expect a genteel kind of piety, a well-bred Christianity that will serve as an example to the little sons and daughters of the town.'[71] The unreliable story provided by Mrs Bentley's diary implicates both her and her husband Philip in the religious and moral hypocrisy of the town; Philip, an uninterested and ineffectual preacher, commits adultery with Judith, a young woman from the town, and the diary also hints at Mrs Bentley's possible adultery with a local liberal humanist who contrasts sharply with her preacher husband. Ross provides many ironic statements in the novel to draw attention to his religious and social critique; when the Bentleys, for largely selfish and concealed reasons, adopt Judith's illegitimate baby after she dies in childbirth, a woman from the town remarks, 'You and your husband are good people. You're real Christians, and I'm glad you're taking the baby.'[72]

Another almost ubiquitous feature of the prairie-realist novel is its representation of evolving gender relations and women's roles in a changing world.[73] Certainly the prairie novel of the period abounds with uncritical representations of women in the traditional roles of wife and mother, yet there are a surprising number of portraits of prairie women found in these same novels that reflect and often bravely advocate new roles for women in modern society. The most obvious and striking feminist portraits appear in the otherwise relatively conservative novels of Nellie McClung, herself a vocal suffragette and a member of the 'famous five' who fought for the legal recognition of women as 'persons,' a goal incredibly achieved only in 1930. In *Purple Springs* (1921), McClung creates the vivid psychological portrait of Pearl Watson, a character who represents many of the feminist aspirations of the time. Not surprisingly, Watson experiences considerable personal conflict as a result of her willingness to challenge normative gender assumptions: 'If Pearl Watson had not a taste for political speeches and debates; if she had read the crochet patterns in the paper instead of the editorials, and had spent her leisure moments making butterfly medallions for her camisoles, or in some other lady-like pursuit, instead of leaning over the well-worn railing around the gallery of the Legislative Assembly, in between classes at the Normal, she would have missed much; but she would have gained something too.'[74] While portraits of women as social activists are rare in Canadian fiction of the period, numerous indirect evocations of feminist ideals appear in other works of prairie realism. Even Stringer's prairie trilogy (1915–22), written in an ironic tone that undercuts many of the assertions of the prairie-diarist narrator, offers a portrait of a woman who is keenly aware of many of the limitations and contradictions of her place in a society dominated by frontier men. On the one hand, her musings offer an authentic exploration of the psyche of a woman who has internalized the values of a patriarchal social order. In *The Prairie Mother*, Chaddie considers the emotional challenges that might face a woman after several years of marriage, and she advocates self-sacrifice as a method of preserving domestic harmony: 'If you are wise you will no longer demand the impossible of him. Being a woman you will still want to be loved.'[75] Yet when her husband's prospects at homesteading fail, Chaddie breaks the stereotype of the passive and effusive female perpetuated in much of the novel and takes action to preserve her family's well-being: 'I haven't surrendered to any sudden wave of emotionalism when I talk about migrating over to that Harris ranch. It's nothing more than good old hard-headed, practical self-preservation.'[76]

Stringer's example demonstrates that it is not always clear whether individual prairie-realist novels offer an endorsement of the changing roles of women in the early twentieth century or simply strive to represent such changes in a vivid, credible, and contemporary manner. But the prairie setting, and the harsh conditions of homesteading life that frequently necessitate that women perform work outside the immediate domestic sphere, would appear to invite exploration of the subject, judging by the number of novels that take up the issue. In one of the best prairie-realist novels, Christine Van Der Mark's almost unknown *In Due Season* (1947), we are offered the portrait of Lina Ashley, a strong and independent woman who through hard work, persistence, and a neglect of many of her own emotional and spiritual needs, achieves material success in spite of the usual travails of prairie existence and the negative influence of her irresponsible and inept husband. Van Der Mark's feminist message in this novel is double-edged; on the one hand, Ashley's material success suggests that motivated women can achieve much in the face of powerful opposition; at the same time, the emotional toll that Ashley's pursuits exact on her suggests that such victories are often pyrrhic.

Numerous prairie novels, like Van Der Mark's, present the homesteading experience almost as a metaphor for the struggle of modern women to endure, physically and psychologically, in the presence of hostile social forces. Some influential thematic readings – with their emphasis upon the relation of *man* to the natural environment – at best treat the subject in universal terms, highlighting the influence of a hostile physical world on the individual. Most often, such studies explore a predominantly masculine experience, stressing, to the exclusion of other interpretations, the at times violent process of wresting subsistence from the land and the imposition of a patriarchal social structure on the untamed landscape. Prairie realists, however, frequently use the prairie experience as a metaphor for the psychological struggle of women to thrive in a male world. Ricou, for example, misses much of the point of McClung's vision and critiques her technique of characterization on the basis of its non-conformity to a unifying theme: 'The image of man in a horizontal world ... seldom seems essential to McClung's conception of character ... McClung apparently feels that the physical environment is important, but she does not reflect upon the possible ... imaginative impact of this distinctive situation.'[77] In many prairie novels, including Stringer's, McClung's, and Van Der Mark's, opposition appears at least as much in the guise of limitations imposed by a traditional social structure upon ambitious modern women as in the form of hostile natural forces. In fact, McClung and many of her contemporaries are being far more imaginative than critics often recognize: they are moving beyond the standard investigation of the individual in a threatening geographic world and adapting this powerful creative opportunity to explore modern feminism.

The formative impact of two world wars on Canadian culture is also a frequent and under-acknowledged subject of prairie-realist fiction. In contrast to the notion of the prairie as an isolated region disconnected from the cataclysmic ideological clashes of the modern age, the impact of the wars is often felt very directly and immediately by prairie individuals and plays a formative role in many of the psychological portraits that prairie realists create. Gander Stake, the unintelligent and self-concerned protagonist of Stead's *Grain* (1926), irrespective of his preoccupations with farming, romance, and achievement of material success, experiences the Great War as a sinister and confusing psychological presence that threatens to disrupt his fortunes: 'He went on working fourteen hours a day in the harvest field … trying to keep the war out of his mind … In all this it is not to be granted that Gander was essentially less patriotic than other young men who responded to the call … He was not lacking in courage, or in a spirit of readiness to defend his home … But Belgium? Gander was unable to visualize a danger so remote.'[78] If Stead's novel presents the Great War largely as background material to connect the prairie to grand, historic twentieth-century forces, other prairie novels do more to incorporate its influence into the central movement of their narrative.

McCourt's novels deal directly with the psychological effects of war on the individual and society, and the war experience is a defining event in the lives of several of his protagonists. In *Music at the Close* (1947), McCourt frames his narrative with reference to both world wars and writes his prairie story within a larger historical context, making it on one level symbolic of the experience of the lost generation in Canada. Neil Fraser, the novel's hero, finds his destiny inalterably bound up in international circumstances beyond his control. The opening chapter presents an orphaned Neil travelling to the homestead of his Uncle Matt, and the indifference of future 'history' to his aspirations is foreshadowed when he encounters a townsperson who hopes the Great War will continue because of the high prices it ensures for his crop: '"Lloyd Peers has been killed. Word just come through this mornin'. Don't know as his people have heard yet." "That so? Too bad ... Matt, if them Huns can just hang on for about two more years we'll all be able to retire. Two years – that's all I ask."'[79] Historical events and personages remain in the background of McCourt's story throughout: the narrative makes reference to 'The Armistice of November 11, 1918,' 'the new Fords that had appeared in the district,' 'T. S. Eliot,' the stock market crash in 'the spring of 1929,' the 'Defence League,' and 'Hitler,' and Neil emerges as a kind of archetypal, modern everyman of the interwar period.[80] In McCourt's final chapter, as Neil lies dying on a battlefield during the Normandy invasion, he muses about the meaning of his wasted life and concludes that his experience is in some respects representative of that of an entire generation: 'And what was true of himself was true of those who died with him. Most men lived and died and left not even a memory of their having been ... Strange that in the irrational, fantastic society of earth, war and war alone could justify the existence of countless millions who in peace were of no importance, not even to themselves.'[81] The commentary that ends *Music at the Close* links the fictional prairie of the novel to the disillusioned modern world of which it is unmistakably a part.

The modern concerns and issues that are an integral part of these and other works demonstrate that the prairie realists were as much informed by a 'modern sensibility' as any writers of Canadian fiction of the period. On this basis alone, the prairie realist shared defining, twentieth-century ideas and assumptions with other modernists. But prairie realism comprises much more than a general modern outlook on the world and a willingness to engage modern subjects in fiction. Perhaps the most unfortunate effect of the critical emphasis upon geographical themes in prairie fiction is not its tendency to close out modern issues and concerns, but the very emphasis upon *theme* itself. The modern-realist aesthetic, as it is defined in the 1920s manifestos and applied in works of fiction from all parts of Canada, consists of a number of formal and technical characteristics that have little or nothing to do with either theme or subject matter. Prairie realism, as its name suggests, is usually considered a regional form of fiction, dedicated to the mimetic and faithful representation of a particular locale, or grouping of locales. From the very start, critics have foregrounded its regional concerns, and defined it by virtue of its otherness to the literature of the rest of Canada and the modern world. This tendency may well have its origins in the prevalent literary tastes of the era when early prairie realists were writing and publishing: as Gordon Roper contends in *Literary History of Canada*, 'the other striking phenomenon of the literary taste of the period was the appetite for local colour, or regional fiction. It was the fashion that affected more Canadian writers of this period than any other. The purpose of the local colourist was to capture in a short story or in a book made up of related sketches the particular flavour of his chosen locality.'[82]

Both major Canadian literary magazines of the 1920s approached prairie fiction with the criteria outlined by Roper in mind. *Canadian Bookman*, with its assertion that new fiction ought to be true to the details of a particular contemporary setting, indirectly privileged regional subject matter, although it clearly indicated that such realist portraits of particular locales were a feature of the larger, national movement in Canadian literature. *The Canadian Forum* implied that prairie writing, with its supposed geographical emphasis and referentiality, was inferior to the cosmopolitan writing of eastern Canada and Anglo-American literary modernism and dismissed it in a quest for a national literature that looked more like those of other countries. Even McCourt, despite having already written his own prairie novel concerned with international issues – *Music at the Close* (1947) – emphasized the regional nature of prairie writing above all else in *The Canadian West in Fiction* (1949): 'There is a remarkable unity of spirit prevailing among prairie dwellers; and a way of life as distinctive as the region which fosters it.'[83] Critics writing after McCourt have done relatively little to alter the regional characterization of prairie realism.[84] According to the regional and referential definition, prairie realism is concerned primarily with the surface details of everyday life on the recognizable Canadian prairie: as Ricou writes, 'the writer discovers a new sensitivity to the minutest details of life. In the absence of landscape spectacle the artist must sharpen his observation and detect those nuances which are the essence of art.'[85] Abiding attention to region means that the exploration of human psychology and consciousness, considered a hallmark of high-modernist literatures, is seldom considered a concern of the prairie realists.

Of course, the psychological emphasis of much prairie fiction has not gone entirely unnoticed.[86] Consistent with their thematic and regional emphases, however, discussions of psychology in the prairie-realist novel have usually limited themselves to a study of characterization and the various ways that prairie landscape shapes the mind of the prairie inhabitant. In most of these instances, critics are shifting their focus slightly to include the representation of a regional experience within a larger notion of prairie literature as a representation of a regional environment. The psychologies of individual characters in many traditional readings become extensions of the prairie setting itself, part of a larger, overwhelming, regional geography. As Kreisel suggests, 'Man, the giant conqueror, and man, the insignificant dwarf always threatened by defeat, form the two polarities of the state of mind produced by the sheer physical fact of the prairie.'[87] In his discussion of *Wild Geese* (1925), Arnason notes that Ostenso creates 'exquisite types whose experiences of isolation, landscape, and love are acted out on a vast and heroic scale, identified with the mournful cry and urgent quest of the wild geese.'[88] In the 'Afterword' to Grove's *Settlers of the Marsh,* Kristjana Gunnars remarks that 'the setting is the prairie ... Consequently a sense of isolation and silence sets in ... People who are too isolated and wrapped in silence are, in Prairie fiction, often reduced to suicide or even murder.'[89] Sandra Djwa, in her discussion of Ross's *As For Me and My House,* argues that 'the wind makes Mrs. Bentley feel that she has been lost and abandoned.'[90] In all of these cases, critics are not discussing psychological realism as a modern form with links to the epistemological experiments of modernist authors: they are discussing regional representations of landscape reflected in the minds of fictional characters.

Such readings of the prairie mind are neither inappropriate nor inaccurate. But they do tend to ignore psychological subjects that have little or nothing to do with landscape or geography. Even in one of the earliest prairie-realist novels, *The Homesteaders* (1916), Stead offers much traditional landscape description but creates psychologically 'real' characters who exist independently of their prairie environment. Stead's novel, one of the first prairie works to depart from the conventions of romantic and adventure writing – a genre that includes his first work, *The Bail Jumper* (1914) – offers characters whose psychological experiences are recognizable, believable, intense, and unexplained by regional circumstance: 'He would not allow his mind to be drawn into speculation – the thing was the remembrance, now, when it was offered him. Old lullabies stole into his brain; a deep peace encompassed him, and consciousness faded thinner and thinner into the sea of the infinite.'[91] More interesting are the experimental techniques employed by prairie realists to explore psychological states. One general method is the symbolic distortion of landscape to reflect the psychological experience and development of characters. While many readings suggest that landscape is reflected in the psychological portraits the prairie realists create, more often than not the reverse is true: landscape is symbolically manipulated by the prairie realist so that it reflects and reinforces the thoughts of independent characters, often in an elaborate and sustained form of pathetic fallacy. Some of the most successful examples of this technique can be found in W.O. Mitchell's *Who Has Seen the Wind* (1947). In this novel, the thoughts and emotions of characters are projected onto the prairie landscape, not determined by it: 'Ben had about as much moral conscience as the prairie wind that lifted over the edge of the prairie world.'[92] In Mitchell's simile, the state of mind of the character is obviously reflected, not passively moulded by environmental influence. Another technique used in the same novel is the symbolic manipulation of landscape to add psychological intensity to particular scenes, as in this example where one of Mitchell's characters is having his moral convictions challenged: 'A gentle wind stirred the leaves on the poplars, setting disks of shadow dancing over Hislop's earnest face.'[93] In numerous passages that strive for psychological character development, Mitchell offers subtle landscape symbols juxtaposed with psychological commentary to nuance his psychological portraits. In this example, the novel's child protagonist struggles to understand the meaning and impact of his father's death, and the prairie environment is shaped by his emotional state: 'Nothing seemed any different, thought Brian O'Connal ... The fall wind was gentle at his window screen; carelessly it stirred a tissue of sound through the dry leaves of the poplar outside. He wondered what his mother was thinking alone in her room.'[94]

In other situations, prairie realists manipulate their descriptions of landscape more dramatically to build the psychological intensity of dramatic situations. In this scene, from Eggleston's *The High Plains* (1938), a character is hopelessly lost in a prairie blizzard, and the narrator describes the environment, not in the precise and specific terms that one might expect of the prairie realist, but in expressionistic, vivid, and visual language that reflects the psychological confusion of the situation: 'It was useless to look aloft for guidance. The sun was heavily obscured in clouds. The horizon on every side was blotted out by swirling drifts. The only constant thing was the wind. No doubt it still blew from the west. David felt no panic. He had managed to keep from freezing so far; and he still had some reserve of strength.'[95] In *Dry Water* (1935), Stead infuses the prairie landscape with symbolic sexual imagery to bring out the undertones of repressed carnal desire, as this awkward courtship scene demonstrates: 'He smiled assurance in answer to her question, and spoke to his horses; the traces tightened; the crackle of roots came up from the shares; two long, smooth, earthen streams began to flow back ... she suited her pace to the plow, watching the colters as they ruthlessly cut through the sod, regardless of the prairie flowers that blossomed on its breast ... she saw the moist, glazed, straight line of the furrow.'[96] In response to her observation of this sexually charged landscape, Clara playfully asks permission to pick Donald's 'strawberry blossoms': 'You don't mind my picking a few on your estate, Mr. Big Farmerman?'[97]

In other passages, prairie writers create landscape scenes that symbolically reflect, in a sustained and general way, the temperaments, or general psychological profiles, of their characters. Grove's *Fruits of the Earth* (1933) draws attention to the mental state of the cold, practical, industrious Abe Spalding by mirroring it in the landscape that he surveys. Crucially, this technique reveals that Abe has not been shaped by his prairie environment. Instead, he has imposed his own will upon his surroundings: 'Abe's eye swept over the landscape beyond his fences ... Rarely, during the first years of his life on the prairie, had he given the landscape any thought. It had offered a clear proposition, unimpeded by bluffs of trees or irregularities ... the trees he wanted he had planted where he wanted them.'[98] In a more emotionally charged passage, the orphaned Neil Fraser of McCourt's *Music at the Close* (1947) travels toward his new home on the prairie and finds his own feelings of fear and nostalgia reflected in another symbolic landscape. In this passage, McCourt's river is not brought to life through vivid description, but through an evocation of its archetypal and symbolic significance: 'The word river stirred something in Neil's blood. All the way from the bleak little prairie town he had been looking, much of the time instinctively rather than consciously, for water ... Back home there had been streams everywhere, a river winding through the very heart of the village where Neil had gone to school. And because the word river suggested something he had left behind, the boy's eyes were shining with expectation.'[99]

In all of these cases, psychological realism, not regionalist, mimetic representation of place, is the aesthetic concern that guides the prairie realist's rendering of geography. These prairie writers are broadening the definition of realism to include the psychological and recreating the prairie in imaginative, fictional, symbolic, and modern terms. The realism of many of the prairie realists is much like the modern realism of Knister, true to universal concerns and broad human experiences, rather than to a particular geographical reality. Much as members of the Group of Seven 'claimed that their wellspring and the forms of their art came not from art but from the land itself' just as they engaged in a highly aestheticized process of interpreting the land and imposing individual and borrowed artistic sensibilities onto it, so, too, were the prairie realists writing with agency, individuality, and influence, and not at the mystical behest of prairie geography.[100] But the symbolic manipulation of landscape is a limited technique, and the concern of prairie writers to achieve psychological realism leads to numerous other forms of experiment and technical innovation.

Traditional realism, with its third-person narratives, makes it challenging for prairie writers to do more than offer detached psychological character analysis. While third-person narrative certainly enables referential descriptions of geography and landscape, it makes mimetic representations of human consciousness extremely difficult to achieve. In other words, prairie realists interested in modern psychology encounter an incompatibility between the traditionally objectivist thrust of realistic writing, concerned with fact, detail, and detached observation, and their desire to create portraits that are psychologically credible, and therefore admittedly subjective. Centre-of-consciousness narrative, discussed earlier in relation to Raymond Knister and his attempts to overcome a similar challenge, is the most common technique used to depict human consciousness in prairie-realist fiction. The versions of this device used by various prairie authors, however, vary dramatically. Two early and primitive centre-of-consciousness forms appear in Stead's *Grain* (1926). Although Stead's narrative aims for a detached and objective point of view, his narrator has a perceptible if vaguely defined personality, and portions of the novel are coloured by the narrator's ironic perspective, especially in humorous passages, including many of those that offer physical descriptions of characters: 'During the next year or two Gander stretched up into a lanky youth ... his Adam's apple became the feature of his long neck; it jumped and gulped and hopped about with prodigious activity.'[101] Stead's narrator's persona, however at odds it may be with the novel's generally objective point of view, enables him to explore the mind of his main character, Gander Stake, through an unconventional form of centre-of-consciousness writing in which the narrator appears to speak Gander's thoughts aloud in the act of directly addressing the character: 'Gander never had shot a goose;

this was his chance at sudden glory. Steady, Gander, steady! What will they say at home when you carry in a great grey goose – maybe two of them? What will they say at school? What will that detested brother Jackie say, who is forever belittling your marksmanship? Gander raised his gun slowly.'[102] A more familiar version of the same technique is used by Stead elsewhere in the same novel. To present the flow of thoughts running through the mind of Gander's father, Jackson Stake, Stead places his thoughts in quotation marks. While the section is written in mimetic dialogue, obviously trying to emulate dialect and speech patterns, it is not meant to represent words actually spoken aloud, but rather thoughts passing through the character's mind: 'Time enough. An' if the crop comes off all right I'll slip him a little cash after threshin'; maybe a twenty dollar bill to do as he likes, an' no questions asked.'[103]

Less idiosyncratic centre-of-consciousness methods are found in other well-known prairie novels of the period. In Grove's *The Master of the Mill* (1944), a sustained impression of thoughts passing through a character's mind is achieved through a subtle shift in tone and diction in the middle of long narrative passages. The third-person narrative voice is not abandoned, but redirected slightly so that the objective narrator begins to speak largely from the point of view of an individual character, in this case forwarding the main narrative while expressing the individual biases of Samuel Clark: 'All that he would change. He would begin by building a huge hall with a gymnasium, with rooms for games and reading, with a swimming pool and a lecture hall. He would raise wages and give the men a voice in the administration.'[104] In Durkin's *The Magpie* (1923), this technique is used even more effectively. The thoughts of Craig Forrester, and the psychological issues he confronts, are foregrounded by the use of sustained centre-of-consciousness narrative and extremely pared-down writing that all but negates the presence of the dominant narrative voice, giving the impression, despite the use of third-person perspective, that the passage is rendered in the first person: 'But why could he not do that and keep fresh the young love that brought him and Marion together? He could. He would not permit himself to think he couldn't ... He would not give a place to the thoughts that had arisen in his mind since dinner. He would sweep them out of his mind.'[105]

McCourt, whose comments on the regional and thematic properties of prairie writing I have already critiqued, would eventually become one of the most ardent proponents of the centre-of-consciousness technique. In *The Wooden Sword* (1956), McCourt writes almost entirely in a centre-of-consciousness mode, and the main narrative voice almost never completely escapes the consciousness of the main character, Steven Venner, a poetry professor whose loneliness, feelings of sexual inadequacy, and haunting memories of the Second World War colour almost everything the third-person narrator communicates. Detached narrative, in this novel, is kept to a bare minimum, usually appearing as a single line of description indicating action followed by a long centre-of-consciousness passage: 'Steven looked at the members of the Faculty ... It would shock them to know that they taught for the love of God. But that was true. The believers, the agnostics, the atheists were all alike in this ... Why else did they accept the material harassments which were the inevitable accompaniment of the academic treadmill.'[106] While these and numerous other examples of the centre-of-consciousness technique are clearly striving to achieve a heightened form of psychological realism, they nevertheless obviously rely upon many of the traditional conventions of third-person narrative. Despite a concerted effort made to mimic the flow of consciousness from thought to thought at points in these novels, their authors make no sustained attempt to experiment with language along the lines of the high modernists in their impressionistic writing and stream-of-consciousness passages. The result is a form of writing that allows numerous subjective perspectives to appear within the framework of an objective narration, without offering more than a fleeting impression of the epistemological workings of any individual human consciousness.

In an important departure from most applications of the centre-of-consciousness technique, Brooker's *Think of the Earth* (1936) moves even closer to conveying the impression of thoughts actually passing through the mind of an individual with the use of a temporary first-person narrative voice within a larger third-person narrative, and periodic modulation into the present tense in a narrative written predominantly in the past tense. Some of these passages take the form of characters, in effect, thinking aloud in sections enclosed by quotation marks: 'He seems to have gotten under my skin. And yet I can get nothing down but a lot of gabble – a lot of dry old doctrine. Somehow he made this thing a matter of life and death. What's the matter with me that I can't answer him in his own terms? I must be getting old-fashioned.'[107] In other passages, incorporated into the main body of his narrative rather than separated by quotation marks, Brooker maintains the third-person point of view but shifts to the present tense and heightens the psychological mimesis of his writing with language that abandons much of the rhetoric of traditional written narrative. These passages attempt to represent thoughts as they occur, not using the patterns of speech, but in the epistemological style of stream-of-consciousness narrative. Brooker further emphasizes that his characters are 'thinking' rather than 'talking' with unconventional punctuation and fragmentary sentence structure: 'A deep, penetrating voice. A splendid talker. He stirred you. There was almost a hint of greatness in the way he spoke – the ringing conviction – the prophetic fervour in his voice. Somewhere – in the right place – he would be an outstanding man ... What a pity! – a man like that throwing his life away – hiding his light under a bushel.'[108] The prevalence of these attempts at psychological writing in a body of work so often characterized as traditional, regional, and geographical is significant. In one respect, these passages indicate that prairie realists were profoundly concerned with representing more than a particular geographic landscape in their works; psychological realism, in fact, appears in many cases to be the primary literary aim of the prairie realist. More importantly, these passages reveal that prairie writers were willing, even compelled, to experiment with the realist form as they knew it and accordingly shared important assumptions about writing with modern writers from outside of their geographic region.

Curiously, while many of these writers were willing to go to considerable lengths to find ways of incorporating subjective points of view into their novels, only a tiny handful of prairie-realist works are narrated in the first person. The same holds true for modern-realist works in general, underlining a key problem for the modern realist: how can both subjective states and impersonal narrative exist in the same work of fiction? The first-person narrative form would seem to mitigate the all important objectivity of modern-realist writing advocated in its manifestos. The third-person narrative form requires tireless and difficult manipulation if it is to encompass a wide range of individual perspectives. This problem sheds light on many of the experiments and failures of the prairie realists and their other modern-realist counterparts: many of their techniques ought to be viewed as individual attempts to broaden the framework of the modern-realist novel to include both purportedly objective and subjective modes of expression, rather than as dim reflections of the most subjective forms of modernist expression, including impressionistic, multi-vocal, perspectivist, expressionistic, and stream-of-consciousness writing. The modern realists are not 'falling short' in an amateurish attempt to depict wholly subjective states: they are refusing to abandon their impulse toward objectivity entirely and struggling to make their impersonal form more inclusive. An examination of some of the very few works of prairie realism written in the first person helps to illustrate and clarify this tension between subjective and objective modes. Psychological perspectivism, when brought together with the more objective aspects of prairie realism through first-person narration, would win great critical acclaim for at least one prairie novel, Ross's *As For Me and My House* (1941).

Before discussing Ross's novel in the context of modern realism, it is useful to consider Stringer's prairie trilogy, *The Prairie Wife* (1915), *The Prairie Mother* (1920), and *The Prairie Child* (1922). In spite of their having appeared over a period of eight years, these three novels have a common narrator and the same ongoing chronological plot – each picks up exactly where the former leaves off, without any contextualizing passage that would make any instalment stand alone. The trilogy takes the form of a first-person diary written by the wife of a Scottish emigrant, and while the traditional tribulations of the settler experience provide much of the drama of the novels, and details of everyday life intrude into the narratives with frequency, the creation of a vivid psychological portrait is Stringer's primary concern throughout. He seizes upon the first-person perspective as a way of bringing his vivid, albeit romantic, patronizing, and at times almost misogynist, portrait of a woman of refined sensibilities to life: 'Isn't it wonderful to wake love in a man, in a strong man? To be able to sweep him off that way, on a tidal wave ... It's like taking a match and starting a prairie-fire and watching the flames creep and spread until the heaven's roaring! I wonder if I'm selfish? I wonder? But I can't answer that now, for it's supper time.'[109] While his portrait of Chaddie McKail is certainly colourful, Stringer falls short of providing the objective and detached rendering of the prairie locale demanded by many critics of prairie realism. But in 1915, works of prairie realism were few and far between, and the initial manifestos of the *Bookman* were still almost half a decade in the future. Whether the realistic depiction of the prairie locale was indeed Stringer's aim is debatable, but it seems unlikely considering the prevalent romantic thrust of Canadian writing that was still in full force at the time.

Without a body of discourse on prairie realism, or realism in Canadian writing in general, and without the third-person convention later established by other prairie realists, Stringer was able to carry out one of the most original literary projects yet seen in Canada. But some critics with regionalist expectations have been dismissive of Stringer's work. Eggleston, writing in *Literary Friends*, recalls encountering Stringer's prairie trilogy as a young man and aspiring prairie realist: 'I was disappointed in his interpretation of the prairie *milieu*, and the prairie people; but I had to admit that [his prairie novels] were highly readable, witty, entertaining, diverting.'[110] McCourt, in *The Canadian West in Fiction*, did not see Stringer, despite his psychological realism, as a realist at all: 'Stringer does not convey any strong impression of a peculiar regional atmosphere.'[111] While other prairie novels that evoke 'regional atmosphere' now rest near the centre of the prairie-realist canon, Stringer, whose psychological realism was unmatched in his day, is now treated as an afterthought by critics, so apparently unconvincing was his portrait of the prairie region. Of course these facts again stress the regional biases many readers bring to prairie realism. They also suggest reasons why almost no prairie realist would use the first-person narrative form again until the contemporary period, despite an unmistakable and ongoing concern with psychological realism. The modern-realist aesthetic, with its uncompromising interest in exploring the contemporary world, favoured a form of narrative objectivity. While the prairie realists, as artists, clearly realized from the beginning that literature had to do more than describe physical reality, hence their psychological emphasis, they recognized possibilities for achieving their aims within the traditional objective framework of the realist novel and set about experimenting with the realist form. Their projects were ambitious in scope and they usually sought to represent the subjective perspectives of a whole range of individuals, something that surely appeared impossible to achieve with a first-person narrator. The third-person perspective at least held out the promise of achieving both literary aims in the same work, and perhaps the prairie realists' failures in this regard are only readily apparent to a contemporary audience wary of terms such as 'objectivity' and accustomed to varied forms of contemporary writing that experiment with the possibilities of subjective narration. For the modern realist wholly to abandon the impulse toward objectivity would have seemed a backward turn to romanticism – the mode of writing against which the realist aesthetic was contrasted in manifesto after manifesto of the period – rather than a modern comprehension of the new realist form proliferating in Canada at the time amid much acclaim and deliberation.

The next prairie realist seriously to explore the possibilities of first-person narration was Sinclair Ross in *As For Me and My House* (1941), more than twenty years after Stringer, but this time with much more success and recognition. Ross's novel makes the importance of Stringer's work clear, even if the prairie trilogy apparently had little direct impact on the other prairie realists and critical conceptions of prairie writing. Ross's novel is undeniably structured on Stringer's work,[112] as the numerous similarities between the two efforts reveal: the female prairie diarists in both novels write at length of their powerful emotional attachments to unloving husbands; both women indirectly and perhaps unwittingly reveal their husbands' adulterous affairs; both women remark frequently upon the sense of isolation and entrapment associated with their prairie houses; both narrators reveal their unreliability through discussions of pregnancy; both women develop suggestive but vaguely defined romantic attachments to intellectual neighbours with similar names; both husbands escape their unhappy wives by secluding themselves in their studies; both wives write of avoiding sexual relations by pretending to be sleeping when their husbands come to bed at night. Ross, perhaps, sensed the possibilities for the prairie writer concerned with psychological realism suggested by Stringer's trilogy and fused this influence with what he had taken from the two decades of third-person prairie novels written since the last instalment of Stringer's trilogy. *As For Me and My House* comes closer to achieving the balance between subjective and objective expression, sought by the modern realist, than any other prairie novel written before 1950. Almost none of the technical fumbling apparent in many of the centre-of-consciousness novels is present in Ross's work, and, while he does not undertake a grand-scale representation of prairie life in his novel, the prairie town of Horizon, its surrounding physical reality, and the psychological portrait of Mrs Bentley come alive side by side, in numerous evocative passages: 'The sand and dust drifts everywhere ... I watch the little drifts form ... if the wind has been high and they have outdrifted themselves, then I look at them incredulous, and feel a strange kind of satisfaction, as if such height were an achievement for which credit was coming to me.'[113]

To be sure, Ross's critics have frequently noted his achievement in this novel. *As For Me and My House* is unquestionably the most written about novel of the period, and critics often remark upon both its psychological realism and graphic representation of the prairie, sometimes in the same comment. D.G. Jones, in *Butterfly on Rock* (1970), writes that 'the land which embodies the authentic life of the Rev. and Mrs. Bentley becomes the more sinister and haunting as it reveals unconsciously their own suppressed vitality.'[114] Such comments draw well-deserved attention to Ross's achievement in balancing objective mimetic presentation and subjective psychological states in the same work, something earlier prairie realists apparently believed was unachievable in the first-person form. They also demonstrate that psychological realism in the prairie novel is most easily recognized when it is inseparable from the representation of the physical aspects of region. The first-person form makes it impossible to discuss Ross's interpretation of the prairie environment without acknowledging Mrs Bentley's subjective perspective: as Harrison writes, 'we place Ross's *As For Me and My House* as the central expression of the prairie experience, because Ross's narrator ... expresses so well the defensive function of the imagination confronting the prairie.'[115] In the many third-person examples of prairie realism, the subjective perspectives are muted and easily detached by critics in search of a prairie landscape portrait or a particular prairie theme. Interestingly, Ross's novel, which perhaps marks the most sustained and successful realization of a key modern-realist aim in fiction – the bringing together of the modern, objective rendering of place with a subjective, psychological perspective – is also considered to mark a new beginning in Canadian writing: as Robert Kroetsch declares, 'Mrs. Bentley ... writes the beginning of contemporary Canadian fiction.'[116]

Critics often identify an inescapable deterministic force associated with prairie geography that shapes both the lives of characters in prairie novels and the form and subject matter of the prairie-realist novel itself. Calder points out that many see prairie realism and the deterministic influence of landscape to be inseparable: 'Criticism of prairie realism is predicated on a belief in the primacy of the land. Geographic determinism is evident even in the critical label: *prairie* realism.'[117] Similarly, the regionalist interpretation of prairie realism foregrounds a geographic determinism that explains the particular characteristics of a given regional experience. As Frank Davey argues, 'the reliance of regionalist ideology on environmental determinism, on a belief that landscape has – or should have – effects on the personalities and perspectives of its inhabitants, leads to the assumption that these effects should have greater importance to the individual than do other possible grounds of identity.'[118] Accordingly, both thematic and regionalist interpretations consider the psychological and dramatic action of the prairie-realist novel the result of environmental influences. This deterministic focus, together with a tendency to characterize the prairie as indifferent and destructive, leads critics to posit what Calder calls a 'tragic view of human existence.'[119] Many readings of prairie novels emphasize this 'tragic view,' depicting prairie individuals as doomed, Sisyphean figures, condemned to struggle with the land in a perilous natural world, their ultimate failure predetermined by forces larger than themselves. These readings are generally convincing until they imaginatively broaden the influence of prairie landscape so that not just fictional individuals, but prairie writers themselves, become isolated victims, overwhelmed by a prairie subject that forces them into a referential mode of expression. Harrison, for example, suggests that early prairie realists had little hand in shaping their aesthetic: 'The bleak solitude of the plains seems to have stirred the imagination,' but in 'most of the [early prairie] fiction, the writer's imagination could hardly be said to have engaged the new environment, let alone assimilated it into artistic form.'[120]

Such statements suggest that the prairie subsumes its writers and determines their subject matter and mode of expression. In this view, the geographical presence of the prairie does not merely provide the ordinary, straightforward, everyday subject matter of the prairie-realist novel; it also strips prairie writers of their artistic licence and predetermines a bare, direct, unembellished form of literary realism. This model locates the source of the unifying themes associated with prairie realism, not in the creative imagination, but in the personified prairie landscape, and suggests that these themes underlie the realist aesthetic of prairie writers: as Ricou argues, 'the landscape and man's relation to it, is the concrete situation with which the prairie artist initiates his re-creation of human experience.'[121] Following this argument, all prairie literature must necessarily be considered regional as it deals fundamentally with a human response to a particular geographic locale. As regional writing is by its very nature referential, the mimetic, realist aesthetic is the predetermined mode for all prairie writing. Placed in such a passive role, prairie writers cease to be artists in the fullest sense of the word, and they become mere transcribers, as fated to be traditional realists as the fictional prairie settler is to succumb to hostile and imposing natural forces. Curiously, some readers have tended to equate the mimetic, referential writing that results from the prairie writer's supposed passivity with aesthetic imitation, as if literary influence and geographic determinism are identical forces: as Eggleston writes, 'because of the isolation of [prairie] writers ... from the main forces of literary activity in other parts of the world, a tendency to be imitative and derivative was inescapable.'[122] There is an obvious contradiction here. Literary imitation implies a concerted effort to recreate another artistic style and, by extension, a keen awareness of that style. If prairie writers are passively applying a geographically determined literary style, then they cannot imitate. If prairie writers are imitative and derivative then their style is not geographically determined.

Obviously, both the 'imitative' and 'deterministic' interpretations of prairie writing ignore its experimental phases. As some of my readings of individual prairie novels have suggested, prairie realists are often actively engaged in transposing their own meanings and symbols onto the prairie landscape. This indicates that the prairie subject was often viewed by the prairie realists not as a monolithic, deterministic force, but as a creative opportunity that allowed them to carry out their literary experiments in relative freedom. Given the number of prairie stories taking up modern issues and with a concern for psychological realism at their centre, the prairie appears to have been viewed as a kind of open canvas, deterministic only as it effectively required that the modern writer experiment with literary form to represent it artistically. Contemporary readers will certainly find such a characterization of the prairie enormously problematic – not least because of its colonial erasure of Aboriginal cultures – but the modern realists do appear to have approached the prairie as a new and experimental possibility, and whatever literary influence informed their projects was almost entirely European and American. Like so many of the emergent subjects of the modernist age – world war, the city, feminism, radical and reactionary political philosophies – the prairie subject was so new to writers (of European descent) that it effectively demanded a new literary form. The significant number of experimental approaches to the prairie environment suggests that it is one of the most conducive subjects awaiting the creative whim of the modern realist, not an oppressive and fixed subject resisting all but the most mimetic and referential forms of expression.

While the influence of geographic determinism on the prairie-realist aesthetic has been overemphasized, it is impossible to deny the thematic presence of this force in many prairie-realist works where the pressures of prairie life are depicted as a challenge to imported cultural notions and an influence upon social behaviour. Stereotypical portraits of practical, hard-working, isolated, and emotionally stunted settlers abound in prairie realism – Niels Lindstedt, Lina Ashley, Abe Spalding, Caleb Gare, Gander Stake, to name a few. The harshness of settler life clearly has a degenerative impact on many of these individuals, and by extension much of their hardship can be traced to the influence of the prairie landscape. Arising from this geographical influence, it is possible to identify an essentially 'tragic view' of prairie existence, even if one ignores the fact that many of the so-called tragic prairie novels provide 'happy' endings. In her 'preface' to *In Due Season* (1947), Van Der Mark provides an outline of her novel that emphasizes many traditional characteristics of the prairie-realist novel, including isolation, hardship, spiritual decline, and the idea of nation-building: 'This is the story of a woman, alone, forced to work ... to wrest a living from the land. This is also the story of a pioneer community. There is the constant passing of seedtime and harvest, and the pushing back of the wilderness. The community grows and develops; the woman degenerates in spirit. For it is the very soul, as well as human blood and bone, which goes into the building of a new land.'[123] However, this general pattern of the prairie-realist novel holds true for only a limited number of the relatively few prairie novels that posit deterministic influences in the first place. In other works, the deterministic forces that drive plot and psychological character development have little to do with geographic pressures. Instead, they are the result of individual psychological factors, or sociological concerns, or historical circumstances.

The central character in Grove's *Our Daily Bread* (1928), John Elliott, actually triumphs over the travails placed in his path by the prairie environment. The tragedy in this novel results from Elliott's psychological flaws and his failure to develop healthy relationships with his children. If *Our Daily Bread* is deterministic, then this determinism has little or nothing to do with geography. Several of Grove's prairie novels, in fact, appear to derive much of their sense of determinism from European naturalism, an almost scientific approach to realism that among other things emphasizes heredity, evolution, social influences, historical circumstances, and an exploration of many of the more traditionally taboo aspects of human existence, including sexuality, psychological disturbance, and animal impulses. Irene Gammel, in *Sexualizing Power in Naturalism: Theodore Dreiser and Frederick Philip Grove*, reads Grove's writing as part of a North American naturalist renaissance rooted in European tradition: 'Though naturalism is often seen as a nineteenth-century European literary reaction to the industrial and Darwinian revolution, the twentieth century witnessed a renaissance of naturalist forms in North America at a time when modernism, with its formal and generic experimentations, was about to establish itself as the dominant paradigm of literature.'[124] Although it is difficult to trace the specific influence of naturalism on prairie writers other than Grove, owing to a dearth of critical and archival material, in many cases the determinism of prairie novels appears to derive from an attempt by their authors to offer a kind of 'scientific' study of the individual in the modern world, rather than from a regional, geographic interest. McCourt's *Music at the Close* (1947) offers the story of Neil Fraser, a twentieth-century everyman who appears fated to die a meaningless death in the Second World War, and many of the major events of his life anticipate his end. Craig Forrester of Durkin's *The Magpie* (1923) sees his idealistic hopes systematically destroyed by twentieth-century social and historical forces much larger than himself and his prairie environment. Stead's *Dry Water* (1935), despite its depression-era setting, equates the Strand family's demise not with geographically imposed hardship, but with large economic forces and swift social and political change. And even some of the prairie-realist novels that *do* depict a kind of geographic determinism at work often suggest that this force is not the product of physical environment alone: as Gunnars writes of Grove's *Settlers of the Marsh* (1925), '[Neils] is not sure whether he can control his own fate ... [he] is at the mercy of circumstance, origin, and time.'[125]

As these examples reveal, the prairie realists, rather than passively rendering tales in which geographic determinism is the catalyst behind plot and character development, frequently structure their novels around their own dramatic concerns. In Grove's *Fruits of the Earth* (1933), the structure and subject matter reflect a highly personal artistic vision. Like *Our Daily Bread, Fruits of the Earth* explores not the influence of environment on the individual but the influence of the individual, in this case Abe Spalding, on the environment: 'With his mind's eye he looked upon the district from a point in time twenty years later.'[126] Grove's novel has all of the makings of a grand-scale sociological and psychological study in the naturalistic style. The author superimposes his own aesthetic vision over the prairie landscape, prefacing the novel with a 'Map of the Spalding District' that lays out the imaginary geography of his fictional world. Grove also draws attention to his own almost scientific approach to writing in his 'Author's Note,' explaining that he offers a 'composite impression' that came into being after he had 'investigated' the 'history' of farms similar to the one he depicts in the novel. Spalding is less a product of the prairie milieu than a man who imports his own hereditary and cultural values into a more or less blank geographic space. Grove's 'Author's Note' hints at Abe's heredity and agency, likening him to 'a race of giants.'[127] Abe comes to Manitoba from Ontario, bringing with him his own predispositions and a 'land hunger' that reflects his desire to control his new world: 'He dreamt of a time when he would buy up the abandoned farms ... he saw himself prosperous ... Abe was a man of economic vision.'[128] Furthermore, Grove's novel depicts the closed social world typical of the naturalistic novel in which authors carry out their creative social experiments. Abe Spalding is the central figure, and the action of the whole novel supports his psychological development as he becomes increasingly successful materially and increasingly incapable of developing and maintaining emotional attachments. His eventual defeat appears predetermined, coming after his heroic efforts to subdue his world. But, in true naturalistic fashion, it results from his own inabilities to alter innate patterns of behaviour: 'He had meant to do what, in his weariness, seemed fulfilment of his desires. True resignation meant accepting one's destiny; to him it meant accepting the burden of leadership ... His own life had been wrong, or all this would not have happened.'[129] Grove's novel, in spite of its ironically earthy title, has little to do with the prairie environment. It is a sustained character study, written largely in accordance with the traditions of European naturalism, and as such offers a key example of a prairie realist using the creative possibilities of the prairie subject to suit his own artistic aims.

As a culturally neutral (for the writer of European descent) and, in the early twentieth century, largely unexplored subject, the prairie provided a curiously timeless and receptive space in which the prairie writer could create stories of psychological intensity, often with little attention to spatial markers and geographic mimesis. In an especially perceptive reading of *Wild Geese* (1925), Keahey remarks that Ostenso uses the creative freedom afforded by prairie in just this way, inscribing the region with her own artistic vision: 'For a novel in which "place" plays such a central role, Ostenso seems not to have wanted to "place" it. The desire to have the setting unmarked by explicit regional or national location may be linked ... to the fact that she was writing it specifically for the purpose of submission to the best North American novel contest ... In other words, an explicit rural Manitoba setting may have been regarded as too "regional" ... for Ostenso's "international" aspirations.'[130] The result of Ostenso's refusal to 'place' *Wild Geese* is a story of remarkable psychological depth for its period, and Ostenso uses the open prairie subject to reflect the temperaments of her vivid characters. The prairie she describes is symbolic, often reflecting her character's mental states, and more a product of her own literary imagination than a landscape portrait drawn from careful observation: 'As he rode along, a mood of loneliness overtook him ... A steady blue was creeping over the prairie in place of the magnificent light that had been there the moment before ... He lifted his face up to catch the strange sound that was passing over him, a great summoning trumpet-call, that seemed to hollow out the heavens.'[131]

For prairie writers concerned with an exploration of the most modern of human concerns, the prairie can be shaped to become an almost mythical, archetypal, 'everyplace' in which grand-scale twentieth-century concerns are easily explored. The prairie of the early twentieth century, to the non-aboriginal writer or settler, was often a place without cultural baggage, large-scale social structures, mythological codes, or literary tradition. Accordingly, it freed prairie writers to explore their own cultural values, sociological interests, symbolic patterns, and aesthetic forms in an uninhibited space. In Eggleston's *The High Plains* (1938), a modern form of 'wasteland' symbolism is ascribed to the prairie, and the author manipulates the prairie landscape to make it reflect his broader concerns with the modern sense of malaise and disillusionment that results from major historical events of the twentieth century: 'A progressive deterioration of the countryside was under way ... the finer grasses and flowers were disappearing ... The villages shrivelled in sympathy ... The dance hall burned down and was not rebuilt'; 'Robert had returned from Germany ... There was an ugly scar across his forehead almost to his ear. His right arm was amputated above the elbow. He was thin and drawn, and his eyes were often dark with pain.'[132] The prairie of Eggleston's novel is not a photographic reproduction of a 'real' space; it is a fictional creation that exists to mirror larger sensibilities and the psychological impact of modern events upon individuals.

McCourt is less subtle in his attempts to make the lives of his prairie characters stand representative of the modern human condition, and he too takes advantage of the cultural neutrality of the prairie to infuse his character studies with larger historical significance. To emphasize the broad thrust of his stories, McCourt links them to a larger twentieth-century experience through the frequent use of historical reference and allusion. His *Music at the Close* (1947), already discussed for its representations of the world wars, details the life of a man who becomes disillusioned with the modern world and is senselessly destroyed by political forces larger than himself. In this novel, key allusions mark progressive stages in the protagonist's process of disillusionment. In one passage, Neil Fraser reads the poetry of T.S. Eliot, though, as a young man, he has only begun to be critical of the world around him and he finds the poetry unsatisfying: 'He found Eliot at first incomprehensible. But as he read on, the words, which in themselves seemed without meaning, began to weave a strange and sinister spell. He was first depressed then savagely rebellious. Surely the end of poetry was not to plunge men into black despair? But "The Hollow Men" and "The Love Song of J. Alfred Prufrock" could have been intended to serve no other purpose.'[133] A more complex pattern of literary allusion runs throughout McCourt's later novel, *The Wooden Sword* (1956), in which the protagonist is pushed to the edge of mental breakdown by, among other things, his inability to deal with horrifying memories of his Second World War past. McCourt links the experiences of Steven Venner to the grand-scale experience of the twentieth century by juxtaposing literary allusions, and references to well-known historical events, with Venner's own private history: 'Abe Lincoln died, Grandad died, Mother died, and death was corruption ... No trumpets sounding. Only the bell in the church-tower that I heard from my bedroom window then for a long time afterwards. Never ask for whom the bell tolls. *Here, coffin that slowly passes, I give you my sprig of lilac*. Spring and lilac-time and death.'[134] McCourt perhaps overuses the technique of allusion, and at times the contrast between his evocative mythological images and their prairie background appears too striking: 'The cloud rose up like a great wave, like a fringed black scarf flung soundlessly skywards, like the upraised hair of some fierce Maenad lusting to envelop and destroy.'[135] Yet McCourt is clearly exploiting the receptiveness of the prairie subject, even as late as 1956, to suit his own artistic intentions and to tell a kind of 'universal' story.

The prairie realists held individual, creative, and experimental conceptions of how the prairie might be represented, and of how the prairie milieu could be used to explore the same issues and concerns that interested their modern-realist contemporaries in other parts of Canada and beyond. The prairie subject offered a full range of creative opportunities, and presented an environment that, for the most traditional prairie realists, provided everyday, observable details and activities to represent. For the writer with experimental inclinations, the prairie offered a chance to explore modern concerns, be they psychological, sociological, historical, or purely imaginative, within limits defined only by the individual artist. While criticism of prairie realism has encouraged the identification of unifying geographical and thematic patterns, it is the experimental and eclectic individualism of the prairie realist that is perhaps most significant to the development of modern fiction in Canada. I have explored this subject in broad terms in this chapter, with attention to the contribution of prairie realism to the modern-realist movement and Canadian modernism more generally. In the next chapter, I explore this same 'experimental and eclectic individualism' in the oeuvre of the most infamous of the prairie realists.

5

Frederick Philip Grove's Eclectic Realism and 'The Great Tradition'

Frederick Philip Grove is an uncooperative and inconvenient modern realist. The well-known inconsistencies of his life story aside, his novels offer a troublesome mixture of some of the most ambitious experiments and spectacular failures in all of Canadian literature. He wrote some of the best-known and representative modern-realist novels, and some of the most atypical, peculiar, misunderstood, and ignored examples of the genre. Grove derived his writerly principles from an idiosyncratic melange of half-understood and partially assimilated aesthetics, including various nineteenth-century realisms and naturalisms, several forms of Anglo-American modernism, romanticism, classical drama, and all three major sub-genres of Canada's modern realism: prairie realism, social realism, and urban realism. Complicating matters further, his prolific and often misleading critical statements on modernity and realism in literature are filtered through a frequently defensive, deceptive, and self-conscious persona: as Margaret Stobie writes, 'Grove liked to pontificate, but it often meant little.'[1] Grove's lack of formal critical training results in his imprecise application of literary terminology, making most of his critical statements appear convoluted, ambiguous, at times even contradictory or opaque. Yet Grove is a giant on the Canadian literary scene of the early twentieth century, probably its highest-profile writer of fiction, and there is scarcely an aspect of the modern-realist movement that does not bear his imprint: he contributed to both *Canadian Bookman* and *The Canadian Forum* in their early years, he was discussed more frequently than any other new modern writer in Canada during the 1920s and '30s, he corresponded with most of the other major modern realists, he wrote numerous manifesto-style articles outlining his thoughts on modernity and realism in Canadian and foreign writing, he travelled widely in Canada lecturing to the general public about countless literary subjects (including modern realism), he had a hand in publishing some of Canada's modern-realist fiction, and he was one of the most prolific modern-realist authors of the period, writing well-known examples of both social realism and prairie realism.

In spite of the varied and eclectic nature of Grove's work, he is most often considered a prairie realist. He is without a doubt the pre-eminent prairie writer of his generation: he wrote more prairie novels than any of his contemporaries except Stead, and the body of critical work on his prairie fiction is large. Grove's works are considered at length in all major critical surveys of prairie realism; there have been several book-length studies that consider his prairie works exemplary of their genre; and his four prairie novels – *Settlers of the Marsh* (1925), *Our Daily Bread* (1928), *The Yoke of Life* (1930), and *Fruits of the Earth* (1933) – were among the most widely read and discussed Canadian novels of their day. No other prairie realist came close to achieving the literary recognition that Grove enjoyed: his two books of nature sketches, *Over Prairie Trails* (1922) and *The Turn of the Year* (1923), were among the most reviewed books in Canada upon their release. He took three much-publicized national reading tours of Canada in 1928–9 and received more official acknowledgment than any of his contemporaries. He was awarded the Lorne Pierce Medal in 1934, was elected to the Royal Society of Canada in 1941, and won the Governor General's Award for his penultimate published work, *In Search of Myself*, in 1946. While all of these circumstances have led to a portrait of Grove as the archetypal prairie realist – the strategies critics have employed in their examinations of Grove's work have greatly influenced the critical reception of prairie realism in general – he was not singly, or even predominantly, a prairie writer. His own comments reveal that he saw himself as a 'modern' writer, working in an international 'tradition,' and he certainly did not consider himself a member of a 'school' of prairie realists.

Apart from four prairie novels and two books of prairie nature sketches, Grove published widely in his lifetime, including two novels set in Ontario; a volume of essays on literary, cultural, and political matters; an allegorical science fiction novel about an ant colony; a volume of autobiography; a vaguely autobiographical novel set predominantly in the United States; and, under his real name, Felix Paul Greve, two German novels entitled *Fanny Essler* (1905) and *Mauermeister Ihles Haus* (1906), which have been translated into English. This chapter explores Grove's eclectic realism in relation to the larger modern-realist movement. Rife with fascinating contradictions, Grove's critical statements begin to explain his elusive and problematic literary aesthetic when examined in the context of modern realism. Grove's work embodies tensions between highly traditional and experimental impulses, between regional and 'universal' subjects and concerns, between referential and symbolic modes of expression, and between a modern-realist and a highly individualistic literary identity. This chapter, while exploring Grove's expression and negotiation of these various tensions, reads his often misunderstood realism and elucidates his 'modernity.' The image of Grove that emerges remains enigmatic, and many aspects of his writing cannot be accounted for under the rubric of modern realism. But his vocal and individualistic struggles to come to terms with many of the same aesthetic tensions and issues faced by his modern-realist contemporaries, even when his techniques and methods are atypical, reveal much about the movement and genre as a whole.

It is not surprising, given his pre-eminence among prairie realists and many of the critical assumptions about prairie realism discussed earlier, that much Grove criticism articulates a thematic emphasis and offers him up as a paradigmatic writer, dedicated to the regionalist's duty of transcribing a prairie landscape and social environment. As Pacey writes in *Frederick Philip Grove* (1944), the first full-length study of his work, 'life to Grove is a perpetual struggle, a struggle of man to assert his will against the various pressures of the environment.'[2] McCourt echoed these sentiments in *The Canadian West in Fiction* (1949), which berated many of Grove's works and achievements but nevertheless dubiously justified his contribution to Canadian letters on the basis of its regional and documentary significance; many more recent critics have followed suit. Grove's critics have also placed much emphasis on the imitative aspects of his writing, suggesting that his sensibilities and literary forms were derived from European tradition. Often his work is considered a dim reflection of late nineteenth-century European fiction.[3] Much of the broad range of criticism on Grove and his oeuvre generally acknowledges that his traditionalism is creative and eclectic and finds an awkward modernity in his writing. As Ronald Sutherland argues, 'there is a complexity, a multiplicity, indeed a modernity about the man and his writing which have largely escaped critical attention.'[4] Some of Grove's most prolific critics, including Irene Gammel, Klaus Martens, and D.O. Spettigue, have made Sutherland's case convincingly with sustained examinations of Grove's affinities with modern European literatures.[5] On the one hand, then, Grove is sometimes positioned as a traditional realist, labouring to adapt outmoded European forms to a realistic representation of Canada's prairie. On the other, his most perceptive critics identify a 'modern sensibility' in his work, although what this means in precise terms remains, like Grove's life story, an elusive subject open to much speculation and debate. Several studies explain the apparent tension between modern and traditional impulses in his writing by emphasizing its naturalist properties. The questions surrounding Grove's concepts and applications of naturalism have still not been resolved by his critics, and a brief survey of their comments on the subject uncovers numerous emphatic yet remarkably dissonant statements.[6]

On the surface at least, a naturalistic affinity on Grove's part would appear to explain the curious blend of realism and modern experiment in his work. Naturalism, a late nineteenth-century form with its advocacy of an artless, at times formless, brand of realism, might explain the loose, even clumsy structure of most of Grove's novels, most notably *Our Daily Bread* (1928), *The Yoke of Life* (1930), and *Two Generations* (1939). Furthermore, the naturalistic emphasis upon biological and social determinism in characterization and plot seems to account for the inescapable fates of some of Grove's key characters, including John Elliott and Abe Spalding. And naturalism, with its interest in the sordid, vulgar, and taboo aspects of human life, perhaps explains Grove's well-documented, fictional interest in sexual matters. A naturalistic presence is most detectable in two of Grove's prairie works, *Our Daily Bread* (1928) and *Fruits of the Earth* (1933), and many of Grove's comments on the art of fiction demonstrate his affinity with some of the characteristics and aims of naturalism. For example, in a 1929 essay entitled 'The Novel [1],'[7] Grove reveals that his techniques of characterization rely upon psychological determinism: 'The novel presents an emotional crisis in the life of its hero or heroine. But the emotional crisis is not barely "sprung" on the reader; it is led up to from its antecedents in circumstance and character; its unavoidable necessity is shown.'[8] Yet in spite of his rhetoric, Grove openly, and probably unwittingly, rebels against other conventions of naturalism, and according to his critical conception of the term at least, he is definitely *not* a naturalist. In 'Realism and Literature' (1929), Grove draws a distinction between Flaubert, a writer he greatly admires, who, 'growing out of the Romantic School, became a realist,' and Zola, whom he deprecates and labels a 'naturalist': 'With this Flaubert, the mature, self-critical, and austere artist, Zola, the naturalist, has no connection whatever ... A naturalist in English means a scientist ... To him the novel was not an art-form which enabled him to cast on his canvas a picture of life as he saw it; it was a "scientific experiment" ... The moment we examine these scientific pretensions of Zola's ... they appear singularly weak, confused, and altogether lacking in the permanent power of art.'[9] Grove associates literary value with what he calls 'realism,' and he sees realism as an outgrowth of the romantic sensibility. Naturalism, to Grove (and his definition of the term is broadly in line with most accepted definitions), may be modern with its emphasis upon science, but it does not fulfil his requirements for 'realistic' writing and 'the permanent power of art': as Grove says of Zola's naturalism, it 'produced artificially facts and sequences of facts.'[10]

Grove's comments suggest that a conventional view of naturalism only partially defines his aesthetic and does not wholly account for his particular brand of determinism. Naturalism, however broadly defined, cannot account for the broad range of impulses and concerns, both traditional and modern, that make up what Grove repeatedly calls 'realism.' An examination of his works in relation to his critical statements on the subject reveals that realism, to Grove, is a modern and experimental form with its roots nevertheless deeply embedded in literary traditions that go back as far as ancient Greece. Grove supplements the oldest aspects of this heritage, notably the concepts of fate and poetic justice often identified by his thematic critics, with many of the techniques of European naturalism. His critical statements also reveal that he was aware of many of the boldest and most experimental forms of high modernism and had read the works of Woolf, Joyce, Lawrence, Stein, Conrad, Chekhov, and T.S. Eliot, among many others. Importantly, and like other Canadian modern realists, Grove disregards many of the most experimental high-modernist techniques – especially those aimed at the sustained and unmediated representation of subjective states – but undeniably favours innovation in writing, and he argues for a modern and experimental interpretation of the realist novel. Grove sums up his thoughts on realism in terms that are broadly in line with the definitions of modern realism found in the literary manifestos of the 1920s and in the works of many of his contemporaries, including Knister and Callaghan. But in spite of the undeniably modern-realist aspects of his work, Grove cannot be singularly labelled a 'modern realist.' He remains, to a significant degree, an anomalous figure, subscribing to many of the assumptions of the modern realists, yet often neglecting, failing, or refusing to execute their narrative strategies in his work. Most dramatically, and through much ambitious experiment, Grove redirects the central preoccupation of the modern realist – psychological realism and epistemological emphasis – toward a broad, universal, historical probing of the human condition that links contemporary Canada to what he calls 'the great tradition.'[11] In so doing, he demonstrates the flexibility of the modern-realist form in the hands of the innovative writer and reveals himself to be paradoxically one of the most traditional and most experimental modern realists.

In spite of Grove's bold critical statements on the importance of innovation in writing, and his clear alliance of realism with experiment, many critics consider him a conservative writer. Such a characterization is substantiated by many of Grove's claims, and certainly by many of the traditional features of his novels, including their attention to detail, omniscient third-person narratives, and sweeping attempts at social realism reminiscent of nineteenth-century European works, especially those by Balzac, Tolstoy, Dickens, and George Eliot. This orthodox characterization of Grove – which can be traced back at least as far as *The Canadian Forum* and articles such as Robert Ayre's 'Frederick Philip Grove' (1932) discussed earlier – may derive from a misunderstanding of Grove's concept of 'the great tradition.' Interestingly, while Grove discusses a 'Great Tradition' in his 1929 essay 'Literary Criticism,' F.R. Leavis's *The Great Tradition* was not published until the year of Grove's death, 1948. For Grove, literary value depends upon a writer's engagement of works that have come before, and he argues that the critic's job is to evaluate new works of fiction by this seemingly conservative set of criteria: 'True criticism cannot help judging because it refers one thing to another; it measures all things by standards derived from the comparison of many works produced in the past, or derived from the great tradition – which it presumes to be permanent because it denies, outside of that tradition, the essential progress of man. Progress on earth *consists* in that very tradition.'[12] In one sense, Grove is articulating the well-known modernist approach to tradition offered up by T.S. Eliot in his 1919 essay 'Tradition and the Individual Talent': 'Tradition ... involves, in the first place, the historical sense ... and the historical sense involves a perception, not only of the pastness of the past, but of its presence; the historical sense compels a man to write not merely with his own generation in his bones, but with the feeling that the whole of the literature of Europe from Homer and within it the whole of the literature of his own country has a simultaneous existence and composes a simultaneous order.'[13]

Nevertheless, however much Grove may wish to establish his works in a rich literary heritage, his view of history and 'the great tradition' is not entirely Eliotonian: he apparently does not perceive a modern break in the long line of cultural continuity, and his realist aesthetic favours not fragmentation but aesthetic unity, not literary allusion but contemporaneity and attention to the actual lives of living individuals. For Grove, 'the great tradition' represents a kind of universal truth, the sum total of the creation of all great writers through the ages who have aimed at the representation of timeless human experiences. For a work of art to be a part of 'the great tradition' a kind of 'universal' vision must rest at its centre. Curiously, Grove aligns this form of writing, the polar opposite of regional depictions of surface events and details of everyday life, with what he calls 'realism.' The writer becomes a realist, in Grove's opinion, when he treats grand-scale themes and issues, not surface minutiae. As he argues in 'Realism in Literature' (1929), 'the artist – or the realist; for to me, personally ... the two terms are synonymous – must mirror, in his presentation, an emotional response to the outside world and to life which is ... a universal response.'[14] And Grove differentiates between this kind of 'universal' realism and the brand of regional realism often attributed to him and his contemporaries: 'a work produced to-day may hold a great appeal through its very inessentials; through the accuracy, for instance, with which it reproduces, in fiction, certain aspects of modern life.'[15] Ultimately, insists Grove, for a work to be realistic and to have significant literary value, this vague question must be asked and answered in the affirmative: 'Does this work, or does it not, reveal a new corner of the timeless human soul?'[16]

Grove's definition of realism outlined so far is anything but conventional and would appear to have little to do either with the modern world or with modern realism. Stobie disregards the critical value of Grove's comments on the subject altogether, suggesting that 'realism apparently meant whatever Grove happened to like in literature'; 'The distinctions that he drew were arbitrary ones without much validity ... [they] are not very helpful and do not mean much in terms of Grove's own writing.'[17] While many of Grove's individual comments on the subject are indeed misleading, when his statements are viewed in total we see that his definition of realism is more broadly in line with the idea of modern realism put forth in the literary manifestos of the 1920s. A more conventional concept of literary realism is articulated by Grove in 'The Novel [1]': 'Both Short Story and Novel ... deal with *socially sig-*

nificant things from the main stream of life. In them, both characters and happenings must be more or less typical for a given society. They must be the normal, natural growth of given conditions actually existing in our midst. In reading them, we must be living the lives depicted as if they were our own.'[18] This aspect of Grove's definition appears reflective of much traditional nineteenth-century realism, emphasizing the importance of social concerns, the need to create representative characters, and the referential recreation of a given milieu.

Nevertheless, in another essay published in 1929, 'A Neglected Function of a Certain Literary Association,' Grove also links realism implicitly to the new, emerging culture in Canada in the 1920s, employing rhetoric that is reminiscent of the *Bookman* manifestos: 'It is only natural that a nascent literature, arising in a young country which is on every hand surrounded by old civilizations, should, from a spirit of self-assertion, emphasize those features, conditions, mental and spiritual attitudes which distinguish its life and its nationals from those of other and older countries.'[19] Like the *Bookman* critics, Grove considers the emerging realism in Canada an inherent part of the growing sense of cultural nationalism. In an unpublished piece, entitled 'Art and Canadian Life,' he calls for young writers in Canada to reflect this 'spirit' in their new forms of writing: 'We must see the new spirit which indeed is stirring here and there in every trifle that we handle every day.'[20] If Grove's call for a mimetic aesthetic is only implicit in this statement, he makes this aim clear elsewhere in the same article, extolling writers to reflect a clearly recognizable, modern Canada in their works: 'to the writer: Show us Canadian life and make us realise what we feel but dimly; namely that it is a new kind of life, a kind which has never been lived before anywhere on Earth. Let painter and writer do that and we shall concede to them that they stand in the great tradition of all art.'[21] In this example, Grove brings together what on the surface appear to be two contradictory poles of his sense of the new realism in Canada. On the one hand it ought to reflect 'the great tradition'; on the other it ought to represent a 'new kind of life' that is distinctly Canadian. The challenge awaiting the realist, in Grove's view, is to find ways of creating literature that is unmistakably Canadian yet at the same time representative of the 'universal' human truths that he indicates are the subject of all great modern and realistic literature.

All of Grove's major experiments with the realist form, then, grow out of this concern: how can literature mimetically reflect Canada but move beyond the surface details of everyday life to reveal the issues of broader significance underneath? This concern is very similar to that raised by Knister in a letter discussed earlier: 'How to impart a hint of the wonder and mystery behind the circumstances, yet remain true to these latter?'[22] However, the experimental forms of realism that Grove's novels apply toward the exploration of universal human concerns are different from Knister's. Grove's novels reflect contemporary Canadian life, as the modern realist demands, while pursuing his ideal for modern literature and wrestling with the grand-scale subjects worthy of 'the great tradition.' This dual emphasis proves to be a difficult literary enterprise. For his part, Grove tells us that his Canadian novels, and in particular his prairie novels, sought to apply an old tradition to a new context: as he writes in an unpublished address entitled 'Mrs. President * Ladies of the Canadian Club': 'I returned to the pioneers. What was it that drew me? ... In a world gone insane with transportation and speed; in a world forgetting eternal things in the hunt for material things ... these pioneers stand unmoved ... concerned with the eternally valid thing – valid no matter where life is lived, no matter when.'[23] For Grove, the prairie is a creative possibility awaiting his 'realistic' interpretation. In what Grove usually considered a culturally neutral, timeless, receptive, open literary realm of the prairie, he perceives a universalism. Like the 'open' prairie subject of other modern realists who find it conducive to their symbolic and psychological explorations of modern concerns, Grove's prairie, rather than determining his passive interpretation of subject matter, allows him to inscribe his own concerns onto it.

To a degree, this explains the determinism found in Grove's novels, especially the prairie novels, in which his protagonists – Niels Lindstedt, John Elliott, Len Sterner, Abe Spalding – appear driven to their final circumstances by forces largely beyond their control. Pacey makes this point directly in his 1944 book on Grove, although later critics would largely supplant this notion of Grove's tragedy with the naturalistic interpretation: he remarks upon a 'view of man's conduct as determined by forces external to him' before suggesting that 'Grove's conception of these forces ... resembles rather the Greek conception of Fate than the scientific determinism of the naturalists.'[24] If at times Grove's novels appear contrived and unrealistic – the marriage that provides a happy ending to Grove's *Settlers of the Marsh* comes to mind – this may have more to do with his concepts of fate and poetic justice than with a lapse in his realism. In two of his other prairie novels, the endings are not so fortunate, and the declines of Abe Spalding and John Elliott are perhaps governed by Grove's notions of the tragic view of human life, put forth in his 1929 essay 'The Happy Ending': 'It is the universal verdict of mankind at its highest that the feeling released in the human soul by the contemplation of life is tragic; and therefore, by inference, that human life itself is a tragic thing.'[25] It is clear that Grove's fundamental concern with the prairie is not referential or linked to its propensity for regional representations of everyday, ordinary life. Rather, the prairie affords Grove the opportunity to explore his grand tragic and comic 'truths' about human existence. In this sense, Grove may be departing from conventional conceptions of realism, yet he is certainly keeping his own preoccupation with 'the great tradition' and its universal themes at the centre of his artistic vision, thereby being a 'true' realist by his own definitions.

As conservative as many of Grove's concepts of realistic literature may appear, there is little doubt that he considered himself an experimental writer, much as the other modern realists did. Although he wrote poems, short stories, and essays, Grove was fundamentally a novelist, and he saw the novel as a new and highly experimental form of literature, as he makes clear in another unpublished and undated essay, 'The Technique of the Novel': 'Contrary to the belief of some people that the novel, after a career of a hundred and fifty years, has pretty well run its course, I hold that it stands on the very threshold of its potentialities. But, whether I am right in this or not, it certainly is fact that the novel is very much alive today; and this is surely attested to by the fact that it is still highly experimental.'[26] Again, Grove links this experimentalism to the particular aim of realism that he favours: the expression of 'universal truths.' At the same time, Grove considered the novel a distinctly modern art form, and he believed that the realist ought to use the boundless potential of the novel to explore modern themes, concerns, and issues, always with attention to the larger truths that he maintained were the substance of literature in 'the great tradition.' Grove's descriptions of the novel form are strikingly modern and were perhaps derived from his surprisingly broad readings in the genre.[27] In a passage from Grove's unpublished article 'The Novel [2],' he represents the novel in a light that is as true of the European high-modernist example as it is of his own peculiar realism:

> Even as it stands today, experimental, chaotic, the novel is, artistically speaking, the most powerful, the most adaptable form of expression which the human mind and soul have ever devised for themselves. It lends itself

> to every purpose which modern man may wish to see served. It can do what, so far, no other art form has been able to do, namely lay open and view the mainsprings, not only of action but of being as well. It can reveal to us with equal clarity what is conscious in us and what remains subconscious or unconscious ... it can conclusively deal with ... every problem of sociology, morals, or philosophy. There is no limit to its possibilities.[28]

Given the largely traditional form of Grove's own novels, his experimental conception of the novel form at first seems surprising. But if there appears to be a contradiction in Grove's thinking, it is only because his conception of what marks legitimate experimentation in the novel (and this is typical of the Canadian modern realist in general) differs substantially from that of most of the Anglo-American high modernists.

Like his friend and contemporary Raymond Knister, Grove was particular about the kind of literary experiment he approved. While he celebrated the novel as a modern and experimental form, Grove was openly hostile to the most self-consciously experimental fiction produced in his day. At the same time as he openly advocated experiment with the realist form towards the realization of 'universal' concerns, he was put off by literary virtuosity, or what he considered literary experiment for its own sake. In his unpublished radio talk, 'Literary Criticism' (1938), Grove publicly demeaned what critics have retrospectively termed high modernism: 'The critic will recognise the enduring thing no matter how gaudily it be bedecked with the baubles of juvenile antics.'[29] Nevertheless, it is important to note that Grove also called for critics to suspend their judgments about the experimental novel and to recognize that much innovation was happening in fiction that was not easily understood: 'If, in the novel – just now the most experimental of all forms of expression – we meet with things to which we are inclined to deny the attribute of beauty, we should hesitate before passing sentence.'[30] Grove's apparent waffling on this issue of experiment in writing is explained by an examination of his concept of 'modernity.' In accordance with his notion that a modern form of realism brought together universal truth and contemporary circumstances, Grove contended that modernity and experimentation in literature were not new concepts: 'The spirit of true art has always been iconoclastic: to use a modern phrase, it is always "experimental."'[31] While Grove was critical of many modernist writers, including Joyce, Woolf, and Stein, he was a great admirer of earlier modernists, including Conrad and Lawrence. But even in his attempts to describe the technique of Lawrence in his unpublished 'Technique of the Novel,' and in spite of his preference for experimental writing, he again arrives at a seemingly conservative stance: 'In fact, as far as methods are concerned, I am unable to see in Lawrence a great innovator; when I ask myself in just what the greatness of Lawrence consisted, I find no answer but that he managed to do what all great artists have done, namely to pour new wine into old skins. It has always been the criterion of true greatness ... that it is not overscrupulous about being original. Goethe said, "I take what is mine wherever I find it."'[32] In this sense, Grove's notion of experiment is broadly in line with the ideas of other modern realists, including Knister, Callaghan, and the *Bookman* manifesto writers. For the modern realist, literary experiment and technical innovation are neither characteristic nor atypical of the modern; a modern literature is involved in a representation of its contemporary environment by whatever technical means necessary. For Grove, modernity and experiment are relative terms. They are characteristic of every age. Writers are modern and experimental, or, in Grove's lexicon, 'realistic,' not when they strive for virtuosity, but rather through identification with an eternally modern spirit.

Grove's realism emphasizes the 'universal' subject matter he favours and suggests that he believes writing is experimental when it seeks to reconcile such an emphasis with contemporary circumstances. But Grove has much to say about exactly how, technically, this aim is to be realized in early twentieth-century Canada. As Grove contends, realism is more about technique and form than subject matter: 'But – and this is the important point – realism in this mistaken sense is a matter of the choice of subject, not of literary procedure; realism in my sense is a matter of literary procedure, not of the choice of subject.'[33] If Grove's own statements are taken at face value, the techniques of his modern realism, like those of the other modern realists, fall largely under the heading of psychological realism. Grove wrote of this aspect of fiction in 'The Novel [3]': 'Let me express it this way: you do not see actors; or in other words, the novel aims at *psychologic illusion*.'[34] Still, despite the prominence of psychological realism in Grove's novels – note his intense psychological portraits of Niels Lindstedt, Ruth Spalding, and Len Sterner – its precise nature has proven difficult to define. This is largely because Grove's idea of psychological realism is, not surprisingly, at odds with standard definitions and is bound up both in his notion that universal truth is at the heart of realistic writing and in his guiding principle that the human experience is tragic. In another unpublished essay, 'Some Aspects of a Writer's Life,' Grove discusses the problem of achieving this sort of psychological realism in the novel and reveals that this aim underlies much of his literary experiment: 'One of the strange things about this sort of work is that a given psychological development ... may be perfectly obvious, logical, and cogent to the writer's mind; but he cannot see his way clear towards making this development of this action appear natural, necessary, and inevitable to others. There are, of course, a thousand purely technical devices which he may try; occasionally I had tried scores of them in succession.'[35] For Grove, psychological realism is equated with the act not of mimetically reflecting human consciousness or of depicting modern psychological themes, but rather of making his depiction of universal truth unfold in a convincing, realistic manner, and this remarkably does not necessarily entail the representation of a single mind or psyche. Unlike most of the modern realists and the high modernists in their epistemological phases, the individual human consciousness is not his concern; he is interested in 'universal' psychological truths, and his novels aim to offer objective portraits of individuals or communities that are psychologically driven and derided by the tragic, or tragicomic, nature of the human condition.

Grove's confusing thoughts and aims in this regard are made clearer in his statements on many of the high-modernist experiments of the period that aim for the mimetic representation of human consciousness, including stream-of-consciousness writing. In 'The Novel [3],' Grove explains the shortcomings of subjective forms of modernist writing in a manner that sheds much light on his own literary aims and techniques:

> In the 'first person' novel, the 'thoughts and feelings of ... the focal character ... ten[d] to merge into analysis. Of late, this psychological analysis has, very naturally, assumed a greater and greater importance ... I need only mention ... Proust's *Du Côté chez Swann*, and Joyce's *Ulysses*. In both these the thoughts and feelings of only a single character are given, in fact, nothing else is given at all, except in as much as it is mirrored by these ... The greater, in the development of the novel, the share of analysis became, the more rigorously novelists saw themselves compelled to restrict their focal characters to one or two. It is almost a corollary of this that, the more analysis lost in breadth and variety, the more it gained in detail and depth ... just now, analysis has tended to swamp the novel and to crowd its central element, namely narration, off the scene. It is the common charac-

> teristic of all experimentation to swing from one extreme to the other. In our case, novelists are fully aware that the real formula of the novel has not yet been found; and so they try this and that; and much brilliant effort may be lost because it proceeds in the wrong direction.[36]

The importance of these observations in clarifying Grove's literary aesthetic is difficult to overstate. He draws attention to the importance of psychological analysis in the modernist novel, something he has tried to achieve with his own brand of modern realism. Yet, crucially, Grove highlights what he believes to be the main disadvantage of first-person narrative and narrative depictions of individual consciousness: a narrow subjectivity. Earlier, I speculated on the reasons for the absence of first-person narratives in prairie-realist novels and suggested that many prairie writers – most successfully Ross in *As For Me and My House* – strive to achieve a balance of subjectivity and objectivity that is demanded by a novel that purports to be both an accurate reflection of a contemporary milieu and a convincing exploration of individual human psychology. These observations may also explain a similar rarity of first-person narration in Grove's fiction. But, for Grove, first-person narration would have had the added detrimental effect of mitigating the universality of his grand-scale depictions of human truths. Certainly, Grove employs most of the standard techniques of the modern realists in his attempts to achieve psychological realism. I have already mentioned his impersonal passages of psychological analysis and his frequent use of the centre-of-consciousness technique, which appears in one form or another in almost all of his novels. Grove is preoccupied with maintaining an illusion of narrative impersonality and objectivity in his writing because his notion of psychological realism has little or nothing to do with epistemology. The consciousness that he seeks to depict in action is neither individual nor unique to any particular time and place, but rather part of a kind of historical consciousness, a zeitgeist of sorts.

Grove's most ambitious experiments with psychological realism derive from his attempts to depict what he calls a 'world consciousness' that puts the reader in touch with a larger historical reality. Grove identifies this aim in 'Realism in Literature,' offering a passage that helps to account for his avoidance of overtly subjective perspectives in his work: 'In realistic art the creative spirit as such will never appear in the first person; whatever it has to say it will say indirectly, through the medium of action and character; it will submerge itself in the world of appearances ... realistic art ... will place itself and thereby the reader in the heart of things in such a way that they look on at what is happening from the inside, as if they were themselves a world consciousness.'[37] Grove makes it clear that the reader's own experience of 'universal truth,' or 'world consciousness,' is the aim of modern realism and that third-person, detached writing, with its ability to stand above a situation and explore it from a variety of perspectives, is the only way of achieving this: 'Naturally, then, prose narrative, conceived and written to be read ... is the form most commonly chosen by the artist of to-day as the one most directly adapted to his purpose which is, of course, to waken an emotional reaction and response, in the largest possible number, to a given set of conditions, data, circumstances, events, and characters.'[38] In light of these two pronouncements, a number of the most troublesome aspects of Grove's novels begin to make sense. The awkward characterizations in three of his early prairie novels – *Settlers of the Marsh* (1925), *Our Daily Bread* (1928), and *Fruits of the Earth* (1933) – can be seen to derive from Grove's attempts to make his characters 'archetypal' or historical representations, first, and psychologically 'real' individuals, second. In *The Yoke of Life* (1930) and *Two Generations* (1939), Grove's overlaying of a symbolic structure onto otherwise traditionally realistic novels might best be viewed as an attempt to make his unremarkable characters representative of 'universal' concerns and issues. In *The Master of the Mill* (1944), Grove's awkward manipulation of temporal chronology can be considered an experiment designed to establish the action of his novel within larger, repetitive historical patterns. And his final unfinished and unpublished novel, *The Seasons* (ca 1938–41), with its ambitious attempt to recreate all aspects of human life, can be seen as the culmination of a career aimed at exploring broad human 'truths' in the confined space of a particular locale.

As I have already discussed three of Grove's four published prairie novels in a number of contexts, I will forgo further discussion of them here. *The Yoke of Life* (1930), however, stands out among this group by virtue of its strange coupling of traditional realism and symbolism, making it, in many ways, Grove's most ambitious prairie novel. It is also his least-esteemed effort. W.J. Keith, in 'Grove's "Magnificent Failure": *The Yoke of Life* Reconsidered,' has anticipated much of my interpretation of this novel: 'Only when we become accustomed to the curious shift in the narrative from a basically "realistic" to an unabashedly "symbolic" level will the novel yield up its most satisfying effects.'[39] Grove begins *The Yoke of Life* with a relatively straightforward, realistic narrative that is similar to those of his other three prairie novels; in his opening chapter, the narrator offers detailed physical descriptions of characters and landscape, much mimetic dialogue, bits of social commentary on the lives of pioneers, a centre-of-consciousness technique, and representations of everyday life on the prairies. Yet beneath the surface of this realism there is a symbolic current unlike that found in any of his other novels. As Keith argues, 'Superficially realistic, [the first chapter] is in fact so constructed as to communicate to the careful reader a symbolic digest of the book's major emphases.'[40] Grove suggests larger significance in his characters and setting by supplementing his realistic description with much symbolic content: 'Len saw a huge spruce tree ahead, out-topping the poplars all around. It stood close to the road, guarding like a sentinel a homestead in the margin of the forest.'[41] Yet in this novel Grove is not merely supplementing traditional realism with a vivid symbolism; rather, as the novel moves forward, he increasingly attempts to subsume his realistic world into a larger symbolic pattern with universal emphasis. The characters in the novel cease to behave as 'real' people would and begin to act as representative, archetypal figures. As Sutherland writes of the protagonist's relationship with Lydia, 'soon she becomes symbolic of all the beauty embodied in his visions – the human correlative of his artistic goal in life.'[42] Lydia, who represents many female archetypes to Len at different times in the novel – virgin, fallen woman, mother, sister, nurse – is also clearly representative of Len's artistic vocation. The strange double suicide that ends the novel – Len ties himself to Lydia, and they lie together in the bottom of a boat as it floats down a river to be smashed against the rocks – does not make sense in the context of pure realism, but it does provide a satisfactory symbolic conclusion in which the artist, unable to realize his vocation, sees both himself and his art destroyed in the process. To be sure, critics have criticized this novel for its failure to conform to traditional realism: as an unsigned review that appeared in *The Saturday Review of Literature* in 1930 states, 'we found it a trial ... to witness the death of Len, neither plausible nor inevitable, in a suicide pact with his sweetheart.'[43] But as Keith argues, 'this [critical] neglect is closely related to [the novel's] unique fictional qualities.'[44] *The Yoke of Life* is undoubtedly reflective of Grove's efforts to broaden the scope of realism beyond the merely referential and is more fairly regarded a modern experiment with the realist genre than a romantic mitigation of the realist form.

In *The Master of the Mill*, published in 1944 but written as early as 1933,[45] Grove strives to depict 'world consciousness' and 'universal' human concerns in a different and more successful manner. Less overtly symbolic than *The Yoke of Life* – despite the looming symbolic presence of the mill itself, discussed earlier – this novel manipulates and distorts temporal chronology to establish the action of the novel within a larger framework of human history. Grove, in 'The Technique of the Novel,' indicates his belief that the novel may manipulate time to link the story to a larger 'experience of life': 'A temporal sequence may be perfectly logical and convincing; and, on the other hand, it may be fanciful or even irrational. In neither case can the mere stringing together of many "And then's" make a work of art out of a mere sequence in time.'[46] The temporal sequence of *The Master of the Mill* is notoriously difficult to follow. The narrative shifts awkwardly among numerous time periods that take place between the founding of the mill in the mid-nineteenth century and 1938. The technique used to mark the passage of time is occasionally jarring: 'That, the senator reflected, had been the last time for many years that he had stood face to face with a woman unselfconscious. [New paragraph] But instantly he was back in the past.'[47] Grove's temporal shifting in this novel is reminiscent of techniques used in numerous high-modernist works, most notably Woolf's *To the Lighthouse* (1927). Yet Grove's concern is not solely the subjective, individual experience of temporality. His temporal discontinuity seems awkward if it is meant to represent the memories and recollections of the individual character, Senator Clark. But Grove's movements back and forth through time are not meant to mimic the individual consciousness experiencing history. They instead appear designed to highlight connections between disparate time periods, and to show circular historical patterns as they affect a large-scale society through time. In this sense Grove's novel has more in common with Woolf's more enigmatic work, *The Waves* (1931). The enduring symbol of the mill reveals that, to Grove, historical consciousness is something quite different from historical reality: 'That mill would live on though it might crumble; it would live on in the thoughts of man, for it had demonstrated the possibility of a new way of life.'[48] It is easy to see, given this broad, visionary emphasis, why Grove found traditional realism to be too limiting a form of expression. He wants not merely to reflect the surface details of life, but also to communicate the broad, historical forces that underlie human experience. This is the sense in which Grove perceives a kind of eternal modernity in great writing: writers are modern, realistic, and experimental, by Grove's definitions, when they succeed in representing their own contemporary period in a way that manages to tap in to the larger, spiralling forces that inform the communal experience of history. Grove's key historical image in this novel is not the mill, which may 'crumble,' but the vaguely Yeatsian image of the 'wheel' invoked in the final chapter. Speaking of the grand-scale passage of time, one of the women in the final scene conceives of history as a cyclical process of evolution: "A wheel! ... A wheel that rotates. Attached to that wheel we return to every point at which we have been.'[49] *The Master of the Mill* sees Grove taking the psychological emphasis of the modern-realist novel to a new level: it is an attempt to depict, mimetically, as impossible as this may be, what Grove calls 'world consciousness' in action; as Miss Dolittle reveals in the final line of the novel, 'I have come to place a great confidence in the capacity of the collective human mind.'[50]

While *The Master of the Mill*, by virtue of the sheer ambition of Grove's vision, might appear destined to have fallen short in achieving the representation of 'world consciousness,' it apparently did not deter his efforts, and Grove set himself an even more difficult task in his final, unpublished novel, *The Seasons* (ca 1938–45), which was left unfinished at the time of Grove's death in 1948. The surviving typescript of 469 pages is divided into three sections named after seasons of the year. The first two sections, 'Summer' and 'Fall,' exist in their entirety. At the time of his death, Grove had only finished a draft of the first two sections and a first chapter of section three, 'Winter.' Content in *The Master of the Mill* with temporal distortion as a means of achieving his grand-scale vision, in *The Seasons* Grove sought to distort space to similar ends. In this novel, his general approach to characterization and his tragic view of human life remain essentially unchanged, but his scope is even more ambitious: 'As for "The Seasons" ... I have the deliberate purpose in mind of making it my *magnum opus*, by which I mean that I shall put into it ... the thoughts and fates of the several scores of characters and the hundreds of background figures.'[51] In this novel, Grove seeks to depict, in a single locale, what he conceives to be the sum total of all human experience. Set in and around an Ontario town based on Simcoe, *The Seasons* traces the lives of what seem to be countless individuals (they number more than one hundred) over the course of a single year, the novel being divided into four mammoth sections named after the seasons. Two letters Grove wrote in 1941 reveal his ambitious intentions both in the scope of his subject matter and his technique:

> I have for two years been working on a panoramic novel which will require another two years to finish. In it, I aim at replacing the time sequence by an

> extension in space, giving a whole countryside, with its towns, farms, etc., within the compass of a single year.[52]

> The aim is not to spin out a plot in time, but to extend the scene in space, giving a bird's-eye view of all that happens typically within an area thirty miles square, including the (imaginary) town of Rivers and its whole population and all its activities, from the odd job man to the great industrialist.[53]

Perhaps his most modern book thematically – *The Seasons* explores both human sexuality and socialist politics to a degree unprecedented in his work – it is in many ways his least successful artistically. And for all of Grove's talk about manipulating time and space, the techniques of this novel are ultimately less remarkable and innovative than those of *The Master of the Mill.* The desire for inclusiveness, and the sheer number of characters it produces, mean that few if any well-developed psychological portraits emerge: although Grove throughout his career tended to emphasize 'world consciousness' at the expense of the individual experience, ultimately it is through individual characters – Niels Lindstedt, Abe Spalding, Len Sterner, Senator Clark, Phil Branden – and the use of characteristically modern-realist techniques such as centre of consciousness, that he comes closest to exploring the 'universal' concerns he prefers.

In *The Seasons*, Grove's boldest experiments with realism, rather ironically, return him almost to a traditional form of nineteenth-century realism that sacrifices individual characterization to offer up a cross-section of society. Ultimately, it suggests that Grove considered society, not the individual, the most important subject of the modern novel. But nearly all of the other modern realists, even the social realists discussed in the next chapter, held the opposite opinion: the individual's experience of the world is fundamental. The 'world consciousness' that Grove aims for in *The Seasons*, then, is not psychological realism in the modern-realist sense. In fact, Grove's 'world consciousness' is hard to differentiate from narrative omniscience. Grove is aiming not to offer psychologically 'real' representation of individual characters, but to give the reader a feeling of 'world consciousness,' or a credible experience of a whole society moving through history. Whether *The Seasons*, had it been finished, would have evolved into a more typically modern-realist example of psychological realism is not clear. Yet it is unmistakable from what survives that, almost until the end of his life, Grove's interest in experimenting with the realist form was unshaken and that his efforts were growing more ambitious and eclectic over time.

With his wide variety of creative projects, elaborate personas, and peculiar literary concepts, it is surprising neither that Grove has generated tremendous critical interest nor that he never achieved the kind of recognition in his lifetime that he felt he warranted. It is also not surprising that, after nine decades of criticism, his readers are still in disagreement about the fundamental nature of his realism, the extent and authenticity of his 'modernity,' and his significance in the development of modern Canadian fiction. A reconsideration of Grove's problematic oeuvre in the context of modern realism makes sense of many of his peculiar aims and techniques. His realism was not borrowed from others nor imported wholesale from foreign traditions: it was the product of a highly individualistic, eclectic, and experimental vision, pursued with attention to the new movement in Canada. Grove's awkward modernity consists in his realism, which both explored the contemporary world, like so many modern realists, and sought to connect this world to a timeless, eternal modernity: 'the great tradition.' Some of his most idiosyncratic experiments with literary form can be considered an outgrowth, or individualistic application, of the modern-realist preoccupation with psychological realism. Yet to suggest that modern realism wholly accounts for Grove's complex career fails to do justice (or perhaps gives too much credit) to a writer whose endeavours were not so focused. Like modern realism generally, Grove straddles many traditional boundaries in and of the literature of the period: he was a prairie realist and a social realist, referential and 'universal,' Canadian and international. Like other modern realists, he faced formidable aesthetic challenges and arrived at workable solutions that were at once individualistic and attuned to the modern spirit of the new movement in Canadian writing. Grove's eclectic modern realism is evidence of the complexity, sophistication, flexibility, and vitality of the movement as a whole: these very qualities are what enabled the movement to appeal to such a broad and diverse group of Canadian writers.

6
The Proliferation of Modern Realism in Canada, Part 2: Urban and Social Realism Reclaimed

Canada's first urban-realist collection of short stories, J.G. Sime's *Sister Woman* (1919), appeared as the first manifestos for a modern realism were published in the *Canadian Bookman*. Over the next three decades, Canadian authors produced a body of ambitious, dynamic, eclectic, and often experimental fiction that engaged nearly all of the pressing and grand-scale social issues of the period, and explored life in Canada's rapidly growing urban centres with unprecedented intensity. This fiction is similar in quantity to the prairie realism produced contingently in the same period – about three dozen novels and scattered works of short fiction – yet Canada's urban and social realists, unlike their prairie counterparts, have only rarely been examined as a school of writers. All three relevant chapters in *Literary History of Canada*, for example, play down the significance of urban and social realism. Pacey, in 'Fiction 1920–1940,' mentions two urban realists briefly under the heading 'Some Minor Realists': J.G. Sime and Philip Child. Except for Callaghan, whose work constitutes the only significant 'urban counterpart of Grove's rural realism,' Pacey considers all other urban and social realists propagandists.[1] Hugo McPherson's 'Fiction 1940–1960' mentions a handful of these works but does not perceive a distinct body of urban or social-realist fiction. F.W. Watt's 'Literature of Protest' mentions just two relevant novelists, Callaghan and Baird. Even Willmott, who offers a convincing discussion of 'The Invisible City' in *Unreal Country*, proceeds from the assumption that 'one of the most outwardly striking features ... is the virtual absence of urban settings and preponderance of rural and wilderness settings in Canadian fiction written between 1900 and 1960.'[2] Accordingly, urban and social realism of the period has not yet been the subject of any comprehensive critical study, is scarcely mentioned in the critical surveys of the period, and many of its authors have been forgotten, if they were ever known at all.

This chapter aims to explore these most uncompromising examples of modern realism and to highlight their crucial place in Canada's literary heritage. Modern realism was a truly national movement of writers in both urban and rural contexts, in disparate regions of Canada, with different social and political affiliations, who shared a commitment to contemporary subject matter and particular aesthetic assumptions. For a number of reasons, this chapter also aims to situate Canada's urban and social realists in the context of early twentieth-century literary culture: they wrote many of their best works just as leftist literary culture in Canada was waging war on modernist aesthetics and calling for a new, bold, realistic literature that was willing to take on major social and political issues. Yet leftist literary culture in Canada rejected modern realism even though it did engage these issues, largely because of its similarity to Anglo-American high modernism. More specifically, then, this chapter explores the relationship between modern realism and the socialist realism advocated by the leftist little magazines of the period. Such a comparison reveals the complex manner in which Canada's modern realists explore social, political, and psychological concerns. Also, highlighting the differences between modern and socialist realism affirms the similarities between modern-realist and modernist literary aesthetics, and clarifies the relationship between the broad and often competing impulses and influences that make up modern realism as a whole.

The array of individual works explored in this chapter is insufficiently defined by the terms 'urban realism' and 'social realism.' Still, these terms are useful, indeed unavoidable, as they denote two unmistakable tendencies of modern-realist fiction of the period. In *Social Realism in the French-Canadian Novel* (1977), Ben-Zion Shek offers a loose definition of 'social realism' in accordance with my usage: 'social realism ... must of necessity have as one of its points of reference the economic, social and political conditions ... having existed during the fictional time-span covered by the works in question.'[3] More sophisticated theories of social realism abound and have proven the subject of much critical debate over the decades, although rarely in the context of Canadian literature. A number of critics consider how the form of the European social-realist novel is determined by its leftist content, including Georg Lukács, the most prominent theorist of social realism: 'in the materialist dialectic content is the overriding moment that ultimately determines form.'[4] But the English-Canadian social-realist novel of the period generally examines individuals in relation to the forces outlined by Shek only on a thematic level, de-emphasizing overtly political interpretation of subject matter. To consider these texts 'social-realist' in the sense outlined by Lukács would prove limiting by denying their important formal similarities to other types of modern realism. For example, later I explore various forms of 'reportage' in specific urban and social-realist texts that are typical of modern-realist fiction as a whole. In other words, I discuss social realism as a form of modern realism with a predisposition for a particular subject matter. While the exploration of social and political forces has some impact on the formal properties of the social-realist text, there is no substantive difference between the technique of social-realist fiction and that of other forms of modern realism. In this sense, the generic boundaries of social realism are as arbitrary as those of prairie realism. Similarly, I employ the term 'urban realism' to denote a tendency of much modern-realist fiction to investigate the modern urban experience and to unfold in a realistic cityscape. Yet much as my discussion of prairie realism challenged regional labels applied to a diverse body of texts that can only be partly accounted for in regionalist terms, my discussion of urban realism acknowledges the inadequacy of a generic heading defined by a particular kind of geographical space.

A further indication of the difficulty of categorizing the fiction of the period is suggested by the fact that social and urban realism are closely linked but divergent concepts.[5] While the generic boundaries of social and urban realism overlap – the increasing interest that Canadian writers showed in urban settings and contemporary life in expanding centres of population effectively assured that social and political issues would become more prominent, and the reverse is also true – not all of Canada's social realists were urban realists: for example, many of Grove's novels – *Our Daily Bread* (1928), *Fruits of the Earth* (1933), *The Master of the Mill* (1944) – are profoundly concerned with social issues, but are not examples of urban realism. There are also exemplary urban-realist novels that are set on the prairie – Durkin's *The Magpie* (1923) takes place in Winnipeg, for example – revealing that fiction of the period does not always fall neatly into the categories of 'urban' and 'rural.' Nevertheless, much as it is impossible to deny a 'prairie realism' with its own thematic preoccupations, there is undeniably a body of urban and social-realist fiction in Canada that foregrounds the cityscape and emphasizes political and societal concerns. The very fact that prairie realism is enshrined in Canada's literary canon while urban and social realism are not reveals that such distinctions exist, and to deny them out of convenience would create an arbitrary sense of the coherence of the modern-realist movement as a whole. The terms 'social' or 'urban' realism are most usefully applied to signify general thematic categories of the larger modern realism that includes these and other forms.

While the works of a few individual writers of the period have very occasionally been discussed in the general context of urban and social realism, there has not yet been a full-length study of the English-language novel comparable to Shek's *Social Realism in the French-Canadian Novel*. Unfortunately, notions of urban and social realism have also been distorted by the fact that most of the extant criticism on the subject has focused exclusively on the works of Morley Callaghan, who, despite his predominantly urban settings, is not singularly or even primarily a social realist. Not only has this uneven focus of attention eclipsed the contributions of Callaghan's forerunners and contemporaries, but it also has had the somewhat paradoxical effect of both denying and mischaracterizing fiction of the period. Callaghan is sometimes called the only urban realist, the exception to the rule that Canadians write about landscape, and this leads to the neglect of other works about the city: Justin D. Edwards, for example, argues that 'as Canada's first urban novel, *Strange Fugitive* is an important text not only for exploring the rhetorical changes in articulations of Toronto, but also as a document that constructs and manipulates conceptions of urban space within the Canadian cityscape.'[6] But even before Callaghan created his formative fictional portrait of Toronto in 1928, Sime had written about Montreal in *Our Little Life* (1921), Durkin about Winnipeg in *The Magpie* (1923), Gilbert Knox [Madge MacBeth] about Ottawa in *The Land of Afternoon* (1924), and a contemporary Vancouver had appeared in *The New Front Line* (1927) by Hubert Evans. At the same time, the general critical emphasis on Callaghan generates the impression that any other works of urban and social realism must necessarily pale in comparison: as Pacey writes, 'A few forgotten novels have virtues that lift them above the level of mediocrity ... but even the best of them fall short of the level of ... Callaghan.'[7] Such comparative notions of urban and social realism ensure that the fortunes of the genre as a whole remain bound up in the literary reputation of one writer whose canonical status has been in serious decline for decades, and many of the common critiques of Callaghan's work – moralism, didacticism, heavy-handed symbolism – turn up in critiques of fiction of the period as a whole.

In terms of their genealogical development, urban and social realism are indistinct from the rest of Canada's modern realism: they arise in the 1920s contemporaneously with the modern-realist manifestos, the first distinguished works of prairie realism, and the experimental works of the first major modern realist, Raymond Knister. While the subject matter of the urban and social-realist novel was affected by the heightened attention paid to political issues and flowering of leftist literary culture in the 1930s – as of course were prairie realism and the projects of individual prose authors of the period – this troubled decade did not, as some literary histories suggest, give birth to social realism in Canada. And urban and social-realist authors, again like their prairie-realist contemporaries, began, as mid-century approached and passed, to write with ever-increasing psychological intensity: even a cursory comparison of works such as Ethel Wilson's *Hetty Dorval* (1947), Hugh MacLennan's *The Precipice* (1948), or Brian Moore's *Judith Hearne* (1955), to Callaghan's early works reveals this development in concrete terms. Urban and social realism are also very similar in technique to other forms of modern realism. Aside from the urban realist's heightened interest in contemporary language and speech patterns, and the social realist's occasional preoccupation with creating character types that allow the exploration of social issues (both of which are present but less evident in prairie realism), there is little other than subject matter to separate works such as Stead's *Grain* (1926) from Evans's *The New Front Line* (1927). But the subject matter of urban and social realism is pronounced: its unflinching and daring exploration of even the most weighty and taboo subjects of the age makes it some of the most modern literature produced in the English-speaking world.

Canada's urban realist is concerned with the same topics that interested the Anglo-American modernists and evokes the modern cityscape in a manner that reflects the rapid pace of life of urban centres, the threatening and often destructive forces sometimes associated with city living and urbanization, and the psychological effects of city dwelling on the individual. At times, the urban realist goes to great lengths to capture the vibrancy of the growing Canadian city and to convey the impact of technological development on contemporary life. Sime's *Our Little Life* (1921) generates just such an impression of Montreal: 'He … used to sit in the window of the Lunch Room, and look out at the people passing to and fro on the sidewalk … and watch the unceasing traffic in the street. There were the electric cars making their way down the middle of the street with an unending clang … [and] the great leviathans of motor cars that came rolling through the traffic to the ground bass of their tooting motor-horns.'[8] Urban portraits such as this one convey the sense of optimism regarding technological advance and industrialization present in the minds of many authors in the 1920s and reflected in the language of the manifestos calling for these sorts of celebratory and realistic depictions of modern Canadian life. With the onset of the Great Depression, however, many urban portraits grow noticeably darker, and the urban realist becomes more interested in exploring the ominous and foreboding character of the urban world. In Irene Baird's *Waste Heritage* (1939), Vancouver is an urban wasteland in which many of the social problems of the novel – poverty, class struggle, gender inequality, violence, unemployment – are almost personified: 'He walked up past the harbor, approaching ... by the low road that ran parallel to the railroad tracks. The squalid streets were quiet and steeped in shadow, the high canyons running between the blocks were blacked out except where the moonlight fell in patches, sharpening angles and creating crude planes of light and darkness. These streets that appeared merely dreary and damned by day took on a sinister air by night.'[9] In Callaghan's most sustained work of social realism, *They Shall Inherit the Earth* (1935), the narrator describes Toronto in a manner that conveys both the sordid aspects of big-city life and the inexplicable effects of the metropolis on the mind of the city dweller: 'There was nothing human going on in that city block that she did not understand, the weeping of a girl deserted ... the young man brutally beaten in that room over the poolroom on the corner, the lustful old man coaxing the innocent girl to sit on his knee ... she heard the noises on the street, smelt the gas and oil from the cars, and then looked up, full of joy, at the dark sweep of the city sky.'[10] The urban realists are not unlike the prairie realists in their concern with imaginatively interpreting, rather than merely describing, the landscape or cityscape. The urban realists' concern with universalizing the city and exploring its symbolic possibilities is further indicated in their allusive renaming of well-known Canadian cities: Callaghan's refusal to 'name' Toronto in his novels indicates his desire to have his urban world take on a universal significance; Philip Child, in *God's Sparrows* (1937), renames Hamilton 'Wellington'; Sime's Montreal is called 'Regalia' in *Our Little Life* (1921); and Baird, in *Waste Heritage* (1939), allusively and symbolically renames Victoria and Vancouver 'Aschelon' and 'Gath.'

Novels of the period also unfailingly engage, to varying degrees, dominant and controversial social, political, and moral concerns. While the specific concerns that the urban and social realists raise are many and varied, generally speaking they pertain to the effects of the economic conflict and crisis between the wars – unemployment, labour unrest, capitalist exploitation of the worker, the hardships associated with factory life, poverty – and to issues arising out of social identities and conflicts – exploitation of women, tensions between religion and secular society, racial prejudice, class conflict. While the majority of these works, true to the spirit of modern realism, are structured around the psychology of one or more individuals, they nevertheless take account of social forces in motion on a grand scale. In A.M. Stephen's *The Gleaming Archway* (1929), for example, labour conflict and the socialist movement in British Columbia are analysed in detail and used as a catalyst to the main action of the novel: 'The labour situation in Vancouver was passing through an intense period when the contending forces were active and aggressive. One wing of the party was demanding industrial action – the other counselling prudence and constitutional measures which would find expression at the polls.'[11] More sympathetic to revolutionary causes, and more subtle and convincing as a novel, Baird's *Waste Heritage* (1939) focuses on the lives of two out-of-work, itinerant men during the Depression. While Baird's characterization of Matt Striker, who rides the rods into Vancouver in hopes of taking part in labour demonstrations, and the childlike Eddy whom he befriends, is convincing, the novel is also concerned with depicting larger social forces, rather than merely analysing or describing them. A particularly notable aspect of Baird's technique is her exploration of group psychology. The emotional fluidity of crowds comes across in her many descriptions of demonstrations as she modulates among various levels of detached description and communal centre-of-consciousness points of view: 'As the long line of measured shuffling hardened to a measured tramp the tenement watchers shrilled a cheer; then as they caught sight of the cops' red machines the cheers soured to catcalls and the boys on the billboard joined in … that made handling the crowd a dangerous, thankless job.'[12]

In Nellie McClung's *Painted Fires* (1925), the author tells the story of a Finnish immigrant to Canada named Helmi who confronts both sexism and class discrimination in a variety of social and personal contexts. While McClung exploits her dramatic situations to their fullest as a means of commenting on a variety of social issues of the period, she largely avoids didacticism through the creation of vivid characters who represent various social and political affiliations without losing their psychological credibility, as McClung's portrait of the self-serving and revolutionary minded Anna Milander reveals: 'Miss Anna Milander was locked in a cell at the police station, charged with having maliciously and with intent to hurt hurled a stone at a policeman ... she was well pleased with her afternoon's work. She had struck a blow in Freedom's cause ... Her picture would be in the paper ... the pride of achievement burned in Anna's heart.'[13] In *Earth and High Heaven* (1944), Gwethalyn Graham tells the story of a love affair between a wealthy Christian socialite, Erica Drake, and Marc Reiser, a Jewish lawyer she falls in love with to the displeasure of her family and friends. In the process of exploring an anti-Semitism insidiously rooted in Montreal society, Graham weaves in and out of the minds of her characters and examines the complex interplay of their social, racial, and linguistic identities side by side with the petty psychological motivations and hangups that underlie their prejudices: 'He remembered what a shock he had had when the parents of a Jewish importer whom he had known for years ... the very best type of Jew ... turned out to be pure ghetto.'[14]

MacLennan's first and unpublished novel, *So All Their Praises* (1933) is strikingly unlike his well-known novels of the 1940s: it is highly experimental in form, employing numerous high-modernist literary techniques, and it is set, not in a romanticized Canada, but primarily in Germany during the rise of Nazism, although sections are set in the United States and Nova Scotia. In many ways, *So All Their Praises* is MacLennan's most thematically modern novel: through a generational conflict between the protagonist and his father, the novel explores tensions between modern and Victorian values. But in contrast to his later novels, this work does not endorse a romantic notion of national progress. Instead, the novel expresses a modern anxiety about the decline of traditional and unifying cultural values: as Elspeth Cameron remarks, 'MacLennan emphasizes that the whole age is caught, like his three main characters, in tremendous upheaval.'[15] The range of modern issues raised by the novel is impressive: alcoholism, psychological disturbance, the unconscious mind, prostitution, crime, spiritualism, and the decline of traditional religious values and influence. The plot of the novel centres on three characters: Michael Carmichael, a British writer, Adolf Fabricus, a German student, and Sarah Macrae, a Canadian musician. While the story unfolds in an awkward manner, constructed around the melodramatic intrigues that arise from the love triangle that links the three central characters, the twentieth-century world that the novel evokes is arresting and vivid, infused simultaneously with a sense of psychological intensity and ominous foreboding: 'It was a clear autumn night and the streets of Freiburg were whitened by the moon ... Roof-tops were sharp as knives against the sky and shadows cut the street into clean-edged rhomboids and slanting triangles ... Freiburg was silent except for the occasional scream of a street-car wheel; so it was very silent, for the noise of the river enhanced the tranquillity, being like the noise blood makes in one's head when there is nothing else to hear.'[16] MacLennan contextualizes such passages of psychological realism with sections that are more omniscient and strive to set a contemporary historical stage for his action: 'Nearly eight million people in Germany unemployed, over three million English unemployed ... and everyone talking at the top of his voice.'[17]

Closely related to these explorations of social issues is the social realists' tendency to situate everyday, commonplace occurrences in relation to encompassing historical events and patterns. In one respect, this dual emphasis on the local and the 'universal' recalls the prairie-realist novel discussed earlier and results in a form of social determinism that explores the ways in which the lives of 'real' individuals are bound up in larger forces. But the social-realist novel is not essentially naturalistic, and one gets a sense that writers of the period are concerned more with exploring modern life, and the confused relation of microcosm to macrocosm that it entails, than with putting forth sociological theories. Hugh Garner's *Cabbagetown* (1950) offers an excellent and representative example of some of the ways in which writers of the period situate their stories in history. Garner's novel, as its name suggests, is on one level a portrait of a specific working-class, immigrant quarter of Toronto, firmly grounded in the 'real' world with references to specific landmarks: 'The street names greeted him with long-known familiarity – Sackville, Parliament, Taylor, Oak, Sumach, Sydenham.'[18] But the manner in which Garner structures his story reveals that his intentions are more ambitious, and that Cabbagetown is meant to represent an archetypal urban experience of the Great Depression. In a manner reminiscent of Dos Passos, *Cabbagetown* is epic in scale, and the narrative almost cinematographically moves in and out of the minds of numerous characters, striving for psychological realism on the level of the individual mind, but always subtly emphasizing the connection between the individual life and a Depression-era zeitgeist. The life of the protagonist, working-class Ken Tilling, begins optimistically, with promising prospects for the future: 'Getting a job was an easy step in the early months of 1929. Business and employment were climbing to unprecedented heights.'[19] But soon Tilling and the other characters in the novel are caught up in the maelstrom of changing times: 'One evening in October the newspapers printed extra editions reporting a stock market crash.'[20] Ken Tilling is in stages driven to a life of crime; his father, stripped of his role as breadwinner, withdraws into a non-responsive state; Tilling's mother, unable to cope with economic hardship and its impact on her family, self-medicates with alcohol; and Tilling's impoverished beloved, Myrla Patson, is impregnated out of wedlock by her wealthy boss and driven in stages to prostitution. Garner's novel seeks to explore the effects of the Depression on certain types of individuals: as he remarked in an interview with John Moss, '*Cabbagetown* ... happens to be – it's been called – the best book about the Depression, the Depression and the urban poor, so it will probably remain a sort of textbook of that particular era.'[21] But Garner avoids drawing moral conclusions about the events that take place in the novel, and his characters do not simply function as symbols: Ken Tilling is driven to crime, partly out of need, partly out of greed; his parents are victims of hard economic times but also partly to blame for their own misfortunes; and Myrla's descent occurs not just because of social forces and the influence of others, but also because of her own questionable moral reasoning. What is the relationship between the individual and society? Garner acknowledges that this is a complex and unanswerable question better left to historians and sociologists than novelists. Like most of his modern-realist contemporaries, Garner appears persuaded that convincing characterization is necessary if such social commentary is to appear credible and that social commentary is not the primary concern of the modern realist.

The period of modern-realist proliferation in Canada is roughly bracketed by the two world wars that were defining moments in Canada's national development. Accordingly, the wars are often viewed with ambivalence in the Canadian novel of the period, authors seemingly torn between depicting the devastating effects of war and exploring the nationalism and national sense of 'coming of age' sometimes associated with the war experience. Canada's social realists engage the war subject from a variety of perspectives, sometimes exploring specific social effects of the conflicts, at other times exploiting the weightiness of the war subject to symbolic ends. The 'war novel,' in fact, constitutes a minor sub-genre of modern-realist fiction in its own right. Durkin's *The Magpie* (1923), Stead's *Grain* (1926), and McCourt's *Music at the Close* (1947) are examples of prairie novels also prominently concerned with the war experience. Evans's *The New Front Line* (1927) and Child's *God's Sparrows* (1937) are comparable urban-realist examples. There are also a number of modern-realist war novels that do not fit into either category, including Charles Yale Harrison's *Generals Die in Bed* (1930), Ted Allan's *This Time a Better Earth* (1939), and Irene Baird's *He Rides the Sky* (1941). In one of the most unjustly neglected works of the period, Sime's thematically linked cycle of short stories entitled *Sister Woman* (1919), the Great War is explored for its effects on the lives of women of the period and seen as a historical force inextricably bound up with their daily lives, urban experience, quest for respect and equal rights, and identities. As Sandra Campbell writes in her 'Introduction' to the 1992 Early Canadian Women Writers series reprint of Sime's book, 'many of these women are depicted at work in the occupations open to women in the Montreal of World War I: they struggle to survive as seamstresses, shop clerks, factory, office and domestic workers and even as prostitutes. In their struggle, they experience the evolving psychic and social pressures brought to bear on women as a result of the rapid industrialisation and urbanisation which Georgina Sime witnessed between 1907 and 1919 in Montreal.'[22]

In Durkin's *The Magpie* (1923), social events that cause moral questioning in the mind of the protagonist, Craig Forrester – namely class responsibilities during the Winnipeg General Strike – are posited as effects of the Great War, and in this way the individual, the local, the national, and the international are linked:

> 'The strongest organization in the country during the next few years will be the returned soldiers, the veterans of the Great War ... The men who have come back from the front will just about control the political life of this country for the next generation' ... Craig lighted a cigarette ... Why was it that everybody was so keen to take sides and prepare the ground for a new struggle now that the great struggle had ceased? He didn't want it. He felt the men and women he met in the street day after day were as tired of struggle as he.[23]

Graham's *Earth and High Heaven* (1944) controversially linked the Nazi atrocities committed against Jews in Europe, even while they were still occurring, to her ambitious examination of anti-Semitism in Montreal: 'So long as the Jews of Germany, and after 1938 the Jews of Europe, continued to suffer purely for their Jewishness, then to run down the Jews of Canada was in some way merely to add to that suffering.'[24]

Another novel of the period, Philip Child's *God's Sparrows* (1937), uses the war subject to somewhat more symbolic ends. In this work, Daniel Thatcher, a wealthy, young protagonist from Hamilton, lives out his childhood in relative ease, the most significant conflict in his life occurring on a symbolic level between the two sides of his family, one attached to American ideals, the other to British. But such social conflicts, suggested by Child to represent competing ideas of the 'old Canada,' lose their importance when Daniel goes off to fight in the Great War. He loses many friends in the fighting, loses his beloved in an influenza epidemic, and returns to Canada a broken man. The symbolic function of the war in the story is identified by Dennis Duffy in his 'Introduction' to the New Canadian Library edition: 'This novel is as much about the end of an era in Canadian history as the life of a single family: the novel concerns not only the agonies of an individual, but the destruction of a culture.'[25] Child does what many social-realist authors of the period do: he writes with a muted symbolism that allows his story to transcend the merely topical without compromising its grounding in 'reality.' Some of the best social-realist novels of the period embody a non-oppositional dualism, supplementing 'straight' realism with a symbolic, psychological, or universal thrust.

Such is also the case with many of the 'case study' novels produced by the urban and social realists. These novels generally purport to explore the lives of more or less typical individuals as they negotiate key social or moral problems presented by modern life. In some of these works, the protagonist is a kind of 'everyman' whose struggles represent those of larger segments in society. In another little-known novel of the period, Hubert Evans's *The New Front Line* (1927), we follow Hugh Henderson, a more or less typical young man who returns to Vancouver after the First World War and struggles to reintegrate into society. While Evans's psychological portrait of Henderson is often intense, at times it appears that the author is more concerned with exploring the social problems of the returned soldier in general than with creating a unique character: 'Some returned men he knew were resuming their interrupted university studies. They were attending lectures with young men and women who had been children when the war broke out. Hugh knew his parents would finance him if he wanted to go to University. But he was too honest to accept financial aid.'[26] The most remarkable case-study novels tend to reflect the modern-realist preoccupation with psychological realism more clearly. In Callaghan's novels, for example, the characters nearly always have an air of typicality – they are generally unremarkable, inarticulate, unheroic – yet it is not usually possible to ascertain exactly what, if anything, such individuals are meant to represent. They are both individual, in the sense that they do not stand obviously representative of some larger social group, and paradoxically 'universal' by virtue of their independence from such symbolic functions. This is the situation in Callaghan's best-known case-study novel *More Joy in Heaven* (1937). While Callaghan's psychological portrait of Kip Caley cannot be called subtle, he nevertheless writes a novel in which the effects of the Depression on the individual become manifest in an indirect and idiosyncratic manner. The questioning in the novel is moral, rather than social and political – is redemption possible in the modern world? – and Callaghan's social critique is levelled at a general hypocrisy that runs across all segments of society rather than at a specific class or ideology. Caley, used and discarded by a Depression-era world eager for a positive symbol during a period of hardship, is at once strikingly credible in his response to those who manipulate him and suggestively symbolic in his embodiment of their guilt, selfishness, and hopelessness.

MacLennan's *Man Should Rejoice* (1937) is a more technically innovative case-study novel that attempts to fuse stream-of-consciousness passages and detached, objectivist passages, and makes the central character, David Culver, a representative figure who embodies the zeitgeist of the modern age itself. His story begins in Nova Scotia when he tells us that 'I came here to live because I could think of no other place to go ... and there was a job I had to finish'; the 'job' is writing the dramatic and unreliable story of his life.[27] The son of a wealthy Pittsburgh businessman, David studies at Princeton University, rejects his social background largely because of his artistic temperament, and travels to Paris to become a painter. In Europe, he falls under the influence of socialist friends before returning to America, where he becomes an employee in one of his father's mills. Disaffected by the lives of the working poor and the alienating conditions of factory life, he grows to detest the capitalist system that his father represents, becomes a communist, and returns to Europe to take part in an armed socialist revolution that kills his wife and leaves him a broken man. The first-person narration frequently shows David contemplating events with both deeply personal and broadly historical emphases:

> Being a painter, I see the form and rhythm of things before I see anything else. Now I want to create, in a book, something of the form and rhythm

> of the most rapid transition from one era to another that mankind has ever known. Whether this is possible, whether I can freeze a durable form out of a state of flux, I don't know. If I succeed I may rid myself of the past, not by burying but by recreating it and giving it a separate life of its own. At least it should not be too difficult to set down what happened to my friends and myself as though it had happened to other people, for I see all vividly, as though I were a stranger looking back from a long distance.[28]

Ultimately, however, the first-person form does not always work well for MacLennan. His first-person speaker often sounds like a third-person narrator, and he tells his tale in a manner that is at times too limited to suit the broad historical emphasis of the novel, and at other times too omniscient to be credible: 'How long was it before Arina realized the type of life she had chosen I do not know. They left for Moscow immediately, travelled without a break to London ... then sailed for New York ... The crowds of the cities astonished her; coming from a land of peasants she was half-stunned by the modern world, and in childish obstinacy rebelled against it ... as the ship neared Halifax harbour she was strangely comforted.'[29] Such problems with balancing objective and subjective modes are even more apparent in the few passages where MacLennan *does* strive for epistemological representation. These scenes share a common weakness with many in MacLennan's later, traditional realist novels: they are didactic. More often than not, these passages represent human consciousness, not as an end in itself, not to explore the complexities and anxieties of the modern human mind, but rather to make a particular social or political comment about the modern world, much as a social realist would do more directly in a third-person mode: as David tells us of his factory experience, 'It was like walking in a bad dream to be in this maze of figures and lathes and bolts and engines ... I was tired and they revolved smoothly through my brain like ball-bearings relative to the turning rod until I seem to revolve myself and the slag-illumined sky to revolve too.'[30]

Also indicative of the urban and social realists' efforts to relate both public issues and the private experience of them is their omnipresent examination, from a variety of philosophical and narrative perspectives, of the changing roles of women. Generally speaking, the dramatic changes in women's lives during the period are portrayed with ambivalence: new roles for women become available due to events of the period – we see women working outside of the domestic sphere because of a lack of male labour during the wars or due to economic necessity during the Depression, for example – and these changes are sometimes pictured as liberating. In Sime's 'Munitions!' from *Sister Woman* (1920), Bertha Martin finds personal fulfilment in going to work in a factory during the war: 'the sense of freedom! The joy of being done with cap and apron. The feeling that you could draw your breath – speak as you liked – wear overalls like men – curse if you wanted to.'[31] One of the better-known feminist portraits of the period appears in Hugh MacLennan's *Barometer Rising* (1941). In this novel, Penny Wain, a ship designer, flourishes in a traditionally male profession but must still face constant criticism from her male colleagues, who doubt her abilities. There is no question that she represents on one level the 'new woman' of the period and finds a degree of satisfaction through the actualization of her talent in her work: 'To be a woman and work at a profession pre-eminently masculine meant that she must be more than good. She had to be better than her male colleagues; she had to work longer hours and be doubly careful of all that she did, for a mistake would ruin her. It had taken a war to open such a job for her in the first place, but she was undeceived as to how superior she must be to continue to keep it.'[32] Other works of the period show that the transition from the domestic to public sphere does not offer any form of liberation, and that women go to work out of economic necessity, not desire. In McClung's *Painted Fires* (1925), the psychological pressures of a society with double standards – necessitating that women work but denying them equality – are vividly depicted. In this stream-of-consciousness passage, a maid who has conceived out of wedlock reflects on such injustices, critiquing a hypocritical society and revealing its personal and spiritual toll when it leads her to question her faith in a higher power: 'God couldn't blame her for quitting. Why didn't He make life a little easier for women? God was all powerful – He could make life as He liked ... Why had a baby come to her when she had no home? ... God was mean to women ... no one wants a girl with a baby.'[33] In Callaghan's *Such Is My Beloved* (1934), two young women, Ronnie and Midge, are, like Myrla Patson in *Cabbagetown* (1950), driven to prostitution out of economic necessity. The novel of the period also abounds with portraits of unempowered housewives and mistresses: Vera in Callaghan's *Strange Fugitive* (1928), Faustina in Len Peterson's *Chipmunk* (1949), and Marion in Durkin's *The Magpie* (1923) are three of the most memorable.

Before moving on to a specific examination of the aesthetic of the urban and social-realist novel in the context of leftist literary culture, it is worth remarking upon a few of the peripheral concerns of the novel of the period that indicate the degree to which writers were concerned with engaging the modern world. These references reveal the willingness of the modern realists to broaden the scope of the Canadian novel to include subjects that are controversial and taboo, intensifying their social analyses and heightening their psychological realism. Not least among these subjects is human sexuality, and its frank depiction in a variety of lights, ranging from relatively explicit descriptions of sexual acts – in Peterson's *Chipmunk* (1949) and Garner's *Cabbagetown* (1950) – to direct if unenlightened discussions of homosexuality – in Callaghan's *No Man's Meat* (1931) and *Cabbagetown* – to sordid subjects such as prostitution, venereal disease, and illegal abortion in *Such Is My Beloved* (1934), *They Shall Inherit the Earth* (1935), and *Chipmunk*, respectively. The declining influence of traditional religion finds a place in most of Callaghan's novels, and also in Joyce Marshall's *Presently Tomorrow* (1946) and Graham's *Earth and High Heaven* (1944). Virtually all of the novels of the period make reference to the various and sometimes radical political movements that figured prominently in newspaper headlines, including communism, Marxism, bolshevism, and socialism. Other novels discuss the influence of fascism from various points of view: Henry Kreisel's *The Rich Man* (1948) tells the story of Jacob Grossman, a Jewish Torontonian who visits Vienna in 1935; Child's *Day of Wrath* (1945) and MacLennan's *So All Their Praises* (1933) are set in Nazi Germany; the rise of Nazism provides a backdrop for events in two Montreal novels, *Presently Tomorrow* and *Earth and High Heaven;* and Hilda Glynn-Ward's *The Writing on the Wall* (1921) is a racist propaganda tirade directed at Chinese Canadians, whom the author suggests will soon overrun British Columbia unless prevented. Countless other modern subjects of varying importance appear in these novels: psychoanalysis in *Strange Fugitive* (1928), the flu epidemics in *Our Little Life* (1921), occult spiritualism in *The Gleaming Archway* (1929), professional sports in Callaghan's *The Loved and the Lost* (1951), and modern publishing in Leslie Bishop's fusion of realism and satire, *The Paper Kingdom* (1936), to name a few. But as modern as these subjects may be, the most important kinship between modern realism and the modernist fiction of Europe and America is found in the aesthetic assumptions shared by writers of the two forms. It is necessary, then, to come to terms with the complex interrelationship that existed in Canada among the urban and social realism I have outlined, modern realism as a whole, international modernist aesthetics, and the socialist realism advocated by the leftist literary culture of the period.

As Canada's modern-realist movement entered its second decade, the roaring twenties became the dirty thirties, and dramatic political and social changes occurred in most segments of Canadian culture and society. For the urban and social realists already concerned with representing a contemporary Canada, these changes confirmed their long-held belief that the modern world was a dynamic subject, and they rose to the challenge of probing big concerns and issues in fiction. But the 1930s would also present a host of material and aesthetic obstacles for the modern-realist author. One of the most significant events of the decade for the movement was the rapid decline and eventual demise of the original champion of modern realism: *Canadian Bookman*. The effects of the Great Depression struck hard across the spectrum of Canadian culture, presenting tremendous financial hardship for all of the little magazines. The short runs of the two leftist magazines of the 1930s – *Masses* lasted two years, *New Frontier* only nineteen months – are the best evidence of their financial problems, which are also alluded to in the desperate pleas for renewed subscriptions and apologies for missed issues found in their pages. Even the well-established *Canadian Forum* nearly collapsed in the 1930s. But none of the little magazines suffered a more prolonged and painful demise than the *Bookman*, which, even in the 1920s, had struggled to stay afloat. While the journal fought and failed to publish regularly and showed an interest in modern realism almost until its total collapse in 1939, after 1932 it was a shadow of its former self, and, while it continued to publish occasional pieces on modern realism, it had lost its important place in the literary culture of the period. The decline of the *Bookman* left no single periodical in Canada with a sustained interest in Canadian fiction and no intellectual or creative forum for the discussion of modern realism.

The few magazines that did publish significant critical work during the Depression were all leftist in political orientation and generally uninterested in Canadian prose, both qualities in marked contrast to the *Bookman*, which wrote extensively about fiction and was, as Mulvihill writes, 'essentially apolitical in any overt sense, [and] it remained so even when literature became more preoccupied with politics during the 1930s.'[34] The most polite leftist voices of the era were heard in *The Canadian Forum*, which managed to publish throughout the 1930s and produced a few articles of relevance to modern realism discussed later.

But as the realities of the Depression began to sink in, this repository of cosmopolitanism began to show even less interest in Canadian writing than it had in the 1920s – it engaged primarily and fiercely in political debates – and nearly all of its scant discussion of literature during the decade focused on poetry. Certainly the *Forum* of the 1930s had little to say on the subject of realism in writing, and nothing matching the intensity of the statements found in *Masses* and *New Frontier*. While the *Forum* published no major critical statements on Canadian fiction in the 1930s, there is evidence that a number of *Forum* contributors agreed implicitly with the views published in *Masses* and *New Frontier* with regards to the need for Canadian writing to engage contemporary issues.

Unlike the *Forum*, however, these leftist venues have not usually been granted a significant place by Canada's literary historians, who tend to mention them as examples of the kind of propagandist writing supposedly characteristic of the decade before promptly dismissing them. For example, despite offering rather lengthy discussions of other early twentieth-century Canadian periodicals, Bruce Meyer's entry on 'Literary Magazines in English' in *The Oxford Companion to Canadian Literature* has only the following to add about the two journals: '*Masses* (1932–4) was primarily political. *The New Frontier* (1936–7), which mixed politics with socially oriented poetry and criticism of a more radical cast than the *Forum*, is notable for having published such writers as A.M. Klein, Dorothy Livesay, and Leo Kennedy.'[35] Dean Irvine's recent *Editing Modernity: Women and Little-Magazine Cultures in Canada, 1916–1956* (2008) draws much-needed attention to leftist magazines of the period, including *Masses* and *New Frontier*, in partial response to what he calls the 'wholesale omission of the 1930s from little-magazine-based histories.'[36] In *Comrades and Critics: Women, Literature, and the Left in 1930s Canada* (2009), Candida Rifkind acknowledges the important contribution of these and other magazines to the development of Canadian modernism; she demonstrates that *Masses* 'can be productively read as [an] exampl[e] of the counterpublic sphere of socialist modernism' and argues that '*New Frontier* was in many ways a literary manifestation of the Popular Front,' which has a 'relationship to modernism [that] is more complex because the connections are epistemological rather than purely stylistic.'[37] While it is difficult to defend much of the literary work published in an average issue of either of these magazines on a purely aesthetic level, they certainly deserve recognition as founding periodicals of a vibrant leftist literary tradition in Canada which continues to the present day.

The colourful and polemical pages of *Masses* and *New Frontier* abound with comments on the importance of realism in modern writing, and their contributors engage in testy and frequent debates about the very nature of literary realism in Canada and the rest of the world. For these reasons, these magazines are of crucial significance to the modern-realist movement, which produced some of its finest works in the years during and surrounding their brief runs. But to suggest that *Masses* and *New Frontier* simply pick up with modern realism where the *Bookman* left off would be inaccurate. In fact, two rather remarkable points become apparent when these leftist organs are considered in relation to modern realism: first, while both *Masses* and *New Frontier* unmistakably argued for a new realist literature in Canada – a realistic literature willing to engage the harsh realities of the Depression and its political and social causes and effects – they approached the already extant modern realism with alternating hostility and indifference and defined their own aesthetic largely in direct opposition to it; second, and more significant, the leftist magazines of the 1930s spurned modern realism because they perceived it to share crucial aesthetic assumptions with international modernist forms that they considered indulgent, elitist, escapist, pointlessly experimental, decadent, bourgeois, and reactionary.

Rhetorically, the manifestos for a new realism in *Masses* and *New Frontier* are almost indistinguishable from those that appeared in the *Canadian Bookman* a decade and a half earlier. Such a similarity reveals that modern realism was a remarkably dynamic, receptive, adaptive, and resilient form in the minds of writers of the period. Few if any other modernist forms appealed for so long to such a wide range of writers with such varied ideological dispositions. One common endeavour attracted both the *Bookman* and the leftist critics to realism: they were utterly convinced that writers, to be modern and relevant, had to engage uncompromisingly and realistically the life that was being lived *today* in contemporary Canada. But these two groups of writers, as we shall see, had very different definitions of such an uncompromising realism. While the *Bookman* directed realism towards the representation of a great nation that needed to be celebrated and understood, the leftists found the realist form useful for critiquing the ills and injustices of a sick and hypocritical society to bring about socio-political change. If this shared interest in contemporary life brings the modern realists and the leftists together superficially, in the final analysis their different ideas of what representing contemporary life entails divide them irreconcilably.

In the April 1932 inaugural issue of *Masses*, L.F. Edwards offered a piece called 'Authorship and Canadiana' which allied the appearance of the new magazine with a desperate need for a new writing in Canada that was willing to engage a troubled world in realistic fashion. Edwards's manifesto reflects both the revolutionary tone of the leftist magazine and the sense of distaste with which its writers viewed Canadian writing of the period: 'The total inadequacy of Canadian authors to portray the true ideology of the people in this country, has had the effect of creating an intellectual impasse ... they seem to be totally unaware of the obligation to endeavour to express the feelings and thoughts of their countrymen, here or anywhere else ... No one will deny that the field is here, awaiting but the stroke of the quill to transfer realistic life to the written page.'[38] Other important assumptions underlying the leftist calls for realistic writing that superficially establish their similarity to those of the modern realists are found in the opening, unsigned editorial, 'Our Credentials,' also appearing in the first issue of *Masses*. In this piece, the founders present the magazine as a direct response to the lack of realistic writing in Canada and list some of the general concerns that should be on the minds of Canada's new realists: pressing social questions, the life of the 'common man' or 'worker,' political debates, the interconnection between art and life, the modern and realistic writing of other nations, and a distinctly Canadian character:

> They [the founders] were justifiably disgusted with the barren fields of Canadian bourgeois culture, with the smirking complacency of Canadian artists and writers, with their puerile ignorance of and contempt for social questions, with their snobbish nose-thumbing at the workers and their movements ... [*Masses*] rejects the theory that art can have nothing in common with politics, that art functions only by and for art ... Art is the product of the current (and previous) social and economic conditions ... Are there any honest intellectuals, who will study the life of the workers, who will make the aims of the workers their aims ... Will they do what Gorky is doing, what Gropper is doing, what Dos Passos is doing, what Barbusse is doing? ... MASSES is the first publication of its kind to appear on Canadian soil, produced from the life of Canada's factories, farms – and breadlines.[39]

The concerns and formations that *Masses* wanted the new realists to focus upon – 'social and economic conditions' and 'workers and their movements' – indicate, on the surface at least, only an ideological disagreement with the *Bookman*: the more conservative magazine demonstrated an interest in socio-political forces at work in contemporary society, but not an overtly leftist interpretation of socio-economic conditions, and an interest in everyday life, common people, and ordinary subjects, but not specifically the working class. Minus the distinctly leftist emphasis, most of the demands of the *Masses* manifesto can be found in the modern-realist manifestos of the *Bookman*, and they had already been reflected in modern-realist fiction produced before 1932.

Less radical, but still unmistakably revolutionary in its political orientation, *New Frontier* also linked its very raison d'être with the need to establish a new realism in Canadian writing. This journal, however, had somewhat higher standards for the literature it printed, and its manifesto pieces correspondingly offer more substantial commentary on the aesthetic and stylistic aspects of the new realism. The unsigned opening manifesto of this journal is startlingly astute and demands a Canadian realism that engaged the issues foreground by *Masses* but avoided two of the pitfalls awaiting the modern-realist writer – regionalist representation and excessive virtuosity and experiment – which are offered as reasons that the Canadian realists have not turned their attention sufficiently, or with the right ideological disposition, to 'social realities':

> Though technically adequate, so many interpretations of the Canadian scene in creative writing ... have been singularly disregardful of or unfaithful to the social realities of our time. This effect roots in a diversity of causes. One of these was the re-discovery of the Canadian north country landscape ... with its infinite possibilities for presentation in art, and its eminent suitability as background for sentimental romance. Another, also of geographic *origin*, was the physical isolation in which many domestic creative artists have had to work ... fostering the provincialism of sectional differences ... Allied with and developing from these is the tendency of the ivory tower.[40]

These manifestos, which echo so many of the issues already discussed in other contexts, raise one unavoidable question: why did the leftist magazines neglect the fiction, already produced in Canada, that fit their definitions for new writing in just about every way? They wanted writing that was concerned with society and politics, the common man, and the Canadian scene, and modern realism, especially in its social- and urban-realist phases, was precisely this. Like the modern realists, the leftists were not interested in either regionalist idylls or modernist virtuosity. And both groups wanted a modern, realistic writing that was on par with the literature of other nations. So why did the leftists and modern realists not come together in the 1930s? The reasons that modern realism proved irreconcilable with leftist literary culture are complex, and can be roughly divided into three overlapping categories: political ideology, issues surrounding the material production of literature, and aesthetics.

The ideological reasons that the leftists did not embrace modern realism as it existed are, on the surface, fairly obvious and straightforward. While the modern realists, especially in the social-realist mode, expressed a fundamental concern with social and political issues, *Masses*, and to a lesser degree *New Frontier*, wanted literature that, at the very least, openly expressed a leftist opinion about these same issues. In its opening manifesto, 'Our Credentials,' the founders of *Masses* stated in no uncertain terms that art necessarily had a political purpose: 'Art is propaganda, or more precisely, a vehicle of propaganda.'[41] The opening 'Editorial' of *New Frontier* similarly demanded that art have a political focus, yet conceded that such art ought also to have, as a secondary characteristic, aesthetic worth: 'Certain individual creative artists and groups ... are becoming more interested in the social implications of Canadian life, [and] are turning out work which has both social and artistic value.'[42] Yet the modern-realist novel of the period was not propagandistic and was rarely interested in offering political commentary, or even in explicitly taking sides in the weighty social and political struggles of the day. Callaghan's work produced in the 1920s and 1930s is indicative of the modern realists' general detachment from political ideals. *Strange Fugitive* (1928) focuses on the life of a 'common' man, Harry Trotter, who works in a lumber yard in Toronto. While several of the stock leftist motifs of the period are played out in Callaghan's novel – Trotter is fired for attacking his oppressive boss, for example – the author avoids exploiting such situations for their political implications, and they appear to be included more for their dramatic potential than their ideological import. Similarly, Callaghan's second and third novels, *It's Never Over* (1930) and *A Broken Journey* (1932), invoke a vivid and contemporary urban landscape but avoid explicit discussion of the political conflicts in the air in the years following the crash of 1929, focusing instead on psychological realism. Even his later novels with a more overtly socio-political emphasis – *Such Is My Beloved* (1934), *They Shall Inherit the Earth* (1935), and *More Joy in Heaven* (1937) – explore issues of political substance more for their dramatic possibilities than for their ideological weightiness.

The leftist magazines, to be sure, took Callaghan to task for appearing indifferent to issues of the day. In the October 1936 issue of *New Frontier*, Israel Jordan reviewed Callaghan's collection of short stories, *Now That April's Here* (1936): 'The sensitive artist cannot help reflecting the cruelty and injustice which are invading the most intimate relations between individuals in the present order of society.'[43] But the same reviewer critiqued Callaghan for merely reflecting the injustice of life in the modern world and expressed hopes that in the future Canada's 'foremost living writer' would learn to politicize his work: 'Perhaps when his compassion has passed beyond the contemplative stage and he has begun to formulate a way out for the people whom he describes with such truth, he will be able to write a sustained novel' (he had already published five).[44] For his part, Callaghan, like most of the modern realists, appeared to reject the political novel on the grounds that it was both intellectually and aesthetically limiting. In a 1939 article which appeared in *Saturday Night*, 'Little Marxist, What Now?' he gloated over the dilemma that the Russian-German non-aggression pact had forced upon the culture of the left and stated in no uncertain terms that it was the price to pay for small-mindedness: 'It didn't seem to occur to ... the little communists ... that they were intellectually servile. They were just being good soldiers in their thinking. Well, they should now be thankful that they have such a long training in intellectual servility. For by this time the party line on the Stalin-Hitler deal has probably come through and they can venture on to the streets.'[45] Callaghan's contempt for the radical left, however, appears to derive also from his perception that their politics limited the creative freedom of the modern writer, and one can hardly blame him, considering the kinds of critiques his works were sometimes submitted to. Turning the tables in 'A Criticism,' published in the first issue of *New Frontier* in 1936, Callaghan provided a critique of the short stories published in the magazine at the request of the editors. He was kinder than he would be after the Stalin-Hitler pact in 1939, but stated unequivocally that political subject matter alone did not make for a good story: 'Right here is the place to state emphatically that class consciousness, or an intention directed toward that end is not enough ... It is odd that these ... pieces should have been on one theme – the man out of work. The editors tell me that this was not a deliberate selection, but that nearly all the stories they received were about men who were out of work. If this keeps on it will appear that ... all the young writers of the country are out of work.'[46] The fact that the leftist magazines could muster only muted praise even for the most high-profile of the urban and social realists of the period solely on the grounds that he was not political *enough* is evidence of the degree to which they generally considered political activism the function of the new realism.

Both *Masses* and *New Frontier* located themselves at the centre of the new writing in Canada, and both published poetry, drama, and fiction in an effort to direct this writing in accordance with their ideological aims. So it is hardly surprising that the novel, which for material reasons they were unable to 'control' as easily as poetry, drama, or short fiction, received less critical attention than other literary forms. Both magazines, in fact, give the impression that no novels of literary worth at all were published in Canada during the 1930s. Apart from a tiny handful of reviews of Callaghan's work, there is almost no mention of the Canadian novel of the period in these magazines. This is not altogether surprising. Given the state of Canadian publishing in the decade, very few new writers of any temperament were able to publish novels. As Pacey writes, 'several firms, and notably one of the most ambitious and experimental, Graphic Press of Ottawa, went bankrupt early in the 1930s; others cut back their lists and survived only by acting as agents for foreign houses. Even established Canadian writers such as Morley Callaghan and Frederick Philip Grove found it increasingly hard to get their books published, and new writers could scarcely get a hearing at all.'[47] And it is hard to imagine that the chances of such 'new writers' getting a 'hearing' would be increased if their politics were both more important than their command of literary form and directed against the broad reading public and the capitalist system that any profit-making publishing house indirectly endorsed. So while the output of modern-realist novels actually *increased* and many of the finest works in the genre were produced in the 1930s – Brooker's *Think of the Earth* (1936); Stead's *Dry Water* (1935); Baird's *Waste Heritage* (1939); Grove's *Fruits of the Earth* (1933), *Two Generations* (1939), and *The Yoke of Life* (1930); and most of Callaghan's best-known works, including *Such Is My Beloved* (1934), *They Shall Inherit the Earth* (1935), and *More Joy in Heaven* (1937) – the visibility of the novel in the literary culture of the period declined. Given this state of affairs, there were almost no propaganda novels published in the period – the work of Claudius Gregory, author of *Forgotten Men* (1933), is probably all that fits easily into this category. Clearly, then, the neglect of the novel in *Masses* and *New Fron-*

tier stems partly from the fact that the novels of propaganda, which they endorsed, were not appearing, and they were powerless to make them appear.

But the leftist aversion to the novel derives from more than a rejection of its subject matter. In many articles published in the little magazines, the novel is derided as an indulgent and capitalist literary form and allied with a bourgeoisie seen to be among the enemies of leftist causes. As Edwin Berry Burgum wrote in *New Frontier* in September 1937, 'it is a commonplace of reputable criticism at the present time that the novel culminates in the writers of bourgeois decadence, the Prousts, Manns, and Joyces.'[48] The magazines made it clear, in the discussion of the few novels they did deem worthy of attention, that one had to look outside of Canada for achievement. Jack Conroy wrote in 'New Forces in American Literature,' printed in the April 1936 *New Frontier*, that in the United States 'a solid body of moving novels ... ha[s] been produced' but 'we are still looking to the future.'[49] The vast majority of books reviewed in both *Masses* and *New Frontier* were not by Canadians, and by far the most sustained discussion of any fiction in either magazine occurred in Felix Walter's 'French Novelists of Today,' a substantial column that appeared six times in *New Frontier* between September 1936 and March 1937 and read Jules Romains, Eugène Dabit, André Malraux, and Louis-Ferdinand Céline, with focus on their social relevance. Both *Masses* and *New Frontier*, if the space they allot to discussion of various literary genres is any indication, rank fiction third in importance behind poetry and drama. Poetry, obviously, better suits the space constraints of the little magazine interested in publishing original creative work than does either drama or fiction. But the leftist interest in drama can be accounted for in broader material terms as well: as Ruth McKenzie wrote in her 1939 article entitled 'Proletarian Literature in Canada,' 'the field of drama is more encouraging than that of fiction. Perhaps this is because it is easier in Canada to get a play performed than to get a story published.'[50] Certainly, the popular agitation-propaganda dramatic form of the period lends itself better to the kind of activism advocated by the magazines – involving the audience in a direct and immediate manner – than does fiction, and many of the journalistic pieces in both magazines report on the effects of various performances on proletarian audiences. The leftist disregard of modern realism, then, may be partly a by-product of the lack of attention that the leftist magazines paid to fiction in general, and the novel form in particular.

But the most significant objections that the critics and writers of *Masses* and *New Frontier* raised to modern realism grew out of these political and material concerns, and related to their notions of the very function and form of realistic writing. The contributors to these little magazines, as we shall see, go to great lengths to describe and justify the precise differences that divide the 'socialist realism' they advocated from the 'bourgeois realism' they opposed. While these magazines may be fairly accused of questionable literary standards in terms of what they often allowed to be published in their pages – as might both *Canadian Bookman* and *The Canadian Forum* – their rejection of a so-called 'bourgeois realism' was not arbitrary or simply the result of aesthetic ignorance or indifference, as is sometimes suggested. The leftist writers and critics had very specific reasons for preferring their socialist realism, and these reasons stem not just from political and material concerns, but also from their vehement disagreement with certain practices of both the modern realists and certain of the Anglo-American high modernists: ambiguity, impersonality, experimentalism, and psychological realism. *Masses* and *New Frontier* paid less attention to fiction than to other literary genres, but between them they published a few dozen short stories during their runs, and these works constitute a distinct and significant genre in their own right. Donna Philips's *Voices of Discord: Canadian Short Stories of the 1930s* (1979) gathers together twenty-six of these Depression-era stories of protest, which she argues 'offer a fascinating view of Depression-era experiences,' including 'poverty, the alienation of industrial workers, the memory of world war, the threat of fascism and renewed war.'[51] Even a cursory glance at these short stories reveals that they share both these thematic concerns and many technical aspects with modern-realist fiction: all of them are realist, at least insofar as they discuss real individuals facing pressing issues of the day, and they generally employ straightforward language, engage contemporary subjects, have a descriptive emphasis, and provide idiomatic dialogue. But in spite of these similarities, some very important differences exist between these stories and modern-realist fiction of the same period.

The first of these differences grows out of the socialist-realist belief that literature ought to function as propaganda and critique. While the modern realist, as I have argued, carries out a variety of experiments to permit the inclusion of subjective perspectives within the framework of purportedly objective narration, one function of socialist realism – often called 'proletarian realism' or more inclusively 'proletarian literature' in discussions of the day – is to interpret so-called 'reality' in a creative manner to foreground a particular ideology. As McKenzie writes, '"proletarian literature" is defined as literature which describes the life of the working class from a class-conscious and revolutionary point of view. It is literature in which the worker is regarded as the victim of capitalistic exploitation; as the instrument of revolution by which a new social order will be ushered in. He, himself, is of more importance as a factor in society than as an individual. Our capitalist system is regarded as responsible for the disintegration of society with its attending evils, and as the root of all wars.'[52] In other words, the primary task of the socialist realist is *not* to reflect life as the broad reading public has been used to seeing or experiencing it. This is the revolutionary aspect of his or her art: to record life so that ideological conclusions can easily be drawn by a narrator or reader. As V.F. Calverton wrote in 'Literature as a Revolutionary Force,' an article which appeared in *The Canadian Forum* in March 1935, 'Proletarian literature ... is more than realistic literature. It is a literature dominated by a dynamic *mythos*, carrying within itself the seeds of prophetic conviction and challenge.'[53] In other words, the 'realism' of a given work, or its credibility as a reflection of reality, is enhanced rather than mitigated by the infusion of a 'mythos,' an admittedly subjective element, into the melange: this is the sense in which socialist realism is 'more than realistic literature.'

E. Cecil-Smith's 'Propaganda and Art,' which appeared in *Masses* in January 1934, further reveals that the differences between the two forms of realism lie not simply in an ideological disagreement about how so-called reality ought to be interpreted. Citing the Russian writer N. Bukharin, Cecil-Smith arrives at a clear distinction between the competing ways – one passive, one active – in which the two types of realists supposedly approach their subject matter: 'The following very big difference between socialist and bourgeois realism immediately strikes the eye: bourgeois realism as such is content with reality, with reflecting it. Marx said that bourgeois philosophy interprets the world, while the task of socialism is to remake it. But the remaking of the world by the proletariat is a deeply realistic remaking. It is carried out on the basis of a precise study of the real laws of nature.'[54] Cecil-Smith does not discuss these differences between 'socialist' and 'bourgeois' realism in the context of Canadian literature, but this distinction, judging by the volume of articles published in the 1930s journals that acknowledge it, was widely accepted by writers and critics favouring both forms. A number of articles published in *Masses* and *New Frontier* highlighted this distinction between socialist and bourgeois realism: 'Our Credentials,' the opening editorial of *Masses* (April 1932), called for a new realistic literature in opposition to the 'barren fields of Canadian bourgeois culture,' which 'propagates those ideas which are most acceptable to capitalism.'[55] T. Richardson's 'In Defense of Pure Art' appeared in *Masses* in July-August 1932 and created an opposition between 'socialist realism' and 'modernism ... the dead culture of an effete civilization.'[56] Jack Lind's 'A Significant Turn in Soviet Literature' (*Masses*, March-April 1933) directed 'bourgeois' Canadian writers to employ the socialist realism he detected in Russian writing. Numerous other articles and letters published in *Masses* also drew this distinction implicitly. A legion of articles with very similar conclusions appeared in *New Frontier*, including Eric Duthie's 'Gathering Strength' (April 1936), Sybil M. Gordan's 'Man Alive in the Novel' (April 1937), Margaret Fairley's 'Books' (May 1937), and Edwin Berry Burgum's 'The Outlook for the Novel' (September 1937), among others. Here, then, is the most fundamental difference between socialist realism advocated by the leftist magazines and the modern realism and modernism they critiqued: the first group of writers was actively engaged in remaking reality in their works; the second group was, at least from the point of view of the leftists, concerned with merely reflecting reality.

While both types of realism are concerned with the lives of ordinary individuals and their place in the modern world, the ways in which they approach this subject reflect their differing approaches to how 'reality' ought to be conveyed. The social-realist portraits of the 'common' individual of the period display a remarkable unity of tone and technique: they are *all* written from a third-person, detached, impersonal, omniscient perspective, and their narratives are stark, grounded in unremarkable, everyday happenings, lacking in dramatic incident, and generally resistant to ideological interpretation. Even those novels of the period that deviate from this model to a degree do so in the typical modern-realist fashion: that is, they stretch the boundaries of the realist form to infuse their objectivist portraits with limited subjective perspectives. In Callaghan's *Strange Fugitive* (1928), the life of Harry Trotter is portrayed largely without dramatic incident – we follow him through everyday events of working, drinking, romancing – almost until he is gunned down by gangsters in the melodramatic final chapter of the novel. While the conclusion to Callaghan's novel has a clear symbolic meaning – Trotter's demise is the result of his own moral disintegration brought about both by the effects of modern life and by his own solipsism – it does not provide an ideological conclusion to the story. And, while many of the typical subjects of the leftist story are impersonally rendered in this novel – unemployment, economic hardship, strained family relations – Callaghan chooses to supplement (or compromise) the objective mode of reportage only through an indirect symbolism that has a moral and psychological function.

A later social-realist novel, Len Peterson's *Chipmunk* (1949), also uses a symbolic device to draw attention to his characters' psychological experience of the modern world. Again, we are given a portrait of everyday, working-class individuals whose situations might easily be exploited for their ideological import: the central character, Claude Widgewood, a baker, and his wife Faustina live a working-class life in an archetypal Canadian city of the period. Peterson's intent, on one level at least, is clearly to convey the dreariness of lives lived at the bottom of the economic scale, and this partly explains his title: the protagonist is compared to a 'chipmunk,' which is, of course, 'a tiny, squirrel-like rodent inhabiting the North American continent ... it scurries about, busily collecting and storing ... it is easily trapped; perhaps it is not too intelligent.'[57] Yet as the metaphor suggests, Peterson is critical primarily not of the society in which the Widgewoods live, but of his characters' stupidity and lack of ambition. Peterson's novel is not so much an ideological examination of working-class life as a naturalistic caricature of the working-class man who is derided and ultimately defeated by his society. Although there is a perceptible leftist perspective to the narrative, Peterson, like Callaghan, avoids offering obvious political interpretations of situations. The Communists who encourage Claude to join the struggle for workers' rights, for example, are depicted as small-minded, self-serving, and manipulative. And, while Claude's boss, Mr Cadenza, is constantly concerned with financial matters, he is hardly the stereotypical capitalist boss of the leftist magazine story and is shown to be fair and legitimately concerned with the well-being of his employees. Peterson's novel is exemplary of the social-realist novel of the period: while it is willing to stretch the boundaries of the realist form to symbolic ends, its central preoccupation remains with providing a detached, purportedly objectivist rendering of everyday life in the modern world.

While socialist-realist fiction is certainly more limited in terms of basic subject matter – not only must it render the lives of common, everyday, ordinary individuals, but it must also do so within the context of leftist ideology – it is, perhaps surprisingly, much more varied in form. In fact, the extremes to which the socialist realists go to convey their political message within the confines of the realist form are sometimes remarkable. This is because there appears to be a fundamental conflict inherent in their aesthetic: on the one hand, the socialist realist desires the materiality, authority, objectivity, simplicity, directness, honesty, and credibility of the realist form; on the other hand, the project of 're-making the world,' as outlined by Cecil-Smith, is idealistic, revolutionary, subjective, complex, indirect, propagandist, and likely to be met with incredulity. The result of this conflict is a body of fiction that, while superficially realistic, has very little in common with other forms of realistic writing, including modern realism. Most obviously, this conflict manifests itself in a heavy-handed didacticism that is apparent almost uniformly in the leftist story of the period, and in sharp contrast to the aims of the modern realist. For example, in H. Francis's 'Freedom of Contract,' published in *Masses* in March-April 1933, the out-of-work Ollie Godden – who could be a character in any of the social-realist novels of the period – is presented in a manner that emphasizes neither his psychology nor even the particulars of his own situation. Rather, the author uses the story of Godden as an opportunity to expound on political matters using the catchphrases of leftist culture: 'He was going to work – at the Pogey House. That was why he was not bubbling over with joy, for this day's work would pay no light bills or pay anything else for that matter. Ollie had thought it was work he wanted but now he had discovered that what he wanted was the right to participate in useful production for himself and his family.'[58]

In other stories, a pointed symbolism is employed to similar ends. While the modern realist occasionally employs symbolism to shade an otherwise impersonal narrative, many of the socialist-realist pieces become so symbolic that their realist intentions are all but eclipsed. In James Hinton's 'Meat!' published in *New Frontier* in July-August 1937, the story of two hungry, presumably out-of-work, Canadian men is told in a realistic fashion. Yet a symbolic strain that runs through the story gets out of control, and the two men, to feed themselves, end up stealing meat from a caged bear named 'Trotsky,' while a number of obviously typecast passers-by interfere: 'Then there comes a fat-buttocked policeman with shoulders like the neck of a beer bottle, the embodiment of supercilious insectile buffoonery.'[59] In another example, George Winslade's 'Rainbow Chasing' from the July-August 1932 *Masses*, the realistic narrative begins like so many others: 'Smoky was broke. He had got up early that morning, before the wife and kids were awake. Relief was cut off.'[60] But after Smoky goes to the unemployment office and spends 'the forenoon ... discussing the class struggle in the slave market,' he lands a job on a schooner, and the tale becomes, in effect, a sea yarn. While Smoky does appropriately get caught up in the politics of the longshoremen during his tenure as a member of the crew, by the end of the tale the language of the story has changed entirely and the realistic opening is only a vague memory: 'Smoky was helping the old man pack his clubber, when a chippy walked up the gangplank and inquired for captain Doyle.'[61]

These stories foreground a fundamental difference between the aesthetics of socialist and modern realism. In contrast to the socialist realists, who write texts that first and foremost identify clear problems with ideological import and solutions, the modern realists appear convinced that a kind of moral or spiritual ambiguity is a defining feature of the modern human condition. The modern realist neither sees this state of affairs as a problem nor seeks to analyse it in an endeavour to find 'solutions.' Rather, this ambiguity – which arises out of complex social relations, human psychology, the decline of traditional religion, and a host of other early-twentieth century preoccupations – presents the modern realists with an exciting creative opportunity. Accordingly, the modern realists rise to this challenge, and they present detached, impersonal, purportedly objective portraits of the modern individual in a state of social, psychological, moral, and spiritual crisis: Callaghan's Father Dowling in *Such Is My Beloved* (1934), Graham's Erica Drake in *Earth and High Heaven* (1944), Athanase Tallard in MacLennan's *Two Solitudes* (1945), Craig Forrester in Durkin's *The Magpie* (1923), and Matt Striker in Baird's *Waste Heritage* (1939), to name only some of the most memorable. Issues of social and political importance are raised in these novels but not for their own sake, and the modern-realist story is not rhetorically structured to solve or explore these issues systematically or directly. But such an impersonal, objectivist stance is what the leftist critics, anticipating more contemporary criticisms of experimental modernism, found most distasteful in modern writing of the period. As John Fairfax wrote in one of the few articles on socialist realism to appear in *The Canadian Forum*, 'Art for Man's Sake' (August 1936), 'the present revolt against those who pretend to have achieved a neutral objectivity in their art is based upon three contentions: first, that it is impossible to do anything of the kind; second, that most of the supposedly "objective" artists are in fact biased in favour of the kind of society we have, and implicitly justify its defects as either negligible or ineradicable; third, that those who contend that environment has little to do with shaping character are posing an indefensible thesis.'[62] Yet the socialist realist does not, following the logic of Fairfax's argument, simply attempt to negate detached, impersonal objectivism in fiction; in fact, it is the modern realists with their commitment to representing subjective experiences within their narratives who ultimately come closest to achieving what Fairfax advocates. Rather, the socialist realist supplants a different claim to objectivity over that of the modern realist: my writing is closer to the 'truth,' more 'real,' because I am aware of the reality of the Marxist dialectic and you are not.

This explains a seeming contradiction in the statements of many of the socialist realists who insist almost in the same breath that their art is idealistic and objective. Cecil-Smith, for example, in the July-August 1932 *Masses*, would contrast the revolutionary socialist realism to modernism by identifying an idealist thrust in the former: 'The revolutionary artist today is not the modernist who continues to express the ideology of the ruling class under capitalism ... He is the artist, however poor he may be mechanically, who strives to express the ideas of the future ruling class – the working people.'[63] Yet another *Masses* article, from January 1934, reveals that Cecil-Smith believed, as did so many of the other socialist realists of the period, that such idealism was precisely what characterized their writing as *objective*: 'We, the revolutionary artists, are the true realists; the dynamic realists. They – the static realists, the naturalists, the romanticists – are the ones who can see only part, sometimes a very small part, of the whole picture and therefore can tell only a partial truth.'[64] In one respect, then, socialist realism differs from modern realism in that it seeks to create a realistic portrait of a fictional world, whereas the latter seeks to make a so-called 'real' world into fiction. Ultimately, however, the modern realists did not consider impersonality or objectivity in their writing to be synonymous with, or even closely related to, political neutrality or writerly disinterest in the social import of subject matter. Rather, objectivity and impersonality were part and parcel of a technique, common to all modern-realist fiction, that might loosely be termed 'reportage.' On the simplest level, this meant the kind of detached, omniscient, detailed rendering of events that I have discussed already in a variety of contexts. But the boldest experiments with the modern-realist form also grew out of this interest in reportage; my discussion of the oeuvres of major writers in other chapters reveals a variety of writerly struggles to report things not easily reported: mental states, spiritual experiences, moral questioning, the modern human condition. 'Reportage,' in fact, is perhaps the one concept that most inclusively defines the technique of the modern-realist novel. As we shall see, it is also the characteristic of modernist writing that most outraged the socialist realists.

Reportage, then, is both the feature that most clearly distinguishes modern realism from socialist realism and a larger and encompassing mode that both arises from and necessitates so many modern-realist techniques and assumptions. Rifkind identifies a 'documentary modernism' in 1930s Canadian literary culture and suggests that it achieves some of its most complex expression in the novel, which is among other things 'a documentary in the normally understood sense of a text that draws on the everyday and aspires to honesty and accuracy in its representation.'[65] I contend that a documentary impulse informs three general types of reportage found in the urban and social-realist novel in particular, and the modern-realist novel in general. Each of these types represents a different strategy by which the modern realist attempts to engage the contemporary world from a detached, objectivist stance, while at the same time incorporating a range of subjective perspectives into the narrative. The fundamental importance of these types of reportage to modern realism as a movement cannot be overstated: *every* modern-realist novel employs at least one of these methods, all of the major experiments of the modern realists with literary form grow out of these methods, and they have much in common with related techniques usually associated with experimental modernisms. The most common and least remarkable of these methods might be called 'direct reportage,' something I have indirectly discussed in a variety of contexts while pointing out the simplicity, directness, omniscience, and purported objectivity sought by so many modern realists. In this mode, the writer becomes almost like the imagist poet who attempts to establish a direct connection between language and the subject being represented. These modern-realist texts are at once and somewhat paradoxically concerned with an immediate representation of 'reality,' of the 'thing itself,' and with appearing autotelic. They have no clearly defined narrative persona, and they imply an accuracy of method and honesty of purpose throughout. The narrative in these stories is designed to generate the impression of transparency, extreme impersonality, complete omniscience, and utter objectivity. At the same time, these narratives are not journalistic: they display a profound concern with exploring subjective states within their objectivist frameworks and with telling a story in a manner that is artful. These characteristics, as we shall see in the next chapter, form the core of the Callaghan style, and all of his early novels are examples of direct reportage. So, too, are most of the other urban and social-realist novels of the period, including Hubert Evans's *The New Front Line* (1927), Patrick Slater's *Robert Harding: A Story of Every Day Life* (1938), and Margaret Duley's *Highway to Valour* (1941).

One of the best novels of the period, Irene Baird's *Waste Heritage* (1939), also presents an example of direct reportage. It is worth examining in some detail as it is one of the few social-realist novels to have received some critical attention and is often wrongly called a propaganda novel. In fact, most of the critics who have written in detail on Baird's novel similarly conclude that its social and political concerns are its most significant feature.[66] Granted, Baird's portrait of working-class men taking part in sit-down strikes in Vancouver explores important political and social issues raised by these critics. But Baird strives not to take sides in her story, and her detached narrative throughout offers a classic example of the direct reportage style. Even in situations where ideological comment might easily be provided, Baird maintains the illusion of objectivity: 'Since he stepped inside the hall Matt was experiencing an odd feeling of black-out, as though his identity were being sucked away and absorbed by the powerful currents of an organization. It made him touchy and defensive; at the same time it gave him a sting of excitement. He tried to pick up the atmosphere quickly, the feel of a mass of men, of hurry, of action, of numbers, of detail, of the dangerous anger boiling in the air.'[67] Not surprisingly, given the lengths to which Baird goes to keep didacticism out of her story, she was bothered by critiques of her novel that insisted on talking about it as a work of propaganda, and in an aptly titled 1976 article, 'Sidown, Brothers, Sidown,' she described her technique and implicitly endorsed the direct reportage style: 'I have never been connected with Communism and I have never thought of myself as a radical if being a radical means wanting to overthrow the system we live in in favour of another political system. I think a reader of the novel will find ... that I don't praise or condemn some of the most important people in the novel who are obviously connected with radical politics.'[68] In light of Baird's remarks, the proliferation of the direct reportage style among modern realists is easy to account for: it is the most obvious technical manifestation of 'reportage' in that it resembles the style of journalism, and it allows the writer interested in the contemporary life to approach the subject immediately and directly. Of course, such writers quickly discovered that detached reportage makes it difficult to enter into the minds of characters and to explore the internal, psychological terrain with the same intensity as the outer world. This also explains the ubiquity of the centre-of-consciousness technique in the novel of the period: so many writers came to the direct reportage style as a way of engaging the modern world and had to find a way of bringing real characters to life in a manner that acknowledged subjectivity without appearing less objective.

A much less common narrative form found in the modern-realist novel might be termed 'mediated reportage.' In this mode, the impersonal, authorial presence itself, or the purportedly objective narrator found in the direct reportage mode, reports from or 'through' a sustained subjective perspective. The most obvious method of mediated reportage is also by far the least common: first-person narration. In fact, there is probably not a single social-realist novel of the period written from the first-person perspective, and there are only a handful in all modern-realist fiction. Almost all of the very few first-person, modern-realist novels take either the diary or epistolary form, which of course implies a kind of objective framework surrounding the first-person narrator. The best examples of mediated reportage in the diary form are Ross's *As For Me and My House* (1941) and Stringer's prairie trilogy (1915–22). Another novel by Irene Baird, *He Rides the Sky* (1941), takes the form of letters written by a Canadian RAF pilot in the Second World War to his family and friends. Baird's novel, like Ross's, is one of the most psychologically intense works produced during the period. But the difficulty of maintaining a sustained first-person voice and simultaneously engaging the large-scale concerns of central interest to the modern realist, and the social realist in particular, is obvious, and this no doubt accounts for the lack of first-person narratives in the period.

A more common method of mediated reportage involves the use of a central character who 'experiences' or 'records' for the reader. While this method differs from direct reportage only by degrees, there are clear examples of texts in which the central character is not merely 'reported on,' but rather *acts* as a reporter. In these cases, the story is not told directly in the central character's voice, but rather filtered through his or her perspective by means of either sustained centre of consciousness or simply heightened narrative attention to his or her particular interpretation of events. Another prairie/social-realist crossover, Stead's *The Smoking Flax* (1924), offers a good example of mediated reportage. In this novel, a university graduate in sociology named Cal becomes a lens through which the novel reports life on a prairie farm as it changes in the early twentieth century. A more complex, and almost metafictional, example of this mode is A.M. Stephen's *The Gleaming Archway* (1929), which rather ingeniously both reports and explores the idea of reportage by making the protagonist a reporter who investigates leftist movements in British Columbia. Stephen hints at still another level of reportage to the text by naming his central character Craig Maitland (A.M. Stephen's initials stand for 'Alexander Maitland'). This method allows Stephen to express his own conservative views in this novel without appearing didactic. Maitland explores a full range of leftist positions in the novel, from the moderate to the revolutionary, yet in the end he does not side with the leftists. Maitland, in the closing scenes of the book, is depicted standing aloof, able to view the political movements of the day with a detached eye, like the unattainable ideal of the modern-realist author himself: 'He was withdrawn, impersonal, looking beyond the man who, like a gramophone, repeated the ancient catchwords of his creed – the confession of faith subscribed to by the scientific Socialists – evolution, revolution, the Movement, the Party, class-consciousness, the class struggle, proletariat! ... Yes – but then, so had all Utopias [seemed] to all the starry-eyed dreamers since the morning of time.'[69] Of course, Maitland arrives at his own ideological interpretation of contemporary politics and, as the reporter himself, is depicted as rendering an objective verdict on the situation. Yet he remains a step removed from the narrator, who, in turn, is simply reporting on Maitland's own thought process and conclusions. While the novel offers a reactionary bias, the opinions appear to be those of a character being objectively rendered by an impersonal narrator. Stephen's example draws attention to the fact that the socialist realists were right in their assertions – obvious perhaps to a contemporary reader – that the purported objectivity of the modern-realist text was largely an illusion; but it also suggests that the modern realists were aware of this very fact and were willing to experiment with creative ways of bringing a subjective perspective, for whatever reason, into a work with an objectivist framework.

A third type of reportage is especially useful to the social realist seeking to explore the individual experience of grand-scale social forces. 'Orchestrated reportage' describes the technique of novels in which the overarching structure is manipulated to allow portions of subjective narration to appear within an objectivist framework. Applications of this technique are highly varied in the modern-realist novel and are often approximations of techniques generally associated with high-modernist prose. As discussed in the previous chapter, Grove's

The Master of the Mill (1944) and *The Seasons* (ca 1938–45) manipulate temporal chronology and space to explore the subjective perspectives of a number of individuals while maintaining an impersonal, almost god-like omniscience. Few examples of orchestrated reportage are as ambitious as Grove's, but such experiments, especially in the social-realist novel, are more common and diverse than one might expect. In some of these examples, the manipulation of structure is designed to allow the author to offer social critique without surrendering the pretence to detachment. In MacLennan's *Two Solitudes* (1945), for example, the examination of the lives of several typecast individuals takes place within an epic, mythological framing narrative that depersonalizes the third-person narration to such a degree that much of the novel's didacticism is muted. In Peterson's *Chipmunk* (1949), the reader is distanced from the protagonist by the narrator's persistent use of a derisive symbolism that frequently links the central character to the animal for which the novel is named. Still, the narrative is otherwise impersonal and the narrator does not critique the central characters directly, encouraging readers to draw critical conclusions of their own. In Child's *God's Sparrows* (1937), the narrator borrows one of Joyce's methods from *A Portrait of the Artist as a Young Man* and permits his language to change its tone and level of sophistication with corresponding thematic developments in the novel; this is partly responsible for the creation of a structural irony in Child's story that permits the reader to side voluntarily with and against a critical narrative voice that might otherwise appear too didactic. In Sime's short-story cycle, *Sister Woman* (1920), the individual stories are framed by a prologue and epilogue in which an unnamed man and woman debate 'The Woman's Question,' expressing attitudes that correspond to typical assumptions of their respective genders; the stories related by the woman to the man between these bracketing narratives are not didactic in themselves, but they take on heightened social significance in the context of the book as a whole.

Perhaps the most overtly modernist example of orchestrated reportage appears in MacLennan's unpublished *So All Their Praises* (1933). To depict the large social and historical forces that influence and shape the lives of his characters, MacLennan developed what he called 'kaleidoscopic passages' which incorporate numerous and often competing voices and fragments.[70] More specifically, these 'kaleidoscopic passages' – similar in technique to passages in F. Scott Fitzgerald's *The Beautiful and Damned* (1922) spoken between Beauty and The Voice –

take the form of dramatic dialogues spoken by historical and symbolic individuals:

> Adolph Hitler said: 'Deutschland von Marxismus frei! Jobs for all the middle class can be had if we revenge ourselves on Jews and other traitors.'
>
> Herr Brüning said: 'We must be careful' ...
>
> Mr. Baldwin said: 'I believe in the innate decency of the English. I am also a born optimist.'
>
> The Pope said: 'Birth control is murder.'
>
> Mr. MacDonald said: 'Great steps forward have been taken towards the solidarity of international understanding throughout the whole world' ...
>
> An old man said: 'I envy the youth today. They will see great things. No one is bored any longer.'[71]

MacLennan's goal in these 'kaleidoscopic passages' is to depict large historical forces, or what Grove called 'world consciousness,' in action. *So All Their Praises* despite being an experimental modernist novel, is not essentially different in its aims from many of the more ambitious modern-realist novels, confirming that high modernism and modern realism differ only in terms of the degree to which they are willing to partake of the boldest narrative experiments of the period.

One of the most effective examples of orchestrated reportage is found in Garner's *Cabbagetown* (1950). In this text, the author creates a number of narrative layers that allow him to emphasize both the immediate and broad significance of his story. Some individual scenes are rendered in the direct reportage style. In other scenes there is a perceptible, ironic narrative voice. The individual scenes are precise, detailed, autonomous, almost like photographs, and Garner identifies 'photographic realism' to be a tenet of his work in a 1969 interview with Allen Anderson: 'I think I got the photographic realism from my literary mentor who happens to be hardly known by this generation – John Dos Passos. He influenced me more, I think, than anyone, including Hemingway or any of the others. He of course dealt in photographic realism.'[72] But to enable his narrative to weave in and out of the minds of his characters, and to move from scene to scene, from snapshot to snapshot, he builds a detailed, realistic scaffolding around his story that makes it read almost like a book of history with a detached perspective and broad sweep: there are countless references to 'real,' identifiable places in Toronto's Cabbagetown, and individual sections of the novel are dated. And, predating A.M. Klein's modernist novel *The Second Scroll*, published a year later, Garner employs the 'mythic method' to lend his novel large symbolic significance and an almost Biblical sense of impersonality and authority: large sections of *Cabbagetown* are titled 'Genesis,' 'Transition,' and 'Exodus.'

The orchestrated reportage of Garner and his contemporaries freely included elements such as irony, symbolism, and myth, revealing that the modern realists did not consider themselves reporters in the journalistic sense, or social scientists, or historians. Their aim was not to provide a truthful account of what happened on a phenomenological level. Instead, they wanted to build inventive narrative structures that enabled them to move across a broad range of subjects, in and out of psychological states and across the varied terrain of the physical world, in a manner that was both credible and artful. The modern realists' 'reportage' was designed to enable them to represent any subject, however large or small, or tangible or abstract, that was relevant to their exploration of the modern human condition. Given these aims, it is not difficult to see why Garner credits Dos Passos with providing an important literary influence. In his USA trilogy – *The 42nd Parallel* (1930), *Nineteen Nineteen* (1932), and *The Big Money* (1936) – Dos Passos offers a distinctly modernist example of orchestrated reportage. In these works, sections of direct reportage are juxtaposed with fragments of contextualizing and largely factual 'newsreel' items, 'camera eye' passages that offer up interior monologues rendered from the perspective of the implied author, and biographical sections on the lives of important Americans that contrast sharply with those of the 'common' characters in Dos Passos's story. In comparison with these methods, the modern realists' experiments were generally subdued but their goals and the effects they achieved were similar. Objectivity and impersonality in fiction did not necessitate a style closely resembling journalism: they entailed, for both modern realists and other modernists, a creative manipulation of literary form, often in striking and obviously 'subjective' ways, to tell a larger objective 'truth' about the contemporary world.

All of these types of reportage, so central to the modern-realist aesthetic, are fundamentally different from the standard, journalistic type of reportage that is sometimes associated with the writing of the period. F.W. Watt, in fact, identifies the journalistic form of reportage as a key defining feature of 1930s prose and a catalyst to the 'emergence' of realism in Canadian fiction: 'The events of the 1930s proceeded to channel ... critical reaction along ideological lines [and] the impact on both prose and poetry was marked. There appeared numerous examples of "reportage," a new prose form ... [that] required a certain discipline: a balance between editorializing and artistry, an eye for vivid and telling detail, powers of concentration. Its significance was not so much in itself, however, as in the movement which it symptomized and encouraged: the movement towards contemporaneity and realism in fiction.'[73] Watt identifies Dorothy Livesay's 'Corbin – A Company Town Fights for Its Life,' published in *New Frontier* in June 1936, as a prime example of the reportage of the period. While it is true that the sketch was a relatively widespread prose form of the 1930s,[74] these sketches are simply journalistic pieces, and their form of reportage should not be confused with the modern-realist reportage that, as I have already argued, was *not* a by-product of 1930s ideological concerns, having come into being following the first manifestos for modern realism a decade earlier. It is immediately obvious that Livesay's story does not fit any of the categories of modern-realist reportage; indeed it is not even fiction, but journalism: 'Again, going on relief would have a bad effect on the single men, many of them union leaders, by forcing them out of the town into relief camps. For in spite of the Federal Government's promises, these camps remain open in Alberta and B.C. Lastly, relief would not be granted to all the miners, as a goodly number of them have property in the shape of automobiles bought during the boom days.'[75] Unlike the modern-realist story that strives to generate the impression of objectivity through literary artifice that is often elaborate, Livesay's sketch presumes to be, like good journalism, merely factual and artless.

But most of the little-magazine short fiction of the period is not like Livesay's sketch. One of the characteristics of the socialist-realist short story of the period is the often unsuccessful attempt to achieve authoritative factuality within a fictional narrative. Such stories, because they fail so demonstrably, are very useful for highlighting both the differences between modern-realist and socialist-realist reportage, and the kinds of struggles the modern realists faced in their own variously successful attempts to bring subjectivities into an objectivist narrative. In A. Poole's 'Fish,' a short story which appeared in *Masses* in July-August 1932, the first-person narrator, an unnamed worker who has been placed in a labour camp for reasons that are not made clear in the story, aims to heighten the reader's outrage at the capitalist treatment of the worker. Presumably to make this mistreatment more readily apparent and to heighten its emotional impact on the reader, the mistreatment of the worker takes place in the present tense. Yet the fact that the narrator is engaged in the act of reporting these events just as they occur appears ridiculous; on the one hand we have the narrative voice describing degradation from a highly subjective perspective; on the other hand it is rendered to us coldly, directly, without emotion. The author's attempt to fuse an objective authority with a subjective, personal account of the situation results in the incredibility of both perspectives: 'I am afraid to drink water out of the tin cup. Some of the boys working in the quarry have syphillis [*sic*] and gonorrhea. They drink out of that cup, too. I don't want to get venereal disease, but what can I do? I am thirsty. I drink and trust to luck.'[76] A much better story, J.K. Thomas's 'Production,' published in the July-August 1937 issue of *New Frontier*, embodies the problem of managing perspectives differently. This story, vividly describing the experience of women working in a tomato-peeling factory, begins with the typical detached third-person narrator: 'There was a silence, while they peeled the steamed tomatoes with skilled fingers.'[77] Yet before long, detached reportage is presumably not conveying the political message of the story sufficiently, and a didactic narrative voice intrudes: 'The Canadian government has a maximum hour law for women ... There is no such law for the men who get twenty-cents an hour. They work a fifteen hour day ... so that they can make a living wage.' Next, the narrator shifts jarringly into the first person – 'I had drifted into Burlington, on the shores of Lake Ontario' – before continuing the story with a clumsy intermingling of all three voices.[78]

These leftist magazine stories demonstrate that the modern realists were not the only ones who experienced difficulty reconciling objective and subjective perspectives in their writing. Yet while the modern realist considered such a balancing act a creative challenge and developed complex and varied technical strategies to make it happen, the leftist writers, if their works are a fair indication, all but ignored the problem. This may partly have been due to a lack of skill: the vast majority of contributors to *Masses* and *New Frontier* were amateur writers. But there are also important aesthetic issues that explain the divergent methods of the modern and socialist realists. As my discussion of the various forms of 'reportage' revealed, the modern realists devise numerous narrative strategies to incorporate subjective perspectives into their work, but such perspectives always appear within a larger objectivist framework. The socialist realists, on the other hand, are not interested in the aesthetic distinction between objective and subjective modes of narration, and they include both modes, without a final 'appeal' to objectivity, detachment, or impersonality.

The modern-realist and socialist-realist modes can also be contrasted, perhaps more revealingly, in this way. Behind (or underneath, or around) all of the various subjective layers of the modern-realist narrative, there is an implied objective and impersonal artist, not unlike the modernist author in Joyce's infamous passage from *A Portrait of the Artist as a Young Man* (1916): 'The artist, like the God of the creation, remains within or behind or beyond or above his handiwork, invisible, refined out of existence, indifferent, paring his fingernails.'[79] The modern-realist text, even when it presents subjective and competing perspectives, always implies such a detached author, or reporter, writing the various forms of reportage. In the case of the socialist realist, the author is anything but impersonal, and is frequently involved in the action of the story itself in various ways: authorial intrusion, overtly didactic narration, the obvious manipulation of structure to reflect ideological models. In these stories, the detached, authorial presence is supplanted by the Marxist dialectic itself, which is itself at once an objective, absolute truth, and subjective by virtue of the fact that it is, as Calverton revealed earlier, 'dominated by a dynamic *mythos*, carrying within itself the seeds of prophetic conviction and challenge.'[80] The modern-realist text, then, is governed by a formal aesthetic of impersonality and objectivity that ultimately takes precedence over subject matter. Any subject that is rendered in accordance with such an aesthetic is suitable for the modern realist; this again clearly contradicts notions that modern realists were somehow merely reflecting 'reality' and explains why there is no significant formal difference between the works of rural and urban modern realists. But the socialist-realist aesthetic is *not* defined by any clear formal principles. It is defined, rather, by a particular subject matter that is more important that any formal, stylistic, or technical device or method; by the same token, in the socialist-realist paradigm, objective and subjective modes are conflated.

Accordingly, when the modern realists laboured to reconcile objectivity and subjectivity in accordance with their aesthetic, developing their varied forms of reportage, the socialist realists responded with alternating hostility and indifference. Such technical innovations, to them, were unnecessary distractions from the overriding socio-political functions of literature and were called indulgent, elitist, escapist, pointlessly experimental, decadent, bourgeois, and therefore reactionary. On these grounds, numerous articles in both *Masses* and *New Frontier* reprobated experimental prose and poetry, calling for writers to leave their so-called 'ivory tower' and face the world directly. These articles revealingly equate modern realism with the more obviously experimental forms of modernism. The leftist critique of experimentalism – either modern-realist or modernist – is not the result of a superficial disagreement about the value of experiment itself, or the form of 'reportage' that ought to prevail in the new realism. Calverton summed up the socialist-realist problem with modern realism by drawing attention to two competing aims of literature of the period: 'Literature ... can be *interpreted,* however, in only two ways: psychologically or sociologically ... The psychological approach tends to stress the importance of the individual more than that of the environment; the sociological tends to stress the importance of the environment more than that of the individual.'[81] The socialist realist considered society, and its close connection to politics and ideology, the fundamental concern of literature and the context in which authors must inalterably situate their stories. But the modernists and modern realists, because of their interest in psychological realism, were considered by the leftists to be 'bourgeois,' focusing on the individual rather than the greater good and ignoring the social implications of art in their selfish and indulgent aesthetic exercises.

Accordingly, a considerable amount of space in the critical articles of both *Masses* and *New Frontier* is devoted to critiquing the psychological thrust of modern literature. The leftist critique appears to have derived from the assumption that the sociological and psychological impulses were incompatible. This point of view is summed up by Lukács in a 1932 article, 'Reportage or Portrayal?': 'The bourgeois novel, ever more lost in the psychological depiction of private fears and feelings, was absolutely unsuited to tackling in any way the great and general questions of our time, let alone to adopting an appropriate attitude towards them.'[82] This seminal critique was reflected by Canadian critics of the period writing in the leftist magazines. In an April 1937 article published in *New Frontier*, 'Man Alive in the Novel,' Sybil M. Gordan argued that 'the problem of the individual ... and society can only be solved in the novel when the writer sees the solution clearly in life. The individual can no longer solve the problem simply by looking within himself.'[83] Even more tellingly, Margaret Fairley's 'Books,' published in *New Frontier* in May 1937, linked psychological emphasis to a kind of epistemological 'reportage' in a condemnatory manner and argued that reporting inwardly and outwardly derived from the same indulgent, decadent, 'ivory tower' impulse that ought to be resisted:

> Neither writer nor reader ... can be passive if the art is good ... That is why realistic, photographic, description, whether of factory or drawing-

> room, is not good art, and that is also why the recording in words or paint of dream-images which flit across the mind's eye is not good art. Neither recording, nor playing with, the world as made is a satisfying occupation for the man who is aware in his bones of the effort which goes every day into the remaking of the world for us. In the present time of crisis only the bourgeois artist can deny the urgency of life. He prides himself on remaining aloof, he is sceptical because he is so completely immune from the need of using his energy that he has to waste it on thinking this way and that ... Only by belonging either actually or with full imaginationfi [*sic*] to the class, which has to create or perish, can an artist of today satisfy his own impulse ... literature has become divorced from the most significant effort, and has become merely an enjoyment, a rest, a consolation.[84]

Critiques of epistemological writing such as these reveal the socialist realists to be inalterably opposed to some of the boldest technical experiments of the modernists with psychological realism – stream of consciousness, expressionism, multivocality, internal monologue, impressionism, and symbolism – which they consider methods of heightened 'realistic' reportage. The socialist realists found the modern realists too experimental, too subjectivist to be included in their ranks, even when their works were political, because their emphasis upon psychology led them away from the unambiguous world of the Marxist dialectic. At the same time, the socialist realists found the modern realists too objectivist because, as Fairley's argument reveals, the experiments of the modernists and those of the modern realists arose from the same 'aloof,' 'sceptical,' and 'bourgeois' contentment with the world as it was, and not from an idealistic contemplation of the world as it might be. The leftist critique, then, confirms what I have argued all along: the modern realists were modernists.

The leftist critique also indirectly confirms the claims made by both of the major modern realists discussed so far in depth – Knister and Grove – who also differentiated their own realism from modernism only by degrees, only by virtue of their avoidance of self-conscious or extreme experimentation. But because the distinctions between socialist realism and social realism have not been clearly drawn by critics, the subtle experiments of the modern realists have been easily overlooked, and the important aesthetic assumptions they share with other modernist writers have not been acknowledged. Instead, their urban and social-realist works are conflated with the more infamous socialist realism of the period, which is neither modern – in the sense that modernist experimentalism is modern – nor realist – in the sense that it avoids the romantic subject and seeks to represent an actual, contemporary world in an 'objective' manner. By the same definitions, the modern realists were in their own minds unmistakably modern *and* realist: this entailed, in the broadest sense, balancing the sociological perspective with the psychological, to reinvoke Calverton's terms, and experimenting with the realist form to allow it artfully to include both concerns.

Callaghan's most clear-cut example of social realism, *They Shall Inherit the Earth* (1935), demonstrates one writer's attempt to balance these two concerns. On the surface, this novel is almost a catalogue of the important social concerns of the period: the Depression, the aftermath of the Great War, the urban experience, class warfare, political radicalism, changing moral values, are all discussed in its pages. The central character, Michael Aikenhead (his psychological problems are blatantly alluded to in his name), is a well-educated young man who cannot find work because of hard economic times and his own unwillingness to embrace capitalist values. The entire story is built around one central dramatic event: Michael allows his half-brother to drown in a boating accident after the two have a heated argument which has an underlying sociological cause: 'I hated everything you ever stood for. I hated your soft useless life. I hated you because you were a bum and got away with it and I had to work. I hated you because you didn't have a spark of pride in you. I hated your guts because you never believed in anything but your balls and your belly. I know all about you. Guys like you are all around, just vomited up by a sick class in society.'[85]

Undeniably, there is a certain didacticism inherent in this exchange. Callaghan invites us to see Michael, who speaks these words to his half-brother David as an embodiment of the leftist revolutionary anger at a capitalist system and the bourgeois class it enables. Yet after this incident occurs about a quarter of the way through the book the real story begins to unfold: the psychological aftermath of the murder. Michael, for reasons that are not ideologically grounded, dislikes his father and is unwilling to ask him for help, instead allowing him to be blamed for the death of David. The most compelling sections of the novel are those that describe the guilt of Michael and the psychological alienation of his father: 'Aikenhead came a little late to church, for he did not want to be noticed by the prominent merchants and professional men and their wives who had once been his friends. He wanted to be unobtrusive and quiet this morning, for his loneliness had been greater than he could bear, and now he was going to make a simple, unpretentious gesture toward the world and his God.'[86] The social and political issues found everywhere in the novel refuse to coalesce into any kind of ideological pattern or to offer a sustained social critique. Instead, Callaghan exploits these issues for their dramatic and moral significance. And this novel, despite being Callaghan's most obvious example of social realism, is also his first to employ a sustained centre-of-consciousness technique, revealing that, for the modern realist, a heightened attention to social concerns could in fact *increase* the psychological intensity of the novel.

Given the clear differences between the aesthetics of urban and social realism and the socialist realism of the 1930s, it is unfortunate that the two have been conflated and compacted into a few small spaces in Canada's literary histories. The dominant place of the leftist little magazines in the literary culture of the 1930s, and the fact that they ignored urban and social realism and supplanted it with their own fiction, means that urban and social realism are often dismissed along with the leftist movement that some conservative critics would unfortunately rather forget. As Watt writes about the prose of the period, 'the direct and savagely indignant protests [of 1930s fiction] have no doubt permanently given way to the subtler and more profound probings and ironies of works like Gabrielle Roy's *The Tin Flute*, and Hugh MacLennan's *The Watch That Ends the Night*, but recent novelists (Ethel Wilson, John Marlyn, Earle Birney, Roger Lemelin) have drawn attention to rather than exhausted the richness of the material.'[87] Denigrating or ignoring the urban and social-realist contingent of modern realism also leads to a skewed sense of the types of modern realism that have not been overlooked. Without its urban counterpart, prairie realism becomes a regionalist anomaly on the Canadian literary landscape, and it can easily be concluded that rural representation and realism go hand in hand. As Pacey writes, 'such realism as there was [in Canada between the wars] developed almost exclusively on the prairies, where there was a distinctive pattern of life which could be clearly differentiated from that of Europe and even from that of the United States, and where the conditions of pioneer life were so forbidding that it was impossible to idyllicize them.'[88] And one cannot help but wonder what effect the neglect of this national body of fiction concerned with the largest issues of the twentieth century has had on conceptions of Canadian literature as a whole. In fact, it is only by displacing urban and social realism from its rightful place in Canadian literary history that some of the most enduring readings of Canadian literature as a whole become possible, as George Woodcock reveals:

> During the 1930s a few isolated novels of some merit might have been classified as vaguely 'social realist' … but the main development of Canadian fiction in fact bypasses the matter of realism, European or North American, largely because Canadians, faced with the wilderness on one side and a dangerously powerful neighbour on the other, had little doubt as to the actual nature of their predicament; what they needed was the combination of mythology and ideology that would enable them to emerge from mere escapism and present a countervision more real than actuality. Hence the weakness of realism as a tradition in literature.[89]

Recognizing the full extent to which Canada's realism was modern, however, necessitates an appreciation of the efforts of the urban and social realists, who approached the same subjects as the international modernists with similar aesthetic assumptions and concerns. But why, exactly, did the modern realists en masse reject the boldest experiments of the high modernists in favour of their own, relatively conservative, forms? What is the precise nature of the relationship between international modernisms and modern realism? The example of Morley Callaghan, the one Canadian writer of the period who was both a central figure in the modern-realist movement and a part of the larger phenomenon generally called international modernism, helps to answer these questions.

7
Morley Callaghan's Cosmopolitan Modern Realism

Although Morley Callaghan is the pre-eminent early twentieth-century Canadian social and urban realist, it is impossible to account for his literary aesthetic and influence solely in these contexts. Much of Callaghan's fiction is concerned with the place of the individual within larger social structures, and with exploring many issues of interest to Canada's urban and social realists generally. Yet Callaghan's most important and influential contribution to early twentieth-century Canadian fiction is stylistic, not ideological or thematic. No other Canadian novelist of the period has received nearly as much critical attention, and Callaghan is one of very few Canadian writers of his generation to have stimulated interest outside of Canada. While these facts suggest Callaghan's central place in Canadian fiction of the period, his literary skill and achievement have always been hotly debated, and none of his contemporaries has enjoyed and suffered such extremes of critical appraisal. All of Callaghan's novels, for example, were initially received with profoundly mixed reviews, even by the most nationalistic Canadian magazines. The critical reception of his first novel, *Strange Fugitive* (1928), is a case in point. In September 1928, Cleveland B. Chase wrote in *The New York Times Book Review* that Callaghan's style was 'fresh and vivid' and his characterization 'sharp and convincing,' but he lamented the 'dull and boring characters.'[1] An unsigned review in the *Toronto Daily Star*, entitled 'Strange Fugitive New Type in Canadian Realist Novel' (1928), remarked that the novel was 'the most untraditional piece of fiction ever produced by a Canadian,' but criticized Callaghan's 'totally cynical estimate of most people and … complete disdain of any of the merely artistic elements in writing.'[2] Callaghan's literary reputation remains contested to the present day. Edmund Wilson, in a much cited celebration of Callaghan, called him 'the most unjustly neglected novelist in the English-speaking world,' and many more recent critics continue to echo this claim, albeit usually with less enthusiasm.[3] At the other extreme, an article by John Metcalf, 'Winner Take All,' offers a spirited refutation of those who have praised the Callaghan style and provides a systematic denigration of his technique and modernist credentials: 'Callaghan was not really in the modernist tradition at all … his major impulse was moralistic and didactic and … this impulse was constantly at war within his work against what little artistry he possessed.'[4] The intensity of the debate surrounding Callaghan's work suggests that more than his own literary reputation is being contested by his critics. Many of the debates about Callaghan's work are ultimately about the nature of modern Canadian fiction itself.

The comments just cited are revealing in that they draw attention to a question that underlies much of the discussion of Callaghan's work: was he Canada's international modernist? So much of the praise lavished on Callaghan in his early career appears motivated by a nationalistic desire to prove his (and Canada's) significance in an international literary context. While criticism of early twentieth-century Canadian prose is often unabashedly self-referential and seemingly uninterested in its relation to literatures from other nations, Callaghan's critics frequently compare him to foreign writers and position him conspicuously within international literary circles.[5] Without a doubt, Callaghan's literary connections suggest that he was a significant but relatively minor figure among canonical Anglo-American modernists. For one thing, his list of literary friends and acquaintances reads like a who's who of the modernist age, something no other Canadian prose writer of the period can claim: Ernest Hemingway, James Joyce, F. Scott Fitzgerald, Gertrude Stein, William Carlos Williams, Sherwood Anderson, Ford Madox Ford, Ezra Pound, Sinclair Lewis, Robert McAlmon, among many others. His first published stories appeared in highly regarded literary magazines from Paris and New York with a penchant for the experimental. If we believe Callaghan's own account in *That Summer in Paris* (1963), he received direct affirmation from many of the now canonical modernist figures he encountered in his early years, especially Hemingway and Fitzgerald. But in spite of all of this evidence, the question persists: was Callaghan really a modernist? If not, why the constant comparisons? If so, why is his work almost unflinchingly realistic and seemingly apathetic to the boldest literary innovations of his international friends and contemporaries? This chapter examines

Callaghan's work in the contexts of international modernism and Canadian modern realism. Ultimately, as we shall see, Callaghan was the most internationally connected Canadian prose writer of his generation, and he shared many writerly assumptions with his experimental friends and acquaintances. At the same time, Callaghan's decision steadfastly to remain a realist in the face of the experimental modernist writing he knew well reveals that he was among the most conservative of the modern realists. In coming to terms with this apparent contradiction, we can make sense of Callaghan's idiosyncratic style and further clarify the problematic relation of modern realism to international modernist forms.

It is tempting to trace Callaghan's aesthetic impulses back to the experimental circles he moved in while in Paris in the late 1920s and draw a clear line of literary influence. Hemingway's impact on Callaghan, for example, has been the subject of numerous studies, and something that Callaghan himself has intermittently both acknowledged and denied. In *That Summer in Paris* (1963), Callaghan's memoirs of his 1929 Paris sojourn, he enumerates many of his aesthetic assumptions alongside reconstructions of literary conversations with Hemingway, inviting readers to make the obvious connections. Numerous critics have done just this, arguing for a striking similarity, at least on the surface, between the forms of writing the two authors advocated.[6] But this often-cited autobiographical source on Callaghan's literary preferences provides only a small part of the story. In numerous articles, book reviews, and interviews published in a wide variety of journals and magazines over several decades, Callaghan has offered a full articulation of his literary aesthetic. His fiction undeniably bears a stylistic similarity to the work of Hemingway, and of other writers of the period, both American and Canadian, but his borrowing from Hemingway was, at best, highly selective, intentionally or otherwise. As Metcalf has argued, 'Callaghan was not much influenced by Hemingway and did not really understand Hemingway's stylistic innovations. He certainly never attempted to use or reproduce them.'[7] From Hemingway, Callaghan perhaps drew his unshakable conviction that a plain, direct, and sparse form of writing was required for the representation of the modern world. The literary techniques that grew out of these assumptions, however, reveal that Callaghan had his own idiosyncratic and original conception of what made writing modern and relevant.

Callaghan's probing and self-reflexive commentaries on the works of the most experimental of his contemporaries – published primarily in forgotten issues of *Saturday Night* – reveal that, while he favoured the apparent hyper-simplicity of the Hemingway style, he was outspokenly contemptuous of most other forms of literary innovation. He also revealed in his articles, even as early as the 1920s and somewhat contrary to his own public assertions that he was not essentially a Canadian writer, a surprising awareness of the emerging modern realism in Canada. He lent his support to the new realism in the style of the *Bookman* manifestos, and, like some of the most talented and energetic of his Canadian contemporaries, he concluded that the key characteristic of the new writing in Canada ought to be psychological realism. The image of Callaghan that emerges from his critical statements is surprising: he considered himself a modern writer, not because of his internationalism but because of his (he believed) uncompromising modern realism: only it could engage the contemporary world directly and objectively. For all of his supposed affinities with international modernism, he loudly eschewed most forms of literary experiment which he considered to be at odds with his realistic intentions.

The most often remarked upon aspect of Callaghan's aesthetic is its straightforward, pared-down, 'journalistic' style, a refined and extreme form of the 'direct reportage' method so important to the modern realists generally. For some critics, the emergence of the Callaghan style marked a clear point of development in Canadian prose, leading other writers of the period towards realist expression.[8] To a greater degree than any other Canadian writer of the period, Callaghan writes in the manner prescribed by the manifestos of the *Bookman* and the *Forum* of the 1920s. Unlike Knister and Grove, whose commitments to realism were no less unwavering but whose techniques were constantly evolving, Callaghan's style was evident, confident, steadfast, and almost wholly intact from the very start of his career. Significantly, Callaghan was considered an experimentalist not just by Canadians: his early, hyper-realistic short stories were received eagerly by experimental modernist literary magazines of the period, including Ernest Walsh's *This Quarter* (Paris), Eugene Jolas's *transition* (Paris), and Ezra Pound's *The Exile* (New York). This acceptance validated Callaghan's belief that his brand of realism was indeed modern and experimental. More generally, this affirmation indicates that modern realism, at least as Callaghan practised it, was perceived by those in the know to be markedly different from nineteenth-century realism – so different, in fact, that it could be considered experimental, not just by Canadians but by European and American connoisseurs of modernist writing as well. Accordingly,

Callaghan's work is a bridge between Canadian and international literary circles of the period. While the validation Callaghan received is certainly atypical for a Canadian writer, his style, although more pronounced and consistent than the styles of his contemporaries, is more or less typical of the best Canadian writing of the period. Callaghan, then, can in one respect be considered an exemplary modern realist: in examining his literary aesthetic – with its uncompromising commitment to realism in the context of unparalleled access to modernist circles – we see a number of the issues faced by all of the modern realists amplified and illuminated.

Nowhere is the Callaghan style more apparent than in his early short stories published in various journals and little magazines in the 1920s, including *The New Yorker*, *Harper's Bazaar* (New York), *Saturday Night* (Toronto), *Esquire* (New York), *Household Magazine* (Topeka), *Scribner's Magazine* (New York), *North American Review* (Boston), *American Mercury* (Garden City, NY), *Common Sense* (New York), *Redbook* (New York), *The Atlantic* (Boston), *Story* (New York), *Toronto Star Weekly*, and the experimental publications of New York and Paris mentioned earlier. The direct reportage mode advocated by the 1920s magazines was a fundamental tenet of the new realism in Canada. While many writers of the period apparently heeded the call for this new mode of writing, only Callaghan developed a full-blown literary style based upon direct reportage. He makes the importance of this method clear in *That Summer in Paris* (1963) as he links it to his Hemingwayesque approach to language: 'Writing had to do with the right relationship between the words and the thing or person being described: the words should be transparent as glass, and every time a writer used a brilliant phrase to prove himself witty or clever he merely took the mind of the reader away from the object and directed it to himself; he became a performer. Why didn't he go on the stage?'[9] On the surface, it appears that Callaghan believed naively that words can be straightforward, 'transparent,' factual signifiers, and that the author can achieve objective, realistic, mimetic representation of a given subject simply by choosing appropriate diction. A number of critics have accordingly identified an imagist influence on Callaghan's prose style and suggested that he believed language ought to be a direct link to what Pound famously dubbed 'the thing itself.'[10]

On the simplest level it appears that Callaghan conceived of the modern-realist style in unsophisticated terms: it ought to present an object 'as is' in a direct, referential fashion. Indeed, most of Callaghan's stories appear to do just this, as the opening passage from 'A Wedding Dress,' first published in *This Quarter* in 1927, demonstrates: 'For fifteen years Miss Lena Schwartz had waited for Sam Hilton to get a good job so they could get married. She lived in a quiet boarding-house on Wellesley Street, the only woman among seven men boarders. The landlady, Mrs. Mary McNab, did not want women boarders; the house might get a bad reputation in the neighbourhood, but Miss Schwartz had been with her a long time.'[11] A particularly characteristic trait of Callaghan's writing found in this passage is the use of deliberately bland adjectives ('good job,' 'bad reputation') to convey a sense of the utterly ordinary, of narrative detachment, objectivity, and impersonality, and to avoid creating the impression that words have done more than signify a given situation or subject.

But a fondness for simplicity and direct expression alone hardly constitutes a distinct literary style. Callaghan's entire method is built upon his explicit belief that modern writing ought to be based in contemporary speech patterns, not writerly convention, and that rhythms of speech ought to inform all other aspects of literary style and technique. As he argued in 'The Past Quarter Century,' a retrospective article published in *Maclean's* in 1936, 'if only it could be made clear that if Canadians have a way of thinking, feeling, and expressing themselves it's to be found in the way they use the language in everyday speech; and if writers would only learn to write by ear, then they could be free, then they could learn and it would be time to start worrying about technique.'[12] This passage also draws attention to one sense in which Callaghan links the concept of the modern with a realistic aesthetic: writing is good when it emulates (represents realistically) the immediate, contemporary (modern) language of everyday life. Style, to Callaghan, is not merely a formal approach to subject matter; it is the fusion of form with subject matter, of direct reportage with the contemporary world it explores. As he wrote in *That Summer in Paris*, the writer ought to 'strip the language, and make the style, the method, all the psychological ramifications, the ambiance of the relationships, all the one thing, so the reader couldn't make separations.'[13]

Given that the root of his aesthetic is in contemporary speech, it is not surprising that Callaghan puts his theories into practice most unambiguously when writing dialogue. He was blunt in his assertion that dialogue ought to be mimetic in a 1931 book review of Polish novelist Ferdynand Goetel's recently translated *From Day to Day*: 'Goetel writes dialogue as it ought to be written – no tricks, no continual reiterations of little witticisms, no forced smartness or brightness – in other words he writes conversation rather than "dialogue."'[14] Although representation of everyday conversation is a nearly ubiquitous feature of the modern-realist novel, no writer handles it more convincingly than Callaghan, and few write novels in which dialogue makes up a larger proportion. But this interest in common speech is not unique to the modern realists. As T.S. Eliot wrote in 'The Music of Poetry' (1942), this was a defining feature of his brand of modernist expression: 'Poetry must not stray too far from the ordinary everyday language which we use and hear ... it cannot afford to lose its contact with the changing language of common intercourse.'[15] In a 1927 short story published in *American Caravan*, 'Amuck in the Bush,' Callaghan's dialogue adheres to Eliot's credo and is strikingly reminiscent of Hemingway, at once ordinary and emotionally charged, convincing and dramatic, colloquial and stylized:

> 'I can kick the hell out of Walton,' Gus said finally.
> 'Sure you can, he's not so much.'
> 'Well stick around, I'm going to.'
> 'Sid'll be up at the park at the ball game tonight,' Luke said.
> 'Damn the ball game.'
> 'Don't you want to show him up? Don't you want to have a go at him?'[16]

A more subtle form of speakerly writing appears in many of Callaghan's third-person narratives. Often these passages, written from an impersonal perspective without a clearly defined narrative persona, introduce contemporary colloquial diction to give the narrative an immediate, authentic, and contemporary tone or quality. This is precisely the technique used to generate, in 'Last Spring They Came Over,' published in *transition* in 1927, a quick-paced, metropolitan, urban-realist impression: 'He got thirty dollars a week on the paper and said it was surprisingly good screw to start. For five a week he got an attic room in a big brick house painted brown on Mutual Street. He ate his meals in a quick-lunch near the office.'[17]

Although Callaghan's direct reportage method derives from underlying aesthetic assumptions that distinguish it from journalism, there can be little doubt that his work as a journalist influenced his literary style. Callaghan was a part-time journalist for the *Toronto Daily Star* between 1923 and 1926, where he met and exchanged stories with Hemingway. His most sustained period of journalistic writing was between 1940 and 1948, when he produced a monthly column on a wide variety of topics – including hockey, democracy, humour, Hollywood, Canadian youth, and wrestling – for a news magazine entitled *New World*, published in Toronto. Callaghan's stories are almost invariably told from a detached, omniscient, third-person perspective, and Callaghan himself has often remarked on the desirability of narrative impersonality. This stance recalls that of other modern realists discussed earlier and suggests another point of convergence for modern realists and prominent high-modernists – as Eliot writes of the modernist author in 'Tradition and the Individual Talent,' 'what happens is a continual surrender of himself as he is at the moment to something which is more valuable. The progress of an artist is a continual self-sacrifice, a continual extinction of personality.'[18] Indeed, many of Callaghan's statements reveal that his style arises out of just such an attempt at 'extinction' of the authorial presence: 'I was simply writing in direct contact with my material, you see, so the whole problem of being a literary guy didn't enter into it at all. The question was whether I was telling the truth.'[19] As a result, the Callaghan style often appears so straightforward, so simple, so like journalism, that it is possible to suggest it is not really literature. Metcalf, for example, takes Callaghan's anti-literary, anti-authorial comments at face value and denies that there is an artistic awareness informing his writing at all: 'Callaghan did not seem to grasp the simple point that literature is artifice, that "the truth" and "the way it was" are created by smoke and mirrors.'[20]

While Callaghan's 'smoke and mirrors' can sometimes be unconvincing and ineffective, they do exist, and he is keenly aware that the reportage method requires a writerly approach to subject matter. Callaghan's best writing generates only the '*illusion* of simplicity' as he manipulates language and point of view in a variety of ways to convey subtle subjective impressions within the framework of purportedly objective, realistic narration.[21] It is worth looking at a few of Callaghan's techniques in more detail, as they reflect the types and varieties of literary experiments that the best modern realists undertake under the guise of simplicity, and demonstrate the artistry that underlies the deceptive plainness of the direct reportage mode. Barry Cameron, for example, offers an excellent summary of Callaghan's manipulation of point of view to generate subjective impressions, or 'ambiguity and ambivalence,' in his direct reportage. Specifically, Cameron notes 'his subtle and deliberate modulation within a single piece of fiction among various points of view – from editorial omniscience to selective omniscience to multiple centres of consciousness to a single limited point of view or centre of consciousness. There is ... little distance in Callaghan's fiction between either the implied author and narrator or the implied author and author, and as a result authorial voice is frequently in tension with the voice of a particular centre of consciousness.'[22] Although ultimately Cameron is doubtful about the success of these techniques in Callaghan's writing, he nevertheless draws attention to the indisputable fact that it is not simply journalism. A typical example of a Callaghan passage that functions in the manner outlined by Cameron appears in 'Ancient Lineage,' first published in *The Exile* in 1928. In this example, direct and journalistic on the surface, Callaghan both invites subjective interpretation by his reader and represents the subjective impressions of two interacting characters: 'Mr. Flaherty got red in the face; of course he understood, but to tell the truth he merely wanted to chat with Mrs. Rower. Now he knew definitely he did not like the heavy nose and unsentimental assertiveness of the lower lip of this big woman with the wide shoulders. He couldn't stop looking at her thick ankles. Rocking back and forth in the chair she was primly conscious of lineal superiority; a proud married woman, surely she could handle a young man, half-closing her eyes, a young man from the University indeed.'[23]

One of the most enduring criticisms of Callaghan's work is summed up in a phrase of Cameron's: 'The reader ... is unnecessarily told too often how to feel, how to interpret, how to judge.'[24] Callaghan's passage might appear laden with authorial value judgments that seem to validate Cameron's claim. But who in the passage is passing judgment – 'she was primly conscious,' 'surely she could handle'? As Callaghan's purported objectivity is so immediately apparent, it is easy to assume that these are the opinions of an omniscient narrator. But the shifts in centre of consciousness in the passage indicate that the judgments are those of the characters. The first line of the passage – 'of course he understood, but to tell the truth he merely wanted to chat' – does not offer the journalistic language of the detached observer; it provides a brief, fleeting impression of the psychological processes underlying Mr Flaherty's emotional state; and in the final lines – 'surely she could handle a young man ... a young man from the University indeed' – the quaint, speakerly tone suggests that this is a sample of Mrs Rower's internal monologue. When Callaghan writes, 'He couldn't stop looking at her thick ankles,' this is not an objective description of Mrs Rower's physical attributes but a condensed description filtered through Mr Flaherty's gaze: a less compact description of the scene might read, 'He couldn't stop looking at her ankles because he was impressed by their thickness.'

Of course, readers may decide for themselves exactly how thick the ankles are, and exactly why they so impressed Mr Flaherty, and this is precisely the point. Solicitation of reader involvement is another much overlooked characteristic of Callaghan's prose, and ironically sometimes confused with its opposite: as Metcalf writes, 'Callaghan's approach to his material and to his heroes is dictatorial.'[25] The demand that the reader get involved by interpreting and piecing together fragments of information is yet another assumption that Callaghan shares with his most experimental contemporaries. There can be little doubt that the allusive methods of Joyce, the surrealism of Stein, the dissonant multivocality of Faulkner, the suggestive impressionism of Woolf, the evocative symbolism of Conrad, the fragmentation and juxtaposition of Dos Passos, not to mention the provocative displays of futurists and dadaists, all require the reader's involvement and interpretation in large degrees. Callaghan's plain, banal diction and emphasis of the ordinary can easily be considered to limit, even suppress interpretation of his subject matter and place the reader in a passive mode. But the very lack of detail, the refusal to draw a clear, precise portrait of a situation, or place, or individual suggests that Callaghan was doing something markedly different from more traditional realists: demanding that his readers fill in the blanks. Some of the reviews he wrote in the late 1920s make this very clear. In a 1926 discussion of Hemingway that appeared in *Saturday Night*, he distinguished modern realism (or naturalism) from older modes: 'He is a fine naturalist who, instead of piling up material and convincing by sheer weight of evidence in the manner of Dreiser or Zola, cuts down the material to essentials and leaves it starkly authentic.'[26]

Nowhere is Callaghan's preference for 'essentials' clearer than in his own creative writing, and particularly in his passages that strive for vivid characterization. In 'A Girl with Ambition,' his first published short story which appeared in *This Quarter* in 1926, he tries to bring a character to life with the simplest of details: 'Mary was a neat clean girl with short fair curls and blue eyes, looking more than her age because she had very good legs, and knew it.'[27] A similar method occurs in 'Soldier Harmon,' which first appeared in *Scribner's Magazine* in 1928: 'They were watching Joe Harmon, a big man with a slow grin and a dark smudge under his left eye, and his manager, Doc Barnes, a small, neat man with shiny black hair.'[28] Based on these descriptions, it is easy to see why some of his early reviewers remarked on his 'dull and boring characters.'[29] But Callaghan is not trying to limit interpretations of these characters through such simple descriptions; rather, he relies on these descriptions to leave the characters open-ended, to provide a point of departure for a subjective response in his reader – what are 'good legs?' What is a 'slow grin'? In his 1928 review of Liam O'Flaherty's *The Assassin*, Callaghan explains his belief that the 'elemental quality of genius' entails a willingness and ability to write in such a way: 'It has always amazed me the way he can touch off a character of a man by pointing to one or two characteristic gestures, or the way he simply mentions a woman and she becomes a creature of flesh and blood and passion. Few people writing today can do it so well.'[30] Whether or not Callaghan's willingness to achieve such an effect is matched by his ability remains open to debate. And ultimately the success of such a form of writing depends upon a reader's willingness to enter into the creative process on some level, and I am not sure that Callaghan's 'hard-boiled' style makes this particularly easy or enjoyable – Callaghan's mention of 'good legs' is perhaps more likely to elicit laughter or raise eyebrows than set off a contemplative process in the reader.[31] Regardless, Callaghan's techniques again draw attention to the fact that the modern-realist style is at once conservative and experimental, and characterized by a writerly exploration of a variety of subjective points of view within the framework of objective narration.

Callaghan's fiction approaches setting in a similar fashion. Although his descriptions of the urban environment are among the first and most vivid in Canadian writing, they are rarely specific or detailed in a photographic sense. This passage from *Such Is My Beloved* (1934) offers a fairly typical example of Callaghan's generalized description of Toronto: 'He looked out over the roofs and lights and noises on the streets, over the corners where on Sunday evenings evangelists sang, and over that street where the crowd at this moment was streaming from the labor temple; somewhere out there where the lighted avenues lengthened and the streets criss-crossed, the girls were loafing and hunting.'[32] To Metcalf, such descriptions are clear-cut examples of poor writing: 'His writing, far from engaging and celebrating the observable world, usually paints the world like a crude backdrop. His descriptive writing is typically vague, generalized, and unfocused.'[33] Fraser Sutherland criticizes Callaghan's representation of Montreal in *The Loved and the Lost* (1951) along similar lines: 'Except for its geographical setting – the mountain and the river are skilfully drawn – Callaghan's Montreal might well be Baltimore.'[34] E.K. Brown reveals the regionalist expectations inherent in such comments while lamenting that Callaghan's stories set in Toronto do not evoke a more detailed urban landscape: 'A great opportunity has been refused by Mr. Callaghan – the opportunity of drawing the peculiarities of Toronto in full vividness and force. This is a subject that no writer has yet treated.'[35] But Callaghan is not trying to reproduce Toronto, or Montreal, or Baltimore, or any other city for that matter: the fact that Callaghan's settings take on a universal symbolic quality is precisely the point, and perfectly in keeping with his notions of what modern-realist literature ought to do. In the same article, Brown sums up Callaghan's universalizing technique, although he obviously intends his comments to be critical of Callaghan's writing: 'Mr. Callaghan's Toronto is not an individualized city but simply a representative one. I mean that in reading Mr. Callaghan one has the sense that Toronto is being used not to bring out what will have the most original flavour, but what will remind people who live in Cleveland, or Detroit, or Buffalo, or any other city on the Great Lakes, of the general quality of their own milieu.'[36] Such readings of Callaghan's fiction demonstrate that the urban realists of the period have been subjected to many of the same regionalist criticisms levelled at the prairie realists discussed earlier. But whether writing of the prairie, or the city, or an individual, or a larger society, the modern realist is more often than not telling a universal tale about the kinds of things that tend to *happen* in the modern world, rather than about something specific that is supposed to have *happened* in a particular time and place. Callaghan is the polar opposite of the local colourist concerned with describing the minute details of a recognizable locale. His realism has larger aims. Much as he does with his characters, Callaghan writes about places using deliberately vague language that invites readers to infuse receptive scenes and spaces with their own subjective impressions.

Perhaps owing partly to the fact that Callaghan's settings are so much more (or less) than regional reflections of a particular Canadian environment, his writing is often discussed as though it has little to do with the rest of Canadian literature of the period. Callaghan has, himself, encouraged such interpretations, often claiming that his literary models and influences were not Canadian, and that he had little interest in other Canadian writers: 'It never occurred to me that the local poets had anything to do with me ... I was wonderfully at home in my native city, and yet intellectually, spiritually, the part that had to do with my wanting to be a writer was utterly, but splendidly and happily, alien.'[37] Yet for all his posturing, Callaghan displayed a familiarity with the types of writing being produced by his contemporaries and suggested that young Canadian writers ought to follow his lead in their search for a new national mode of expression. He offered praise for the most realist of his contemporaries, especially Knister,[38] and denounced the romantic thrust of the national literature as a whole, always measuring it against his own literary aesthetic. In a 1928 article which appeared in *Saturday Night*, 'Looking at Native Prose,' Callaghan summed up what he thought was wrong with Canadian writing in terms that echo the *Bookman* and *Forum* manifestos, calling for the mimetic reflection of Canada, and a new realist form, indifferent to the rural and urban divide, capable of such an aim: 'Prose in this country is, I believe, more degraded than in any other civilized country on Earth ... How many prose writers are there in this country who have a feeling for words alone? ... The opportunity awaiting the honest Canadian prose writer is so large that I believe many are appalled, laugh weakly, and prefer to go on writing fairy tales after the fashion of Oscar Wilde. One half of the American world awaits the prose writer, awaits his recording, awaits his acceptance of the new world of the plain, the bush country, and the skyscraper.'[39] But for Callaghan the new realism was much more than mimetic reproduction of landscape, or journalistic writing about modern Canadian life. Callaghan advocated that young writers bring their realist aims to bear not upon a distinctly Canadian landscape but rather on a modern North American way of life. Callaghan considered contemporary language, and the literary style that proceeds naturally from it, to have the power to tap into the spirit of the times, into a vibrant, energetic, modern, North American zeitgeist: 'The way lies through the acceptance of whatever speech we have in this country, and prose employing it will have the colour, the raciness, the flesh and blood of the people of this section of the American continent. And because of the soil we are American. Not United States, but American.'[40] Just such a literary movement, he surmised, was already in full bloom in the United States (with Hemingway, Anderson, and Fitzgerald among others) and beginning in Canada, with the work of a few writers including Knister, Grove,[41] and, by implication, himself: 'The few young men in this country, Raymond Knister, Tom Murtha, etc., who are interested in prose, are attempting to find a beginning on their own soil, and are on absolutely solid ground. The older generation, regarded so seriously now, never found a beginning, were not interested in technique and had no identity ... If any evidence can be found after a canvass of the prose writers in this country, that some writers are aware of modern methods, and are using the speech of the soil, then there should be loud whoops of joy.'[42] Callaghan, then, was aware of the new modern realism in Canada and he lent it his full advocacy. But, to him, this movement was not wholly, or even centrally, Canadian. It was a North American cultural phenomenon.

But why, with all of his exposure to foreign literary modes and models, and with his obvious aesthetic affinities with numerous modernist tenets, did Callaghan remain at core a realist? He might easily have allied himself with any of the experimental writers he encountered in his wide reading of modernist literatures and travels in the literary circles of the day: Joyce, Pound, Ford, Faulkner, or Woolf. Even writing from his urban, North American perspective, Callaghan arrived at essentially the same conclusion about literary experiment as did both Grove and Knister: experiment should not be pursued for its own sake but rather directed to serve the causes of realism; just as he might call Victorian literature, with its adornments and flourishes, excessive and evasive, so too did Callaghan conclude that modernist experiments with language occur at the expense of the 'truth.' Between 1926 and 1940, Callaghan regularly reviewed books for a variety of journals and magazines, and the majority of the works he reviewed were written by foreign writers, many of them among the most canonical modernists. These reviews, most of them published in *Saturday Night*, interpreted works by Woolf, Hemingway, Ford, Williams, Mann, Dos Passos, Huxley, Faulkner, Joyce, and many others, for a Canadian audience. These reviews are the most telling source of Callaghan's opinions on experimental modernisms and reveal much about why Callaghan considered realism the most modern of forms and favoured his speakerly style of direct reportage but rejected other forms of linguistic experiment. They also draw attention to a much overlooked concern of Callaghan's writing: psychological realism. Like Knister and to a lesser extent Grove, Callaghan saw psychological realism as the central aim of the modern novel. These same reviews reveal that some of the more vexing aspects of his writing – moralism, didacticism, melodrama, artlessness – are not the result of artistic indifference or incompetence but of his unconventional efforts to unite two competing ideals in modern fiction: impersonality and psychological realism.

While Callaghan considered modern speech the foundation of the modern-realist aesthetic, he was conservative in terms of the type of linguistic experiment he favoured. The author whose work Callaghan most frequently reviewed was William Faulkner, and while Callaghan no doubt saw him as a remarkable talent, he characterized him not as an avant-garde literary innovator but as an outmoded literary decadent. In a 1940 *Saturday Night* review of *The Hamlet,* he wrote that 'as for the Faulknerian style one can't help thinking that possibly the best way to get even with him would be to write him letters or pieces about his books in his highly artificial manner and then ask him how he liked it. For surely his is the most deliberately mannered style in modern American writing ... those elaborate decorative and decadent redundancies are just plain vulgar.'[43] Clearly, a large part of what Callaghan is rejecting here is literary artifice, or a 'deliberately mannered style.' For Callaghan, 'style' ought to strive to connect the reader directly to the modern world, effacing the author, not drawing the reader's attention to literary artifice, and writing that is self-consciously literary, Callaghan believed, obscured the contemporary subject. He makes this clear in a 1938 review of Faulkner's earlier novel, *The Unvanquished*: 'Pick up almost any one of the earlier and heavier Faulkner books and try reading them aloud and what you feel is the style is something very literary, something almost antique, something a little rotten that doesn't belong in contemporary life at all: the clean straight line was never there: the effect was a crumbling gothic in our time, and not the gothic of the American skyscraper either: it was the crumbling gothic of a dead time.'[44] Callaghan apparently, like Grove, did not equate literary 'experiment' with the 'modern'; Faulkner could be experimental, but 'almost antique.' In Callaghan's view, writers were modern when they engaged contemporary life directly and immediately, and this was only possible with the realistic form of writing, based on contemporary speech, that he favoured. His key critique of Faulkner is the 'very literary' aspect of his style and the attention his writing draws to literature as art at the expense of literature as a reflection of life.

Callaghan was also highly critical of writers who experimented with language in a manner that he *did* consider modern if such experiments failed to engage the contemporary world. Although Callaghan was a great admirer of James Joyce – in *That Summer in Paris,* Callaghan fawningly recounts an evening spent at the Joyce apartment in Paris that was partly spoiled by an overly talkative Robert McAlmon – he was nevertheless highly critical of *Finnegans Wake* in a 1939 review. In this piece, Callaghan spells out his critique of modernist literary experiment in no uncertain terms, calling it a 'literature feeding not on life but on words':

> The tendency toward pure abstraction can only lead finally to the starvation of the medium. It is a gesture of great intellectual pride and spiritual isolation on the part of the artist. But the pursuit has gone on steadily in our time, and it seems to me that the pursuit is continued on page after page of 'Finnegan's Wake': an unholy effort, or if you will, the actual job done, of making pieces of literature with words, simply as words, as the substance ... And that is why you get the impression that in this book you are dealing with the end of something in literature. It isn't just the Ivory tower, it is the Ivory tower with every window shut and every door locked. It is the great artist retreating completely from life and burning his bridges behind him.[45]

Such critiques can also be found in Callaghan's writings on numerous other prominent modernists of the period. In a 1928 review of Woolf's *Orlando*, he wrote: 'It seems to me that the last half of the book is a little too much of a demonstration of marvellous technical competence. I become too conscious of Virginia Woolf, a very clever shrewd and sharp witted author; the reader becomes aware that she is jibing at a certain style of biography, that she is witty, wise, and satirical.'[46] In *That Summer in Paris*, Callaghan was openly contemptuous of Stein's work: 'Abstract prose was nonsense. The shrewd lady had found a trick, just as the naughty Dadaists had once found a trick. The plain truth was, as I saw it, Gertrude Stein now had nothing whatever to say. But she was shrewd and intelligent enough to know it. As for her deluded coterie, well, I had no interest in finding one of them who would lead me shyly to her den.'[47]

In these examples, Callaghan offers a critique of experimental writing that echoes that made by leftist magazines of modernism and modern realism. Joyce's experimentalism, Callaghan argues, represents a 'great artist retreating completely from life,' not a great artist engaging the contemporary world. Callaghan rejects the excesses of modernist innovation from the point of view of the social realist and allies the 'real' with the 'modern.' Indeed, to Callaghan these terms are synonymous: realism is necessarily modern, because its subject is the modern world. While Callaghan's views on this subject are somewhat naive and problematic, it is unfair to suggest that he resists experiment in writing out of ignorance, or what Metcalf calls 'an indifferent command of literary technique.'[48] As he reveals in *That Summer in Paris*, he is anything but indifferent; modern writing must absolutely engage the modern world directly or face dire consequences: 'I remember deciding that the root of the trouble with writing was that poets and storywriters used language to evade, to skip away from the object, because they could never bear to face a thing freshly and see it freshly for what it was in itself ... Tell the truth cleanly. Weren't the consequences of fraudulent pretending plain to anyone who would look around? Hadn't the great slogans of the first World War become ridiculous to me before I had left high school?'[49] Callaghan, then, defines the limits of the modern-realist form as follows: contemporary language is the foundation of the modern-realist style. But so many modernist experiments devolve into mere linguistic wordplay. Experimentalism is not inherently bad. It is even desirable, so long as that experiment does not compromise the fundamental connection between language and the contemporary world, between art and life. Realism, to Callaghan, was a form free of excessive experiment and linguistic indulgence. This meant that it was the best literary form for engaging the contemporary subject. Therefore, it was the most modern form of expression by virtue of its formal conservatism relative to other modernist forms.

Ironically, given that Callaghan is one of the few legitimate Canadian prose stylists of his generation, his own pronouncements on the absolute importance of directness in literary expression sound like calls for a kind of anti-style. In spite of his own willingness to manipulate language and point of view to achieve particular literary effects, Callaghan defines his own style in terms of its conscious avoidance of ostensible artistry. In an interview published in 1990, he remarked in some detail on the deliberate artlessness of his own form and method of composition: 'I write, say, ten pages, and I'm trying to go over it to get it ready for the girl who's typing it. And I just go over that, changing syntax here and there, but all I'm really trying to do is get the thing so she can read it. And that's the style. I mean it sounds utterly plebeian, but that's all I'm trying to do, to get the thing so it will read naturally ... you'll just say: Gee, this is true, it's all true, absolutely true.'[50] Such pronouncements lead Metcalf to conclude, not unreasonably, that Callaghan is the artistically indifferent author of 'stumblebum writing.'[51] It is true that Callaghan, and all of his Canadian contemporaries, often write passages that are flat, dull, unengaging, and, at least to a contemporary audience, naive in terms of the literary effects they try to achieve. Yet the same authors create passages that are highly convincing and demonstrative of a creative ingenuity and willingness to push the realist form to its very limits. Callaghan writes passages that appear hastily composed, but he also, as I have demonstrated in my earlier discussion of his short fiction, often writes with a remarkable degree of both complexity and transparency. Callaghan's above comments reveal not artistic indifference but his belief that writing should *appear* natural and straightforward, and not just on the level of language. In a 1929 review, Callaghan linked what he called the 'modern technique' with a 'lack of artificial arrangement of material that is very often mistaken for form.'[52] A 1928 review of Thomas Mann's short fiction was more explicit on the same point: Mann's book was deemed a 'masterpiece, modern in manner ... devoid of plot, devoid of tricks of style and arrangement, direct and simple.'[53]

Callaghan's belief in the fundamental importance of avoiding excessive artifice meant that he felt a story should not appear overly structured or even consciously emplotted. In general terms, Callaghan suggested that a narrative ought to reflect the realistic passage of time and to appear to follow the natural rhythm of contemporary life. More specifically, Callaghan identified the natural, credible psychological development of the individual as the key concern of modern fiction, and he revealed that his own stories were emplotted along psychological lines:

> These [my] stories start out and you think you know what this theme is, what the story is. But after a while you begin to get really mad because suddenly everything goes off in all the wrong directions. It isn't the story you thought it was at all, and from now on you don't know what the people are going to do. Then you get to the end of the story and the stories don't seem to you to end right. The stories end in terms of the people themselves rather than in terms of the pattern for that kind of material.[54]

Callaghan's concern with psychological realism explains the apparent formlessness of many of his novels, most prominently *It's Never Over* (1930) and *A Broken Journey* (1932), both discussed below: usually he is more concerned with creating credible psychological portraits than with constructing a gripping plot. His concern with the psychological also makes sense of another problematic feature of Callaghan's writing: melodrama. Much as several of Grove's novels discussed earlier – *The Yoke of Life, Two Generations, The Master of Mill* – thwart traditionally realistic emplotment to depict a kind of 'world consciousness' in action, some of Callaghan's novels make more sense as psychodrama than examples of straightforward, realistic fiction. The melodramatic endings that strain the reader's credulity in so many Callaghan works – the 'hit' at the end of *Strange Fugitive* (1928), Father Dowling's breakdown at the end of *Such Is My Beloved* (1934), Kip's death at the end of *More Joy in Heaven* (1937) – are appropriate psycho-symbolic conclusions to novels that have the exploration of an individual's psychological degeneration at their centre.

The Callaghan works that are most fundamentally concerned with human psychology are among his least known. This may be because they are also his works that are least concerned with exploring recognizable Canadian locales and evoking weighty social concerns and issues that lend themselves easily to debate, discussion, and materialist critique. It may also be because the personalities and psychological processes Callaghan uses to structure these works are so ordinary and slow to unfold that they fail to engage readers with other expectations. Although most of these psychological novels have received little attention from critics, they are crucial to a full understanding of his aesthetic and style. Callaghan's second and third novels, *It's Never Over* (1930) and *A Broken Journey* (1932), use deliberately tedious and relatively mundane psychological processes to 'drive' their plot. In the first of these two works, the story focuses on the psychological effects of the execution of a convict upon his friend, John Hughes, and the two women who compete for his affection, Lillian and Isabelle (the latter woman also happens to be the sister of the dead man). Through a series of slow-moving though realistically drawn scenes, the reader becomes aware of Isabelle's deepening conviction that her brother's death has altered her life permanently for the worse, and of her underhanded determination to inflict her unhappiness on John and Lillian. Significant events are few and far between in the novel, and the moments of crisis in the story correspond with important though commonplace moments of psychological development, as in this passage which partly explains John's decision to pursue a new love interest: 'Now, when she would not see him, he wished he was still giving her money, though he had become niggardly, but they might at least have been held together by the common payments. And then he felt more confident.'[55]

A Broken Journey is a love story about two seemingly compatible lovers who are driven apart by circumstance and lack of confidence in one another. This story, a love triangle like *It's Never Over*, moves even more slowly: a young couple, Marion and Peter, travel north, but a back injury confines Peter to bed for the entire vacation (he is pushed down a flight of stairs by a previous love interest earlier on). During his convalescence, the characters have meaningless conversations in which they exchange platitudes and conceal their growing disaffection from one another. Much of Callaghan's narrative takes the form of detached descriptions of internal states juxtaposed with emotionally restrained dialogue: '"Nice fellow, the doctor," he said, as if he had enjoyed a social call from the man. "Of course he's a very stupid man, but he's a nice fellow just the same" ... She had so much sudden resentment, she was afraid to answer him. At the moment she hated him. She wanted to hit him, hurt him, make him cry out and then feel good watching his pain.'[56] Eventually, after a long process of emotional extrication from the central affair, Marion falls in love with another man, a robust Hemingwayesque character who contrasts with her invalid fiancé. While both *It's Never Over* and *A Broken Journey* are occasionally melodramatic, as this passage reveals, the psychological character development that nudges them along is highly convincing, and almost inseparable from the other elements of the novels: even the settings are frequently symbolic and reflective of the internal thought processes the characters are experiencing. While these two novels are also probably Callaghan's least enjoyable, they nevertheless reveal that even early on in his career psychological realism was his primary concern and the driving force behind his plots.

More compelling are the two substantial novellas that initially appeared as the second and third sections of Callaghan's 1929 collection of short fiction, *A Native Argosy*. These works are even more centrally concerned with psychological realism than most of Callaghan's novels. They also deal with psychological issues that are more dramatic and less commonplace. In the first novella, *An Autumn Penitent*, Joe Harding's incest with his niece Ellen, when it is discovered by his wife Lottie, leads to the suicide of both female characters, who only find the horror of the situation compounded by the fundamentalist Christianity they have recently embraced. Although he was critical of their faith before the suicide, Joe is gradually convinced by a manipulative and self-serving minister to take part in a dramatic baptismal ceremony involving other local converts. In the early parts of the novella, a psychological intensity is generated by Callaghan's skilful and unsensational handling of the incest theme, by subtle suggestions that Ellen has become pregnant, by Joe's obsessive and inappropriate interest in Ellen, and by Lottie's manipulative attempts to win religious concessions from Joe as her own faith deepens. In the latter half, Joe's conversion occurs not as an immediate response to the suicide but as the culmination of a personal process involving grief, guilt, and self-doubt: 'In the dark, lying alone in the big bed, he tried to go back to the beginning of things, until his head ached. There he was, lying in bed, outside was the moon and the stars and the lake. Well, what about it, where did it all come from? He remembered learning in school about masses swimming in space and now he thought about it eagerly but got tired.'[57]

The second novella, *In His Own Country*, is among the strangest examples of modern realism. In this work, Bill Lawson, a 'common' man who believes himself to be a modern-day Thomas Aquinas, gradually retreats from his young wife and community as his efforts to 'make a plan of different fields of science and show definitely that it could become one fine system in accordance with a religious scheme' grow more and more detached from reality.[58] Eventually, Bill's endeavours cause him to fall into a catatonic state. The third-person narrative of this story is skilfully modulated to generate sympathy for Bill's wife Flora: it traces her slow emotional development from love and admiration for Bill, into feelings of neglect and rejection, into anger and emotional detachment, into her gradually yielding to the affections of another man, into her decision to leave her marriage, into her feelings of remorse for her infidelity, into her eventual decision to return to her sick husband and become his caretaker. The psychological portrait of Flora as she moves through these phases is vivid: 'It's terrible to have to go in and out all day by yourself, Bill. We were living together and I had only my own thoughts. A woman that's only my age and only married 'bout two years shouldn't never be left like that. She gets thinking and things get all mixed up and it never does her any good. But wasn't I silly to be afraid of you?'[59]

As Callaghan's career moved into the mid-1930s, his concern with social realism intensified, and he began to show less concern with creating individual psychological portraits, and more with exploring the relationship of the individual to a larger social world. While even Callaghan's first novels have a clear social context – *Strange Fugitive* (1928) takes place in an archetypal North American city in the 1920s, disguised as Toronto – it is not until 1935, with the publication of *They Shall Inherit the Earth*, that his stories start to be built as much around specific ideological schemes as psychological concerns. Unfortunately, his novels begin to appear to some readers contrived and didactic as a result. If his early novels appear formless because they are emplotted upon unpredictable psychological processes, his later novels appear contrived because they are constructed to allow Callaghan to explore specific social issues, depict the interaction of various elements in a particular social milieu, and show his characters reacting to powerful social forces.

Such Is My Beloved (1934), marks the boundary between the old psychological fiction and the new social-realist works, combining the most successful elements of both. In this novel, Callaghan again creates a vivid portrait of the archetypal North American city (Toronto), and he raises a host of modern concerns and issues that, while muted in this novel, come to take centre stage in later efforts: class politics, the Depression, socialism, the decline of moral values, urban isolation, and evolving gender roles and relations. But rather than creating character types to explore these concerns, as he does in later works, the novel is structured around the psychology of the main character, Father Dowling, a naive young priest who attempts to rescue two young women, Ronnie and Midge, from their life working the big-city streets, while all the time wrestling with his own moral conscience and repressed sexual desires. A third-person narrator tells the story largely from the perspective of Father Dowling – another example of 'mediated reportage.' The resultant psychological analysis is vivid and convincing. These effects are heightened by a cleverly modulated narrative perspective that permits structural irony, but maintains sympathy with both Father Dowling and the young women, softening the didacticism of the novel's social observations by filtering them through the naive perspective of the young priest: 'As he walked along the crowded streets, with the women carrying parcels coming out of the big stores, he looked earnestly at each one ... He longed to see Ronnie and Midge coming along the street in the crowd, well clothed, with some of the independence and commitment in their faces that he saw in the faces of these women ... He looked up and saw a woman with a mink wrap ... Indignant, he wondered why God saw fit to permit so many people to have wealth and comfort, and so many to remain poor and hungry.'[60] The novel's plot follows the psychological development of Father Dowling as his obsession with the women deepens and culminates in a mental breakdown resulting from his inability to redeem the women, his awareness of the injustice of modern society, and his inability to gratify his lusts. The other characters and situations in the novel, however, are static. While Callaghan's later novels retain this method of portraying the destruction of the individual in the face of an indifferent society, never again does he create a portrait of an individual as psychologically convincing as that of Father Dowling.

The problem with the later novels is that Callaghan's concern shifts to the examination of the individual in society, and his psychological portraits appear to reflect social concerns rather than psychological insight. In *The Loved and the Lost* (1951), for example, Callaghan's characters are as much representatives of larger social groups as of individuals. The psychological development of Jim McAlpine, the central character who struggles with his love for a woman who represents a challenge to both his social position and his opinions on race relations, appears contrived at times, and directed to allow the author an opportunity to make various philosophical points: 'If I had some Negro friends and like them as one human being likes another I think they'd get into the habit of talking frankly in my presence, and I'd hear them talking about little incidents of discrimination going on all over the country in restaurants and trains and hotels. A lot of them are porters and they have these stories of one humiliation after another.'[61] This tendency in Callaghan's novels post-1934 has led to one of the most persistent criticisms of his work, again summed up well by Metcalf: '[Callaghan] is always completely external to the stories he is telling. The reader is not invited to participate in any way; we are not allowed to experience events in a Callaghan story and neither are we allowed to draw our own conclusions. Rather, Callaghan relentlessly tells and explains.'[62] It is impossible to dispute that Callaghan's stories very often have an underlying philosophical concern or social comment guiding the narrative. Yet in the vast majority of these instances, Callaghan is not telling the reader what to think, or raising a moral question and then answering it. Callaghan is guilty, instead, of telling his reader, perhaps too bluntly, not what to think, but rather what his characters are thinking. In *More Joy in Heaven* (1937), for example, we are privy to the thoughts of characters so clearly, entirely, directly, and unambiguously that our narrator appears autocratic, as this glimpse into the thoughts of Julie Evans at a dramatic moment reveals: 'She was watching his face for some sign of incredible violence and cunning. He only looked mild and tired … She remembered how hard he was to defeat, how his eagerness and hopefulness always lifted him up. It brought him out of prison … She began to feel he was a bigger and stronger man than even she with her love had thought him to be.'[63] As direct and objectivist as the passage may appear, it is rendered partly from the perspective of a particular character. And while such a method of psychological exposition may not be to everyone's taste, what the passage lacks in subtlety, it arguably makes up for in clarity.

Such passages as this one may not be wholly convincing, but they do reveal that, even in Callaghan's most didactic and moralistic works, a central concern is with the direct, unambiguous representation of characters' thoughts, and he remains willing to modulate narrative point of view to permit the reader to view situations through the eyes of a variety of different individuals. But such directness and lack of ambiguity may be a liability in fiction with a fundamental concern with psychology. As contemporary readers know, and as Callaghan's international and modern-realist contemporaries tried to demonstrate through the epistemological emphases of their writing, human psychology is inherently ambiguous. Even writers as conservative as McClung, Grove, and MacLennan generally avoided such direct, matter-of-fact verbalizations of psychological states, and they tried instead a number of techniques aimed at reflecting the human consciousness in action: centre of consciousness, Grove's 'world consciousness' passages, MacLennan's 'kaleidoscopic' scenes. These techniques are a step beyond the unambiguous psychological passages found in Callaghan's work: representing a character's mind epistemologically requires a greater degree of experiment with the realist form than does the mere summing up of such thoughts under the guise of objectivity. But Callaghan rejects the first option, except in a few scattered, fleeting moments much more suited to the kind of psychological development found in short fiction than to the sustained character development necessary for the modern novel. Even in Callaghan's most convincing works of psychological realism he seldom if ever mimics the flow of human consciousness; his thought processes happen step by step, in sequential, directly worded summations of states of mind that occur at intervals throughout a novel.

Essentially, this refusal to abandon a pretence to objectivity, even at times when the representation of a subjective state of consciousness appears called for in a given narrative, is the one thing that most strikingly separates Callaghan from most of his modern-realist contemporaries and the international high modernists. Unlike either group, Callaghan is so utterly afraid of 'artifice' in writing, so determined to tell the 'truth,' that he winds up reducing human psychology to a few lines of narrative summation. In a sense, Callaghan is equating objectivity with a lack of ambiguity, although the two are obviously not the same thing. Callaghan, apparently, was unable to accept a modernist notion, perhaps most dramatically explored by European surrealists and expressionists, that the human mind was ambiguous, and that behind conscious perceptions, thoughts, and ethical conclusions, there were many competing and indefinable subjective impulses. Or, perhaps more accurately, Callaghan's idea that modern writing grows out of speech is incompatible with a modernist (and modern-realist) belief that the individual human mind in the process of experiencing 'modernity,' not the language that expresses this experience, should be a fundamental concern of the writer. In his 1938 review of Faulkner's *The Unvanquished*, Callaghan reveals that he believed attempts to mimic human consciousness led away from psychological realism, rather than toward it, because they replace a detached, objective, unambiguous summary of the contents of the mind with a mere reflection of its ambiguous processes: 'The mind begins to hunger for a pause, some moment of illumination into the souls of the characters. That illumination hardly ever comes; the picture, the action keeps flickering before the eyes: get the illumination out of it if you can, but there must be no stop in the visual recording … Faulkner has actually very little illumination of character to offer. Perhaps it has been a mistake to think of him at all as a prober into dark psychological depths.'[64]

Callaghan carried his interpretation of epistemological modes of writing a step further in a 1939 review of Faulkner's *The Wild Palms*:

> All the Faulkner talent for giving you the quality of a moment, or rather the external appearance of a moment, is there … It is there on the page as real as a bright dream, but there is something wrong. Nine times out of ten the thing that is wrong is what was supposed to be going on inside the people. It just isn't true … But sooner or later someone is going to ask one important question not only of William Faulkner but of all American writers. It's a simple question, and it's just this: What is a man, what is he doing on Earth? What's your conception of a man? All the big writers understood that question and tried to give some kind of an answer from Chaucer to Gorki … Try reading this last book of Faulkner's with this question in mind, and various answers, some of them pretty juvenile, will keep popping out from the pages.[65]

Callaghan, the eternal objectivist, is here accusing Faulkner's stream-of-consciousness writing of conveying only the 'external appearance of the moment,' thereby avoiding the all-important 'psychological depths.' Ironically, Callaghan's writing, with its desire to get, in effect, to the psychological heart of the matter, leads to a denial of the psychological complexity of the human mind and misses the mark: his brand of psychological writing, with its direct summations of thoughts, is what conveys only the 'external appearance of the moment,' showing the thought, the mental conclusion, without fully acknowledging the subconscious process that leads to it. Callaghan rejects Faulkner's writing because 'it just isn't true' or it does not pose the questions he believes literature ought to pose. Ultimately it does not offer up an 'answer.' Callaghan is not fundamentally interested in the actual, ambiguous workings of the human mind; he is interested in the influence of the larger, social world on the individual mind and the specific thoughts and choices that arise in an individual's mind when faced with particular situations. How one thinks is not important: he wants to know what and why people think. This contrast draws attention to the essential difference between 'realism,' or that which strives to convey a sense of reality, and 'mimesis,' or that which strives to mimic reality, two impulses in tension in Canadian literature of the period. Callaghan, atypically, was an unqualified realist. Other writers of the period were also realists, but willing to stretch the boundaries of the realist form more readily, sometimes through epistemological mimesis, to admit the subjective perspectives that Callaghan found distracting or unnecessary to his literary aims. In this sense, the modern realists were like many of their high-modernist counterparts.

Callaghan's refusal to abandon the detached, objective mode of narration that he preferred from the very beginning of his career opens his writing to criticism on the grounds that it appears moralistic, monotonous, and heavy-handed. His refusal at all costs to abandon the direct style for psychological mimesis, in one sense, makes him the most conservative of the modern realists. It is perhaps appropriate, given the matrix of contradictions that is modern realism, that its most conservative proponent should also be its most well-connected and well-versed in modernist forms and modes. Revealingly, the same rejection of mimesis that separates Callaghan from many of his modernist contemporaries also divides him from the modern realists of the period, who willingly supplemented their 'direct reportage' with all sorts of epistemological techniques that I have already discussed in a variety of contexts. While the techniques of the modern realists to this end only vaguely approximate those of the most experimental high-modernists – Joyce, Woolf, Faulkner – their works, nevertheless, bear a striking similarity to those of a whole host of other international modernists whose styles are experimental but essentially realist: Hemingway, Lawrence, Fitzgerald, Rhys, Conrad, Camus, among others. This would appear to offer a possible explanation for why so many Canadian writers believed they were being experimental when they wrote in the realist style and why international magazines occasionally validated their assumptions. It also suggests again that modern realism was not simply a response to a nationalist call for regional writing in Canada, but rather one of numerous often competing and contradictory impulses that make up literary modernism. It also explains why Callaghan, the one Canadian prose writer of the period comfortably to straddle the boundary between Canadian and foreign writing, was able to do so effortlessly and unquestioningly.

8
Modern Realism and Canadian Literature

The modern-realist movement that began energetically and unmistakably with the appearance of *Canadian Bookman* and its first loud manifestos in January 1919 did not conclude so unambiguously. The movement was already beginning to wind down by the end of the Second World War. It perhaps came to an end in an absolute sense with Hugh MacLennan's problematic emergence as the first 'contemporary' Canadian writer, despite the deeply traditional realism of his first published novels. All the same, elements and influences of the movement continue well beyond 1945. A number of modern-realist works discussed in this study were published in the 1950s, including Callaghan's *The Loved and the Lost* (1951) and McCourt's *The Wooden Sword* (1956). There are also many works published in the 1950s that incorporate many of the movement's trademark techniques and characteristics: Ernest Buckler's *The Mountain and the Valley* (1952), Ethel Wilson's *The Equations of Love* (1952), Brian Moore's *Judith Hearne* (1955), Mordecai Richler's *Son of a Smaller Hero* (1955), Adele Wiseman's *The Sacrifice* (1956), Robertson Davies's *A Mixture of Frailties* (1958), and MacLennan's *The Watch That Ends the Night* (1959), to name just a few. Indeed, realism certainly remained the dominant mode of serious Canadian fiction at least until the 1970s, and a strong realist tradition persists even today. The realist tradition has been reinvigorated and redirected in recent years by numerous 'ethnic' Canadian writers who, like the modern realists did, often find themselves constrained, challenged, and energized by expectations of literary mimesis. Much as modern realists in the early twentieth century sought to represent the 'new' and unexpressed Canadian experience, so, too, do some of the best contemporary Canadian writers now employ a realist aesthetic to challenge the hegemonic and colonial narratives represented by the modern-realist tradition. Recent high-profile literary awards have been presented most often to Canadian writers who can be considered realists, if not modern realists in the absolute sense outlined in this book. From a literary-historical perspective, then, the temporal boundaries of modern realism are inconvenient: it does not, like some other modernist movements – futurism, for example – end suddenly or spectacularly with the arrival of a seismic historical event or rival aesthetic. Instead, like literary modernism as a general phenomenon, modern realism was exhausted slowly, over many years, and several of its characteristics have proved remarkably enduring. As Bradbury and McFarlane write about European modernisms, 'the broader view of Modernism ... must suggest an extraordinary range of continuities through into present art.'[1]

Suprisingly, given the near absence of Canada's modern realism from literary histories, most of its 'continuities' are glaringly obvious. Many of the best-known late twentieth-century Canadian writers have produced major works with prominent 'realist' characteristics that are founded upon the tradition established by their modern-realist forerunners: Richler, Atwood, Davies, Bissoondath, Mistry, Laurence, Findley, and Munro, among many others. Today, almost a century after *Canadian Bookman* announced the arrival of a 'new era' in its first manifesto, at least two of the fundamental tenets of modern realism remain prominent in the Canadian literary imagination: psychological realism and an interest in representing a contemporary Canada. As a movement, modern realism came to an 'end,' but its aesthetic was never abandoned by a disgruntled group of authors who felt it had 'failed.' Neither was it unseated by a new, competing literary form with combative and antagonistic theories. Instead, it slowly and quietly lost its coherence even as the majority of Canada's serious writers continued to produce realist fiction. By 1950, there were no periodicals or little magazines in Canada that showed more than a remote interest in debating the value and shape of the realist aesthetic. The careers of most of the overt and polemical modern realists had drawn to a close before mid-century, or they had been directed away from self-conscious experiment with the realist form, or they had simply begun to take realism for granted. There are only a very few scattered, mostly retrospective, critical pieces written on modern realism after 1950, including short sections of Callaghan's *That Summer in Paris* (1963) discussed earlier. The new writers who emerged in the 1950s, even when their styles were predominantly realist, gave no indication that they considered themselves a part of a realist movement. By its very definition, a literary movement advocates distinct aesthetic assumptions and methods, often in the face of hegemonic tradition or in opposition to rival forms and formations. The modern-realist movement was initiated by writers who, invigorated by the modern spirit that prevailed in the wake of the Great War, objected to the dominant romanticism in early twentieth-century Canadian fiction, and they aggressively opposed it with their new methods. Many other rebellious modernist movements were ultimately abandoned because they proved too limited or became unfashionable – futurism, Dada, surrealism, vorticism. But modern realism ironically ceased to be a movement after 1950 because of its very success. By mid-century, modern realism had no need of advocacy: it had no serious aesthetic rival on the Canadian literary scene and was established as the dominant and default mode of serious fiction. Few dominant literary aesthetics die a sudden death. Instead, they tend to lose coherence just as they gain a sense of widespread acceptance. The boisterous advocacy of a literary aesthetic ceases to be fashionable or necessary when it has triumphed and entered the mainstream. And modern-realist influences are ubiquitous in Canadian fiction of the present day.

The most dramatic, lasting, and significant aspect of the modern-realist movement – its near total conquest of 'serious' Canadian fiction by 1950 – has been overlooked because it is so apparent. The triumph of realism by mid-century was so absolute in Canada that it seems to have been determined by extra-literary forces: nationalism, colonialism, landscape, region, culture. The modern realists have not received the credit they deserve for commanding the most successful and enduring literary revolution in Canada's history. Instead, they at very best receive muted praise for their 'formative' role: as Pacey writes in *Literary History of Canada*, 'if this period [1920–40] deserves remembering at all, it is as the time when a few novelists first seriously tried to come to terms with their Canadian environment, and to find a suitable style.'[2] Neither have the modern realists received their due for laying the groundwork for contemporary Canadian fiction and the first indisputably world-class achievements by Canadian writers: perhaps the best evidence of the existence of a modern-realism is the vigour of the celebrated Canadian postmodernism that reacts to it. Like other modernist movements, modern realism has both transcended its literary-historical boundaries and continued into the present, and provided a hegemonic structure against which a younger generation of writers could write. But modern realism is not significant solely because it changed the national literature and set the stage for a contemporary fiction. Canada's modern realism, in its own right, constitutes a significant branch of the international collection of movements that makes up literary modernism. The modern realists did more than try 'to come to terms with their Canadian environment': their exploration of the cultural conditions and great subjects of modernity was sustained and uncompromising. Like many of their modernist contemporaries, the modern realists did more than try 'to find a suitable style': they developed an innovative, experimental, complex, workable, and enduring aesthetic. And it was their *own* aesthetic: they did not usually imitate or replicate the methods and techniques of foreign writers. Instead, their interest in bringing subjective perspectives into impersonal and objectivist narratives, in rendering complex human psychology within a 'realistic' exploration of their contemporary world, led them to insist that a Canadian modernism – a modern realism – had to 'happen' in its own way.

The modern-realist movement, and the eclectic oeuvres that it comprises, are perhaps the best indication we have that Canada's early twentieth-century 'isms' – romanticism, naturalism, realism, modernism – ought to be judged on their own terms, something that the modern realists themselves frequently told us and critics such as Willmott have emphasized. This certainly does not mean applying looser or kinder 'standards of criticism,' to reinvoke a phrase from *Canadian Bookman* that was echoed in Frye's 'Conclusion to a *Literary History of Canada*.'[3] But it does entail an end to at least one persistent critical practice that can be traced back to *The Canadian Forum* of the 1920s: looking for modern Canadian writers to mimic foreign models, and then either reprobating or excusing them when they do not. The fact that modernism and realism 'appear' simultaneously and contingently in Canada is only unbecoming or embarrassing if one denies the existence or validity of a Canadian literary tradition that has points of convergence with and divergence from other traditions. Ironically, the quest of many nationalist critics to 'validate' Canadian writing by linking it to foreign literatures, or by denying that such comparisons have any value at all, has contributed to the neglect of some of Canada's own hard-won modernisms.

It is a truism that much high-modernist experiment in other countries developed in reaction to and rejection of nineteenth-century realism. The functional and dynamic coexistence of modernism and realism in the minds of Canada's early twentieth-century writers, however, is proof that these aesthetics are not inherently or irreconcilably opposed, which is something that some contemporary critics of international modernism are exploring. Chris Baldick, one of the most insightful contemporary modernist scholars, does not discuss Canadian writing, but nevertheless reveals how Canada's modern realism might be reimagined relative to international and canonical modernisms:

> The modern movement ... as understood by writers who had grown up with it, was a broad church that embraced a variety of forms, techniques, styles, and attitudes, all of which were in some way innovative and in some way representative of new twentieth-century modes of awareness ... This does not mean that the contrasts often highlighted between the more experimental modernist works and the more traditional realist novels ... are in themselves irrelevant or misleading; only that they can be given a false significance if they tempt us to forget that there are many ways of being modern, or to believe that the experimental and traditional can be segregated cleanly. As the modernist writers themselves understood very well, every literary experiment is necessarily traditional in some sense, just as every 'traditionalist' work of any value is also a new experiment.[4]

The fact that Canadian modern realism has gone almost unnoticed may be partly the result of the polarizing and binary thinking that Baldick challenges. The modern realists demonstrated time and again that they believed the modernist and realist impulses were symbiotic: the incorporation of modernist technique into a larger realist framework could actually *enhance* the 'realism' of the text; and the text could effectively become more 'modern' when realist methods were employed to ground it in what Lionel Stevenson called 'the actual vital spirit of their times, free of outworn conventions and yet avoiding all self-conscious affectation of revolt.'[5]

In this sense, modern realism resembles a more famous, relatively conservative 'branch' of modernism that includes writers such as Ernest Hemingway, Joseph Conrad, Jean Rhys, D.H. Lawrence, Albert Camus, F. Scott Fitzgerald, Thomas Mann, Henry James, Evelyn Waugh, and many others. This international assortment of writers, like their Canadian counterparts, experimented with literary realism. But while they stretched the boundaries of the realist form to be sure, they stopped short of endorsing the boldest high-modernist techniques and strategies. Despite the comparison, the modern realists are better described as 'constructive' modernists than 'conservative' modernists. They did not reject high-modernist strategies because they were reactionary. Rather, they applied the revolutionary and experimental spirit of modernism, not to break violently with an established order but rather to establish their own tradition where they believed one was lacking. This is one sense in which I read differently than Willmott does in *Unreal Country*: 'The formal effects I will ascribe to Canadian works as modernist act to create an innovative experience of incoherence for the reader, typically without the openly alternative or aggressive relationship to conventional form characteristic of canonical texts.'[6] In my view, the modern realists baulked at the boldest modernist methods – extreme fragmentation, dissonant multivocality, the most subjectivist epistemological methods – because they considered them in conflict with the modern-realist conviction that art had to be coherent, clear, and constructive: how else could they establish a modern Canadian fiction rooted in the contemporary world?

The modern realists thus demand a re-examination of some general assumptions about Canadian literature. Several readings of Canadian fiction may derive from a need to explain the proliferation of Canadian realism in the absence of an acknowledgment of a modern-realist movement: if realism did not come into being *because of a conscious and modern literary movement*, how else can one explain its prominence in Canadian literature? Since realism is ubiquitous in Canadian fiction, or at least was during the explosion of nationalist and thematic criticism in the 1950s, '60s, and '70s, it is almost impossible to imagine it ever having to fight to emerge, survive, and flourish. It can seem such a given, such an obvious and defining characteristic of the national literature, that it hardly seems worthy of mention. It can appear on the surface reminiscent of nineteenth-century realism, and be cursorily and summarily dismissed as imitative and outmoded. It can also be perceived as a default aesthetic for writers presumably carrying out nationalist, regional, or referential projects. But the autonomous and calculated aesthetic of the modern realists indicates that geography, nationalism, and foreign influences are perhaps not the deterministic forces they are sometimes thought to be for Canadian writers. That the modern realists arrived independently at methods similar to those of a whole branch of 'conservative' modernists, who were writing in numerous other national contexts, demonstrates their internationalism and relative freedom from such deterministic forces. The interdependence of the various subgeneric forms of modern realism – prairie realism, social realism, urban realism – indicates that Canadian literature is not always productively considered as a collection of regional forms, defined by geographical spaces, and bifurcated along rural and urban lines. Such a regional view of Canadian fiction denies the agency of individual authors, leads to thematic interpretations and overriding national theses, and neglects both aesthetic concerns and relevant international influences. Canada's modern writers were referential: this is undeniable. They were 'realists' after all. But more often than not, they demonstrated that the 'region' is subjected to the creative whim and experiment of the author; the author is not subjected to the creative whim of a personified landscape or region or geographical space. Furthermore, the prominent 'themes' of interest to the modern realists had little to do with region: they were the same ones that interested all sorts of modernists. And even then, modern realism is defined primarily, not by its subject matter, but by its modern aesthetic assumptions: art should be innovative and rooted in the contemporary world, the author ought to be extricated from the text, the mimetic reflection and exploration of the workings of the human mind present a great experimental challenge.

The neglect of modern realism is reflected not just in literary criticism, but also in the early twentieth-century canon. Despite very promising signs such as the inauguration of the *Canadian Literature Collection / Collection de littérature canadienne* and the *Editing Modernism in Canada* project, scandalously few books of the period are in print, and the few that are provide a skewed sense of the modern-realist movement as a whole. Most modern-realist works have never been the subject of any significant critical attention. Such oversights will not be rectified as long as literary histories perpetuate the myth that Canadian realists belong to an antique and insignificant chapter in Canada's literary pre-history. Every time another modern-realist title disappears from the *New Canadian Library*, prevailing conceptions of the period are reinforced, and the 'modern-realist canon' becomes less diverse. It is not necessary to advocate an uncritical celebration of lost and forgotten fiction. I hope this book has been highly critical of most of the modern realists, their works, and their techniques. But however one judges the literary significance or achievement of individual modern-realist works, it is impossible to deny the modern realists' distinct and hard-won aesthetic, commitment to making Canadian literature better, and participation in the twentieth century's remarkable modernist revolution. The modern-realist movement, with all of its imperfections, deserves to take its rightful place in the Canadian literary history it has profoundly changed and among the other international modernisms with which it shares a commitment to innovation and experiment, a deep interest in human psychology, and an indefatigable fascination with the cultural conditions of modernity.

Notes

1: The Modern-Realist Movement: Contexts, Aesthetics, Origins

1 See, for example, George Woodcock, 'Hugh MacLennan,' *Northern Review* 3 (1950), 2–10; Robertson Davies, 'MacLennan's Rising Sun,' *Saturday Night* (28 March 1959): 29–31; Paul Goetsch, 'Too Long to the Courtly Muses: Hugh MacLennan as a Contemporary Writer,' *Canadian Literature* 10 (1961): 7–18; David Arnason, 'Canadian Nationalism in Search of Form: Hugh MacLennan's *Barometer Rising*,' *Journal of Canadian Fiction* 1 (1972): 68–71; T.D. MacLulich, *Hugh MacLennan* (Boston: Twayne, 1983); Mari Peepre-Bordessa, *Hugh MacLennan's National Trilogy: Mapping a Canadian Identity (1940–1950)* (Helsinki: Suomalainen Tiedeakatemia, 1990).

2 Robert Kroetsch, 'A Canadian Issue,' *Boundary* 2 3.1 (1974): 1.

3 Glenn Willmott, *Unreal Country: Modernity in the Canadian Novel in English* (Montreal: McGill-Queen's University Press, 2002), 38.

4 See especially Willmott, *Unreal Country*.

5 Ibid., 42.

6 Adrian MacDonald, 'English Realism to a Canadian,' *Canadian Bookman*, September 1922, 235.

7 Sandra Djwa, '*The Canadian Forum*: Literary Catalyst,' *Studies in Canadian Literature* 1 (1976), 21.

8 Garden City Press, 'Introducing the Canadian Bookman's Bookmen,' *Canadian Bookman*, January 1919, 1.

9 Mary Vipond, 'The Canadian Authors' Association in the 1920s: A Case Study in Cultural Nationalism,' *Journal of Canadian Studies* 15 (1980): 73.

10 Desmond Pacey, 'Fiction 1920–1940,' in *Literary History of Canada: Canadian Literature in English*, ed. Carl F. Klinck. (Toronto: University of Toronto Press, 1965), 168.
11 Lionel Stevenson, 'Manifesto for a National Literature,' in *Towards a Canadian Literature: Essays, Editorials and Manifestos* (Ottawa: Tecumseh, 1984), 207–8.
12 Hilda Glynn-Ward, 'A Plea for Purity,' *Canadian Bookman*, March 1924, 64.
13 Pacey, 'Fiction 1920–1940,' 186.
14 Donald Stephens, 'Novels in English, 1920–1940,' in *The Oxford Companion to Canadian Literature* (Toronto: Oxford University Press, 1997), 817.
15 W.J. Keith, *Canadian Literature in English* (London: Longman, 1985): 121.
16 George Woodcock, *George Woodcock's Introduction to Canadian Fiction* (Toronto: ECW, 1993), 49.
17 E.L. Bobak, 'Seeking "Direct, Honest Realism": The Canadian Novel of the 1920s,' *Canadian Literature* 89 (1981): 86.
18 Ibid., 85–6.
19 T.D. MacLulich, *Between Europe and America: The Canadian Tradition in Fiction* (Toronto: ECW, 1998), 9.
20 Alison Calder, 'Reassessing Prairie Realism,' *Textual Studies in Canada* 12 (1998): 56.
21 Desmond Pacey, *Creative Writing in Canada* (Toronto: Ryerson, 1952), 1–3.
22 Douglas Mao and Rebecca L. Walkowitz, *Bad Modernisms* (Duke University Press, 2006), 1.
23 Chris Baldick, *The Oxford English Literary History*, vol. 10: *The Modern Movement* (Oxford: Oxford University Press, 2004), 4–5.
24 John Moss, Introduction to *The Canadian Novel*, vol. 3: *Modern Times: A Critical Anthology* (Toronto: New Canada, 1982), 10.
25 Ibid.
26 Willmott, *Unreal Country*, 42.
27 Ibid., 5.
28 Ibid.
29 Ibid., 6.
30 Ibid., 5.
31 Dennis Duffy, 'Losing the Line: The Field of Our Modernism,' *Essays on Canadian Writing* 39 (1989): 165.
32 Ibid., 166.
33 Frank Davey, 'Sheila Watson,' in *The Oxford Companion to Canadian Literature* (Toronto: Oxford University Press, 1983), 822.
34 MacLulich, *Between Europe and America*, 100.
35 Ibid., 88–9.

36 Vassiliki Kolocotroni et al., 'Introduction,' in *Modernism: An Anthology of Sources and Documents* (Edinburgh: Edinburgh University Press, 1998), xix.
37 Colin Hill, 'Critical Introduction,' in *Waste Heritage* by Irene Baird (Ottawa: University of Ottawa Press, 2007), ix–lvii.
38 Robert Lecker, *Making It Real: The Canonization of English-Canadian Literature* (Toronto: Anansi, 1995), 4.
39 E.H. Dewart, 'Introductory Essay to *Selections from Canadian Poets*,' in *Towards a Canadian Literature: Essays, Editorials and Manifestos*, ed. Douglas M. Daymond and Leslie G. Monkman (Ottawa: Tecumseh, 1984), 55.
40 William Douw Lighthall, *Songs from the Great Dominion: Voices from the Forests and Waters, Settlements and Cities of Canada* (London: Scott, 1889), 5.
41 Pacey, 'Fiction 1920–1940,' 168.
42 Cal Smiley, 'Novels in English 1900 to 1920,' in *The Oxford Companion to Canadian Literature*, ed. William Toye (Toronto: Oxford University Press, 1983), 570–1.

2: Manifestos for a Modern Realism: *Canadian Bookman* and *The Canadian Forum* in the 1920s

1 Mary Vipond, 'The Nationalist Network,' *Canadian Review of Studies in Nationalism* 7.1 (1980): 32.
2 'Among the Booksellers,' *Canadian Bookman*, January 1919, 83.
3 For critical discussions of the *Bookman*'s nationalism and boosterism, see Desmond Pacey, 'The Writer and His Public, 1920–1960,' in *Literary History of Canada: Canadian Literature in English*, ed. Carl F. Klinck (Toronto: University of Toronto Press, 1965), 3–21; T.D. MacLulich, *Between Europe and America: The Canadian Tradition in Fiction* (Toronto: ECW, 1988); James Mulvihill, 'The "Canadian Bookman" and Literary Nationalism,' *Canadian Literature* 107 (1985): 48–59.
4 Wynne Francis, 'The Expanding Spectrum: Literary Magazines,' *Canadian Literature* 57 (1973): 6–17.
5 Mary Vipond, 'The Canadian Authors' Association in the 1920s: A Case Study in Cultural Nationalism,' *Journal of Canadian Studies* 15 (1980): 69, 66.
6 'Standards of Criticism,' *Canadian Bookman*, April 1919, 7.
7 Ibid.
8 W. Garland Foster, 'On Reflecting Canadian Life,' *Canadian Bookman*, December 1924, 249.
9 A.E.S.S., 'A Prairie Essayist,' *Canadian Bookman*, May 1924, 111.
10 Anne Burke, ed., 'Some Annotated Letters of A.J.M. Smith and Raymond Knister,' *Canadian Poetry: Studies, Documents, Reviews* 11 (1982): 122.

11 'Bookishness in Canada,' *Canadian Bookman*, January 1919, 11.
12 Barker Fairley, 'Artists and Authors,' *The Canadian Forum*, December 1921, 460.
13 Douglas Bush, 'Making Literature Hum,' *The Canadian Forum*, December 1926, 72–3.
14 Vipond, 'The Canadian Authors' Association in the 1920s' 69–70.
15 Mulvihill, 'The "Canadian Bookman" and Literary Nationalism,' 51.
16 Janet Lyon, *Manifestoes: Provocations of the Modern* (Ithaca, NY: Cornell University Press, 1999), 9.
17 'The New Era,' *Canadian Bookman*, January 1919, 1.
18 Ibid.
19 Ibid.
20 Ibid.
21 Ibid.
22 Douglas M. Daymond and Leslie G. Monkman, eds., *Canadian Novelists and the Novel* (Ottawa: Borealis, 1981), 173.
23 J.M. Gibbon, 'The Coming Canadian Novel,' *Canadian Bookman*, July 1919, 13–14.
24 Ibid., 14–15.
25 Ibid., 15.
26 Ibid., 14.
27 Ibid., 15.
28 Ibid., 14.
29 Beaumont S. Cornell, 'The Essential Training of the Novelist,' *Canadian Bookman*, June 1921, 46.
30 Ibid., 46.
31 Adrian MacDonald, 'English Realism to a Canadian,' *Canadian Bookman*, September 1922, 234.
32 Ibid.
33 Ibid., 235.
34 Ibid.
35 Ibid., 234.
36 Ibid.
37 Ibid., 234–5.
38 Ibid., 235.
39 Ibid.
40 Ibid.
41 Lorne Pierce, 'Canadian Literature and the National Ideal,' *Canadian Bookman*, September 1925, 143.
42 Ibid., 144.

43 Lorne Albert Pierce and Albert Durrant Watson, *Our Canadian Literature: Representative Prose and Verse* (Toronto: Ryerson Press, 1922), xiv, xvii.
44 Ibid., 144.
45 Ibid.
46 Francis Dickie, 'Realism in Canadian Fiction,' *Canadian Bookman*, October 1925, 165.
47 Ibid.
48 Ibid.
49 A.H.B., 'To the Lighthouse,' *Canadian Bookman*, September 1927, 277.
50 John H. Creighton, 'The Fiction of James Joyce,' *The Canadian Forum*, July 1926, 309.
51 John Hurley, 'Mr. Elliott's [*sic*] Wasteland,' *Canadian Bookman*, May 1923, 126.
52 Lionel Stevenson, 'The Fatal Gift,' *Canadian Bookman*, September 1923, 235.
53 Ibid.
54 Lionel Stevenson, 'The Outlook for Canadian Fiction,' *Canadian Bookman*, July 1924, 157.
55 Ibid., 158.
56 Ibid.
57 Lionel Stevenson, 'Is Canadian Poetry Modern?' *Canadian Bookman*, July 1927, 195.
58 Ibid., 195.
59 Ibid., 196.
60 Ibid.
61 Ibid.
62 Unsigned review of *The Cow Puncher* by Robert J.C. Stead, *Canadian Bookman*, January 1919, 69.
63 Unsigned review of *Blue Pete: Half Breed* by Luke Allan, *Canadian Bookman*, September 1921, 59.
64 Unsigned review of *God's Green Country* by Ethel Chapman, *Canadian Bookman*, February 1923, 43.
65 Georges Bugnet, 'Two New Western Books,' review of *Settlers of the Marsh* by Frederick Philip Grove, and *Wild Geese* by Martha Ostenso, *Canadian Bookman*, December 1925, 203.
66 T.D. Rimmer, 'Recent Canadian Novels,' *Canadian Bookman*, October 1926, 307.
67 'Land and Weather,' unsigned review of *The Pioneers of Old Ontario* by W.L. Smith, *Over Prairie Trails* by Frederick Philip Grove, and *Nature In American Literature* by Norman Foerster, *The Canadian Forum*, May 1923, 248.
68 'A New Anthology,' *The Canadian Forum*, November 1923, 58.

69 W.S.M., 'A Literary Tramp,' review of *Wild Honey* by Frederick Niven, *Canadian Forum* May 1927, 252.
70 See Djwa, '*The Canadian Forum*: Literary Catalyst,' 7–25.
71 *The Oxford Companion to Canadian Literature*, ed. William Toye (Toronto: Oxford University Press, 1983), s.v. '*The Canadian Forum*.'
72 Raymond Knister, 'Canadian Letter,' in *The First Day of Spring: Stories and Other Prose*, ed. Peter Stevens (Toronto: University of Toronto Press, 1976), 379.
73 Raymond Knister, 'The Canadian Short Story,' *Canadian Bookman*, August 1923, 203–4.
74 Ibid., 204.
75 Ibid., 203.
76 Djwa, '*The Canadian Forum*: Literary Catalyst,' 21.
77 A.J.M. Smith, 'Introduction to *The Book of Canadian Poetry*,' in *Towards a Canadian Literature: Essays, Editorials and Manifestos*, vol. 2., ed. Douglas M. Daymond and Leslie G. Monkman (1943; repr., Ottawa: Tecumseh, 1984), 338.
78 'Three Years Have Passed,' *The Canadian Forum*, October 1920, 3.
79 Ibid.
80 Huntley K. Gordon, 'Canadian Poetry,' *The Canadian Forum*, March 1921, 178–80.
81 Ibid., 178.
82 Fairley, 'Artists and Authors,' 460.
83 Ibid.
84 J. Addison Reid, 'The Canadian Novel,' *The Canadian Forum*, June 1922, 658.
85 Alfred Gordon, 'Canadian Culture?' *The Canadian Forum*, March 1922, 558.
86 Creighton, 'Fiction of James Joyce,' 310.

3: Raymond Knister: Revolutionary Modern Realist

1 Robert Lecker, *Making It Real: The Canonization of English-Canadian Literature* (Toronto: Anansi, 1995), 4.
2 See David Arnason, 'Preface,' *Journal of Canadian Fiction* 4.2 (1975): 7–10; Anne Burke, 'Some Annotated Letters of A.J.M. Smith and Raymond Knister,' *Canadian Poetry: Studies, Documents, Reviews* 11 (1982): 98–135.
3 Raymond Knister, 'Canadian Letter,' in *The First Day of Spring: Stories and Other Prose*, ed. Peter Stevens (Toronto: University of Toronto Press, 1976), 378.
4 Ibid., 380.

5 Raymond Knister, 'Canadian Literature: A General Impression,' *Journal of Canadian Fiction* 4.2 (1975): 169–74.
6 Raymond Knister, 'Canadian Literati,' *Journal of Canadian Fiction* 4.2 (1975): 160.
7 Ibid., 161.
8 Raymond Knister, ed., *Canadian Short Stories* (Toronto: Macmillan, 1928), xi, xviii.
9 Frederick Philip Grove to Raymond Knister, 15 November 1929, in *The Letters of Frederick Philip Grove*, ed. Desmond Pacey (Toronto: University of Toronto Press, 1976).
10 Knister, 'Canadian Literature: A General Impression,' 172.
11 Raymond Knister, 'List of Books Read by J. Raymond Knister From September 14 to Mid 1924,' box 8, The Raymond Knister Collection, McMaster University.
12 Raymond Knister to Lorne Pierce, 23 November 1925, box 2, The Raymond Knister Collection, McMaster University.
13 Peter Stevens, Introduction to *The First Day of Spring: Stories and Other Prose*, ed. Peter Stevens (Toronto: University of Toronto Press, 1976), xii.
14 Leo Kennedy, 'Raymond Knister,' *The Canadian Forum*, September 1932, 461.
15 See Norah Story, ed., *The Oxford Companion to Canadian History and Literature* (Toronto: Oxford University Press, 1967); Philip Child, introduction to *White Narcissus* by Raymond Knister (1929; repr., Toronto: McClelland and Stewart, 1962), 7–16.
16 Raymond Knister, *White Narcissus*, New Canadian Library (1929; repr., Toronto: McClelland and Stewart, 1962), 110.
17 Raymond Knister, 'The One Thing,' in *The First Day of Spring: Stories and Other Prose*, 158.
18 Raymond Knister to W.A. Deacon, 11 October 1923, file 84, The Raymond Knister Collection, Victoria College, University of Toronto.
19 Raymond Knister, 'The Loading,' in *The First Day of Spring: Stories and Other Prose*, 79.
20 Raymond Knister, 'Indian Summer,' in *The First Day of Spring: Stories and Other Prose*, 90.
21 Paul Denham, 'Beyond Realism: Raymond Knister's *White Narcissus*,' *Studies in Canadian Literature* 3 (1978): 71.
22 Raymond Knister, 'Mist Green Oats,' in *The First Day of Spring: Stories and Other Prose*, 58.
23 Knister, 'The Loading,' 83.
24 Knister, 'Indian Summer,' 86–7.

25 Knister, 'Mist Green Oats,' 59.
26 Knister, 'Canadian Literature: A General Impression,' 171.
27 Raymond Knister to Elizabeth Frankfurth, 11 April 1924, box 1, The Raymond Knister Collection, McMaster University.
28 Knister, ed., *Canadian Short Stories*, xiii–xiv.
29 Raymond Knister, 'Dissecting the "T.B.M,"' *Saturday Night*, 6 September 1930, 5. Knister's response to an earlier *Saturday Night* article entitled 'Why Be True to Life' in which S. Laycock writes: 'It is a curious form of relaxation to go home after a day's monotonous grind and read an account of someone else's monotonous grind' (qtd in 'Dissecting' 5). Knister's article defends fiction that offers the 'truth about life' and is one of his most revealing manifestos on realism.
30 Child, introduction to *White Narcissus*, 8.
31 Raymond Knister, 'Grapes,' in *The First Day of Spring: Stories and Other Prose*, 98.
32 Ibid., 106.
33 Raymond Knister, 'Banking Hours,' ts. box 6, The Raymond Knister Collection, McMaster University, 2.
34 Ibid., 3–7.
35 Ibid., 1.
36 Raymond Knister, 'Eric Mirth, or the Larger I,' *Journal of Canadian Fiction* 4.2 (1975): 98.
37 Ibid., 97.
38 Ibid.
39 Ibid., 100.
40 Raymond Knister to W.A. Deacon, file 84, The Raymond Knister Collection, Victoria College, University of Toronto.
41 Raymond Knister, 'The Strawstack,' in *The First Day of Spring: Stories and Other Prose*, 192.
42 Ibid., 187.
43 Ibid.
44 Centre of consciousness is a term defined by Maurice Beebe as part of his discussion of Henry James in *Ivory Towers and Sacred Founts: The Artist as Hero in Fiction from Goethe to Joyce* (New York: University Press, 1964). Centre of consciousness is less epistemological than stream of consciousness as a narrative form as it involves a shift of tone and point of view, but does not attempt to step outside of the central narrative and does not involve a mimetic representation of the direction and flow of consciousness in a character's mind. The narrative voice in a centre-of-consciousness passage, usually third-person omniscient, abandons a degree of impersonality and

speaks from the point of view of a particular character. This technique is sometimes called 'free indirect discourse,' though I prefer the first term because it draws attention to the psychological aims of this device.

45 Raymond Knister, 'The Fate of Mrs. Lucier,' in *The First Day of Spring: Stories and Other Prose*, 180–1.

46 Ibid., 184.

47 As Denham summarizes in 'Beyond Realism,' 'much of the scant commentary on *White Narcissus* has seen it as an early experiment in realism' (70).

48 Knister, *White Narcissus*, 20.

49 Ibid., 126.

50 Ibid., 133.

51 Kennedy, 'Raymond Knister,' 460.

52 Raymond Knister to Elizabeth Frankfurth, 11 April 1924, box 1, The Raymond Knister Collection, McMaster University.

53 Knister, *Group Portrait*, Ts. folders 9–10, the Raymond Knister Papers, Queen's University, 1.

54 Ibid.

55 Ibid., 40.

56 Ibid., 43.

57 Kennedy, 'Raymond Knister,' 459.

58 Ernest Walsh to Raymond Knister, 23 April 1925, folder 1, The Raymond Knister Papers, Queen's University.

59 Raymond Knister to Ernest Walsh, 12 May 1925, box 3, The Raymond Knister Collection, McMaster University.

60 Raymond Knister to Ernest Walsh, 3 June 1925, box 3, The Raymond Knister Collection, McMaster University.

61 Raymond Knister to Merrill Denison, 3 May 1923, box 1, The Raymond Knister Collection, McMaster University.

62 Raymond Knister to Elizabeth Frankfurth, 19 November 1925, box 1, The Raymond Knister Collection, McMaster University.

63 Raymond Knister to Frederick Philip Grove, 9 February 1931, box 1, The Raymond Knister Collection, McMaster University.

64 See Marcus Waddington, 'Raymond Knister: A Biographical Note,' *Journal of Canadian Fiction* 4 (1975): 175–92.

65 Raymond Knister, 'Via Faust,' folder 24, The Raymond Knister Papers, Queen's University, 1.

66 Raymond Knister to Elizabeth Frankfurth, 11 April 1924, box 1, The Raymond Knister Collection, McMaster University.

67 Knister, 'Via Faust,' 1.

4: The Proliferation of Modern Realism in Canada, Part 1: Prairie Realism Re-evaluated

1 Edward McCourt, *The Canadian West in Fiction* (Toronto: Ryerson Press, 1949), v.
2 Laurence Ricou, *Vertical Man, Horizontal World: Man and Landscape in Canadian Prairie Fiction* (Vancouver: University of British Columbia Press, 1973), ix.
3 Dick Harrison, *Unnamed Country: The Struggle for a Canadian Prairie Fiction* (Edmonton: University of Alberta Press, 1977), ix.
4 Deborah Lou Keahey, *Making It Home: Place in Canadian Prairie Literature* (Winnipeg: University of Manitoba Press, 1998), 6–7.
5 See, for example, Susan Jackel, 'Prairie Writing,' in *The Oxford Companion to Canadian Literature*, ed. Eugene Benson and William Toye (Toronto: Oxford University Press, 1997), 960–3; Robert Thacker, *The Great Prairie Fact and Literary Imagination* (Albuquerque: University of New Mexico Press, 1989); Terry Angus ed., *The Prairie Experience*, Themes in Canadian Literature (Toronto: Macmillan, 1975); A.T. Elder, 'Western Panorama: Settings and Themes in Robert J.C. Stead,' *Canadian literature*, 17 (1963): 44–56; Robert G. Lawrence, 'The Geography of Martha Ostenso's *Wild Geese*,' *Journal of Canadian Fiction* 16 (1976): 108–14; Salvatore Proietti, 'Frederick Philip Grove's Version of Pastoral Utopianism,' *Science-Fiction Studies* 19.3 (1992): 361–77; Hallvard Dahlie, *Isolation and Commitment: Frederick Philip Grove's Settlers of the March* (Toronto: ECW, 1993).
6 Jackel, 'Prairie Writing,' 960–3.
7 See Rudolf Bader, 'Frederick Philip Grove and Naturalism Reconsidered,' in *Gaining Ground: European Critics on Canadian Literature*, ed. Robert Kroetsch and Reingard M. Nischik (Edmonton: NeWest, 1985), 222–3; Rosalie Murphy Baum, 'Martha Ostenso's *Wild Geese*: More Insight into the Naturalistic Sensibility,' *Journal of Canadian Culture* 1.2 (1984): 117–35; Irene Gammel, *Sexualizing Power in Naturalism: Theodore Dreiser and Frederick Philip Grove* (Calgary: University of Calgary Press, 1994); Mac Fenwick, 'Niels's Saga: Colonial Narrative and Nordic Naturalism in *Settlers of the Marsh*,' *English Studies in Canada* 23.3 (September 1997): 297–314; Frank Birbalsingh, 'Grove and Existentialism,' *Canadian Literature* 43 (1970): 67–76; Thomas Gerry, 'Dante, C.D. Burns and Sinclair Ross: Philosophical Issues in *As For Me and My House*,' *Mosaic* 22.1 (Winter 1989): 113–22; John Ming Chen, 'The Politics of Social Realism in English-Canadian Novels (1920–55)' (PhD diss., University of Calgary, 1989); Isobel MacKenna, 'As They Really Were: Women in the Novels of Grove,' *English Studies in Cana-*

da 2 (1976): 109–16; Lorraine McMullen, 'Women in Grove's Novels,' in *The Grove Symposium*, Reappraisals Canadian Writers, ed. John Nause (Ottawa: University of Ottawa Press, 1974), 67–76; Elizabeth Potvin, '"The Eternal Feminine" and the Clothing Motif in Grove's Fiction,' *Studies in Canadian Literature* 12.2 (1987): 222–38; Helen Buss, 'Who Are You, Mrs. Bentley? Feminist Re-vision and Sincalir Ross's *As For Me and My House*,' in *Sinclair Ross's As For Me and My House: Five Decades of Criticsm*, ed. David Stouck (Toronto: University of Toronto Press, 1991), 190–209; Terry Goldie, 'W.O. Mitchell and the Pursuit of the Homosocial Ideal,' in *Magic Lies: The Art of W.O. Mitchell*, ed. Shelia Latham and David Latham (Toronto: University of Toronto Press, 1997), 100–9.

8 Alison Calder, 'Reassessing Prairie Realism,' *Textual Studies in Canada* 12 (1998): 51.

9 Donna Bennett, 'Conflicted Vision: A Consideration of Canon and Genre in English-Canadian Literature,' in *Canadian Canons: Essays in Literary Value*, ed. Robert Lecker (Toronto: University of Toronto Press, 1991), 146.

10 See for example Alison Calder and Robert Wardhaugh, 'Introduction: Where Is the Prairie?' in *History, Literature, and the Writing of the Canadian Prairies*, ed. Alison Calder and Robert Wardhaugh (Winnipeg: University of Manitoba Press, 2005), 3–24; Aritha Van Herk, 'Prairie Writing 1983 to 1996,' in *The Oxford Companion to Canadian Literature*, 963–5.

11 W.J. Keith, *Canadian Literature in English* (London: Longman, 1985), 121.

12 H.M.R., 'New Furrows,' review of *New Furrows* by Flos Jewell Williams, *Canadian Bookman*, January 1927, 21.

13 Robert Ayre, 'Frederick Philip Grove,' *Canadian Forum*, April 1932: 255–6.

14 Ricou, *Vertical Man*, 8.

15 Calder, 'Reassessing Prairie Realism,' 58–9.

16 'Land and Weather,' review of *The Pioneers of Old Ontario* by W.L. Smith, *Over Prairie Trails* by Frederick Philip Grove, and *Nature in American Literature* by Norman Foerster, *Canadian Forum*, May 1923, 248.

17 Ibid.

18 'The Turn of the Year,' review of *The Turn of the Year* by Frederick Philip Grove, *Canadian Forum*, 1924, 152.

19 'Four Novels,' review of *The Kays* by Margaret Deland, *The Dark Dawn* by Martha Ostenso, *Grain* by Robert J.C. Stead, and *The Time of Man* by Elizabeth Madox Roberts, *Canadian Forum*, January 1927, 121.

20 Ibid., 122.

21 Paul A.W. Wallace, 'The Romance of the West,' *Canadian Forum*, March 1923, 174.

22 Robert Ayre, 'The Pollyanna Farmer,' *Canadian Forum*, November 1930, 56.

23 Ibid.
24 Ibid., 57.
25 Ibid.
26 Ibid., 59.
27 Ibid.
28 Frederick Philip Grove, 'Apologia Pro Vita et Opere Suo,' *Canadian Forum*, August 1931, 420–1.
29 Frederick Philip Grove, *In Search of Myself* (Toronto: Macmillan, 1946), 5–6.
30 Wilfrid Eggleston, *Literary Friends* (Ottawa: Borealis, 1980), 146.
31 Ibid., 1–2.
32 McCourt, *The Canadian West in Fiction*, 5.
33 'Members Admitted to the Canadian Authors' Association,' *Canadian Bookman*, September 1921, 56.
34 Arnason, 'The Development of Prairie Realism: Robert J.C. Stead, Douglas Durkin, Martha Ostenso and Frederick Philip Grove,' PhD diss., University of New Brunswick, 10–11.
35 See Margaret R. Stobie, *Frederick Philip Grove*, Twayne's World Author Series (New York: Twayne, 1973).
36 Jackel, 'Prairie Writing,' 691.
37 David Arnason, afterword to *Wild Geese* by Martha Ostenso, New Canadian Library (Toronto: McClelland and Stewart, 1989), 304.
38 'The Cow Puncher,' review of *The Cow Puncher* by Robert J.C. Stead, *Canadian Bookman*, January 1919, 69.
39 'The Heart of Cherry McBain,' review of *The Heart of Cherry McBain* by Douglas Durkin, *Canadian Bookman*, October 1919, 23.
40 B.K. Sandwell, 'Portrait of a Fine Canadian Woman,' review of *The Prairie Mother* by Arthur Stringer, *Canadian Bookman*, December 1920, 84.
41 Austin Bothwell, 'Nellie Puts Herself in a Book,' *Canadian Bookman*, December 1921, 16.
42 Unsigned review of *Neighbours* by Robert J.C. Stead, *Canadian Bookman*, November 1922, 293.
43 'Durkin's New Novel,' review of *The Magpie* by Douglas Durkin, *Canadian Bookman*, February 1924, 43.
44 Georges Bugnet, 'Two New Western Books,' review of *Settlers of the Marsh* by Frederick Philip Grove, and *Wild Geese* by Martha Ostenso, *Canadian Bookman*, December 1925, 203.
45 T.D. Rimmer, 'Four Canadian Novels,' *Canadian Bookman*, January 1927, 15–16.
46 A.S.M., review of *Fruits of the Earth* by Chas. W. Peterson, *Canadian Bookman*, March 1929, 71.

47 Chas. W. Peterson, *Fruits of the Earth: A Story of the Canadian Prairies* (Ottawa: Ru-Mi-Lou, 1928), 7.

48 Kathleen K. Bowker's 'Robert Stead: An Interview,' *Canadian Bookman*, April 1923, details some of Stead's literary involvement with several Canadian newspapers. Other articles, including Robert Stead's 'Literature as a National Asset,' *Canadian Bookman*, December 1923, and 'Third Annual Convention, C.A.A.: Address by the President,' *Canadian Bookman*, July 1924, present the words of Stead spoken in his official role as president of the CAA, addressing a national audience and calling for new forms of writing in Canada. In 'An Interview with Nellie McClung,' C.I.D. demonstrates McClung's links to other Canadian writers of the period, including Laura Goodman Salverson. 'A Cup of Tea with Nellie McClung,' by A. Ermatinge Fraser, reads like a popular fan-magazine piece in its discussion of McClung's literary connections and an afternoon spent with McClung during the 1928 Calgary CAA convention. A biographical sketch, initialled W.K., outlining the since disproved narrative of Grove's life, appeared in April 1925, indicating a growing interest in Grove, who himself had become an occasional contributor to the *Bookman* by the mid-1920s. Grove's addresses are mentioned in articles such as 'Philip Grove at the Empire Club' that describe his extensive author tour for the Canadian Club. Despite the indications of a literary community that these and other articles provide, it is important to note that the tone of many of these pieces indicates that their authors are perhaps trying hard to *create* a literary community in the very act of suggesting that one exists.

49 Judith Skelton Grant, 'Gordon, Charles William,' *The Oxford Companion to Canadian Literature*, 307.

50 Bowker, 'Robert Stead: An Interview,' 99.

51 Dick Harrison, 'Stead, Robert J. C.,' *The Oxford Companion to Canadian Literature*, 771–2.

52 Ricou, *Vertical Man*, ix.

53 Ibid., vii.

54 Harrison, *Unnamed Country*.

55 Robert J.C. Stead, *Grain*, New Canadian Library (1926; repr., Toronto: McClelland and Stewart, 1993), 47.

56 Wilfrid Eggleston, *The High Plains* (Toronto: Macmillan, 1938), 120.

57 Frederick Philip Grove, *The Master of the Mill* (Toronto: Macmillan, 1944), 20–1.

58 Robert J.C. Stead, *The Homesteaders* (Toronto: Musson, 1916), 85–6.

59 Eggleston, *The High Plains*, 135.

60 Bertram Brooker, *Think of the Earth*, ed. Glenn Willmott (1936; repr., Toronto: Brown Bear, 2000), 4.

61 Vera Lysenko, *Yellow Boots* (1954; repr., Edmonton: NeWest, 1992), 291.
62 Robert J.C. Stead, *Dry Water* (Ottawa: Tecumseh, 1983), 158.
63 Robert J.C. Stead, *The Smoking Flax* (Toronto: McClelland and Stewart, 1924), 95.
64 Ibid., 298–9.
65 Douglas Durkin, *The Magpie* (Toronto: Hodder, 1923), 95.
66 Frederick Philip Grove, *Our Daily Bread* (Toronto: Macmillian, 1928), 5.
67 Ibid., 350, 390.
68 Brooker, *Think of the Earth*, 45.
69 Ibid., 238.
70 Ibid., 289.
71 Sinclair Ross, *As For Me and My House*, New Canadian Library (1941; repr., Toronto: McClelland and Stewart, 1989), 5.
72 Ibid., 211.
73 For critical discussions of gender in prairie realism see MacKenna's 'As They Really Were'; McMullen's 'Women in Grove's Novels'; Potvin's '"The Eternal Feminine"'; Buss's 'Who Are You, Mrs. Bentley?'; and Goldie's 'W.O. Mitchell and the Pursuit of the Homosocial Ideal.'
74 Nellie McClung, *Purple Springs* (Toronto: T. Allen, 1921), 228.
75 Arthur Stringer, *The Prairie Mother* (Indianapolis: Bobbs, 1920), 11.
76 Ibid., 42.
77 Ricou, *Vertical Man*, 17.
78 Stead, *Grain*, 121.
79 Edward McCourt, *Music at the Close*, New Canadian Library (1947; repr., Toronto: McClelland and Stewart, 1966), 18.
80 Ibid., 46, 56, 128, 136, 148, 200.
81 Ibid., 217.
82 Gordon Roper, 'New Forces: New Fiction, 1880–1920,' in *Literary History of Canada: Canadian Literature in English*, vol. 1, ed. Carl F. Klinck (Toronto: University of Toronto Press, 1965), 296.
83 McCourt, *Canadian West in Fiction*, v.
84 D.O. Spettigue links the prairie novel unqualifiedly with a regional impulse: 'The novel seems inseparable from what we call realism … it reveals something about the hero as he reacts with or against his environment.' *Frederick Philip Grove* (Toronto: Copp Clark, 1969), 79. Roy Daniells denies the existence of any kind of national movement in Canadian literature of the period altogether, suggesting that prairie realism must be considered individually and defined by its own particular regional characteristics: 'Analysis of the Canadian scheme of things must be regional, or at least begin by being regional.' 'Literature: I, Poetry and the Novel,' in *The Cul-*

ture of Contemporary Canada, ed. Julian Park (Ithaca, NY: Cornell University Press, 1957), 40. Terry Angus emphasizes the influence of a regional geography on the prairie writer and considers this limited subject matter to be far more important in defining prairie realism than technique: 'The literature of the Canadian prairies reflects the geographical nature of the west … . Snow, drought, floods, wind, and extremes in temperature are central events; geography and climate dominate the imagination of the prairie artist.' *The Prairie Experience*, 1. And, more generally, major literary surveys of Canadian literature, including both *Literary History of Canada* and *The Oxford Companion to Canadian Literature*, insist upon discussing prairie realism as a separate, partitioned, regional form of expression that has little in common with the rest of the national literature. In the latter reference work, for example, Donald Stephens's entry entitled 'Novels in English 1920 to 1940' is subdivided into three sections that represent the types of Canadian fiction produced during the period: 'Western Novels,' 'Historical Fiction,' and 'Other Fiction' (571–3). These isolationist characterizations of prairie writing have proven enduring. As Calder writes, 'prairie realism is, by definition, regional; it is *prairie* literature. When it comes under the label of "regional" … it is perceived in a specific way. Regional literature, at least in Canada, is defined as being both realistic and referential. Its value resides in its ability to mirror a specific environment, to show what real "life" is like in, as Edward McCourt says, "a limited and peculiar environment."' 'Reassessing Prairie Realism,' 59.

85 Ricou, *Vertical Man*, 8.

86 See, for example, Henry Kreisel's 'The Prairie: A State of Mind,' in *Contexts of Canadian Criticism*, ed. Eli Mandel (1968; repr., Toronto: University of Toronto Press, 1971), 254–66.

87 Ibid., 256.

88 Arnason, afterword in *Wild Geese*, 305.

89 Kristjana Gunnars, afterword in *Settlers of the Marsh*, by Frederick Philip Grove, New Canadian Library (Toronto: McClelland and Stewart, 1989), 267.

90 Sandra Djwa, 'No Other Way: Sinclair Ross's Stories and Novels,' in *Sinclair Ross's As For Me and My House: Five Decades of Criticism*, ed. David Stouck (1971; repr., Toronto: University of Toronto Press, 1991), 60.

91 Robert J.C. Stead, *The Bail Jumper* (Toronto: Briggs, 1914), 267.

92 W.O. Mitchell, *Who Has Seen the Wind* (Toronto: Macmillan, 1947), 30.

93 Ibid., 29.

94 Ibid., 236.

95 Eggleston, *High Plains*, 17.

96 Stead, *Dry Water*, 88.
97 Ibid.
98 Fredrick Philip Grove, *Fruits of the Earth* (Toronto: J.M. Dent, 1933), 35–6.
99 McCourt, *Music at the Close*, 17.
100 David P. Silcox, *The Group of Seven and Tom Thomson* (Toronto: Firefly, 2003), 29.
101 Stead, *Grain*, 69.
102 Ibid., 21.
103 Ibid., 45.
104 Grove, *Master of the Mill*, 39.
105 Durkin, *The Magpie*, 109.
106 Edward McCourt, *The Wooden Sword*, New Canadian Library (1956; repr., Toronto: McClelland and Stewart, 1975), 199–200.
107 Brooker, *Think of the Earth*, 6.
108 Ibid., 24.
109 Arthur Stringer, *The Prairie Wife* (Toronto: McLeod, 1915), 15.
110 Eggleston, *Literary Friends*, 25–6.
111 McCourt, *Canadian West in Fiction*, 78, 81.
112 I have written about this at length in 'As For Me and My Blueprint: Sinclair Ross's Debt to Arthur Stringer,' in *The Canadian Modernists Meet*, ed. Dean Irvine, Reappraisals: Canadian Writers (Ottawa: University of Ottawa Press, 2005), 251–74.
113 Ross, *As For Me and My House*, 97.
114 D.G. Jones, *Butterfly on Rock: A Study of Themes and Images in Canadian Literature* (Toronto: University of Toronto Press, 1970), 38.
115 Harrison, *Unnamed Country*, ix.
116 Robert Kroetsch, afterword in *As For Me and My House*, by Sinclair Ross, New Canadian Library (1941; repr., Toronto: McClelland and Stewart, 1989), 217.
117 Calder, 'Reassessing Prairie Realism,' 56.
118 Frank Davey, 'Towards the End of Regionalism,' *Textual Studies in Canada* 12 (1998): 4–5.
119 Calder, 'Reassessing Prairie Realism,' 51.
120 Dick Harrison, 'The Beginnings of Prairie Fiction,' *Journal of Canadian Fiction* 4.1 (1975): 159.
121 Ricou, *Vertical Man*, xi.
122 Eggleston, *Literary Friends*, 8.
123 Christine Van Der Mark, *In Due Season* (Toronto: Oxford University Press, 1947), ii.
124 Gammel, *Sexualizing Power in Naturalism*, 1.

125 Gunnars, afterword in *Settlers of the Marsh*, 270.
126 Grove, *Fruits of the Earth*, 4.
127 Ibid., vi.
128 Ibid., 4–5.
129 Ibid., 333.
130 Keahey, *Making It Home*, 15.
131 Martha Ostenso, *Wild Geese*, New Canadian Library (1925; repr., Toronto: McClelland and Stewart, 1989), 55–6.
132 Eggleston, *High Plains*, 169, 174.
133 McCourt, *Music at the Close*, 128.
134 McCourt, *Wooden Sword*, 199–200.
135 Ibid., 7.

5: Frederick Philip Grove's Eclectic Realism and 'The Great Tradition'

1 Margaret R. Stobie, *Frederick Philip Grove*, Twayne's World Authors Series (New York: Twayne, 1973), 95.
2 Desmond Pacey, *Frederick Philip Grove*, Canadian Men of Letters (Toronto: Ryerson Press, 1944), 123.
3 See, for example, Frank Birbalsingh, 'Grove and Existentialism,' in *Writers of the Prairies*, ed. Donald G. Stephens (Vancouver: University of British Columbia Press, 1973), 57–66.
4 Ronald Sutherland, *Frederick Philip Grove*, Canadian Writers, New Canadian Library (Toronto: McClelland and Stewart, 1969), 5.
5 See especially Irene Gammel's *Baroness Elsa: Gender, Dada, and Everyday Modernity* (Cambridge: MIT Press, 2002); Klaus Martens's *F.P. Grove in Europe and Canada: Translated Lives* (Edmonton: University of Alberta Press, 2001); Spettigue's *F.P.G.: The European Years* (Ottawa: Oberon, 1973).
6 See Rudolf Bader, 'Frederick Philip Grove and Naturalism Reconsidered,' in *Gaining Ground: European Critics on Canadian Literature*, ed. Robert Kroetsch and Reingard M. Nischik (Edmonton: NeWest, 1985), 222–33; Stanley E. McMullin, 'Evolution versus Revolution: Grove's Perception of History,' in *The Grove Symposium*, Reappraisals Canadian Writers, ed. John Nause (Ottawa: University of Ottawa Press, 1974), 77–88; Irene Gammel, *Sexualizing Power in Naturalism: Theodore Dreiser and Frederick Philip Grove* (Calgary: University of Calgary Press, 1994).
7 Grove wrote three essays entitled 'The Novel,' all of which receive consideration in this section. Despite their identical titles, these essays are not multiple drafts of the same work; each stands alone and offers its own insights into Grove's thoughts on the genre. To distinguish among these

three essays in my discussion, I have numbered them [1], [2], and [3]. 'The Novel [1],' is the published essay that appears in Grove's 1929 collection of essays, *It Needs to Be Said* (Toronto: Macmillan, 1929). 'The Novel [2]' is a manuscript that appears in box 20, folder 21 of the Frederick Philip Grove Collection. 'The Novel [3],' is a manuscript from box 20, folder 22 of the same archival source. Various references in these drafts to works of fiction and well-known facts of Grove's life almost certainly indicate that these addresses were written for his Canadian Club lecture tour in 1928–9.

8 Grove, 'The Novel [1],' in *It Needs to Be Said*, 122.

9 Grove, 'Realism in Literature,' in *It Needs to Be Said*, 55–6.

10 Ibid., 56.

11 Grove, 'Literary Criticism,' in *It Needs to Be Said*, 33.

12 Ibid., 33.

13 T.S. Eliot, 'Tradition and the Individual Talent,' in *Modernism: An Anthology of Sources and Documents*, ed. Vassiliki Kolocotroni, Jane Goldman, and Olga Taxidou (1919; repr., Edinburgh: Edinburgh University Press, 1997), 367.

14 Grove, 'Realism in Literature,' 63.

15 Grove, 'Literary Criticism,' 36.

16 Ibid.

17 Stobie, *Frederick Philip Grove*, 92.

18 Grove, 'The Novel [1],' in *It Needs to Be Said*, 120.

19 Grove, 'A Neglected Function of a Certain Literary Association,' in *It Needs to Be Said*, 3.

20 Grove, 'Art and Canadian Life,' ts. box 20, folder 5, Frederick Philip Grove Collection, University of Manitoba, 8.

21 Ibid., 6.

22 Raymond Knister to Elizabeth Frankfurth, 11 April 1924, Box 1, The Raymond Knister Collection, McMaster University.

23 Grove, 'Mrs. President * Ladies of the Canadian Club,' unpublished address, ts. box 20, folder 8, Frederick Philip Grove Collection, University of Manitoba, 9–10.

24 Pacey, *Frederick Philip Grove*, 124.

25 Grove, 'The Happy Ending,' in *It Needs to Be Said*, 86.

26 Grove, 'The Technique of the Novel,' ts. box 20, folder 27, Frederick Philip Grove Collection, University of Manitoba, 1–2.

27 The fact that Grove borrowed many of the novels he read from friends through the mail means that his letters provide an indication of the breadth of his reading of modern and traditional works. The following pieces of correspondence offer just a few examples. In a letter to Richard

Crouch dated 24 November 1934, Grove thanks his friend for the loan of numerous works by 'Marx,' 'Scott,' 'Gide,' 'Plato,' and T.S. 'Eliot.' On 13 January 1935, Grove again wrote to Crouch, asking to borrow a copy of D.H. Lawrence's *Lady Chatterley's Lover*. On 12 November 1937, Grove wrote to Crouch thanking him for the loan of two novels by Virginia Woolf, and one book by Gertrude Stein (Pacey's editorial notes speculate that the Woolf novels were probably *The Waves* [1931] and *The Years* [1937], and that the Stein book was possibly one of the three she had published in the 1930s), remarking that 'I am very glad to see what sort of things these women do. Neither seems to me of any fundamental importance, such as attaches to Joyce or Lawrence, let me say' (322).

28 Grove, 'The Novel [2],' 2.
29 Grove, 'Literary Criticism,' ts. box 20, folder 20, Frederick Philip Grove Collection, University of Manitoba, 4.
30 Grove, 'Art and Canadian Life,' ts. box 20, folder 5, Frederick Philip Grove Collection, University of Manitoba, 7.
31 Ibid., 7.
32 Grove, 'The Technique of the Novel,' ts. box 20, folder 27, Frederick Philip Grove Collection, University of Manitoba, 2.
33 Grove, 'Realism in Literature,' 53.
34 Grove, 'The Novel [3],' 1.
35 Grove, 'Some Aspects of a Writer's Life,' ts. box 20, folder 26, Frederick Philip Grove Collection, University of Manitoba, 2.
36 Grove, 'The Novel [3],' 9.
37 Grove, 'Realism in Literature,' 76.
38 Grove, 'The Novel [1],' 118.
39 W.J.Keith, 'Grove's "Magnificent Failure": *The Yoke of Life* Reconsidered,' *Canadian Literature* 89 (1981): 104–17.
40 Ibid., 104.
41 Frederick Philip Grove, *The Yoke of Life* (Toronto: Macmillan, 1930), 10.
42 Sutherland, *Frederick Philip Grove*, 52.
43 Unsigned review of *The Yoke of Life* by Frederick Philip Grove, *The Saturday Review of Literature*, 25 October 1930, 274. See also Stobie, *Frederick Philip Grove*, 88.
44 Keith, 'Grove's "Magnificent Failure,"' 104.
45 Frederick Philip Grove to Lorne Pierce, 24 May 1939, *The Letters of Frederick Philip Grove*, ed. Desmond Pacey (Toronto: University of Toronto Press, 1976).
46 Grove, 'The Technique of the Novel,' ts. box 20, folder 27, Frederick Philip Grove Collection, University of Manitoba, 6.

47 Grove, *Master of the Mill*, 62.
48 Ibid., 328.
49 Ibid., 332.
50 Ibid.
51 Frederick Philip Grove to Desmond Pacey, 2 February 1941, *The Letters of Frederick Philip Grove*, 401.
52 Frederick Philip Grove to Desmond Pacey, 20 January 1941, *The Letters of Frederick Philip Grove*, 400.
53 Frederick Philip Grove to Lorne Pierce, 13 March 1941, *The Letters of Frederick Philip Grove*, 403.

6: The Proliferation of Modern Realism in Canada, Part 2: Urban and Social Realism Reclaimed

1 Desmond Pacey, 'Fiction 1920–1940,' in *Literary History of Canada: Canadian Literature in English*, vol. 2, ed. Carl F. Klinck (Toronto: University of Toronto Press, 1965), 193–7.
2 Glenn Willmott, *Unreal Country: Modernity in the Canadian Novel in English* (Montreal: McGill-Queen's University Press, 2002): 146.
3 Ben-Zion Shek, *Social Realism in the French-Canadian Novel* (Montreal: Harvest House, 1977), 15.
4 Georg Lukács, 'Reportage or Portrayal,' in *Essays on Realism*, ed. Rodney Livingstone (1932; repr., Cambridge: MIT Press, 1980), 59.
5 See George J. Becker, *Realism in Modern Literature* (New York: Ungar, 1980), 12.
6 Justin D. Edwards, 'Strange Fugitive, Strange City: Reading Urban Space in Morley Callaghan's Toronto,' *Studies in Canadian Literature / Études en littérature canadienne* 23 (1998), 213–14.
7 Pacey, 'Fiction 1920–1940,' 168.
8 J.G. Sime, *Our Little Life: A Novel of To-Day*, Early Canadian Woman Writers Series (1921; repr., Ottawa: Tecumseh, 1994), 128.
9 Irene Baird, *Waste Heritage* (New York: Random House, 1939), 231.
10 Morley Callaghan, *They Shall Inherit the Earth*, New Canadian Library (1935; repr., Toronto: McClelland and Stewart, 1969), 140–1.
11 A.M. Stephen, *The Gleaming Archway* (London: Dent, 1929), 123.
12 Baird, *Waste Heritage*, 44.
13 Nellie McClung, *Painted Fires* (Toronto: T. Allen, 1925), 20–1.
14 Gwethalyn Graham, *Earth and High Heaven*, New Canadian Library, (1944; repr., Toronto: McClelland and Stewart, 1969), 130–1.
15 Elspeth Cameron, *Hugh MacLennan: A Writer's Life* (Toronto: University of Toronto Press, 1981), 84.

16 Hugh MacLennan, *So All Their Praises*, 1933, box 3, folder 19–20, The Hugh MacLennan Papers, McGill University, Rare Books and Special Collections, 5.
17 Ibid., 57.
18 Hugh Garner, *Cabbagetown* (1950; repr., Toronto: McGraw-Hill Ryerson, 1968), 6.
19 Ibid., 3.
20 Ibid., 36.
21 John Moss, 'A Conversation with Hugh Garner,' *Journal of Canadian Fiction* 1.2 (1972): 50–5.
22 Sandra Campbell, introduction to *Sister Woman* by J.G. Sime (Ottawa: Tecumseh, 1992), vii–viii.
23 Douglas Durkin, *The Magpie* (Toronto: Hodder and Stoughton, 1923), 33.
24 Graham, *Earth and High Heaven*, 74.
25 Dennis Duffy, introduction to *God's Sparrows* by Philip Child (Toronto: McClelland and Stewart, 1978), 6.
26 Hubert Evans, *The New Front Line* (Toronto: Macmillan, 1927), 40.
27 Hugh MacLennan, *Man Should Rejoice*, 1937, box 3, folder 1-3. The Hugh MacLennan Papers, McGill University, Rare Books and Special Collections, 1.
28 Ibid., 2.
29 Ibid., 8.
30 Ibid., 5.
31 J.G. Sime, 'Munitions!' in *Sister Woman* (Ottawa: Tecumseh, 1992), 43.
32 Hugh MacLennan, *Barometer Rising*, New Canadian Library (1941; repr., Toronto: McClelland and Stewart, 1991), 11.
33 McClung, *Painted Fires*, 222–3.
34 James Mulvihill, 'The "Canadian Bookman" and Literary Nationalism,' *Canadian Literature* 107 (1985): 49.
35 Bruce Meyer, 'Literary Magazines in English,' in *The Oxford Companion to Canadian Literature*, ed. William Toye (Toronto: Oxford University Press, 1983), 458.
36 Dean Irvine, *Editing Modernity: Women and Little-Magazine Cultures in Canada, 1916–1956* (Toronto: University of Toronto Press, 2008), 13.
37 Candida Rifkind, *Comrades and Critics: Women, Literature, and the Left in 1930s Canada* (Toronto: University of Toronto Press, 2009), 45, 89.
38 L.F. Edwards, 'Authorship and Canadiana,' *Masses* 1.1 (April 1932): 7.
39 'Our Credentials,' *Masses*, April 1932, 1.
40 'Editorial,' *New Frontier*, April 1936, 3.
41 'Our Credentials,' *Masses*, April 1932, 1.
42 'Editorial,' *New Frontier*, April 1936, 3.

43 Israel Jordan, 'Now That Callaghan's Here,' review of *Now That April's Here* by Morley Callaghan, *New Frontier* 1.6 (October 1936): 29.
44 Ibid., 29–30.
45 Morley Callaghan, 'Little Marxist, What Now?' *Saturday Night*, 16 September 1939, 24.
46 Morley Callaghan, 'A Criticism,' *New Frontier* 1.1 (1936): 24.
47 Desmond Pacey, 'The Writer and His Public, 1920–1960,' in *Literary History of Canada: Canadian Literature in English*, vol. 2., ed. Carl F. Klinck (Toronto: University of Toronto Press, 1965), 12.
48 Edwin Berry Burgum, 'The Outlook for the Novel,' *New Frontier* 2.4 (September 1937): 25.
49 Jack Conroy, 'New Forces in American Literature,' *New Frontier* 1.1 (April 1936): 22.
50 Ruth McKenzie, 'Proletarian Literature in Canada,' *Dalhousie Review* 19.1 (1939): 59.
51 Donna Philips, *Voices of Discord: Canadian Short Stories from the 1930s* (Toronto: New Hogtown, 1979), 9.
52 McKenzie, 'Proletarian Literature in Canada,' 49.
53 V.F. Calverton, 'Literature as a Revolutionary Force,' *Canadian Forum*, March 1935, 225.
54 E. Cecil-Smith 'Propaganda and Art,' *Masses* 2.11 (January 1934): 10.
55 'Our Credentials,' *Masses* 1.1 (April 1932): 1.
56 T. Richardson, 'In Defense of Pure Art,' *Masses* 1.4–5 (July-August 1932): 4.
57 Len Peterson, *Chipmunk* (Toronto: McClelland and Stewart, 1949), 1.
58 H. Francis, 'Freedom of Contract,' *Masses* 1.8 (March-April 1933): 12.
59 James Hinton, 'Meat!' *New Frontier* 2.3 (July-August 1937): 7.
60 George Winslade, 'Rainbow Chasing,' *Masses* 1.4–5 (July-August 1932): 7.
61 Ibid., 8.
62 John Fairfax, 'Art for Man's Sake,' *Canadian Forum*, August 1936, 24.
63 E. Cecil-Smith, 'What Is "Pure" Art?' *Masses* 1.4–5 (July-August 1932): 5.
64 Cecil-Smith, 'Propaganda and Art,' 11.
65 Rifkind, *Comrades and Critics*, 162–4.
66 See Robin Mathews, Anthony Hopkins, and R.L. Hyman, 'Wasted Heritage and *Waste Heritage*: The Critical Disregard of an Important Canadian Novel,' *Journal of Canadian Studies* 17.4 (1982): 74–87.
67 Baird, *Waste Heritage*, 28–9.
68 Irene Baird, 'Sidown, Brothers, Sidown,' *Laurentian University Review* 9 (1976): 82.
69 Stephen, *Gleaming Archway*, 288–9.

70 Hugh MacLennan to Frances MacLennan, 19 March 1933, box 13, folder 6, The Hugh MacLennan Papers, McGill University, Rare Books and Special Collections.
71 MacLennan, *So All Their Praises*, 58.
72 Hugh Garner, 'An Interview with Hugh Garner,' interview by Allen Anderson, *Tamarack Review* 52.3 (1969): 21.
73 F.W. Watt, 'Literature of Protest,' in *Literary History of Canada*, vol. 2: 487.
74 The best sketches of the period were published in *New Frontier*, including Livesay's 'Corbin – A Company Town Fights for Its Life,' *New Frontier*, June 1936, 8; Barry Mather's 'It Is Wonderful!' September 1936, 10; Bernard Rawlinson's 'Cornwall: The Diary of a Strike,' October 1936, 15–17, 23; William E. Kon's 'Boom Town into Company Town: The Story of Sudbury,' November 1936, 6–9; J.J. McGeer's 'Vancouver Underground,' November 1936, 12–13; Ted Allan's 'Blood for Spanish Democracy' 1.10 (February 1937): 12–13.
75 Livesay, 'Corbin,' 8.
76 A. Poole, 'Fish,' *Masses*, July-August 1932, 5–6.
77 J.K. Thomas, 'Production,' *New Frontier*, July-August 1937, 24.
78 Ibid., 24.
79 James Joyce, *A Portrait of the Artist as a Young Man* (1916; repr., London: Penguin, 1992), 233.
80 Calverton, 'Literature as a Revolutionary Force,' 225.
81 Ibid., 221.
82 Lukács, 'Reportage or Portrayal,' 46.
83 Sybil M. Gordan, 'Man Alive in the Novel,' *New Frontier*, April 1937, 24.
84 Margaret Fairley, 'Books,' *New Frontier*, May 1937, 26.
85 Callaghan, *They Shall Inherit the Earth*, 62.
86 Ibid., 215–16.
87 Watt, 'Literature of Protest,' in *Literary History of Canada*, 488.
88 Pacey, 'Fiction 1920–1940,' 186.
89 George Woodcock, 'Possessing the Land: Notes on Canadian Fiction,' in *The Canadian Imagination: Dimensions of a Literary Culture*, ed. David Staines (Cambridge: Harvard University Press, 1977), 20.

7: Morley Callaghan's Cosmopolitan Modern Realism

1 Cleveland B. Chase, 'Morley Callaghan Tells What a Bootlegger Thinks About,' in *Morley Callaghan*, ed. Brandon Conron (Toronto: McGraw-Hill Ryerson, 1975), 24–6. First published in *The New York Times Book Review*, 2 September 1928.

2 'Strange Fugitive New Type in Canadian Realist Novel,' *Toronto Star Daily*, 29 September 1928, 13.

3 Edmund Wilson, 'Morley Callaghan of Toronto,' in *Morley Callaghan*, 106–19. First published in *The New Yorker*, 26 November 1960, 106.

4 John Metcalf, 'Winner Take All,' *Essays on Canadian Writing* 51–2 (1993): 143.

5 See Victor Hoar, *Morley Callaghan* (Toronto: Copp Clark, 1969); Conron ed., *Morley Callaghan*; and Fraser Sutherland, *The Style of Innocence: A Study of Hemingway and Callaghan* (Toronto: Clark, 1972).

6 See Harry Salpeter, 'The First Reader,' *The World*, 18 August 1928, 9; Ruth Suckow, 'Canadian Short Stories: A Promise of Vigor,' review of *Canadian Short Stories*, ed. Raymond Knister, *The World*, 9 December 1928, 11; Douglas Bush, 'Is There a Canadian Literature?' *Commonweal*, 6 November 1929, 13; Charles G.D. Roberts, 'A Note on Modernism,' in *Open House*, ed. William Arthur Deacon and Wilfred Reeves (Ottawa: Graphic, 1931), 23–4; Joseph Warren Beach, *The Twentieth Century Novel: Studies in Technique* (New York: Appleton, 1932); Sutherland, *The Style of Innocence*; Tom Marshall, 'Tragic Ambivalence: The Novels of Morley Callaghan,' *University of Windsor Review* 12 (1976): 33–48; Ray Ellenwood, 'Morley Callaghan, Jacques Ferron, and the Dialectic of Good and Evil,' in *The Callaghan Symposium*, Reappraisals Canadian Writers, ed. David Stains (Ottawa: University of Ottawa Press, 1981), 37–46; T.D. MacLulich, 'Colloquial Style and the Tory Mode,' *Canadian Literature* 89 (1981): 7–22.

7 Metcalf, 'Winner Take All,' 118.

8 See Desmond Pacey, 'Fiction 1920–1940,' in *Literary History of Canada: Canadian Literature in English*, vol. 2, ed. Carl F. Klinck (Toronto: University of Toronto Press, 1965), 168–204.

9 Morley Callaghan, *That Summer in Paris*, Laurentian Library (1963; repr., Toronto: Macmillan, 1976), 21.

10 See especially Victor Hoar and Gary Boire, 'Morley Callaghan and His Works,' in *Canadian Writers and Their Works*, eds. Robert Lecker, Jack David, and Ellen Quigley (Toronto: ECW, 1990), 79–145.

11 Morley Callaghan, 'A Wedding Dress,' in *Morley Callaghan's Stories* (Toronto: Macmillan, 1959), 56. First published in *This Quarter* 1.2 (1927).

12 Morley Callaghan, 'The Past Quarter Century,' *Maclean's*, 15 March 1936, 38.

13 Callaghan, *That Summer in Paris*, 21.

14 Morley Callaghan, 'Novel and Diary,' review of *From Day to Day* by Ferdynand Goetel, *Saturday Night*, 22 August 1931, 7.

15 T.S. Eliot, 'The Music of Poetry,' in *On Poetry and Poets* (1942; repr., New York: Farrar, 1957), 21.

16 Morley Callaghan, 'Amuck in the Bush,' in *Morley Callaghan's Stories*, 87–92. First published in *The American Caravan: A Yearbook of American Literature*, ed. Van Wyck Brooks et al. (New York: Macaulay, 1927), 89.
17 Morley Callaghan, 'Last Spring They Came Over,' in *Morley Callaghan's Stories*, 38. First published in *transition* 3 (1927).
18 T.S. Eliot, 'Tradition and the Individual Talent,' in *Modernism: An Anthology of Sources and Documents*, ed. Vassiliki Kolocotroni, Jane Goldman, and Olga Taxidou (1919; repr., Edinburgh: Edinburgh University Press, 1997), 369.
19 Robert Weaver, 'A Talk with Morley Callaghan,' *The Tamarack Review* 7 (1958): 4.
20 John Metcalf, 'Winner Take All,' 122.
21 Ibid., 118.
22 Barry Cameron, 'Rhetorical Tradition and the Ambiguity of Callaghan's Narrative Rhetoric,' in *The Callaghan Symposium*, Reappraisals Canadian Writers, ed. David Staines (Ottawa: University of Ottawa Press, 1987), 73.
23 Morley Callaghan, 'Ancient Lineage,' in *Morley Callaghan's Stories*, 170. First published in *The Exile* 3 (1928).
24 Cameron, 'Rhetorical Tradition,' 73.
25 Metcalf, 'Winner Take All,' 140.
26 Morley Callaghan, 'Introducing Ernest Hemingway,' review of *In Our Time* and *The Torrents of Spring* by Ernest Hemingway, *Saturday Night*, 7 August 1926, 7.
27 Morley Callaghan, 'A Girl with Ambition,' in *Morley Callaghan's Stories*, 238. First published in *This Quarter* (1926).
28 Morley Callaghan, 'Soldier Harmon,' in *Morley Callaghan's Stories*, 180. First published 11 January 1930 in *Toronto Star Weekly*.
29 Chase, 'Morley Callaghan Tells What a Bootlegger Thinks About,' 26.
30 Morley Callaghan, 'The Soul of a Killer,' review of *The Assassin* by Liam O'Flaherty, *Saturday Night*, 8 September 1928, 8.
31 The term 'hard-boiled' was first used to describe Callaghan's style by Cleveland B. Chase in an often-cited 1928 review of *Strange Fugitive* for *The New York Times Book Review*.
32 Morley Callaghan, *Such Is My Beloved*, New Canadian Library (1934; repr., Toronto: McClelland, 1957), 95–6.
33 Metcalf, 'Winner Take All,' 120–1.
34 Sutherland, *Style of Innocence*, 77.
35 E.K. Brown, 'The Problem of a Canadian Literature,' in *On Canadian Poetry* (Toronto: Ryerson Press, 1943), 33.
36 Ibid., 11.

37 Callaghan, *That Summer in Paris*, 22.

38 In 'Looking at Native Prose' *Saturday Night*, 1 December 1928, 3, Callaghan singled out Knister for praise and counted him, with himself, among the most experimental of the new writers in Canada. In a 1957 interview with Robert Weaver, he suggested that he and Knister had a common approach to writing that made them stand apart from other Canadian writers. In *That Summer in Paris* (1963), Callaghan again remarked on Knister's experimentalism, but, perhaps in an attempt to elevate himself above his early contemporaries, he resorted to some rather tasteless personal attacks on Knister.

39 Morley Callaghan, 'Looking at Native Prose,' *Saturday Night*, 1 December 1928, 3.

40 Ibid.

41 Callaghan saw Grove as 'the best' of the older generation of Canadian writers and offered mitigated praise of his work in 'Looking at Canadian Prose' (ibid.)

42 Ibid., 3.

43 Morley Callaghan, 'Faulkner's Fabulous World,' review of *The Hamlet* by William Faulkner, *Saturday Night*, 11 May 1940, 9.

44 Morley Callaghan, 'Civil War Story,' review of *The Unvanquished* by William Faulkner, *Saturday Night*, 14 May 1938, 15.

45 Morley Callaghan, 'Into the Dream World,' review of *Finnegan's Wake* by James Joyce, *Saturday Night*, 27 May 1939, 21.

46 Morley Callaghan, 'Breaking New Ground,' review of *Orlando* by Virginia Woolf, *Saturday Night*, 29 December 1928, 8.

47 Callaghan, *That Summer in Paris*, 184.

48 Metcalf, 'Winner Take All,' 115.

49 Callaghan, *That Summer in Paris*, 19–20.

50 Morley Callaghan, 'Eternal Style,' interview by Ray Ellenwood, *Idler* 30 (1990): 37–8.

51 Metcalf, 'Winner Take All,' 144.

52 Morley Callaghan, 'Lyrical Realism,' review of *The Wanderer* by Alain Fournier, *Saturday Night*, 5 January 1929, 8.

53 Morley Callaghan, 'Impressive Short Stories,' review of *Children and Fools* by Thomas Mann, *Saturday Night*, 23 June 1928, 9.

54 Donald Cameron, 'Morley Callaghan: There Are Gurus in the Woodwork,' in *Conversations with Canadian Novelists*, vol. 2. (Toronto: Macmillan, 1973), 25.

55 Morley Callaghan, *A Broken Journey* (Toronto: Macmillan, 1932), 112.

56 Ibid., 189.

57 Morley Callaghan, 'An Autumn Penitent,' in *An Autumn Penitent*, Laurentian Library (Toronto: Macmillan, 1973), 1–79. First published in *The Second American Caravan: A Yearbook of American Literature*, ed. Alfred Kreymborg et al. (New York: Macaulay, 1928), 67.
58 Morley Callaghan, 'In His Own Country,' in *An Autumn Penitent*, Laurentian Library (Toronto: Macmillan, 1973), 87. First published in *Scribner's Magazine*, January-March, 1929.
59 Ibid., 153.
60 Callaghan, *Such Is My Beloved*, 41.
61 Morley Callaghan, *The Loved and the Lost* (1951; repr., Toronto: Stoddart, 1953), 148.
62 Metcalf, 'Winner Take All,' 140.
63 Morley Callaghan, *More Joy In Heaven*, New Canadian Library (1937; repr., Toronto: McClelland and Stewart, 1967), 145.
64 Callaghan, 'Civil War Story,' 15.
65 Morley Callaghan, 'Faulkner Riddle Is Solved,' review of *The Wild Palms* by William Faulkner, *Saturday Night*, 28 January 1939: 20.

8: Modern Realism and Canadian Literature

1 Malcolm Bradbury and James McFarlane, 'The Name and Nature of Modernism,' in *Modernism: A Guide to European Literature, 1890–1930*, ed. Bradbury and McFarlane (London: Penguin, 1991), 52.
2 Desmond Pacey, 'Fiction 1920–1940,' in *Literary History of Canada: Canadian Literature in English*, ed. Carl F. Klinck. (Toronto: University of Toronto Press, 1965), 168.
3 See Northrop Frye, 'Conclusion to a *Literary History of Canada*,' in *The Bush Garden: Essays on the Canada Imagination* (Concord: Anansi, 1995), 215–53.
4 Chris Baldick, *The Oxford English Literary History: The Modern Movement* (Oxford: Oxford University Press, 2004), 4–5.
5 Lionel Stevenson, 'Is Canadian Poetry Modern?' *Canadian Bookman*, July 1927, 196.
6 Glenn Willmott, *Unreal Country: Modernity in the Canadian Novel in English* (Montreal: McGill-Queen's University Press, 2002): 41.

Bibliography

Archives

Frederick Philip Grove Collection, University of Manitoba, Winnipeg.
The Hugh MacLennan Papers, Rare Books and Special Collections, McGill University, Montreal.
The Raymond Knister Collection, McMaster University, Hamilton.
The Raymond Knister Collection, Victoria College, University of Toronto.
The Raymond Knister Papers, Queen's University, Kingston.

Sources

A.E.S.S. 'A Prairie Essayist.' *Canadian Bookman*, May 1924, 111.

A.H.B. 'To the Lighthouse.' *Canadian Bookman*, September 1927, 277.

Allan, Ted [Alan Herman]. 'Blood for Spanish Democracy.' *New Frontier* 1.10 (February 1937): 12–13.

– *This Time a Better Earth*. New York: Morrow, 1939.

'Among the Booksellers.' *Canadian Bookman*, January 1919, 83.

Anderson, J. Ansel. 'The Coward.' *The Canadian Forum*, August 1925, 338, 340.

Angus, Terry, ed. *The Prairie Experience*. Themes in Canadian Literature. Toronto: Macmillan, 1975.

Arnason, David. Afterword to *Wild Geese* by Martha Ostenso. New Canadian Library. Toronto: McClelland and Stewart, 1989. 303–9.

– 'Canadian Nationalism in Search of Form: Hugh MacLennan's *Barometer Rising*.' *Journal of Canadian Fiction* 1 (1972): 68–71.

– 'The Development of Prairie Realism: Robert J.C. Stead, Douglas Durkin, Martha Ostenso and Frederick Philip Grove.' PhD diss., University of New Brunswick, 1980.

– 'Preface.' *Journal of Canadian Fiction* 4.2 (1975): 7–10.

A.S.M. Rev. of *Fruits of the Earth* by Chas. W. Peterson. *Canadian Bookman,* March 1929, 71.

Ayre, Robert. 'Frederick Philip Grove.' *Canadian Forum,* April 1932, 255–7.

– 'The Pollyanna Farmer.' *Canadian Forum,* November 1930, 56–60.

Bader, Rudolf. 'Frederick Philip Grove and Naturalism Reconsidered.' In *Gaining Ground: European Critics on Canadian Literature,* edited by Robert Kroetsch and Reingard M. Nischik. Edmonton: NeWest, 1985. 222–33.

Baird, Irene. *He Rides the Sky*. Toronto: Macmillan, 1941.

– *John*. Philadephia: Lippincott, 1937.

– 'Sidown, Brothers, Sidown.' *Laurentian University Review* 9 (1976): 81–6.

– *Waste Heritage*. New York: Random House, 1939.

Baldick, Chris. *The Oxford English Literary History,* vol. 10: *The Modern Movement*. Oxford: Oxford University Press, 2004.

Baum, Rosalie Murphy. 'Martha Ostenso's Wild Geese: More Insight into the Naturalistic Sensibility.' *Journal of Canadian Culture* 1.2 (1984): 117–35.

Beach, Joseph Warren. *The Twentieth Century Novel: Studies in Technique*. New York: Appleton, 1932.

Beattie, Robert. 'Island Night.' *The Canadian Forum,* November 1920, 52–4.

Becker, George Joseph. *Realism in Modern Literature*. New York: Ungar, 1980.

Beebe, Maurice. *Ivory Towers and Sacred Founts: The Artist as Hero in Fiction from Goethe to Joyce*. New York: New York University Press, 1964.

Bennett, Donna. 'Conflicted Vision: A Consideration of Canon and Genre in English-Canadian Literature.' In *Canadian Canons: Essays in Literary Value,* edited by Robert Lecker. Toronto: University of Toronto Press, 1991. 131–49.

Birbalsingh, Frank. 'Grove and Existentialism.' In *Writers of the Prairies,* edited by Donald G. Stephens. Vancouver: University of British Columbia Press, 1973. 57–66.

Bishop, Leslie. *The Paper Kingdom*. Toronto: Heineman, 1936.

Bobak, E.L. 'Seeking "Direct, Honest Realism": The Canadian Novel of the 1920s.' *Canadian Literature* 89 (1981): 85–101.

Boeschenstein, Hermann. 'Hugh MacLennan, ein kanadischer Romancier.' *Zeitschrift für Anglistik und Amerikanistik,* 8 (1960): 117–35.

Boire, Gary. 'Morley Callaghan and His Works.' In *Canadian Writers and Their Works,* edited by Robert Lecker, Jack David, and Ellen Quigley. Toronto: ECW, 1990. 79–145.

'Bookishness in Canada.' *Canadian Bookman,* January 1919, 11–12.

Bothwell, Austin. 'Nellie Puts Herself in a Book.' *Canadian Bookman,* December 1921, 19–20.

Bowker, Kathleen K. 'Robert Stead: An Interview.' *Canadian Bookman*, April 1923, 99.

Bradbury, Malcolm, and James McFarlane. 'The Name and Nature of Modernism.' In *Modernism: A Guide to European Literature, 1890–1930*, edited by Bradbury and McFarlane. London: Penguin, 1991. 19–55.

Brooke, Francis. *The History of Emily Montague*. 1796. Toronto: McClelland and Stewart, 1995.

Brooker, Bertram. *Think of the Earth*. 1936. Edited by Glenn Willmott. Toronto: Brown Bear, 2000.

Brown, E.K. 'The Problem of a Canadian Literature.' In *On Canadian Poetry*. Toronto: Ryerson Press, 1943.

Bugnet, Georges. *Nipsya*. Montreal: Garand, 1924.

– 'Two New Western Books.' Review of *Settlers of the Marsh* by Frederick Philip Grove and *Wild Geese* by Martha Ostenso. *Canadian Bookman*, December 1925, 203.

Buitenhuis, Peter. *Hugh MacLennan*. Canadian Writers and Their Works. Toronto: Forum, 1969.

Burgum, Edwin Berry. 'The Outlook for the Novel.' *New Frontier* 2.4 (September 1937): 25–6.

Burke, Anne, ed. 'Some Annotated Letters of A.J.M. Smith and Raymond Knister.' *Canadian Poetry: Studies, Documents, Reviews* 11 (1982): 98–135.

Bush, Douglas. 'Is There a Canadian Literature?' *Commonweal*, 6 November 1929, 13.

– 'Making Literature Hum.' *The Canadian Forum*, December 1926, 72–3.

Buss, Helen M. 'Who Are You, Mrs. Bentley? Feminist Re-vision and Sinclair Ross's *As For Me and My House*.' In *Sinclair Ross's 'As For Me and My House': Five Decades of Criticism*, edited by David Stouck. Toronto: University of Toronto Press, 1991. 190–209.

Calder, Alison. 'Reassessing Prairie Realism.' *Textual Studies in Canada* 12 (1998): 51–60.

Calder, Alison, and Robert Wardhaugh. 'Introduction: Where Is the Prairie?' In *History, Literature, and the Writing of the Canadian Prairies*, edited by Alison Calder and Robert Wardhaugh. Winnipeg: University of Manitoba Press, 2005. 3–24.

Callaghan, Morley. 'Amuck in the Bush.' In *Morley Callaghan's Stories*, 87–92. First published in *The American Caravan: A Yearbook of American Literature*, ed. Van Wyck Brooks et al. (New York: Macaulay, 1927), 89.

– 'An Autumn Penitent.' In *An Autumn Penitent*, 1–79. First published 1928 in *The Second American Caravan: A Yearbook of American Literature*, edited by Alfred Kreymborg et al. New York: Macaulay.

– *An Autumn Penitent*. Laurentian Library. Toronto: Macmillan, 1973.
– *Ancient Lineage*. In Morley Callaghan's Stories, 173. First published in *The Exile* (1928).
– 'Breaking New Ground.' Review of *Orlando* by Virginia Woolf. *Saturday Night*, 29 December 1928, 8.
– *A Broken Journey*. Toronto: Macmillan, 1932.
– 'Civil War Story.' Review of *The Unvanquished* by William Faulkner. *Saturday Night*, 14 May 1938, 15.
– 'A Criticism.' *New Frontier* 1.1 (1936): 24.
– 'Eternal Style.' Interview with Ray Ellenwood. *Idler* 30 (1990): 33–8.
– 'Faulkner Riddle Is Solved.' Review of *The Wild Palms* by William Faulkner. *Saturday Night*, 28 January 1939, 20.
– 'Faulkner's Fabulous World.' Review of *The Hamlet* by William Faulkner. *Saturday Night*, 11 May 1940, 9.
– 'Impressive Short Stories.' Review of *Children and Fools* by Thomas Mann. *Saturday Night*, 23 June 1928, 8–9.
– 'In His Own Country.' In *An Autumn Penitent*, 83–171. First published January-March 1929 in *Scribner's Magazine*.
– 'Into the Dream World.' Review of *Finnegan's Wake* by James Joyce. *Saturday Night*, 27 May 1939, 21.
– 'Introducing Ernest Hemingway.' Review of *In Our Time* and *The Torrents of Spring* by Ernest Hemingway. *Saturday Night*, 7 August 1926, 7–8.
– *It's Never Over*. 1930. Laurentian Library. Toronto: Macmillan, 1972.
– 'Last Spring They Came Over.' In *Morley Callaghan's Stories*, 38–45. First published 1927 in *transition* 3.
– 'Little Marxist, What Now?' *Saturday Night*, 16 Septemeber 1939, 24.
– 'Looking at Native Prose.' *Saturday Night*, 1 December 1928, 3.
– *The Loved and the Lost*. 1951. Toronto: Stoddart, 1953.
– 'Lyrical Realism.' Review of *The Wanderer* by Alain Fournier. *Saturday Night*, 5 January 1929, 8.
– *More Joy in Heaven*. 1937. New Canadian Library. Toronto: McClelland and Stewart, 1967.
– *Morley Callaghan's Stories*. Laurentian Library. Toronto: Macmillan, 1959.
– 'Mr. and Mrs. Fairbanks.' In *Morley Callaghan's Stories*, 227–31. First published September 1933 in *Harper's Bazaar*.
– *A Native Argosy*. Toronto: Macmillan, 1929.
– *No Man's Meat*. 1931. Toronto: Macmillan, 1978.
– 'Novel and Diary.' Review of *From Day to Day* by Ferdynand Goetel. *Saturday Night*, 22 August 1931, 7.
– *Now That April's Here and Other Stories*. New York: Random House, 1936.

– 'The Past Quarter Century.' *Maclean's*, 15 March 1936, 36, 38.
– 'Soldier Harmon.' In *Morley Callaghan's Stories*, 180–91. First published 11 January 1930 in *Toronto Star Weekly*.
– 'The Soul of a Killer.' Review of *The Assassin* by Liam O'Flaherty. *Saturday Night*, 8 September 1928, 8.
– *Strange Fugitive*. 1928. Laurentian Library. Toronto: Macmillan, 1973.
– *Such Is My Beloved*. 1934. New Canadian Library. Toronto: McClelland and Stewart, 1957.
– *That Summer in Paris*. 1963. Laurentian Library. Toronto: Macmillan, 1976.
– *They Shall Inherit the Earth*. 1935. New Canadian Library. Toronto: McClelland and Stewart, 1969.
– 'A Wedding Dress.' In *Morley Callaghan's Stories*, 56–61. First published 1927 in *This Quarter* 1.2.
Calverton, V.F. 'Literature as a Revolutionary Force.' *Canadian Forum*, March 1935, 221–7.
Cameron, Barry. 'Rhetorical Tradition and the Ambiguity of Callaghan's Narrative Rhetoric.' In *The Callaghan Symposium*, edited by David Staines. Reappraisals, Canadian Writers. Ottawa: University of Ottawa Press, 1981. 67–76.
Cameron, Donald. 'Morley Callaghan: There Are Gurus in the Woodwork.' In *Conversations with Canadian Novelists*. Vol. 2. Toronto: Macmillan, 1973. 17–33.
Cameron, Elspeth. *Hugh MacLennan: A Writer's Life*. Toronto: University of Toronto Press, 1981.
Campbell, Sandra. Introduction to *Sister Woman* by J.G. Sime. Ottawa: Tecumseh, 1992. vii–xxviii.
'Canadian Book Trade's Golden Era.' *Canadian Bookman*, April 1922, 130–1.
Cecil-Smith, E. 'Propaganda and Art.' *Masses* 2.11 (January 1934): 10–11.
– 'What Is "Pure" Art?' *Masses* 1.4–5 (July-August 1932): 5.
Chapman, Ethel. *God's Green Country: A Novel of Canadian Rural Life*. Toronto: Ryerson Press, 1922.
– *The Homesteaders*. Toronto: Ryerson Press, 1936.
Chase, Cleveland B. 'Morley Callaghan Tells What a Bootlegger Thinks About.' In *Morley Callaghan*, edited by Brandon Conron. Toronto: McGraw-Hill Ryerson, 1975. 24–6. First published 2 September 1928 in *The New York Times Book Review*.
Chen, John Ming. 'The Politics of Fiction: Social Realism in English-Canadian Novels (1920–55).' PhD diss., University of Calgary, 1989.
Chen, Zhongming, and Isobel MacKenna. 'As They Really Were: Women in the Novels of Grove.' *English Studies in Canada* 2 (1976): 109–16.
Child, Philip. *Day of Wrath*. Toronto: Ryerson Press, 1945.

– *God's Sparrows*. 1937. New Canadian Library. Toronto: McClelland and Stewart, 1978.

– 'Introduction.' In *White Narcissus* by Raymond Knister. New Canadian Library. Toronto: McClelland and Stewart, 1962. 7–16.

Connor, Ralph. *Black Rock: A Tale of the Selkirks*. Toronto: Westminster, 1898.

– *The Man from Glengarry*. Toronto: Westminster, 1901.

– *The Sky Pilot: A Tale of the Foothills*. Toronto: Westminster, 1899.

Conron, Brandon. *Morley Callaghan*. Twayne's World Authors Series. New York: Twayne, 1966.

– *Morley Callaghan*. Critical Views on Canadian Writers. Toronto: McGraw-Hill Ryerson, 1975.

Conroy, Jack. 'New Forces in American Literature.' *New Frontier* 1.1 (April 1936): 22.

Cornell, Beaumont S. 'The Essential Training of the Novelist.' *Canadian Bookman*, June 1921, 46.

– *Lantern Marsh*. Toronto: Ryerson Press, 1923.

– *Renaissance*. Toronto: Macmillan, 1922.

'The Cow Puncher.' Review of *The Cow Puncher* by Robert J.C. Stead. *Canadian Bookman*, January 1919, 69.

Creighton, John H. 'The Fiction of James Joyce.' *The Canadian Forum*, July 1926, 309–10.

Dahlie, Hallvard. *Isolation and Commitment: Frederick Philip Grove's Settlers of the Marsh*. Toronto: ECW, 1993.

Daniells, Roy. 'Literature: I, Poetry and the Novel.' In *The Culture of Contemporary Canada*, edited by Julian Park. Ithaca, NY: Cornell University Press, 1957. 1–80.

Davey, Frank. 'Sheila Watson.' In *The Oxford Companion to Canadian Literature*, edited by William Toye. Toronto: Oxford University Press, 1983. 822–3.

– 'Towards the End of Regionalism.' *Textual Studies in Canada* 12 (1998): 1–17.

Davies, Robertson. 'MacLennan's Rising Sun.' *Saturday Night*, 28 March 1959, 29–31.

Daymond, Douglas M., and Leslie G. Monkman, eds. *Canadian Novelists and the Novel*. Ottawa: Borealis, 1981.

Denham, Paul. 'Beyond Realism: Raymond Knister's *White Narcissus*.' *Studies in Canadian Literature* 3 (1978): 70–7.

Dewart, E.H. 'Introductory Essay to *Selections from Canadian Poets*.' 1864. In *Towards a Canadian Literature: Essays, Editorials and Manifestos*, edited by Douglas M. Daymond and Leslie G. Monkman. Vol. 1. Ottawa: Tecumseh, 1984. 50–9.

Dickie, Francis. 'Realism in Canadian Fiction.' *Canadian Bookman*, October 1925, 165.

Djwa, Sandra. '*The Canadian Forum*: Literary Catalyst.' *Studies in Canadian Literature* 1 (1976): 7–25.

– 'No Other Way: Sinclair Ross's Stories and Novels.' 1971. In *Sinclair Ross's 'As For Me and My House': Five Decades of Criticism*, edited by David Stouck. Toronto: University of Toronto Press, 1991. 55–65.

Dos Passos, John. *The 42nd Parallel*. 1930. Boston: Houghton, 2000.

– *The Big Money*. New York: Harcourt, 1936.

– *Nineteen Nineteen*. 1932. Boston: Houghton, 2000.

Duffy, Dennis. 'Losing the Line: The Field of Our Modernism.' *Essays on Canadian Writing* 39 (1989): 164–90.

Duley, Margaret. *Highway to Valour*. 1941. Toronto: Griffin, 1977.

Duncan, Sara Jeannette. *The Imperialist*. 1904. New Canadian Library. Toronto: McClelland and Stewart, 1990.

Durkin, Douglas. *The Heart of Cherry McBain*. Toronto: Musson, 1919.

– *The Magpie*. Toronto: Hodder and Stoughton, 1923.

'Durkin, Douglas.' Review of *The Lobstick Trail* by Douglas Durkin. *Canadian Bookman*, December 1921, 24.

'Durkin's New Novel.' Review of *The Magpie* by Douglas Durkin. *Canadian Bookman*, February 1924, 43.

Duthie, Eric. 'Gathering Strength.' Review of *American Writers' Congress*, edited by Henry Hart. *New Frontier* 1.1 (April 1936): 30–1.

Edel, Leon. 'The Eternal Footman Snickers.' *The Canadian Forum*, December 1930, 96, 98.

'Editorial.' *New Frontier* 1.1 (April 1936): 3.

Edwards, Justin D. 'Strange Fugitive, Strange City: Reading Urban Space in Morley Callaghan's Toronto.' *Studies in Canadian Literature / Études en littérature canadienne* 23 (1998): 213–27.

Edwards, L.F. 'Authorship and Canadiana.' *Masses* 1.1 (April 1932): 7.

Eggleston, Wilfrid. *The High Plains*. Toronto: Macmillan, 1938.

– *Literary Friends*. Ottawa: Borealis, 1980.

Elder, A. T. 'Western Panorama: Settings and Themes in Robert J.C. Stead.' *Canadian Literature*, 17 (1963): 44–56.

Eliot, T.S. 'The Music of Poetry.' 1942. In *On Poetry and Poets*. New York: Farrar, 1957. 17–33.

– 'Tradition and the Individual Talent.' 1919. In *Modernism: An Anthology of Sources and Documents*, edited by Vassiliki Kolocotroni, Jane Goldman, and Olga Taxidou. Edinburgh: Edinburgh University Press, 1997. 366–71.

– 'The Waste Land.' 1922. *The Waste Land and Other Poems*. London: Faber, 1940. 25–52.

Ellenwood, Ray. 'Morley Callaghan, Jacques Ferron, and the Dialectic of Good and Evil.' In *The Callaghan Symposium*, edited by David Staines. Reappraisals, Canadian Writers. Ottawa: University of Ottawa Press, 1981. 37–46.

Elliott, T.R. [Thomas Rose]. *Hugh Layal: A Romance of the Up Country*. New York: Macmillan, 1927.

Evans, Hubert. *The New Front Line*. Toronto: Macmillan, 1927.

Fairfax, John. 'Art for Man's Sake.' *Canadian Forum*, August 1936, 23–4.

Fairley, Barker. 'Artists and Authors.' *The Canadian Forum*, December 1921, 460–3.

Fairley, Margaret. 'Books.' *New Frontier* 2.1 (May 1937): 26–7.

Faulkner, William. *Absalom, Absalom*. New York: Random House, 1936.

– *As I Lay Dying*. New York: J. Cape and H. Smith, 1930.

– *The Sound and the Fury*. New York: J. Cape and H. Smith, 1929.

– *The Wild Palms*. London: Chatto and Windus, 1939.

Fenwick, Mac. 'Niels's Saga: Colonial Narrative and Nordic Naturalism in Settlers of the Marsh.' *English Studies in Canada* 23.3 (September 1997): 297–314.

Fitzgerald, F. Scott. *The Beautiful and Damned*. 1922. New York: Macmillan, 1986.

Foster, W. Garland. 'On Reflecting Canadian Life.' *Canadian Bookman*, December 1924, 249.

'Four Novels.' Review of *The Kays* by Margaret Deland, *The Dark Dawn* by Martha Ostenso, *Grain* by Robert J.C. Stead, and *The Time of Man* by Elizabeth Madox Roberts. *Canadian Forum*, January 1927, 121–2.

Francis, H. 'Freedom of Contract.' *Masses* 1.8 (March-April 1933): 12.

Francis, Wynne. 'The Expanding Spectrum: Literary Magazines.' *Canadian Literature* 57 (1973): 6–17.

Frye, Northrop. 'Conclusion to a *Literary History of Canada*.' In *The Bush Garden: Essays on the Canada Imagination*. 1965. Concord: Anansi, 1995. 215–53.

Gammel, Irene. *Baroness Elsa: Gender, Dada, and Everyday Modernity: A Cultural Biography*. Cambridge: MIT Press, 2002.

– *Sexualizing Power in Naturalism: Theodore Dreiser and Frederick Philip Grove*. Calgary: University of Calgary Press, 1994.

Garden City Press. 'Introducing the Canadian Bookman's Bookmen.' *Canadian Bookman*, January 1919, 1.

Garner, Hugh. *Cabbagetown*. 1950. Toronto: McGraw-Hill Ryerson, 1968.

– 'An Interview with Hugh Garner.' Interview with Allen Anderson. *Tamarack Review* 52.3 (1969): 19–34.

Gerry, Thomas. 'Dante, C.D. Burns and Sinclair Ross: Philosophical Issues in *As For Me and My House*.' *Mosaic*, 22.1 (Winter 1989): 113–22.

Gibbon, J.M. 'The Coming Canadian Novel.' *Canadian Bookman*, July 1919, 13–15.

Glynn-Ward, Hilda. 'A Plea for Purity.' *Canadian Bookman*, March 1924, 64.

– *The Writing on the Wall*. 1921. Toronto: University of Toronto Press, 1974.

Goetsch, Paul. Introduction to *Hugh MacLennan*, edited by Paul Goetsch. Critical Views on Canadian Writers. Toronto: McGraw-Hill Ryerson, 1973. 1–10.

– 'Too Long to the Courtly Muses: Hugh MacLennan as a Contemporary Writer.' *Canadian Literature* 10 (1961): 7–18.

Goldie, Terry. 'W.O. Mitchell and the Pursuit of the Homosocial Ideal.' In *Magic Lies: The Art of W.O. Mitchell*, edited by Sheila Latham and David Latham. Toronto: University of Toronto Press, 1997. 100–9.

Gordan, Sybil M. 'Man Alive in the Novel.' *New Frontier* 1.12 (April 1937): 24–5.

Gordon, Alfred. 'Canadian Culture?' *The Canadian Forum*, March 1922, 558–9.

Gordon, Huntley K. 'Canadian Poetry.' *The Canadian Forum*, March 1921, 178–80.

Graham, Gwethalyn. *Earth and High Heaven*. 1944. New Canadian Library. Toronto: McClelland and Stewart, 1969.

Grant, Judith Skelton. 'Gordon, Charles William.' In *The Oxford Companion to Canadian Literature*, edited by William Toye. Toronto: Oxford University Press, 1983. 306–8.

Grove, Frederick Philip. 'Apologia Pro Vita et Opere Suo.' *Canadian Forum*, August 1931, 420–2.

– 'Art and Canadian Life.' Ts. box 20, folder 5. Frederick Philip Grove Collection, University of Manitoba, Winnipeg.

– *Consider Her Ways*. Toronto: Macmillan, 1947.

– *Fanny Essler*. Translated by Christine Helmers, A.W. Riley, and D.O. Spettigue. Ottawa: Oberon, 1984.

– *Fruits of the Earth*. Toronto: J.M. Dent, 1933.

– 'The Happy Ending.' In *It Needs To Be Said*, 79–90.

– *In Search of Myself*. Toronto: Macmillan, 1946.

– *It Needs to Be Said*. Toronto: Macmillan, 1929.

– *The Letters of Frederick Philip Grove*. Toronto: University of Toronto Press, 1976.

– 'Literary Criticism.' In *It Needs to Be Said*, 23–46.

– *The Master Mason's House* [*Maurermeister Ihles Haus*]. Translated by Paul P. Gublins. Ottawa: Oberon, 1976.

– *The Master of the Mill*. Toronto: Macmillan, 1944.

– 'A Neglected Function of a Certain Literary Association.' In *It Needs to Be Said*, 1–22.
– 'The Novel.' In *It Needs To Be Said*, 115–32.
– *Our Daily Bread*. Toronto: Macmillan, 1928.
– *Over Prairie Trails*. Toronto: McClelland and Stewart, 1922.
– 'Realism in Literature.' In *It Needs to Be Said*, 47–78.
– *A Search for America*. Ottawa: Graphic, 1927.
– *Settlers of the Marsh*. New York: Doran, 1925.
– *Tales from the Margin: The Selected Stories of Frederick Philip Grove*, edited by Desmond Pacey. Toronto: Ryerson Press, 1971.
– *The Turn of the Year*. Toronto: McClelland and Stewart, 1923.
– *Two Generations: A Story of Present-day Ontario*. Toronto: Ryerson Press, 1939.
– *The Yoke of Life*. Toronto: Macmillan, 1930.
Gunnars, Kristjana. Afterword to *Settlers of the Marsh* by Frederick Philip Grove. New Canadian Library. McClelland and Stewart: Toronto, 1989. 267–75.
Hémon, Louis. *Maria Chapdelaine*. Toronto: Macmillan, 1921.
Harrison, Charles Yale. *Generals Die in Bed*. New York: W. Morrow, 1930.
Harrison, Dick. 'The Beginnings of Prairie Fiction.' *Journal of Canadian Fiction* 4.1 (1975): 159–77.
– 'Stead, Robert J.C.' In *The Oxford Companion to Canadian Literature*, edited by William Toye. Toronto: Oxford University Press, 1983. 771–2.
– *Unnamed Country: The Struggle for a Canadian Prairie Fiction*. Edmonton: University of Alberta Press, 1977.
'The Heart of Cherry McBain.' Review of *The Heart of Cherry McBain* by Douglas Durkin. *Canadian Bookman*, October 1919, 23.
Heidenreich, Rosmarin. 'Narratological Structures and Ideology: The Case of Hugh MacLennan's *Two Solitudes*.' In *Hugh MacLennan*, edited by Frank M. Tierney. Reappraisals, Canadian Writers. Ottawa: University of Ottawa Press, 1994. 125–34.
Hill, Colin. 'As For Me and My Blueprint: Sinclair Ross's Debt to Arthur Stringer.' In *The Canadian Modernists Meet*, edited by Dean Irvine. Ottawa: University of Ottawa Press, 2005. 251–74.
– 'Critical Introduction.' In *Waste Heritage: A Novel by Irene Baird*, edited by Colin Hill. Ottawa: University of Ottawa Press, 2007. ix–lvii.
Hinton, James. 'Meat!' *New Frontier* 2.3 (July-August 1937): 6–8.
H.M.R. 'New Furrows.' Review of *New Furrows* by Flos Jewell Williams. *Canadian Bookman*, January 1927, 21.
Hoar, Victor. *Morley Callaghan*. Toronto: Copp Clark, 1969.
Hoar, Victor, and Gary Boire. 'Morley Callaghan and His Works.' In *Canadian*

Writers and Their Works, edited by Robert Lecker, Jack David, and Ellen Quigley. Toronto: ECW, 1990. 79–145.

Hopkins, Anthony. 'Thematic Structure and Vision in *Waste Heritage*.' *Studies in Canadian Literature* 1 (1986): 77-85.

Howard, Victor. *Morley Callaghan*. Toronto: Copp Clark, 1969.

Hurley, John. 'Mr. Elliott's [*sic*] *Wasteland*.' *Canadian Bookman*, May 1923, 126.

Innis, Mary Q. 'The Quarrel.' *The Canadian Forum*, August 1922, 722–3.

Irvine, Dean. *Editing Modernity: Women and Little-Magazine Cultures in Canada, 1916–1956*. Toronto: University of Toronto Press, 2008.

Jackel, Susan. 'Prairie Writing.' In *The Oxford Companion to Canadian Literature*, edited by William Toye. Toronto: Oxford University Press, 1983. 677–9.

– 'Prairie Writing.' *The Oxford Companion to Canadian Literature*, edited by Eugene Benson and William Toye. Toronto: Oxford University Press, 1997. 960–3.

Jones, D.G. *Butterfly on Rock: A Study of Themes and Images in Canadian Literature*. Toronto: University of Toronto Press, 1970.

Jones, John T. 'Wagon Wheels.' *The Canadian Forum*, October 1926, 403–4, 406.

Jordan, Israel. 'Now That Callaghan's Here.' Review of *Now That April's Here* by Morley Callaghan. *New Frontier* 1.6 (October 1936): 29–30.

Joyce, James. *Dubliners*. 1914. Cambridge: Cambridge University Press, 1995.

– *Finnegans Wake*. New York: Viking Press, 1939.

– *A Portrait of the Artist as a Young Man*. 1916. London: Penguin, 1992.

– *Ulysses*. 1922. London: Picador, 1997.

Keahey, Deborah Lou. *Making It Home: Place in Canadian Prairie Literature*. Winnipeg: University of Manitoba Press, 1998.

Keith, W.J. *Canadian Literature in English*. London: Longman, 1985.

– 'Grove's 'Magnificent Failure': *The Yoke of Life* Reconsidered.' *Canadian Literature* 89 (1981): 104–17.

Kennedy, Leo. 'Portion of Your Breath.' *The Canadian Forum*, January 1930, 123–5.

– 'Raymond Knister.' *The Canadian Forum*, September 1932, 459–61.

– 'We All Got to Die.' *The Canadian Forum*, December 1930, 99–100.

Klein, A.M. 'Friends, Romans, Hungrymen.' *New Frontier* 1.1 (April 1936): 16, 18.

– *The Second Scroll*. 1951. New Canadian Library. Toronto: McClelland and Stewart, 1961.

Knister, Raymond. 'Canadian Letter.' In *The First Day of Spring*, 377–82.

– 'Canadian Literati.' *Journal of Canadian Fiction* 4.2 (1975): 160–8.

– 'Canadian Literature: A General Impression.' *Journal of Canadian Fiction* 4.2 (1975): 169–74.

– ed. *Canadian Short Stories*. Toronto: Macmillan, 1928.
– 'The Canadian Short Story.' *Canadian Bookman*, August 1923, 203–4.
– 'Dissecting the "T.B.M."' *Saturday Night*, 6 September 1930, 5.
– 'Eric Mirth, or the Larger I.' *Journal of Canadian Fiction* 4.2 (1975): 97–106.
– 'The Fate of Mrs. Lucier.' In *The First Day of Spring*, 178–85. First published 1925 in *This Quarter* 1.2.
– *The First Day of Spring: Stories and Other Prose*, edited by Peter Stephens. Toronto: University of Toronto Press, 1976.
– 'Grapes.' In *The First Day of Spring*, 97–113.
– 'Indian Summer.' In *The First Day of Spring*, 84–96.
– 'The Loading.' In *The First Day of Spring*, 75–83. First published January 1924 in *The Midland*.
– 'Mist Green Oats.' In *The First Day of Spring*, 58–74. First published August-September 1922 in *The Midland*.
– *My Star Predominant*. Toronto: Ryerson Press, 1934.
– 'The One Thing.' In *The First Day of Spring*, 151–64. First published January 1922 in *The Midland*.
– 'Peaches, Peaches.' *The First Day of Spring*, 8–57.
– 'The Strawstack.' In *The First Day of Spring*, 186–94. First published October 1923 in *The Canadian Forum*.
– *White Narcissus*. 1929. New Canadian Library. Toronto: McClelland and Stewart, 1962.

Knox, Gilbert [Madge MacBeth]. *The Land of Afternoon*. Ottawa: Graphic, 1924.

Kolocotroni, Vassiliki, Jane Goldman, and Olga Taxidou. 'Introduction.' In *Modernism: An Anthology of Sources and Documents*. Edinburgh: Edinburgh University Press, 1998. xvii–xx.

Kon, William E. 'Boom Town into Company Town: The Story of Sudbury.' *New Frontier* 1.7 (November 1936): 6–9.

Kreisel, Henry. 'The Prairie: A State of Mind.' 1968. In *Contexts of Canadian Criticism*, edited by Eli Mandel. Toronto: University of Toronto Press, 1971. 254–66.
– *The Rich Man*. 1948. New Canadian Library. Toronto: McClelland and Stewart, 1948.

Kroetsch, Robert. Afterword to *As For Me and My House* by Sinclair Ross. 1941. New Canadian Library. Toronto: McClelland and Stewart, 1989. 217–21.
– 'A Canadian Issue.' *Boundary 2* 3.1 (1974): 1–2.

'Land and Weather.' Review of *The Pioneers of Old Ontario* by W.L. Smith, *Over Prairie Trails* by Frederick Philip Grove, and *Nature in American Literature* by Norman Foerster. *Canadian Forum*, May 1923, 248, 250.

Lawrence, Robert G. 'The Geography of Martha Ostenso's *Wild Geese*.' *Journal of Canadian Fiction*, 16 (1976): 108–14.

Leavis, F.R. *The Great Tradition: George Eliot, Henry James, Joseph Conrad*. London: Chatto and Windus, 1948.

Lecker, Robert. *Canadian Canons: Essays in Literary Value*. Toronto: University of Toronto P, 1991.

– *Making It Real: The Canonization of English-Canadian Literature*. Toronto: Anansi, 1995.

Lighthall, William Douw. *Songs from the Great Dominion: Voices from the Forests and Waters, Settlements and Cities of Canada*. London: Scott, 1889.

Lind, Jack. 'A Significant Turn in Soviet Literature.' *Masses* 1.8 (March-April 1933): 10.

Livesay, Dorothy. 'Beach Sunday.' *The Canadian Forum*, January 1931, 138, 140.

– 'Corbin – A Company Town Fights for Its Life.' *New Frontier* 1.3 (June 1936): 6–8.

Lowry, Malcolm. *Under the Volcano*. London: Cape, 1947.

Lucas, Alec. *Hugh MacLennan*. Canadian Writers, New Canadian Library. Toronto: McClelland and Stewart, 1970.

Lukács, Georg. 'Reportage or Portrayal.' 1932. *Essays on Realism*, edited by Rodney Livingstone. Cambridge: MIT Press, 1980. 45–75.

Lyon, Janet. *Manifestoes: Provocations of the Modern*. Ithaca, NY: Cornell University Press, 1999.

Lysenko, Vera. *Yellow Boots*. 1954. Edmonton: NeWest, 1992.

MacDonald, Adrian. 'English Realism to a Canadian.' *Canadian Bookman*, September 1922, 234–5.

MacKay, L.A. 'No Escape.' Review of *More Joy In Heaven* by Morley Callaghan. *Canadian Forum*, March 1938, 427.

MacKenna, Isobel. 'As They Really Were: Women in the Novels of Grove.' *English Studies in Canada* 2 (1976): 109–16.

MacLennan, Hugh. *Barometer Rising*. 1941. New Canadian Library. Toronto: McClelland and Stewart, 1991.

– *Each Man's Son*. 1951. New Press Canadian Classics. Toronto: Stoddart, 1993.

– *The Precipice*. 1948. Toronto: Popular Library, n.d.

– *Two Solitudes*. 1945. New Press Canadian Classics. Toronto: Stoddart, 1993.

– *The Watch That Ends the Night*. 1959. Toronto: Stoddart, 1991.

MacLulich, T.D. *Between Europe and America: The Canadian Tradition in Fiction*. Toronto: ECW, 1988.

– 'Colloquial Style and the Tory Mode.' *Canadian Literature* 89 (1981): 7–22.

– *Hugh MacLennan*. Twayne's World Authors Series. Boston: Twayne, 1983.

Mao, Douglas, and Rebecca L. Walkowitz. *Bad Modernisms.* N.p.: Duke University Press, 2006.

Marshall, Joyce. *Presently Tomorrow.* Boston: Little-Brown, 1946.

Marshall, Tom. 'Tragic Ambivalence: The Novels of Morley Callaghan.' *University of Windsor Review* 12 (1976): 33–48.

Martens, Klaus. *F.P. Grove in Europe and Canada: Translated Lives.* Edmonton: University of Alberta Press, 2001.

– 'Nixe on the River: Felix Paul Greve in Bonn.' *Canadian Literature* 151 (1996): 10–43.

Mather, Barry. 'It Is Wonderful.' *New Frontier* 1.5 (September 1936): 10.

Mathews, Robin. '*Waste Heritage*: The Effect of Class on Literary Structure.' *Studies in Canadian Literature* 6 (1981): 65–81.

McClung, Nellie. *Clearing in the West: My Own Story.* Toronto: T. Allen, 1935.

– *Painted Fires.* Toronto: T. Allen, 1925.

– *Purple Springs.* Toronto: T. Allen, 1921.

– *Sowing Seeds in Danny.* Toronto: Briggs, 1908.

McCourt, Edward. *The Canadian West in Fiction.* Toronto: Ryerson Press, 1949.

– *The Flaming Hour.* Toronto: Ryerson Press, 1947.

– *Home Is the Stranger.* Toronto: Macmillan, 1950.

– *Music at the Close.* 1947. New Canadian Library. Toronto: McClelland and Stewart, 1966.

– *Walk through the Valley.* Toronto: McClelland and Stewart, 1958.

– *The Wooden Sword.* 1956. New Canadian Library. Toronto: McClelland and Stewart, 1975.

McGeer, J.J. 'Vancouver Underground.' *New Frontier* 1.7 (November 1936): 12–13.

McKenzie, Ruth. 'Proletarian Literature in Canada.' *Dalhousie Review* 19.1 (1939): 49–64.

McMullen, Lorraine. 'Women in Grove's Novels.' *The Grove Symposium*, edited by John Nause. Reappraisals, Canadian Writers. Ottawa: University of Ottawa Press, 1974. 67–76.

McMullin, Stanley E. 'Evolution Versus Revolution: Grove's Perception of History.' In *The Grove Symposium*, edited by John Nause. Reappraisals, Canadian Writers. Ottawa: University of Ottawa Press, 1974. 77–88.

McNaught, Eleanor. 'September Sonata.' *The Canadian Forum*, March 1932, 217–20.

McPherson, Hugo. 'Fiction 1940–1960.' In *Literary History of Canada: Canadian Literature in English*, edited by Carl F. Klinck. Vol. 2. Toronto: University of Toronto Press, 1965. 205–33.

'Members Admitted to the Canadian Authors' Association.' *Canadian Bookman*, September 1921, 56–8.

Metcalf, John. 'Winner Take All.' *Essays on Canadian Writing* 51–2 (1993): 113–45.

Meyer, Bruce. 'Literary Magazines in English.' In *The Oxford Companion to Canadian Literarure*, edited by William Toye. Toronto: Oxford University Press, 1983. 455–63.

Mitchell, W.O. *Who Has Seen the Wind*. Toronto: Macmillan, 1947.

Montgomery, Lucy Maud. *Anne of Green Gables*. 1908. Toronto: McClelland and Stewart, 1989.

Moodie, Susanna. *Roughing It in the Bush; or, Life in Canada*. London: R. Bentley, 1852.

Moore, Brian. *Judith Hearne*. Toronto: McClelland and Stewart, 1955.

Moss, John. 'A Conversation with Hugh Garner.' *Journal of Canadian Fiction* 1.2 (1972): 50–5.

– Introduction to *The Canadian Novel*, vol. 3: *Modern Times: A Critical Anthology*, edited by John Moss. Toronto: New Canada, 1982. 7–15.

Mount, Nick. *When Canadian Literarture Moved to New York*. Toronto: University of Toronto Press, 2005.

'Mrs. Dalloway.' *The Canadian Forum*, July 1926, 318.

Mulvihill, James. 'The "Canadian Bookman" and Literary Nationalism.' *Canadian Literature* 107 (1985): 48–59.

'A New Anthology.' *The Canadian Forum*, November 1923, 58.

'The New Era.' *Canadian Bookman*, January 1919, 1–2.

Niven, Frederick. *A Wilderness of Monkeys*. London: Secker, 1911.

O'Flaherty, Liam. *The Assassin*. New York: Harcourt, 1928.

O'Hagan, Howard. *Tay John*. 1939. New Canadian Library. Toronto: McClelland and Stewart, 1974.

Olafsen, Olaf. 'The Victim.' *The Canadian Forum*, July 1924, 309, 316.

Ostenso, Martha. *Wild Geese*. 1925. New Canadian Library. Toronto: McClelland and Stewart, 1989.

'Our Credentials.' *Masses* 1.1 (April 1932): 1.

'Over Prairie Trails.' *The Canadian Forum*, May 1923, 248–9.

Pacey, Desmond. *Creative Writing in Canada*. Toronto: Ryerson, 1952.

– 'Fiction 1920–1940.' In *Literary History of Canada: Canadian Literature in English*, edited by Carl F. Klinck. Vol. 2. Toronto: University of Toronto Press, 1965. 168–204.

– *Frederick Philip Grove*. Canadian Men of Letters. Toronto: Ryerson Press, 1944.

– 'The Writer and His Public, 1920–1960.' In *Literary History of Canada: Cana-

dian Literature in English, edited by Carl F. Klinck. Vol 2. Toronto: University of Toronto Press, 1965. 3–21.

Peepre-Bordessa, Mari. *Hugh MacLennan's National Trilogy: Mapping a Canadian Identity (1940–1950)*. Helsinki: Suomalainen Tiedeakatemia, 1990.

Peterson, Chas. W. *Fruits of the Earth: A Story of the Canadian Prairies*. Ottawa: Ru-Mi-Lou, 1928.

Peterson, Len. *Chipmunk*. Toronto: McClelland and Stewart, 1949.

Philips, Donna. *Voices of Discord: Canadian Short Stories from the 1930s*. Toronto: New Hogtown, 1979.

Pierce, Lorne. 'Canadian Literature and the National Ideal.' *Canadian Bookman*, September 1925, 143–4.

Pierce, Lorne Albert, and Albert Durrant Watson. *Our Canadian Literature: Representative Prose and Verse*. Toronto: Ryerson Press, 1922.

Poole, A. 'Fish.' *Masses* 1.4–5 (July-August 1932): 5–6.

Potvin, Elizabeth. '"The Eternal Feminine" and the Clothing Motif in Grove's Fiction.' *Studies in Canadian Literature* 12.2 (1987): 222–38.

Proietti, Salvatore. 'Frederick Philip Grove's Version of Pastoral Utopianism.' *Science-Fiction Studies* 19.3 (1992): 361–77.

Proust, Marcel. 1914. *Du côté de chez Swann*. Paris: B. Grasset, 1914.

Rawlinson, Bernard. 'Cornwall: The Diary of a Strike.' *New Frontier* 1.6 (October 1936): 15–17, 23.

Ray, Margaret. 'St. George and the Dragon (A Modernized Version).' *The Canadian Forum*, December 1927, 458, 460–1.

Reid, J. Addison. 'The Canadian Novel.' *The Canadian Forum*, June 1922, 658–60.

Review of *Blue Pete: Half Breed* by Luke Allan. *Canadian Bookman*, September 1921, 59.

Review of *God's Green Country* by Ethel Chapman. *Canadian Bookman*, February 1923, 43.

Review of *Neighbours* by Robert J.C. Stead. *Canadian Bookman*, November 1922, 293.

Review of *The Yoke of Life* by Frederick Philip Grove. *The Saturday Review of Literature*, 25 October 1930, 274.

Richardson, T. 'In Defense of Pure Art.' *Masses* 1.4–5 (July-August 1932): 4.

Richler, Mordecai. *Son of a Smaller Hero*. London: Deutsch, 1955.

Ricou, Laurence. *Vertical Man, Horizontal World: Man and Landscape in Canadian Prairie Fiction*. Vancouver: University of British Columbia Press, 1973.

Rider, Peter E. Introduction to *The Magpie* by Douglas Durkin. Toronto: University of Toronto Press, 1974. vi–xiv.

Rifkind, Candida. *Comrades and Critics: Women, Literature, and the Left in 1930s Canada*. Toronto: University of Toronto Press, 2009.

Rimmer, T.D. 'Four Canadian Novels.' *Canadian Bookman*, January 1927, 15–16.

– 'Recent Canadian Novels.' *Canadian Bookman*, October 1926, 307–8.

Roberts, Sir Charles G.D. 'A Note on Modernism.' In *Open House*, edited by William Arthur Deacon and Wilfred Reeves. Ottawa: Graphic, 1931. 23–4.

Robins, J.D. 'David, Son of Thalia.' *The Canadian Forum*, December 1928, 88, 90–2.

– 'The Walls of Jericho.' *The Canadian Forum*, July 1921, 304–7.

Roper, Gordon. 'The Kinds of Fiction, 1880–1920.' In *Literary History of Canada: Canadian Literature in English*, edited by Carl F. Klinck. Vol. 1. Toronto: University of Toronto Press, 1965. 298–326.

– 'New Forces: New Fiction, 1880–1920.' In *Literary History of Canada: Canadian Literature in English*, edited by Carl F. Klinck. Vol. 1. Toronto: University of Toronto Press, 1965. 274–97.

Ross, Sinclair. *As For Me and My House*. 1941. New Canadian Library. Toronto: McClelland and Stewart, 1989.

– *The Lamp at Noon and Other Stories*. New Canadian Library. Toronto: McClelland and Stewart, 1968.

– *The Well*. Toronto: Macmillan, 1958.

Roy, Gabrielle. *The Tin Flute*. New Canadian Library. Toronto: McClelland and Stewart, 1947.

Salpeter, Harry. 'The First Reader.' *The World*, 18 August 1928, 9.

Salverson, Laura Goodman. *The Dark Weaver*. Toronto: Ryerson Press, 1937.

Sandwell, B.K. 'Portrait of a Fine Canadian Woman.' Review of *The Prairie Mother* by Arthur Stringer. *Canadian Bookman*, December 1920, 84.

Scott, Duncan Campbell. *In the Village of Viger*. 1896. New Canadian Library. Toronto: McClelland and Stewart, 1983.

Shek, Ben-Zion. *Social Realism in the French-Canadian Novel*. Montreal: Harvest House, 1977.

Silcox, David P. *The Group of Seven and Tom Thomson*. Toronto: Firefly, 2003.

Sime, J.G. 'Munitions!' In *Sister Woman*. Ottawa: Tecumseh Press, 2004. 35–45.

– *Our Little Life: A Novel of To-Day*. 1921. Early Canadian Woman Writers Series. Ottawa: Tecumseh, 1994.

– *Sister Woman*. 1920. Early Canadian Women Writers Series. Ottawa: Tecumseh, 1992.

Simpson, J. H. 'Orchard Way.' *The Canadian Forum*, August 1931, 416–17.

Slater, Patrick. *Robert Harding*. Toronto: Thomas Allen, 1938.

Smart, Elizabeth. *By Grand Central Station I Sat Down and Wept*. 1945. London: Flamingo, 1992.

Smiley, Cal. 'Novels in English 1900 to 1920,' in *The Oxford Companion to*

Canadian Literature, edited by William Toye. Toronto: Oxford University Press, 1983. 569–71.

Smith, A.J.M. 'Introduction to *The Book of Canadian Poetry*.' 1943. In *Towards a Canadian Literature: Essays, Editorials and Manifestos*, edited by Douglas M. Daymond and Leslie G. Monkman. Vol. 2. Ottawa: Tecumseh, 1984. 336–40.

Spettigue, D.O. *F.P.G.: The European Years*. Ottawa: Oberon, 1973.

– *Frederick Phillip Grove*. Toronto: Copp Clark, 1969.

Staines, David. 'Mapping the Terrain.' *Mosaic* 11.3 (1978): 137–51.

'Standards of Criticism.' *Canadian Bookman*, April 1919, 7–9.

Stead, Robert J.C. *The Bail Jumper*. Toronto: Briggs, 1914.

– *The Cow Puncher*. Toronto: Musson, 1918.

– *Dennison Grant*. Toronto: Musson, 1920.

– *Dry Water*. Ottawa: Tecumseh, 1983.

– *Grain*. 1926. New Canadian Library. Toronto: McClelland and Stewart, 1993.

– *The Homesteaders*. Toronto: Musson, 1916.

– 'Literature as a National Asset: A Radiographed Message.' *Canadian Bookman*, December 1923, 343.

– *Neighbours*. Toronto: Hodder and Stoughton, 1922.

– *The Smoking Flax*. Toronto: McClelland and Stewart, 1924.

– 'Third Annual Convention, C.A.A.: Address by the President.' *Canadian Bookman*, July 1924, 164.

Steele, James. 'History Repeating Itself as Fiction: Oxyrhynchus and the Novels.' In *Hugh MacLennan*, edited by Frank M. Tierney. Reappraisals, Canadian Writers. Ottawa: University of Ottawa Press, 1994. 109–24.

Stephen, A.M. *The Gleaming Archway*. London: J.M. Dent, 1929.

Stephens, Donald. 'Novels In English, 1920–1940.' In *The Oxford Companion to Canadian Literature*, 2nd ed., edited by Eugene Benson and William Toye. Toronto: Oxford University Press, 1997. 817–20.

Stevens, Peter. '*The Canadian Forum*.' In *The Oxford Companion to Canadian Literature*, edited by William Toye. Toronto: Oxford University Press, 1983. 101.

– Introduction to *The First Day of Spring: Stories and Other Prose*, edited by Peter Stevens. Toronto: University of Toronto Press, 1976. xi–xxvi.

Stevenson, Lionel. *Appraisals of Canadian Literature*. Toronto: Macmillan, 1926.

– 'Is Canadian Poetry Modern?' *Canadian Bookman*, July 1927, 195–201.

– 'The Fatal Gift.' *Canadian Bookman*, September 1923, 235–6.

– 'Manifesto for a National Literature.' In *Towards a Canadian Literature: Es-*

says, Editorials and Manifestos, edited by Douglas M. Daymond and Leslie G. Monkman. Vol. 1. Ottawa: Tecumseh, 1984. 203–8.

– 'The Outlook for Canadian Fiction.' *Canadian Bookman*, July 1924, 157–8.

Stobie, Margaret R. *Frederick Philip Grove*. Twayne's World Authors Series. New York: Twayne, 1973.

Story, Norah, ed. *The Oxford Companion to Canadian History and Literature*. Toronto: Oxford University Press, 1967.

'Strange Fugitive New Type in Canadian Realist Novel.' *Toronto Star Daily*, 29 September 1928, 13.

Stringer, Arthur. *The Prairie Child*. Toronto: McClelland and Stewart, 1922.

– *The Prairie Mother*. Indianapolis: Bobbs, 1920.

– *The Prairie Wife*. Toronto: McLeod, 1915.

Suckow, Ruth. 'Canadian Short Stories: A Promise of Vigor.' Review of *Canadian Short Stories*, edited by Raymond Knister. *The World*, 9 December 1928, 11.

Sutherland, Fraser. *The Style of Innocence: A Study of Hemingway and Callaghan*. Toronto: Clarke, Irwin, 1972.

Sutherland, Ronald. *Frederick Philip Grove*. Canadian Writers, New Canadian Library. Toronto: McClelland and Stewart, 1969.

Thacker, Robert. *The Great Prairie Fact and Literary Imagination*. Albuquerque: University of New Mexico Press, 1989.

Thomas, J.K. 'Production.' *New Frontier* 2.3 (July-August 1937): 24–5.

'Three Years Have Passed.' [Prospectus of the first issue]. *The Canadian Forum*, October 1920, 3.

Tierney, Frank, ed. *Hugh MacLennan*. Ottawa: University of Ottawa Press, 1994.

Tolstoy, Leo. *War and Peace*. Translated by Constance Garnett. New York: Carlton House, 1930.

'The Turn of the Year.' Review of *The Turn of the Year* by Frederick Philip Grove. *Canadian Forum*, 1924, 152.

Van Der Mark, Christine. *In Due Season*. Toronto: Oxford University Press, 1947.

van Herk, Aritha. 'Prairie Writing 1983 to 1996.' In *The Oxford Companion to Canadian Literature*, edited by Eugene Benson and William Toye. Toronto: Oxford University Press, 1997. 963–5.

Vipond, Mary. 'The Canadian Authors' Association in the 1920s: A Case Study in Cultural Nationalism.' *Journal of Canadian Studies* 15 (1980): 68–79.

– 'Canadian Nationalism and the Plight of Canadian Magazines in the 1920s.' *Canadian Historical Review* 58 (1977): 43–63.

– 'The Nationalist Network.' *Canadian Review of Studies in Nationalism* 7.1 (1980): 32–53.

Waddington, Marcus. 'Raymond Knister: A Biographical Note.' *Journal of Canadian Fiction* 4 (1975): 175–92.

Wallace, Paul A.W. 'The Romance of the West.' *Canadian Forum*, March 1923, 174–6.

Waterston, Elizabeth. *Survey: A Short History of Canadian Literature*. Toronto: Methuen, 1973.

Watson, Sheila. *Deep Hollow Creek*. New Canadian Library. Toronto: McClelland and Stewart, 1999.

– *The Double Hook*. 1959. New Canadian Library. Toronto: McClelland and Stewart, 1992.

Watt, F.W. 'Literature of Protest.' In *Literary History of Canada: Canadian Literature in English*, edited by Carl F. Klinck. Vol. 2. Toronto: University of Toronto Press, 1965. 473–89.

Weaver, Robert. 'A Talk with Morley Callaghan.' *The Tamarack Review* 7 (1958): 3–29.

Williams, Flos Jewell. *New Furrows: A Story of the Alberta Foothills*. Ottawa: Graphic, 1926.

Willmott, Glenn. Introduction to *Think of the Earth* by Betram Brooker. Toronto: Brown Bear, 2000. ix–xx.

– *Unreal Country: Modernity in the Canadian Novel in English*. Montreal: McGill-Queen's University Press, 2002.

Wilson, Edmund. 'Morley Callaghan of Toronto.' In *Morley Callaghan*, edited by Brandon Conron. Toronto: McGraw-Hill Ryerson, 1975. 106–19. First published 26 November 1960 in *The New Yorker*.

Wilson, Ethel. *The Equations of Love*. 1952. New Canadian Library. Toronto: McClelland and Stewart, 1990.

– *Hetty Dorval*. Toronto: Macmillan, 1947.

Winslade, George. 'Rainbow Chasing.' *Masses* 1.4–5 (July-August 1932): 7.

Woodcock, George. *George Woodcock's Introduction to Canadian Fiction*. Toronto: ECW, 1993.

– 'Hugh MacLennan.' *Northern Review* 3 (1950): 2–10.

– *Hugh MacLennan*. Toronto: Copp Clark, 1969.

– 'A Nation's Odyssey: The Novels of Hugh MacLennan.' *Canadian Literature* 10 (1961): 7–18.

– 'Possessing the Land: Notes on Canadian Fiction.' In *The Canadian Imagination: Dimensions of a Literary Culture*, edited by David Staines. Cambridge: Harvard University Press, 1977. 18–39.

Woolf, Virginia. *To the Lighthouse*. 1927. London: Triad, 1977.

– *The Waves*. 1931. London: Oxford University Press, 1992.

W.S.M. 'A Literary Tramp.' Review of *Wild Honey* by Frederick Niven. *Canadian Forum* 7.80 (1927): 252, 254.

Yeats, William Butler. 'The Second Coming.' In *Selected Poetry*, edited by Timothy Webb. London: Penguin, 1991. 124.

Zichy, Francis. 'MacLennan and Modernism.' In *Hugh MacLennan*, edited by Frank M. Tierney. Ottawa: University of Ottawa Press, 1994. 171–80.

Index

www.ingramcontent.com/pod-product-compliance
Lightning Source LLC
LaVergne TN
LVHW090153080826
844660LV00013B/784/J

9781442640566